CW00944686

THE KINGDOM OF

Northumbria

AD 350–1100

The opening page of St Luke's Gospel from the Lindisfarne Gospels

THE KINGDOM OF

Northumbria

AD 350–1100

N. J. Higham

ALAN SUTTON

First published in the United Kingdom in 1993 by
Alan Sutton Publishing Limited
Phoenix Mill · Far Thrupp · Stroud · Gloucestershire

First published in the United States of America in 1993 by
Alan Sutton Publishing Inc. · 83 Washington Street · Dover · NH 03820

British Library Cataloguing in Publication Data

Higham, N.J.
The Kingdom of Northumbria.
I. Title
942.8

ISBN 0-86299-730-5

Library of Congress Cataloging in Publication Data

Higham, N. J.
    The kingdom of Northumbria / N.J. Higham.
    Includes bibliographical references and index.
    ISBN 0-86299-730-5 : $34.00
    1. Northumbria (Kingdom) – History.   2. Anglo-Saxons–
    Northumbria (Kingdom)   I. Title.
DA670.N813H54   1992
942.8′01–dc20
                                                        92–9825
                                                            CIP

Typeset in 11/12 Sabon.
Typesetting and origination by
Alan Sutton Publishing Limited.
Colour separation by Yeo Valley Graphic Reproductions, Wells.
Printed in Great Britain by
Butler and Tanner, Frome, Somerset.

Contents

Acknowledgements   vii
Abbreviations   ix

1   Before the English: An Introduction   1
2   Catastrophe or Continuity?   43
3   The English Take-over   76
4   Politics and the Conversion   105
5   A Christian Kingdom: Northumbria 685–867   140
6   The Viking Age   173
7   Northumbria and England: 954–1054   211
8   The Destruction of Northumbria   233
9   Settlement and Landscape: A Postscript   252

Further Reading   273
Picture Credits   285
Index   287

To My Parents
With Thanks

Acknowledgements

This volume would have been impossible to write without the vast amount of historical and archaeological scholarship which has been lavished on the region over the last few decades. Although it might be thought iniquitous to pick out individuals, Professor Emeritus Rosemary Cramp has been the inspiration behind this and other projects. Similarly, it is a pleasure to acknowledge the contribution made by John Hurst and Professor Emeritus Maurice Beresford, the originators of the Wharram Research Project. Both my colleagues at Manchester University and my students over the last decade have done much to stimulate my own research on early English history. Many other researchers have aided me with their advice and with their photographic archives among whom I would particularly like to thank Lindsay Allason-Jones, Eric Cambridge of the University of Durham, Andrew Foxon of Hull City Museums, Richard Hall and Katie Jones of the York Archaeological Trust, Elizabeth Hartley of the Yorkshire Museum, Peter Hill, Jill Ivy of the Dean and Chapter Library, Durham, Professor Barri Jones, Lloyd Laing, Gordon Maxwell, Michael Metcalf and Philip Nixon for the use of his superb photographs. Without the skills and unfailing patience of Alan Sutton, Roger Thorp and Clare Bishop, the volume would have progressed far less smoothly to completion but my greatest debt is, as ever, to my family – Felicity and Naomi – who have lived and travelled with this book for many years. To all, my grateful thanks.

Abbreviations

EH   *The Ecclesiastical History of the English People*, Bede, 731, ed. and trans. B. Colgrave and R.A.B. Mynors. Oxford University Press, Oxford, 1969

HB   *The History of the Britons*, sometimes attributed to Nennius, early ninth century, ed. and trans. J. Morris in *Nennius, British History and The Welsh Annals*, Phillimore, Chichester, 1980

AC   *Annales Cambriae (The Welsh Annals)*, perhaps tenth century, ed. and trans. J. Morris in *Nennius, British History and The Welsh Annals*, Phillimore, Chichester, 1980

Cow Green Reservoir, Teesdale

CHAPTER 1

Before the English: An Introduction

The shires of northern England and southern Scotland, pre-1974

The county structure of northern England and southern Scotland, post-1974

The Geography of Northumbria

There is nothing which today corresponds to Northumbria – a kingdom which had its genesis in the conquest of Deira (East Yorkshire) and various British kingdoms by Æthelfrith of Bernicia. His successors massively expanded the area of their direct rule until it stretched from the Whitham to the Tay in the east, and from the Mersey to the Southern Uplands of Scotland in the west. Beyond these boundaries were client-rulers and Northumbria's greatest kings did battle to establish themselves as 'overkings' of all Britain. At its greatest extent, the direct rule of Northumbrian kings encompassed thirteen modern English counties (nine pre-1974) and five Scottish ones (thirteen pre-1974).

Their challenge ceased abruptly in AD 685, when King Ecgfrith was killed by the Picts near Forfar. Thereafter Northumbria was in retreat, losing control of southern Scotland and Lindsey, but it is in this late period that the name 'Northumbrians' was coined. In the preamble of the Council of Hatfield (680), quoted verbatim by Bede, Ecgfrith, Æthelfrith's grandson, was described as king of the 'Humberfolk'. This title reflects his rule of areas on both sides of the Humber, and it was only after the permanent loss of Lindsey that the title was adjusted to 'Northumbrians'. The name seems to have been still novel when Bede wrote his *Ecclesiastical History* (731) but was abandoned in the Viking Age, when the kingdom ceased to exist as a single unit.

'Northumbria' was revived as the title of the late English earls under Cnut and Edward the Confessor but was extinguished during the reign of William the Conqueror, who broke up the region into its constituent parts. The great plains and rolling hills beside the Humber which had formed the heartland were renamed, becoming *EurvicScire* (Yorkshire) after the walled city which served as the focus of the Anglo-Scandinavian earldom. Beyond the North York Moors, the power of

1

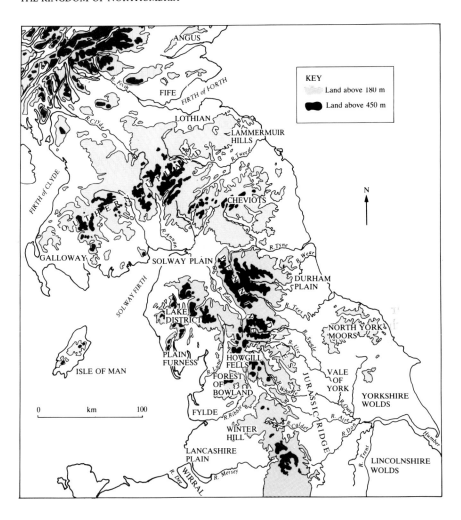

Topography, drainage and the regions
of the north

the Bishops of Durham encouraged the transfer of the name of their *burh*
and principal seat to the region. Thereafter, the name of the old kingdom
survived only north of the Tyne, where it was attached to the most
northerly of the early Norman earldoms, incongruously distant from the
Humber by 150 km. West of the Pennines, areas which had been detached
from Northumbria remained a part of Scotland or were regained only by
force – as Cumberland, the 'land of the Britons' (of Strathclyde). Neither
Westmorland nor Lancashire existed before the twelfth century.

Notwithstanding these problems of geography, this volume will
concentrate on the history and archaeology of a region which focuses
on England north of the Humber and the Mersey, but also includes
Scotland south and east of a line between Stirling and Wigtown.

The Making of the Landscape

Northumbria lies close to the north-western limits of the temperate
climatic zone within which the natural vegetation is deciduous woodland. It is one of the more mountainous parts of Britain, with a higher
proportion of upland than any other area ruled by Anglo-Saxon kings.
The agricultural value of its land varies dramatically over comparatively
short distances, with large tracts virtually worthless as farmland.

Composed of Carboniferous rocks, the Pennine uplands form a
near-continuous spine which begins south of Northumbria's frontier in

2

the Peak District and ends in Rothbury Forest. The uplands form a broken and much-eroded barrier of limestone and gritstone between the two coastal plains, with a variety of distinctive landscapes. The hills are closer to the Irish than the North Sea and steeper on the west side.

Igneous activity has been widespread, as in the Whin Sill, at Bamburgh and on the Farne Islands, and has caused block-faulting, resulting in the fault-lines which provide characteristically steep scarps on the edges of several major valleys. The highest and bleakest hills are concentrated in the northern half of the range, where Cross Fell is only marginally below 900 m high.

The North York Moors form an isolated area of upland east of the Pennines which consist of much younger Jurassic sand and mudstones nowhere higher than 450 m, but fringed by bold scarps to the landward side. The Pennines are continued to the north and west by the Lake District, Cheviot Hills and Southern Uplands, which collectively dominate northern Northumbria. The Lake District mountains are the highest in England, but otherwise the older and more eroded mountain ranges are not distinguished by their height. It is their wide extent and hostile climate which make them such formidable obstacles to human settlement.

The lowlands of Northumbria were already established 200 million years ago so that deposition continued thereafter in marine conditions. In County Durham, magnesian limestone was succeeded by quickly eroded sandstones, marls and mudstones, and similar red sandstones survive beneath the Cumbrian and Lancashire lowlands. The Jurassic and Carboniferous sandstones of North Yorkshire overlay these deposits, as does the still younger chalk of the Yorkshire Wolds, with their downland landscape.

The Whinsill in Northumbria, topped by Hadrian's Wall

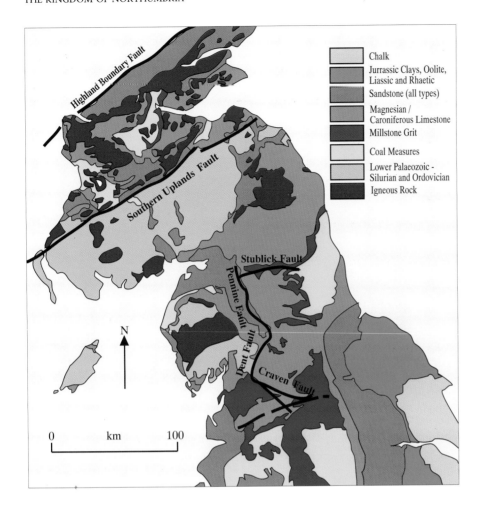

Chalk

Jurrassic Clays, Oolite, Liassic and Rhaetic

Sandstone (all types)

Magnesian / Caroniferous Limestone

Millstone Grit

Coal Measures

Lower Palaeozoic - Silurian and Ordovician

Igneous Rock

The geology of Northumbria

The principal uplands divide the lowlands into five unequal parts. The largest lies in Yorkshire and this region has long tended to dominate. Beyond the North York Moors a narrower and discontinuous plain extends to the Lammermuir Hills, beyond which the plains of Lothian extend along the Firth. West of the Pennines an extensive lowland centres on the Solway and the Eden Valley. The Howgill Fells separate it from the southern Cumbrian lowlands, Lonsdale and the Lancashire Plain, which have tended to be associated in a single unit.

Recent erosion, faulting and uplift has combined with successive glaciations to reshape the landscape. During the last glacial maximum the region was covered with ice-sheets. Ice from Scandinavia and Scotland invaded but both ice-flows were diverted from northern England by local ice centres, of which the Lake District was by far the most active.

The melting of these ice-sheets led to the deposition of substantial quantities of glacial debris across northern England. Glacial erosion has left its mark on many upland areas, but particularly the Lake District, where the over-deepening of valleys and deposition of end-moraines has created numerous lakes. Boulder clay from ice-sheets and water-sorted sands and gravels subsequently covered the lowlands. Melt-water trapped between retreating ice and high ground escaped via channels which were considerably deepened in consequence. In the west, glacial till was responsible for the raising of much of the Solway Plain, the Fylde and the south-west Lancashire lowlands above sea level.

Langdale, a glaciated valley in Lakeland. From the screes Neolithic communities collected the raw material from which they fashioned a widely distributed range of stone axes

Landscape and Land-use

The physical landscape had a more pervasive influence on human activity in Northumbria than in the other large Anglo-Saxon kingdoms. Many terrains offered few opportunities to the peasant farmer, whose homes could be established only in the more hospitable niches. Most countrymen grew only sufficient grain to feed themselves and depended heavily on livestock, using seasonal pastures in the uplands or on lowland mosses (transhumance), inhabiting shielings (graziers' huts) in the summer months. Dense settlement was limited to the few extensive areas of hospitable lowland.

These constraints resulted from a complex interaction between man and the landscape over several millennia. During early prehistory mixed deciduous woodland had spread across the region. This woodland stabilized the soil and moderated the effects of high rainfall.

It takes no more than an excursion along the central sections of the M62 to realize that the uplands are today characterized by open moorland, peat bogs, podsols and thin acid soils, through which stone and rock outcrop. It was a subtle mix of human and natural agencies which had already created this environment even before Northumbria's history began.

The earliest clearances were probably made in the Middle Stone Age by hunter-gatherers but, from the Neolithic Revolution onwards, farmers cleared the forests to obtain access to the vast store of cultivable soils which had developed over thousands of years. By the Bronze Age a hundred generations of farmers had removed trees from many areas. Archaeological monuments dating from the period are commonly found on sites with a seriously degraded environment. The removal of the woodland exposed fragile soils to the heavy rainfall characteristic of the uplands. The result was a rapid loss of topsoil, layers of which were swept into the rivers and lakes. Unregulated surface water cut new channels and deepened existing ones, or leached the soil as it drained downwards. Peat formed and bogs grew across land which had hitherto supported trees, both on upland sites and across poorly drained lowlands, on the Fylde, Merseyside, Teesside and Humberside.

Bronze Age settlements on the Cheviots are characteristically between 210 and 380 m above sea level, and their common association with small fields implies the cultivation of cereals at these altitudes. Thereafter, communities abandoned the high moorlands, regrouping their scattered settlements below the 300 m contour. If this evidence were to be extrapolated across the region, it implies a vast loss of habitat. Agriculture was henceforth to be concentrated on the shoulders of the better drained valleys and in those parts of the lowlands with free-draining soils – as most particularly on the Yorkshire Wolds.

Small-scale climatic variations have important implications for agricultural potential in the region. Most terrains offered conditions as favourable to the agriculturalist in the Roman period as today, but rather fewer opportunities in the centuries before c. 300 BC. The climate of Northumbria is characterized by its regional variability. Although

Unenclosed hut circles and field remains at Shap, which probably date from the Bronze Age. The site is threatened by the expansion of the adjacent quarry

Flooded peat cuttings in Chat Moss, the largest of the great mosses which fronted the Mersey throughout the medieval period

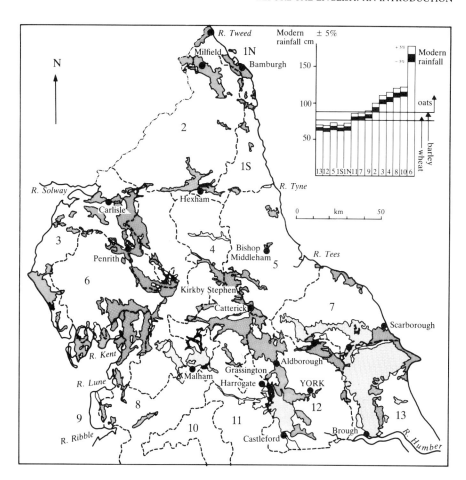

The regionalized agricultural climate of northern England, illustrating the variability of rainfall. The darker areas represent free-draining soil, the lighter areas limestone or chalk

A glacial erratic perched on moorland at Heathwaite Fell, near Coniston Water

modern climatic data is not directly or precisely relevant to the past, it does provide an insight into regional variation, and an indication of the opportunities offered by different areas.

There is a marked contrast between the climate east of the Pennines/Cheviots and that of other areas, and a strong link between altitude and climate. Wheat and barley are intolerant of rainfall over 75 cm annually. The eastern lowland plains are the only areas where such low levels were the norm. The length of the grazing season varies enormously. The regionalism of the climatic regime consistently favoured the eastern lowlands. Had the distribution of free-draining soils compensated for the variability of climate then its effects would have been slight, but the best agricultural soils are similarly concentrated east of the uplands, particularly in eastern Yorkshire.

All the signs are that the Wolds had already been extensively cleared of trees by the Late Bronze Age, when the area was divided up by massive dyke systems. The region was clearly experiencing intensive land-use pressures even before the Roman Conquest.

During the period c. 300 BC–AD 300, woodland clearance intensified, with existing clearance extended and new areas affected. The inception of clearance has been identified in the fifth and sixth centuries BC on Teesside and the terraces of the middle Mersey, followed by Humberside, but carbon-dated clearance levels elsewhere suggest that the process gained little momentum before c. 100 BC.

This general economic expansion should be associated with growing population. There are several factors which may have contributed to the process, apart from advantageous environmental changes. The advent of iron tools offered opportunities to the farmer and local smelting may have rendered iron equipment cheaper and easier to acquire than bronze – a complex alloy requiring imported tin. New crop species were becoming available, alongside new strains of domesticated livestock. The typical British farmer in the last century before Christ had more choice than ever before as to how to manage his farm. Rising productivity and better climatic conditions reduced mortality rates. As population expanded, so communities invested in enclosure systems which gave them greater control over their farmland.

It extended to the whole region, this picture of economic expansion is wildly over-optimistic. Evidence of ironworking and of new clearance is limited to the eastern plains until the second century AD, and there is little evidence for a spread of iron tools to Lakeland farmers at all. Even so, settled farmsteads were in occupation in parts of County Durham, Northumberland and Lothian when the Roman occupation occurred, and the discovery of ard or plough marks under Roman forts and the banks of the Hadrianic *vallum* (a flat-bottomed ditch) implies that agriculture was widespread before the military occupation. When the legions arrived, large tracts of north-east England and south-east Scotland were open country, studded with small farms and enclosed settlements, around some of which enclosure was already extensive.

Long Meg, a standing stone adjacent to the largest stone circle in northern England, at Hunsonby, near Penrith

Limestone pavement on Orton Scar, featuring the undated, but possibly early medieval, enclosed settlement of Castle Folds

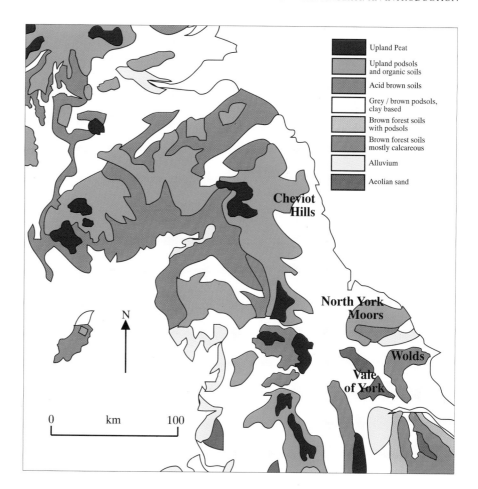

Upland Peat

Upland podsols
and organic soils

Acid brown soils

Grey / brown podsols,
clay based

Brown forest soils
with podsols

Brown forest soils
mostly calcareous

Alluvium

Aeolian sand

Cheviot
Hills

North York
Moors

Wolds

Vale
of York

N

0   km   100

The soils of Northumbria, generalized
and simplified

The Cheviot Hills, which mark the
boundary of medieval Northumberland
with Scotland

Social Hierarchies and State Formation

During the Late Bronze Age, northern communities responded to rising social tensions by developing more complex social hierarchies, headed by warrior-nobles, whose weapons dominated the output of late bronze-smiths. Bronze was expensive and generally used to manufacture weapons, not tools. Enclosed settlements were constructed to provide a degree of security. The earliest were palisaded and many have been identified on good defensible positions where they form the earliest defensive circuit of later hill-forts. Most were small but, during the middle centuries of the first millennium, defences became progressively larger in scale and more labour-intensive, with stone walls or earth banks and ditches replacing timber palisades. Most examples were eventually to boast multiple ditch systems and were permanently occupied, perhaps by an aristocracy.

A minority of hill-forts were far larger. A string of them – including Woden Law – stretch along the edge of the Cheviots in Northumberland and along Teviotdale. These can plausibly be interpreted as minor *oppida*, functioning as defensible foci for clans or sections of a tribe. At the very apex of this hierarchy are a small number of widely dispersed and exceptionally large hill-forts. The largest of these (15–20 ha) are in the north-east of our region, at Traprain Law and Eildon Hill, which have been interpreted as the tribal *oppida* of the Votadini and Selgovae respectively. Each required an exceptional input of labour to construct the defences, and their very existence implies the presence of extensive authority.

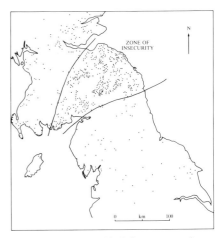

The distribution of hill-forts in northern England and southern Scotland

Woden Law, a large and well-defended hilltop enclosure above Teviotdale

Leck Castle, a small hill-fort or large defended farmstead in northern Lancashire

In other areas the largest sites were significantly smaller, with Burnswark (Dumfries and Galloway), for example, barely topping 7 ha, and Carrock Fell (Cumbria) just 2.1 ha, reflecting, perhaps, the smaller labour forces available in these western areas. Hill-forts are very unevenly distributed within Northumbria, with the majority lying on the edges of the Cheviots and Southern Uplands. The incidence of complex defences is similarly lower elsewhere. East of the Pennines sites are scarce. The largest example is that at Almondbury, near Huddersfield, where an entire hilltop was encircled by strong earthwork defences. The site may have offered a focus for communities across a substantial part of the West Riding, although a case has been made for another large hill-fort only 35 km distant under the village of Barwick-in-Elmet.

South of Cheviot, few, if any, of these hill-forts were constructed after the mid-millennium. Communities on the Wolds seem to have been the first to have abandoned defences. Indeed, few were ever developed and where they have been dated they belong to the period 1200–500 BC. Since evidence of human activity is particularly widespread and dense in this, the richest part of the region, the early abandonment of defences may be significant.

By about 450 BC, Pennine communities also seem to have abandoned significant defences. The best documented example remains Almondbury, which was slighted and abandoned probably during the fifth

century, but beyond the Tyne sites were being re-equipped with ramparts for several more centuries.

This contrast may be important, given that the greatest density of late prehistoric metalwork is in eastern Yorkshire, where hundreds of ditched farm sites have been identified, excavated examples of which were typically founded in the last century or two before Christ. Enclosed trackways and ditch-defined enclosure systems imply intensive land-use. The tribal population here was more densely settled and more productive than that of any other part of the region, although it is important to note that recent research has much expanded our knowledge of settlement and land-use in Teesdale, where excavation at Thorpe Thewles has uncovered a complex pre-Roman settlement sequence.

At about the time that Almondbury was abandoned, an exotic culture was established on the Yorkshire Wolds. This 'Arras culture' was introduced from France, either by continental immigrants or by a more complex network of close contacts between the two regions. The culture is defined by its metalwork and mortuary rites, with its regular use of square-ditched, accompanied inhumation under barrows, the richest of which have been found to contain chariot or cart burials. Elsewhere in the north late prehistoric mortuary traditions are barely identified and communities appear to have used methods of corpse disposal which are impervious to archaeological identification.

If the collapse of hill-fort construction in the Pennines may be linked with the cultural distinctiveness of the Wolds, the Wolds communities

Ingleborough, a site with magnificent natural fortifications which were enhanced in the mid- to late Bronze Age by the construction of a box rampart round the edge of the summit

Part of a hoard of Bronze Age metalwork from Heathery Burn (Co. Durham)

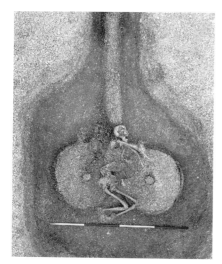

Chariot burial at Wetwang Slack on the Yorkshire Wolds

Almondbury, near Huddersfield, a large hill-fort of the fifth century BC which was adapted as a castle site in the Norman period

may have established a hegemony throughout England between the Humber/Mersey and central Northumberland, the profits from which they exchanged for luxury goods from Gaul and the Rhineland. This culture offers the earliest tangible evidence of a political system encompassing Northumbria.

The name recorded for the tribe occupying East Yorkshire by Ptolemy – the Parisi – must derive from this period of transmarine contact. The name has survived in France – hence Paris – and is unique in northern Britain in being an import. A large settlement developed at North Ferriby, the ferry terminal and trading port on the Humber, and this may have developed some urban characteristics during the last generations before the Conquest.

This people had, however, already lost whatever pre-eminence they had enjoyed when Ptolemy was writing. By the end of the millennium, weapons were being deposited in graves of the Arras culture and a 'warrior cult' may be implied by the finding of chalk figurines of armed men, but economic and demographic trends were arguably against the Parisi. Had Ptolemy written his *Geographia* two centuries earlier, he might have described the Parisi as stretching from sea to sea. As it was, it was the Brigantes, focused in the second century AD at Aldborough (*Isurium Brigantum*) who were to be the dominant force in northern Britain until the Roman Conquest.

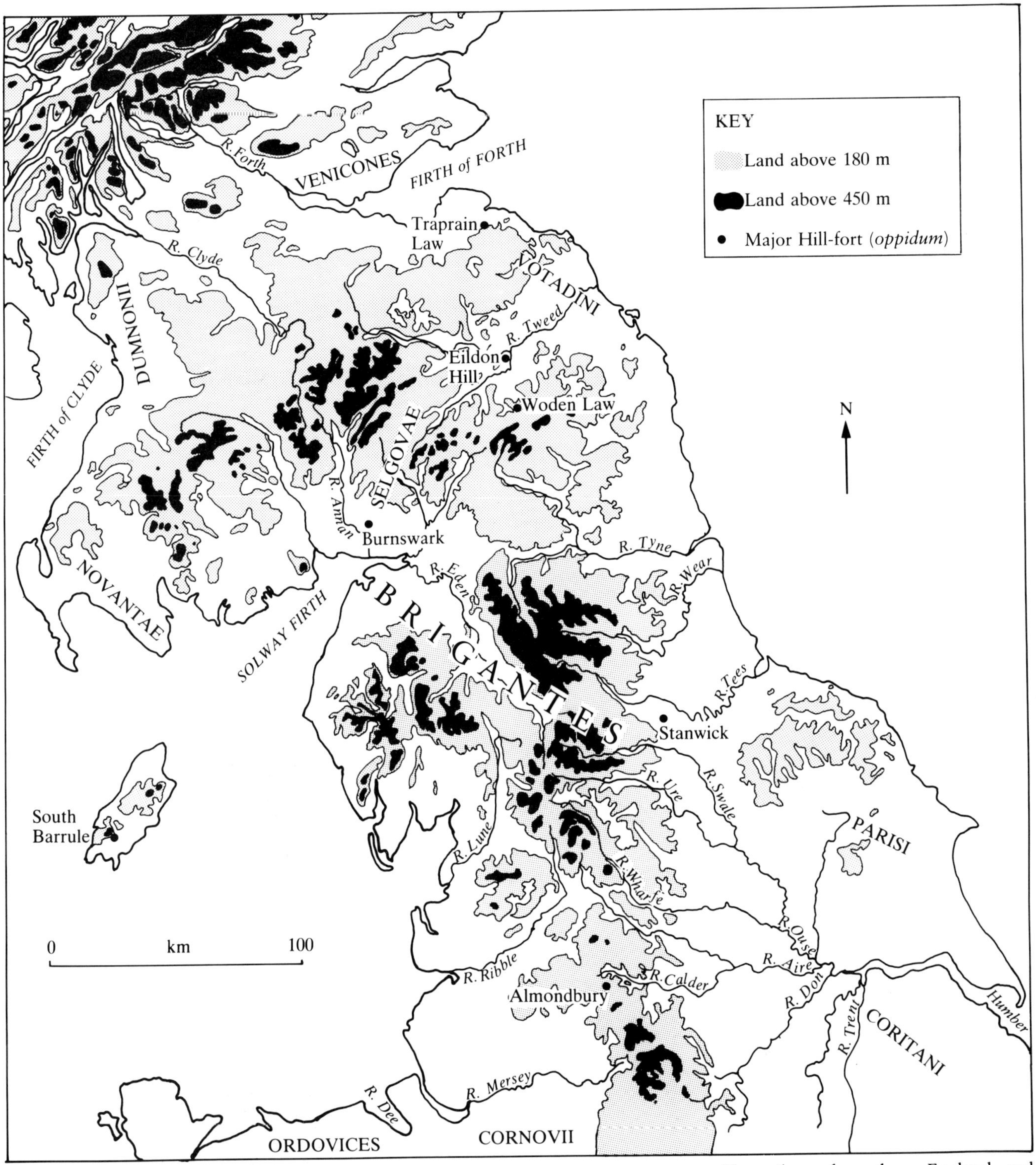
KEY
Land above 180 m
Land above 450 m
Major Hill-fort (*oppidum*)
N
0 km 100
R. Forth
VENICONES
FIRTH of FORTH
Traprain Law
R. Clyde
VOTADINI
DUMNONII
R. Tweed
Eildon Hill
FIRTH of CLYDE
Woden Law
SELGOVAE
R. Annan
Burnswark
R. Tyne
R. Wear
R. Eden
NOVANTAE
SOLWAY FIRTH
BRIGANTES
R. Tees
Stanwick
R. Ure
R. Swale
South Barrule
PARISI
R. Lune
R. Wharfe
R. Ouse
R. Aire
R. Ribble
R. Calder
Almondbury
R. Don
R. Trent
CORITANI
Humber
R. Mersey
R. Dee
ORDOVICES
CORNOVII

The tribes of northern England and southern Scotland, after Ptolemy

That the Brigantes ('High-Ones') were already known by their Ptolemaic name in the centuries before Christ seems unlikely. Changes in tribal status seem often to have been accompanied by name changes on the edge of the Roman world. The Brigantes belong to the dawn of the Roman period, when the long arm of Rome first reached across the Humber to the north. Henceforth, coastal vessels would have far easier access to the North Sea coastline and both carriers and diplomats were beginning to push up the old trackways and new Roman roads which were reaching out inexorably to the Humber crossings.

Rome and the Brigantes

Wharfedale in autumn. Woodland and rough grazing drop steeply from Grassington's fells to the river and steep tributary streams act as manorial and township boundaries

In AD 43 a Roman expeditionary force made a rather hesitant crossing of the Channel and began the conquest of Britain. Before AD 50 a legion was operating in the east Midlands. By AD 60 *legio IX Hispana* was

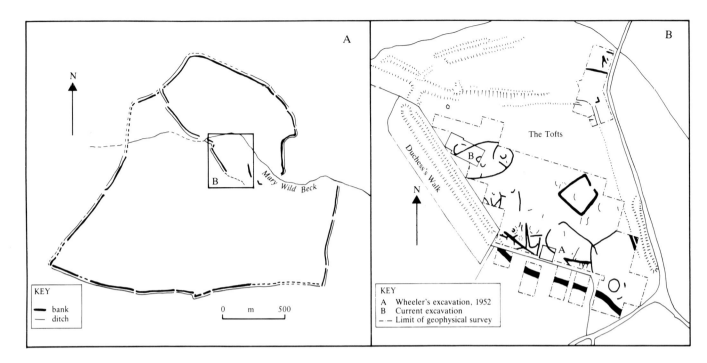

KEY
■— bank
— ditch

0   m   500

KEY
A   Wheeler's excavation, 1952
B   Current excavation
- - Limit of geophysical survey

stationed at Lincoln and its commanding officer was in control of the Coritani, whose northern boundary lay on the Humber.

Beyond it, Roman governors recognized a client-kingdom of the Brigantes, among whom, by AD 51 at the latest, Cartimandua was queen. She repaid the governor's confidence by trapping and surrendering the British leader, Caratacus, and maintained cordial relations with several Roman governors to their mutual advantage. Their willingness to sustain her implies that they had little inclination to occupy her poorly developed realm.

Cartimandua used her wealth and Roman support to ride roughshod over domestic sensibilities, set aside her capable husband and take a new one. In the ensuing civil war Venutius was forced into an anti-Roman stance and, despite his tribal support, Cartimandua's stratagems and Roman troops proved decisive (Tacitus, *Annales*, XII, 40). The queen ruled until the critical year of four Emperors (AD 69) but Venutius then raised Brigantia and the queen had to be evacuated.

The Brigantes pose problems of interpretation, despite the name being widely recorded in classical writings. There were profound differences between the client-kingdom and the subsequent Roman tribe or *civitas*. Most references are to the latter but some writers used the term 'Brigantes' in two different contexts: one pertained to the whole community of the Humber–Cheviot region – 'the most numerous of the whole province' (Tacitus, *De Vita Agricolae* XVII), 'stretching from sea to sea' (Ptolemy, *Geographia*, II, 3, 10); the other to the later and smaller *civitas*. Before the loss of their powers, the rulers of the Brigantes enjoyed hegemonic power over their neighbours. Brigantia has, therefore, significant parallels with early medieval Northumbria. Both were umbrella organizations embracing numerous local 'peoples' and both were focused on overgrown royal households sited east of the Pennines.

Cartimandua's court was the extended *oppidum* of Stanwick. The ramparts of this vast complex are a unique monument of the ultimate prehistoric in northern Britain. The site is of such importance that it

The enclosed *oppidum* at Stanwick, Teesdale

One of the massive banks of the Stanwick *oppidum*

was chosen as a research project by Sir Mortimer Wheeler in 1951/2, and has recently been the subject of an archaeological re-appraisal run from Durham University.

Stanwick is a low-lying site, on and around the Mary Wild Beck, of *c.* 310 ha, being enclosed by successive banks that were, in part, stone-faced and fronted by ditches cut from earth and rock. It was a feat of engineering on a scale that advertised the authority and coercive powers of its proprietor. Imported pottery was present before AD 50 and ceased about the time the client-government collapsed.

The siting of this *oppidum* was clearly important. Political control of the north has generally lain within a short distance of Scotch Corner, and Stanwick was no exception. From it, the client-ruler exercised control over her disparate 'kingdom': to it came her tribute and the labour to build it; from it she controlled the flow of exotic manufactures into the hinterland.

In 1844 a large hoard of metalwork was found very near the Stanwick earthworks. It had been assembled slightly after the mid-first century and contained in excess of ninety items of bronze, iron and a little gold. Although current opinion favours interpretation as a smith's hoard, it might represent part of the queen's possessions which she was forced to abandon in AD 69. Although Mortimer Wheeler interpreted Stanwick as Venutius' hosting camp, it was probably not used by him. There was to be no siege and the defences survived. The site thereafter fell into disuse.

Excavations on The Tofts at Stanwick, carried out by a team from Durham University in 1989, showing the round houses

Selected items from the late Iron Age hoard found at Stanwick

The conquest of Venutius was the first military priority of Petillius Cerealis, who built on incursions by his predecessor, Bolanus. Starting from the Humber crossings at North Ferriby and Brough-on-Humber, the Roman army established a string of forts, from Brough to Malton and York, which isolated the heartland of the Brigantes from the Parisi. With the Yorkshire lowlands partitioned and garrisoned, Cerealis pursued Venutius across the north and it says much for anti-Roman sentiment that the latter was able to attract support sufficient for several battles. By AD 74 the north was under Roman military control. Cerealis' successor was free to turn to conquests in Wales.

The Military Occupation

Agricola was appointed as governor in AD 78 and immediately smashed the resistance of the Ordovices in North Wales. In the next year he turned to the north, campaigning on both sides of the Pennines from bases at Chester and York. Tacitus was able to boast on his behalf that 'no previous Roman governor had ever taken in so much territory so easily to the province' (*Agricola*, XX). The erstwhile clients of the Brigantes did not resist, nor did the Selgovae and Votadini of southern

OPPOSITE: The Flavian occupation of northern Britain, which reached its furthest expansion under Julius Agricola, governor of Britain in the early 80s

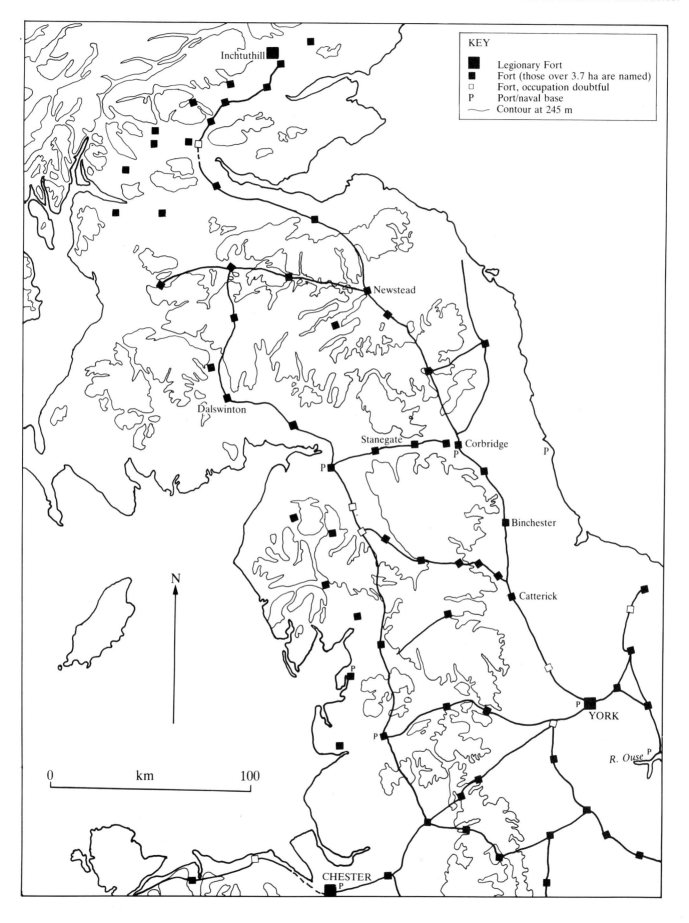

KEY

■ Legionary Fort
■ Fort (those over 3.7 ha are named)
□ Fort, occupation doubtful
P Port/naval base
⌒ Contour at 245 m

Inchtuthill

Newstead

Dalswinton

Stanegate   Corbridge
                        P   P
         P

                              Binchester

                              Catterick

N

                                        YORK
                                    P

                                          R. Ouse P

0   km   100

CHESTER
P

Scotland. Agricola occupied the Clyde–Forth lowlands, and pushed on northwards.

Behind his armies, Agricola began the construction of the road-system which was to be developed and redeveloped over the next century and a half. The main routes were eventually to be well-engineered roads, crossing rivers on substantial masonry bridges, such as that of which the abutments survive at Piercebridge. Between the coastal plains there developed a series of cross-Pennine roads. Along the arterial route across Stainmore, a line of signal stations are extant, and it is possible that a signalling system once ran from York to Carlisle, and even along the Lune Valley road, since a possible example is known at Middleton Hall.

Along these roads were established a series of forts, initially of timber, but ultimately rebuilt in stone. Agricolan forts were relatively few and thinly spread along the main roads. Agricola overcame the northern tribes at *Mons Graupius* in AD 83 but the next few decades saw progressive withdrawals of Roman troops from Britain. Inchtuthil was abandoned unfinished and the Gask Ridge watch-towers may represent the first attempt to construct a frontier within Britain. By AD 90 the army had abandoned Fife and begun to pull back to the Tyne–Solway isthmus and a makeshift frontier or *limes* on Stanegate. In the hinterland forts were constructed to control movement in areas hitherto barely garrisoned.

There are indications of war in northern Britain during the second century. The difficulties of the terrain and successive troop withdrawals

The central section of Hadrian's Wall, looking east towards Housesteads

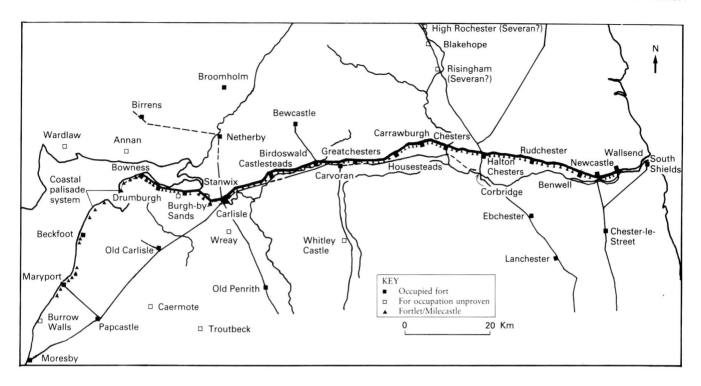

Hadrian's Wall

Milecastle 37, on the central section of Hadrian's Wall

may have enabled tribesmen to revert to raiding. Roman troops acted as police but faced problems characteristic of a colonial power operating against local men with the backing of the local community.

The Walls

Hadrian arrived in Britain in AD 122/3 and set in commission the wall which bears his name (hereafter, the Wall). The new system supplemented the Stanegate Road and forts with a continuous wall built on commanding ground, equipped with mile-fortlets and intervening turrets. During construction, the decision was made to move the garrisons to the Wall and construct forts on the southern side. Various other changes were incorporated during building, which took the best part of two decades. A military ditch fronted it, wherever practicable, and a *vallum* was dug on the south side, probably to distinguish the province from the military corridor.

The frontier was no sooner completed than abandoned. Hadrian's elderly and unmilitary successor ordered a fresh advance to the Forth–Clyde isthmus on his elevation in AD 139. His expansion of the province provided the emperor with a timely military success. His purpose was presumably political but the choice of Britain may be significant. Some northern tribes may have been actively hostile and the building of new frontier works emphasized Roman might.

The new wall was quickly constructed of turf and earth, with closely spaced forts. The Wall garrisons were redeployed to the new frontier, the gates of the abandoned forts left open and the *vallum* slighted. The route system beyond Hadrian's Wall was recommissioned. The phase 4B fort at Corbridge on Dere Street shows close structural similarities with the stone and timber Antonine Wall forts. In northern England the garrisons were thinned to supply the necessary manpower.

Roman occupation of southern Scotland wobbled ominously in the 150s, when troops were pulled back, and, although the farther wall was temporarily re-occupied, it was abandoned for good when Antoninus Pius died. The garrisons returned to the Hadrianic frontier and its outliers, whence the army maintained surveillance over the tribes for many decades to come.

The north saw successive military campaigns over the next two generations and the frontier was under considerable strain in the 180s. Dio recorded that tribes crossed the Wall, killed a Roman general and did great damage (LXIII, 8). Tribal war-bands were ill placed to attack or besiege Roman forts and most confrontations probably occurred in the countryside, unless they found a military installation all but unguarded.

The garrisons of the north were probably much reduced by Clodius Albinus when he took the British army to the continent in AD 196 in a rather too leisurely bid for empire. Dio recorded that the first Severan governor bought peace from the Maeatae (LXXV, 5) and his name occurs in several inscriptions recording fort rebuilding. In AD 208 Severus arrived at the head of an imperial expedition, but it is unclear whether he did this to combat enemy action, as Herodian reported, or to remove his sons from decadent Rome (Dio, LXXVI, 13). Severus and Caracalla used South Shields and Corbridge as their springboards to establish a new campaign base at Carpow beyond the Forth, and enjoyed considerable success before the war was ended by Severus' death. This campaign had a major impact on the northern tribes, who left the province in peace for most of the next century. The Tyne–Solway *limes* was secured and northern England finally pacified.

Kaims Castle, a fortlet which was part of the system of outposts north of the Antonine Wall. The photograph was taken after light snow

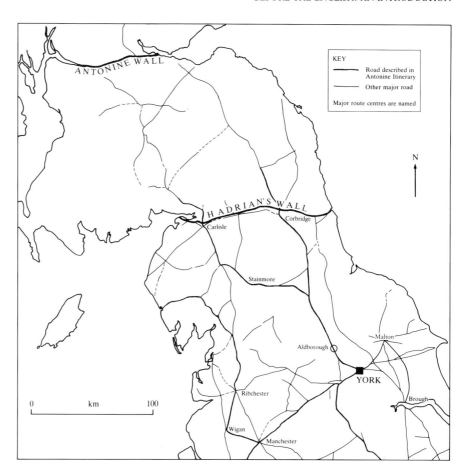

The Roman walls and the road network of the north

The putative Roman road on Blackstone Edge, running diagonally across the picture. If it was Roman, and not medieval, in origin, it would have carried traffic between York and Manchester

Beyond the Wall, Roman forces supervised the tribes south of the Forth, with what were probably regular tribal gatherings at stipulated sites sanctioned by the colonial power. Diplomacy, gifts and interference in the internal workings of the local tribes rendered the region an effective buffer zone. Roman practice in this respect probably mirrored that of the Brigantes before them.

Romanization and the North

Rome exported its own cultural, social and economic system towards the periphery of its military and political control. The provinces tended to adopt the cultural habits and greater specialization of the Roman world, arriving with the soldiers, administrators and merchants. This process is very visible in southern Britain, where a civil province settled into a Roman mould within the first century. In the north, the process was delayed – to an extent even stillborn. Romanization was hindered by low levels of social stratification at the conquest. Despite recent advances, the agricultural base was less productive than in the south and so less able to support a cash economy. Lastly, the continuing presence of the Roman garrisons gave the region a distinctive structure which impeded the development of civil hierarchies and economic specialization by sucking in imports. Northern England remained a peripheral part of the Roman world, whatever criteria are applied.

Government and Social Order

It was the commander of *legio IX Hispana* (after *c.* AD 122, *VI Victrix Pia Fidelis*) at York who was the political successor of the client-rulers of Brigantia. To this officer fell the task of disarming, administering, taxing and policing the newly won territory and overseeing the numerous garrisons. The legionary fortress was the most important centre in the north for more than three centuries.

The Severans sub-divided Britain into two provinces and raised the civilian settlement outside the fortress (*Colonia Eboracensis* by AD 237) to the status of a *colonia*, making it the provincial capital of Britannia Inferior – the north-east Midlands and the north. Until the separation of civil jurisdiction from military command under Justinian, the commander of the legion was the governor. Despite Brough-on-Humber and a harbour near Bridlington, York was the most important port in the north, linked via the Humber and Ouse to coastal traffic in the North Sea and via the Trent to the east Midlands. Although the earliest civil settlement was east of the Ouse, it was the area of

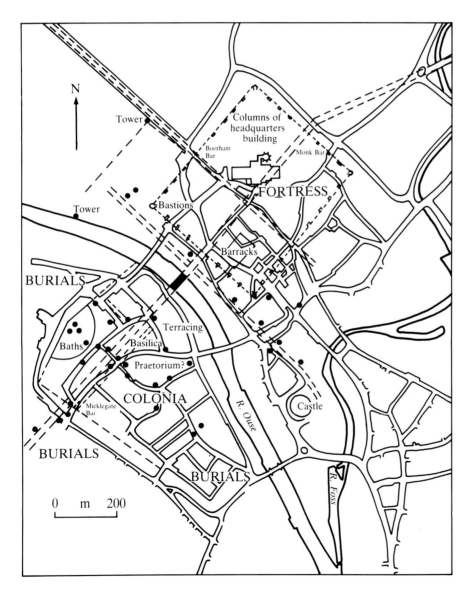

Roman York. The modern road system is simplified

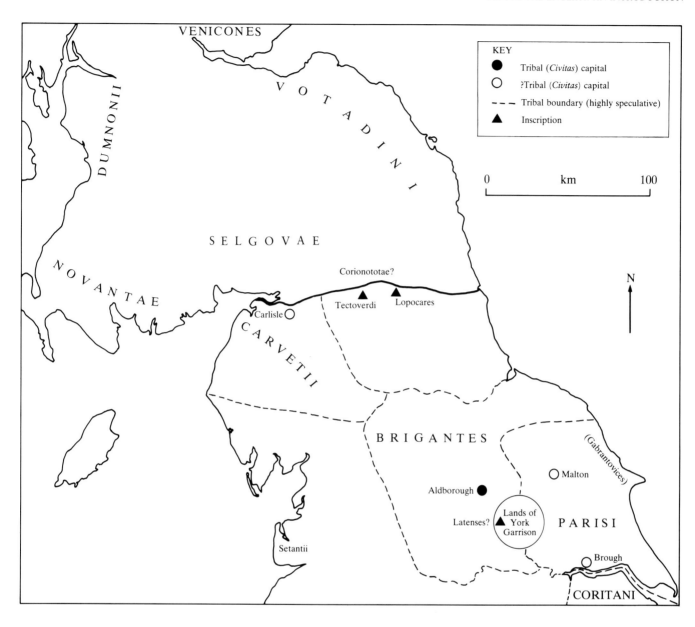

Tribes of the Roman north. All tribal boundaries are hypothetical

An internal tower on the north-west perimeter wall of the fortress at York, built before c. AD 200

Micklegate and Bishophill where the civil settlement eventually developed and was circumscribed by a masonry wall. Although on a lesser scale and overshadowed by the fortress, the site has parallels with London and some buildings were adorned with imported marble. However, it was the fortress which remained the more important site throughout, and the authority of its commander *vis-à-vis* the civil governor was emphasized by the building of new flanking towers along the riverside during the early fourth century – most probably under Constantine the Great, whose acclamation occurred here.

The density of garrisons in some parts of the north – particularly the Tyne–Solway area – suggests that large parts of the better agricultural lands were requisitioned by the soldiery. In addition, access to quarries, ores and other resources cut across pre-existing land rights. It is not difficult to find reasons for long-continuing antagonism towards the Romans on the part of the indigenous population. Be that as it may, the north was the last region to be granted local self-government in Roman

Britain, and many areas were never released from direct military administration.

The Parisi were apparently separated from the Brigantes and organized as a *civitas* before Ptolemy's sources were compiled. Briganita otherwise retained its integrity to this point, but Pausanias recorded that they were 'deprived . . . of most of their territory because they had entered on a war of aggression by invading the *Genounian* part' (*Description of Greece*, VIII, 43). Whoever it was they attacked the punishment deprived them of erstwhile clients to the north and west.

The Carvetii ('deer-people') in Cumbria are unlikely to have been given self-government until the Severan period, although some planned urban development had been postulated at Carlisle a generation before. When the Brigantes achieved the same status depends on interpretation of the poorly-researched Aldborough (*Isubrigantum* in the Antonine Itinerary), which probably originated as a Flavian fort. The *civitas* may have come into existence under Hadrian but it seems unlikely that the military authorities relinquished direct control before the Severan campaigns, and romanization was slight before *c*. AD 200. The Carvetian tribal territory was probably defined by the Wall, Stainmore and central Lakeland but there are no known limits to the *civitas* of the Brigantes and, despite the general view that it encompassed the bulk of the north, there is a good case for defining it far more narrowly. It was certainly not wide, limited as it was by the Carvetii, and by the military *prata* (expropriated territory) of the York legion to the south-east,

The southern Pennines in winter

Tombstone from the Roman period cemetery outside the auxiliary fort at Brougham

which may have extended as far as Tadcaster. There is no evidence that any of the other tribes enjoyed self-government. All Lancashire, the bulk of the Pennines, much of Durham and the south Lakes with Furness probably remained under military rule throughout the Roman occupation.

Urbanization

Roman civilization was urban in character, and urbanization is a useful measure of romanization. It began late in the north and the results never matched the density and sophistication of towns in southern England. None existed beyond Hadrian's Wall. Within, Brough-on-Humber, Malton, York, Aldborough, Catterick and Piercebridge represent two-thirds of the more plausible candidates. Even among these, urban facilities such as water conduits, *fora* (market-places), temples, theatres and baths were far from uniform.

The best-equipped town was York, the capital of Britannia Inferior, across the Ouse from the legionary fortress. An imperial palace may have been present, particularly given the recent discovery of masonry on a massive scale. Literary evidence implies that a palace or *praetorium* was built for Severus early in the third century. If it survived thereafter it can have seen only occassional use until the Diocletianic reforms separated the governorship from command of the legion, but recent excavations on the Queen's Hotel site may have revealed a fragment of this building. The *colonia* was well provided with baths from the second century onwards and late Victorian excavations revealed a *basilica* close to the river which may be associated with the *forum*. The presence of a bishop implies an as yet unlocated Christian church. York housed a cosmopolitan community, among whom locals need not have been either prominent or influential.

The civil settlement began to supply the needs of the legionaries in the fortress. An intimate relationship with the military was typical of northern towns, which generally developed on sites vacated by soldiers. The latter often retained an interest. At Catterick, a core of government buildings attracted shops and workshops. These were refurbished in stone in the third century, but its position on the military supply network reflects the movement of goods to the garrisons. Within

One of the military granaries at Corbridge. Even with the development of a town on the site, the military retained facilities here and its role as a port and supply centre for the Wall dominated the civil settlement

Vindolanda (Chesterholm), an auxiliary fort and its *vicus* on Stanegate

Corbridge town was a large military compound with storehouses and workshops. The site served as a port for the Wall, as did Carlisle in the west. Such communities were not so different from the *vicani* who occupied settlements outside the walls of many forts. At Old Carlisle and *Vindolanda* (Chesterholm), for example, were long-lived, well-built masonry strip-houses, end-on to the roadways and supplying various services to the soldiers.

In his *Geographia*, Ptolemy attributed the *polis* of *Petuaria* at Brough-on-Humber to the Parisi. The civil site began as a fort, stores depot and port which then attracted civilian settlement. In the mid- to late second century the town was defended and boasted a theatre. Inscriptional evidence incorporated in the fourth-century naval base may denote its status as a tribal capital but this is contested. Similarities between its defences and the Antonine Wall forts imply that the former were the work of the army and later walls bear comparison with the Saxon Shore forts. Within, the principal structures so far located were workshops, denoting an economy similar to that of the numerous refitting depots of southern and central Lancashire, where metal-working was common – again probably for a military market.

Malton is a better candidate as the Parisian capital as the Arras culture was concentrated on the north-east Wolds: a *vicus* developed early outside a fort of the Conquest period and was walled by around AD 200; suburbs or ribbon development also occurred across the river at Norton, where pottery kilns were concentrated. The *vicus* achieved a high degreee of romanization: water was piped into the settlement; a

goldsmith was resident; and the so-called 'Town House' boasted mosaics, hypocausts, and painted wall-plaster.

Throughout the northern towns of Roman Britain, evidence for prosperous, urbanized tribal gentry is sparse. A scatter of mosaics at Aldborough testify to the presence of housing of this standard in the regular street-grid around the central *forum*, and mosaics at Toft Green (York) may be products of the same workshop. Several properties at the tribal capital of Carlisle appear to have been well-accoutred town-houses, although the total absence of villas in the region may imply that these were the homes of immigrant traders. A scatter of sites in the York *colonia* have produced comparable evidence.

All these examples may have been commissioned by incoming bureaucrats or merchants. Excluding these sites and Malton there were few such residences. Vicinal buildings were often stone-founded and comparatively large but they had few other characteristics of romanized accommodation. A cultured lifestyle was available, therefore, in the provincial and tribal capitals, where Roman-style temples, public baths and even theatres were concentrated, Latin was spoken, and a Roman education available. *Vicani* presumably knew enough Latin to communicate with the soldiers but local recruitment may have gradually reduced the need for Latin in the *vici*. Town life thinned dramatically to the north and west where romanization was at its weakest.

Mosaic from a Roman house under excavation at Clementhorpe, York

Religion and Burial

When the Roman Conquest occurred the religions of the northern tribes were similar to that of other Celtic tribes, characteristically localized, associated with water, animals or animalism, or hilltops. Animal names used in tribal names imply that totemism was common but pre-Roman cults left no physical remains so religious customs are poorly evidenced. It is from the Roman period that most information derives. Local cults survived unusually well and attracted Roman-style dedications, becoming an important strand in the mêlée of religious practices which characterized relations between man and the supernatural within the Empire.

Brigantia, or Bregans, was a pseudo-eponymous deity of the Brigantes. The distribution of dedications has been used to speculate concerning the geography of the client-kingdom but most dedications were by officials in the third century, and Brigantia was coupled with imported Roman gods such as Victory and Caelestis. This interest in Brigantia may have been rekindled by the creation of the new northern province, for which administrators may have sought a precedent in the erstwhile client-kingdom.

Other local spirits of the Wall zone had a distinctly higher profile than parallel deities in southern Britain but civilian dedications are scarce. Most were commissioned by soldiers or *vicani*, many of whom were probably immigrants. It may have been local recruitment to the soldiery which brought together Roman styles of dedication and a respect for local cults. Some occur within tightly defined areas which may represent tribal territories. Dedications to the horned Belatucadrus are concentrated in the territory of the Carvetii. Mars

Romano-Celtic cults in northern England

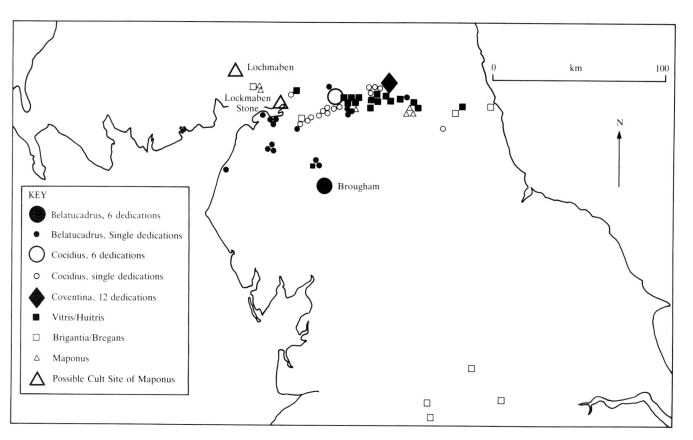

KEY

⬤ Belatucadrus, 6 dedications

• Belatucadrus, Single dedications

◯ Cocidius, 6 dedications

○ Cocidius, single dedications

◆ Coventina, 12 dedications

■ Vitris/Huitris

□ Brigantia/Bregans

△ Maponus

⧍ Possible Cult Site of Maponus

Lochmaben

Lockmaben Stone

Brougham

The temple of Mithras at Carrawburgh

Rigas, at Malton, may have been a Parisian deity. Dedications to Vitris or Huitris are concentrated on the central sections of the Wall, and to Cocidius along the western sections and at Bewcastle. The centre of the cult to Maponus may be at *locus Maponi* in Dumfries and Galloway. Rather different is the well of Coventina, at Carrawburgh, where twelve dedications have been recovered to a deity unknown elsewhere, apparently the tutelary divinity of a specific spring.

In other respects local dedications mirrored the religious practices characteristic of other areas of the Roman world. The Roman army brought with them the official religions of the Empire, and dedications to the Capitoline Triad played an important role in the official religion of the garrisons. As many as sixteen such dedications were discovered buried beside the parade-ground outside the fort at Maryport. Some emperors had a special attachment to or association with specific deities, such as the triple association evidenced in stone at Carlisle between Commodus, Victory and Hercules. The presence of a college of *Augustales* at York is demonstrated by two inscriptions, so there was presumably a shrine of the imperial cult established there.

Other groups in the frontier region brought with them or utilized religious practices drawn from diverse parts of the vast pantheon of Greek and Roman religion, which were specifically adapted to their own specialisms within the Roman system. Perhaps the best known of

OPPOSITE: Old Carlisle, a Roman auxiliary fort and its *vicus* in the hinterland of the Wall

A stone lion, now in Corbridge Museum, from the mausoleum at Shorden Brae

the religions brought in from the east is Mithraism, which attracted a distinguished but select following from among the military élite. Small, church-like temples were constructed for the celebration of the rites, of which an as yet unlocated example existed at York. The *mithraeum* at Carrawburgh was a long-lived and much refurbished structure, within which the principal altars were dedicated by the commander of the garrison.

The presence of such cults reflects a substantial imperial community in the region, whose polyglot ideologies had a profound impact on the garrison forts and the urban communities. Outside such centres were grouped the burials of the inmates, ranged in large cemeteries along the roads. Grave styles conformed to the gradual development of Roman funerary customs – shifting slowly from cremation to inhumation, for example, during the second and third centuries. Grave markers were an important area of employment for the masons responsible for inscriptions and temples, and they are particularly numerous in the region, albeit commissioned largely by immigrants. The graves of a few individuals attracted rather more resources, with the construction of elaborate mausolea, such as that at Shorden Brae cemetery, outside Corbridge, with a tower built on a 10 m² base inside a precinct ornamented with sculptures of lions crouching over stags.

The most complete cemetery so far excavated in the north is that at Trentholme Drive, York, used from *c.* AD 140 until the late fourth

century, wherein about 350 individuals were buried. Both cremations and inhumations were found, the shift from the former to the latter having occurred gradually during the period *c.* AD 180–280. The absence of tombstones and the presence of only two sarcophagi coincided with evidence of massive recutting of graves by later gravediggers to suggest that the cemetery was utilized by a relatively poor quarter of the *colonia*. Most, if not all, of the extra-mural graves arguably contained the remains of members of the garrisons, their dependants or town-dwellers. How the corporal remains of countryfolk were disposed of remains a mystery.

A lowland farm site at Yanwath, near Penrith. Fields and an approach track are visible as crop marks to the right of the main settlement

The Countryside

Throughout the Roman period the vast bulk of the indigenous population lived and worked in the countryside, inhabiting farms which owed little to Roman stereotypes. Examples are best preserved on the edges of the uplands, on marginal land which has not since seen intensive agriculture. Until the use of aerial photography became widespread little indigenous settlement had been identified in the valleys and plains of the region. Now, however, site discovery on the better drained soils of the lowlands has completed the logical pattern of settlement. Voids do still exist but in most instances these are explicable either by problems of identification or by the presence of poor upland soils or lowland peat. The most easily identified form of farm site is an enclosed yard, with buildings, internal divisions and minor structures, surrounded by a bank and ditch or stone wall – the method of enclosure generally dependent on the materials to hand. Settlements were enclosed rather than defensible. The small number of narrow gaps through the perimeter barrier were generally closed with a simple gate.

When excavated, such sites generally yield small numbers of Roman artefacts. The quantity of finds depends on the length of occupation, regional siting and the proximity of markets. Beyond the Wall, finds are minimal and, outside the Antonine period, there was insufficient penetration of Roman goods to provide a reliable dating mechanism for sites of low status. Elsewhere, finds concentrate in particular periods but excavators often suspect aceramic occupation occurring at other times. Dating evidence is at its most prolific in Yorkshire, and particularly on and around the Wolds, where a long-lived pottery industry provided for a local market and eventually achieved considerable export success along the Wall. A survey of Wharram demonstrated that

A ditched promontory settlement at Great Woolden Hall, Irlam. Excavation by the Greater Manchester Archaeological Unit produced pottery of the Roman period

larger and more important sites were occupied from the late pre-Roman Iron Age through the Roman period and on into the early to mid-Saxon period. Studies in the area of Kielder Dam provide similar evidence of repeated reconstruction of settlements.

Such farms adhered tenaciously to specific sites over long periods even stretching back into tribal prehistory. Neither their enclosures nor their houses owed much to romanization, except where farmers opted for the rectilinear building style of the Roman world, sometimes roofed with clay tiles. Such minor adaptation to more romanized forms occurred in East Yorkshire during the second century but did not spread elsewhere until other regions had also become *civitates*.

Individual farm sites are scattered across the more hospitable terrains, sometimes in small groups sharing field systems. There are few instances of groups of farms sufficiently united to be described as a village, although settlement at Wharram Percy was larger than is commensurate with a single farmstead. Another candidate is at Grassington in Wharfedale, where two groups of farms existed alongside isolated settlements. Many settlements were associated with roadways, although it is rarely clear whether the road preceded or post-dated establishment of the settlement. Few occur above *c*. 300 m but there is a tendency for sites to congregate on the interface between land reserved for open grazing and arable. In the vicinity of Kirkby Stephen, turf-constructed dykes seem to have marked this interface but, despite excavation, they have not been securely dated. Similar problems pertain to many of the linear earthworks which divide up large blocks of the Wolds.

A turf dyke on Crosby Garrett Fell, near Kirkby Stephen, which appears to distinguish the arable land associated with three farm sites from open grazing on the fell

A farmstead under excavation on Fingland Rigg, on the Solway Plain

Land-use

Deforestation peaked during the Roman period, when large tracts of countryside had little more woodland than is present today. Palisaded settlements used a great deal of timber, and woodland was cleared rapidly around them. It may be for this reason that subsequent rebuildings resorted to either ditch-and-bank systems or stone walls. Elsewhere, grazing livestock reduced woodland to open or scrubby grassland.

Throughout much of the north, the characteristic field system was small in scale, and associated with one or a very small number of settlements. Agriculture was probably limited to a few acres immediately adjacent to the farmyard in closes protected by walls, hedges or ditches, in which manuring enabled annual cropping to be maintained. Where evidence has survived, barley seems to have been the commonest grain grown in the region outside the Wolds, where wheat was probably more widely sown. Seasonal exploitation of moorland pastures – known as transhumance – enabled farmers to conserve pasture close to home for hay.

Extensive enclosed landscapes were in use during the Roman period as far north as southern Cumbria but are most widespread in the limestone Pennines, the Wolds and in South Yorkshire. One at Austerfield was cut by a Roman road, demonstrating that it was pre-Roman, and this evidence is in line with the dating of so-called 'ladder' systems of small fields, which are widespread in eastern Yorkshire.

Farmsteads and fields on Aughertree Fell

They have only been identified across a small proportion of the region, characteristically in well-drained areas where deforestation was early. Such landscapes were capable of producing significant surpluses, in grain or livestock. They are not closely associated with villas and were probably an indigenous phenomenon. Some were abandoned during the Roman period but others probably remained in use after the collapse of Roman Britain. Aerial photography of parts of the Wolds has established the contemporaneity of Roman roads and field systems. At Wharram, abandonment of several 'ladder' systems has been inferred from the absence of Roman pottery. The distribution of pot-sherds from manuring suggests that large-scale agriculture occurred, probably within prehistoric boundaries. On the north-eastern Wolds some 40 km^2 were enclosed and Roman pottery scatters imply settlement and manuring in the later Roman period.

Most such complexes are now visible only from the air or through field-walking and excavation, but within the Yorkshire Dales there are extensive stretches of landscapes which bear the heavy imprint of activity within the Roman period, and these are far easier to visit and comprehend. The best-preserved fringe Wharfedale approximately at their most visible around Grassington. These landscape remains can be traced sporadically over c. 180 ha of enclosed rough grazing land on a limestone plateau, between about 300 and 350 m above OD. The fields, settlements and roadways are picked out by collapsed stone walls or stony banks, while lynchets imply intensive cultivation of some enclosures. The density of settlement was clearly impressive and land-use intense.

A tumbled field wall at Grassington under light snow. Note the slight curve of this arable field and the terraced effect resulting from plough cultivation

38

Romanization within the Countryside

The development of romanized farms and country houses, or villas, is another measure of cultural adaptation. The adoption of rectilinear building plans, half-timbered or stone-walled construction, or roof-tiles was eventually widespread, starting in East Yorkshire where it quickly followed the appearance of Roman pottery, glassware and metalwork. Yet round houses remained widespread throughout the period and coins are rarely found on farm sites.

A small minority of sites saw the building of more romanized structures, with substantial and multi-roomed houses sporting hypocausts, mosaics and wall-paintings, often associated with rectilinear agricultural buildings. Most such villas were constructed on pre-existing settlements and were arguably commissioned by the indigenous gentry, although land-purchase by immigrant bureaucrats, merchants or veterans cannot be ruled out. Villas occur on good agricultural land and were probably funded by the sale of grain in the towns and *vici*, or

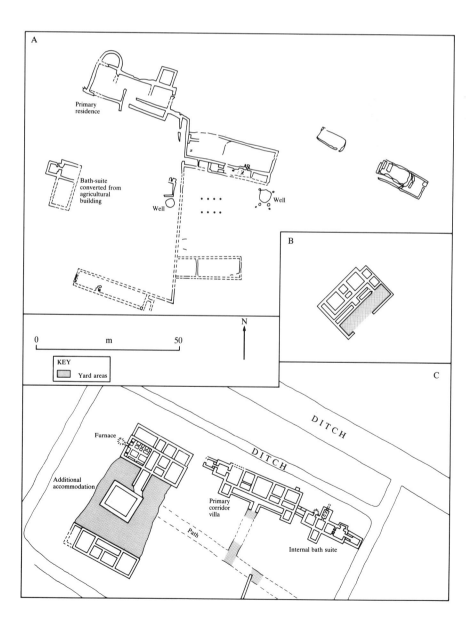

Romanized country houses or villas in the north. A: Dalton Parlours; B: Drax; C: Gargrave (A, C after Hartley and Fitts, 1988; B after Branigan, 1980)

to the government. Villas were primarily the homes of a social élite of tribal patrons and landlords.

The Venus Mosaic from the Roman villa at Rudston

Villas developed only slowly in the north. At both Holme House and Old Durham (the most northerly example yet identified), circular structures built in stone reflect the interface between Roman and native styles of building. These particular structures may have been linked to a shift towards more intensive exploitation of grain crops under the stimulus of military demand. Garstang was founded soon after the fort at Slack and the corn dryers at Wharram Percy, Langton and Welton Wold certainly suggest a shift to intensive corn production.

Most villas were built in the late third or early fourth centuries, more than ten generations after the initial conquest of Brigantia. Although none attained the palatial proportions of some in the Cotswolds, they were built in the same corridor-style and on the same sort of scale as numerous minor southern villas. The basic designs used travelled up from the Midlands. Many were decorated with mosaics. A handful of these are examples of skilled workmanship within a classical genre – the charioteer mosaic at Rudston is the obvious example – but most were crudely executed and simple in conception. Some mixed classical with Celtic motifs, as does the so-called 'Venus Mosaic', also from

Rudston, with its rusticated anthropomorphic and animal figures. Several villas had large detached bath-suites or pools, as at Dalton Parlours and Well respectively, where facilities were provided for use by visitors, tenants and dependants who were not normally residents within the villa-house, for whom there were internal bath-suites. Other villas were extremely small, barely more than romanized cottages, such as that identified at Drax.

The distribution of villas is uneven. They were concentrated in the lowland region in the south-east of Brigantia, in Yorkshire. None have been located west of the Pennines, and the spread thins dramatically north of the Tees. There are barely fifty known in all, of which approximately half lie in Parisian territory, east of York. Villas are found in the same areas as the wealthy tribal aristocracy of the pre-Roman era. The level of agricultural yields was a factor in both distributions. There are concentrations of villas around Malton and Brough-on-Humber but those adjacent to Bridlington, York and Aldborough are fewer, with none particularly close to the latter, around which land may have been farmed from within the *civitas* capital. The environs of York pose special problems of identification, owing to the subsequent deposition of flood silts across the plain, so the pattern of settlement is probably seriously under-recorded. Those around Malton, York and Brough were well placed to exploit the social and commercial opportunities offered by urban markets and most others were sited within easy reach of Roman roads and the military supply network which used them.

A Roman corn-drying kiln at Wharram Percy

Rome and the North

For several centuries, the Roman Empire surrounded itself with a military shell. Within it, the bulk of the provinces adopted a civilian social and economic system focused on towns and on gentry residences in the countryside. On both, romanized goods and coinage can be readily uncovered. The bulk of northern England remained part of the outer shell, dominated by large garrisons. Graphically highlighted by some of the writing tablets excavated at *Vindolanda*, their needs constituted the greatest single economic force in the region, omitting only the basic subsistence of the local population. A large amount of land was controlled by the army, imperial officers or outside contractors in charge of mineral extraction. There was little scope for an indigenous élite, such as that which is archaeologically visible in the south-east of the region, south of the Tees. It was here that the civilian towns and villas were sited, close to the provincial capital and two of the three cantonal capitals. Yet even here, the penetration of Roman culture was slower than in most of southern Britain, and local farmers were barely integrated into the Roman economic system.

Throughout the first 250 years of the Roman period, the north of England ran a trade deficit in manufactured goods with the south and the continent. This was paid for by southern taxes to resource the soldiers concentrated in the north. The effect was an ongoing subsidy from the richer regions of the island to the periphery, where it was released into the markets in the *vici* and towns. The wages of soldiers and administrators were sufficient to attract outsiders from all parts of the Empire, bringing with them many of the trappings of romanization.

Around them, rural communities retained a lifestyle that owed more to later prehistory than to the Romans. They presumably paid whatever taxes were demanded of them – perhaps in livestock – but romanized goods entering the farm gate were few and cheap. The indigenous people of northern Britain were little affected by romanization as far as their culture, language and economy were concerned. There were more of them than hitherto and new settlements had come into being but many still inhabited farms founded before the Romans crossed the Channel. The villas and towns in the south-east of the region remained islands – important islands but islands none the less – within a hinterland which was at least as Celtic as it was Roman.

CHAPTER 2

Catastrophe or Continuity?

The degree of specialization in the late Empire was far greater than among its barbarian neighbours: military skills were the monopoly of a professional army which was paid, supplied and recruited from a large but generally passive civilian populace, regimented and governed by a complex bureaucracy. During the early fifth century this system broke down, not only in Britain but throughout much of the western Empire. The result was a crisis of unprecedented scale in which the complex and interlocking Roman social structure ceased to operate. Local communities were left without effective government or defence and, with the exchange economy in ruins, were forced to adjust as best they could.

The reasons for this collapse remain a matter of debate. Scholars have sought the causes in the army itself, in pressures from barbarian neighbours, in climatic, demographic and economic shifts and in deep-seated changes within the Roman system of administration and government. It seems likely that no single factor can, on its own, offer an adequate explanation of the end of Rome in the west, which appears to have resulted both from a long-drawn crisis of under-production and over-government and from a temporary convergence of several causal factors – climatic change, rebellion within the Empire and invasion from without. The Empire suffered from many of the same problems of totalitarianism which were prevalent in the twentieth-century Communist bloc and the difficulty of shedding these problems was no less in the ancient world than in the modern. The mixed market economy of the second century had degenerated by the fourth century to one dominated by state conscription, forced labour, bureaucracy and governmental regulation. The low rates of return which characterized rural production in the West could not sustain such onerous governmental pressures.

In the short term, the collapse was a consequence of the ending of the diocesan government. Honorius' government of the West failed to re-establish control of Britain after the failure of the rebellion of

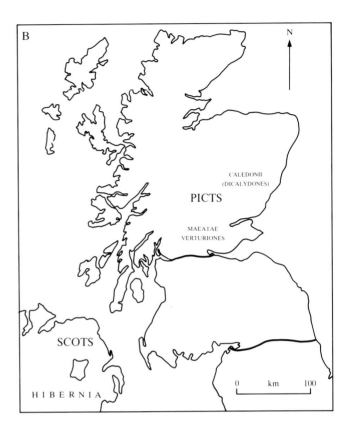

Constantine III (*c.* 406–10) and Britain was never again ruled by the representatives of an emperor based beyond the Channel.

Regional considerations were also important within the diocese. The frontier status of the northern province and the low levels of romanization attained across much of it both left their mark on the process.

The tribes of northern Britain. A: according to Ptolemy; B: as portrayed in third- and fourth-century Roman literature. In the *Ravenna Cosmography* the Picts of the fourth century were superimposed on to the Ptolemaic tribes

Rome and the Northern Barbarians

One of the functions of the northern province had always been to act as a buffer between the richer and more romanized south and barbarians beyond the Wall. During the fourth century, the latter regained the initiative and became more demanding in their relationship with the Empire, with the result that new programmes were instituted to restrain them.

In the mid-second century, Ptolemy named twelve tribes in Britain beyond the Forth. By the early third century, these had been consolidated into two tribal groups – the Maeatae (probably focused on Fife and Angus) and the Caledones of the far north. By the end of the third century, Roman writers were referring to the Picts (*Picti*) to describe the inhabitants of the whole region. In his description of events in the 360s, Ammianus Marcellinus noted that the Picts constituted two nations, the Dicalydones and the Verturiones. The Picts of the fourth century were presumably the Caledonians and Maeatae of the third.

This consolidation into ever larger political units was probably encouraged by Roman administrators who found it convenient to deal with the minimum number of barbarian leaders, keeping them attached to the Roman interest by diplomatic gifts, trading monopolies and subsidies. Such terms may have been components of the treaties with Rome broken by the Picts and the Scots (of Ireland) in the mid-fourth century. When diplomacy failed to satisfy barbarian demand for Roman goods, then their leaders came under increasing pressure to send raiding parties to bring back booty, which in turn assisted in maintaining their own leadership of what were highly competitive hierarchies.

Raiding by sea-borne tribesmen from Ireland and Pictland became a major threat to the British provinces during the late third and fourth centuries. The bases from which both communities made their attacks were generally beyond the reach of counter-measures – although in his *Chronicon Gratiani* (IV), Prosper Tiro implied that Magnus Maximus struck at the southern Picts, and Stilicho was credited with naval action against barbarian pirates in defence of Britain.

In AD 360 the threat posed by the Picts and Scots laying waste places near the frontiers was sufficient to bring the 'Master of Armies', Lupicinus, across the Channel in mid-winter to restore the situation. Severe raiding was documented in 365 and 367, when Ammianus makes it clear that the northern garrisons failed to halt a large-scale raid by the Celtic tribes on southern Britain (*Historia*, XXVII, 8). However, the widespread evidence for destruction among the northern forts, which was linked by an earlier generation of scholars to this barbarian conspiracy, has now largely evaporated, leaving only a handful of forts and Corbridge as possible but uncertain candidates for destruction at this date. Barbarians are more likely to have raided the countryside than to have attacked walled centres but destruction was not common at this stage even among the villas of Yorkshire. The major weight of the attacks of the Picts and Scots was probably directed at the south, sweeping past the coasts of the north in search of richer pickings beyond. Some of these raiders were later attacked by incoming Roman forces in Kent.

The south-west corner tower of the fortress at York, rebuilt to imposing standards in the early fourth century. The larger masonry blocks equipped with arrow slits in the top third were added in the medieval period

The Frontier Army

The British garrisons lost out in the process of army re-organization during the fourth century. As frontier forces (*limitatenses*), they were paid less than soldiers in the new field armies and they probably did less well in the internal competition for resources and manpower. The northern British army had lost large numbers of units and men during the third and early fourth centuries, including those redeployed to confront the menace from pirates or Saxons on the Channel. Evidence of 'chalet'-type accommodation from Wallsend, Housesteads and elsewhere suggests that the total number of troops stationed in some Wall forts had declined by up to 90 per cent, the survivors perhaps being housed with their dependants in family units. The Roman soldiers defending the north may have numbered fewer than six thousand for much of the fourth century.

Despite this, the northern army showed itself to be flexible and professional, investing in new dispositions and adopting novel strategies as appropriate. Modern attempts to characterize it as a farmer militia are poorly founded.

In the *Notitia Dignitatum*, a late Roman collection of administrative documents, York remained the command post of the *dux* ('duke') and the sixth legion, and archaeological evidence confirms continuing

Maryport, an auxiliary fort on the Irish Sea equipped with at least one external bastion in the fourth century

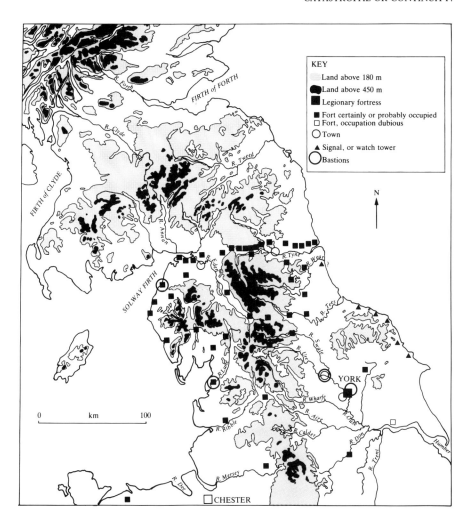

The military defences of the north in the late Roman period

occupation throughout the period. New flanking towers – provided perhaps on the orders of Constantine the Great – emphasized the stature of the fortress where it confronted the civil *colonia* across the Ouse. These and the mid-fourth-century bastions on the town wall at Aldborough imply that provision was made for the use of catapults in the defence of key centres. Archaeological evidence for such *ballistae* at High Rochester and Lanchester and aerial photographic evidence at Maryport suggest that exposed garrisons were given better protection at this stage, but most forts seem not to have been equipped with artillery, even where extensive rebuilding occurred in the Theodosian period. It seems likely that the improvements to the walls of the legionary fortress and the tribal capital were undertaken more for reasons of status than of military necessity.

The Theodosian period saw widespread rebuilding among the forts along the Wall, all of which were retained in use at some level, although some of the intervening installations – milecastles and turrets – remained derelict. Almost all the forts were listed in the *Notitia*.

In line with contemporary practice, new work was undertaken by drafts of labourers supplied as part of their obligations to the state by the individual *civitates* of the diocese, among whom the Catuvellauni of Hertfordshire, the Durotriges of the central south of England, the Dumnonii of the south-west and, perhaps, the Brigantes themselves recorded their involvement in inscriptions. A reduction in the size and number of the gates of several forts implies a new emphasis on habitation and defence, and there were changes in the use of the central buildings in several forts during the last decades of the century, the Binchester *praetorium* (headquarters building), for example, losing its organizational functions and becoming a slaughter-house.

Until successive troop withdrawals to the continent under Magnus Maximus (AD 385–8) and Stilicho (AD 398), occupied forts were still numerous in the hinterland. Several sites, such as Binchester, Piercebridge and Catterick, saw substantial refitting after AD 360, the latter apparently in order to provide accommodation for cavalry. According to the long-obsolete lists recorded in the fifth century in the *Notitia*, mounted units predominated among the hinterland forts, offering a swifter response to raids than infantry, albeit at a greater expense. However, many second-century forts were totally abandoned.

The last decades of the fourth century saw a major overhaul of coastal defence and of internal security along the arterial roads. A shift of resources to the coasts had already begun early in the century. A unit of bargemen from the Tigris was deployed at South Shields before *c.* AD 325 and a similar group has been identified defending the Lune in the vicinity of Lancaster. Perhaps as early as the 340s Lancaster itself was equipped with a new fortress defended by a massive new wall, known as the Wery Wall, built to specifications familiar among the

Military dispositions in northern Britain as portrayed in the *Notitia Dignitatum*

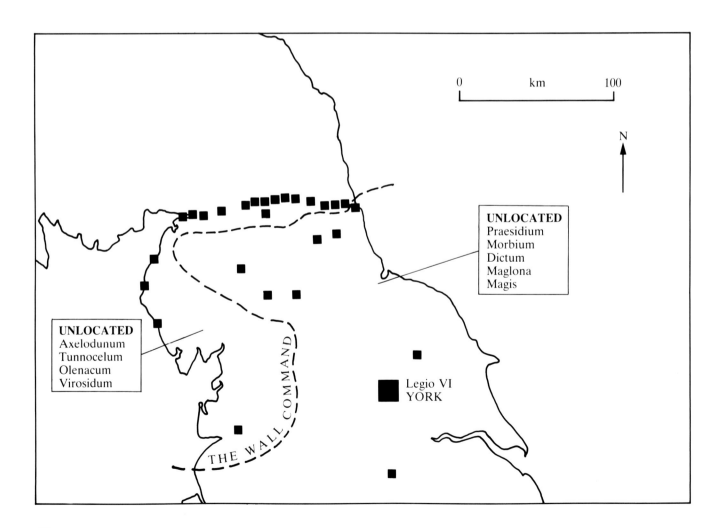

UNLOCATED
Praesidium
Morbium
Dictum
Maglona
Magis

UNLOCATED
Axelodunum
Tunnocelum
Olenacum
Virosidum

THE WALL COMMAND

Legio VI
YORK

0   km   100

N

The fast-eroding North Sea coast at Huntcliff was the site of a Roman watch-tower

Saxon Shore forts of the south. This was presumably a fleet base and was probably the command post for a Roman fleet covering the northern Irish Sea coasts. It might also be linked to the role of the *areani* or *arcani*, who were the scouts or agents whose treachery was held responsible for the disaster of AD 367. The western coastal defences were further strengthened by a re-occupation of the second-century forts on the Cumbrian coast at Ravenglass and Burrow Walls, associated with some signs of late activity at Bowness-on-Solway and several of the second-century mile-fortlets nearby.

The naval station at Brough-on-Humber became inoperative during the fourth century as a consequence of silting but surveillance was maintained by a string of large watch-towers, ruined examples of which survived into this century at five locations in Yorkshire from Filey northwards to Huntcliff. More may originally have been constructed along the now much-eroded coast of County Durham as far as the Wall. The massively constructed towers may have been as much as 30 m high, providing a much improved view to sea. In a period when sailors preferred to hug the land, they were strategically sited to provide an oversight of coastal waters. Forewarned, local fleet units could intercept and chase off raiders before they could pass by or reach land. The title of the unit at Malton, the *numerus supervenientium Petuariensium*, suggests that it derived from Brough and that its role was to 'anticipate' raids. This unit may have been the base from which the coastal towers were manned and organized. These towers have been firmly attributed to the Theodosian period but the coin evidence starts somewhat earlier.

Inland, attempts were made to establish better control over the major arterial routes by the construction of fortlets, such as those at Wreay Hall and Barrock Fell between Carlisle and Penrith. It has been suggested that these acted as signal stations, and late Roman signal stations were certainly constructed alongside this stretch of the A6. These sites, however, were probably block-houses, serving a police function. Individual signal stations in the Lune Valley and along the Ribble/Aire gap imply a massive investment in rapid communication systems, but it is unclear to what period these belong.

Towns, Trade and the Social Hierarchy

Few of the *vici* outside the forts are known to have remained in occupation after the 360s. At Chesterholm (*Vindolanda*), the final stages of occupation were characterized by a decline in the removal of refuse from the site; it was described by the excavator as 'squalid'. Civilians may have found room within some of the northern forts, but this suggestion remains unproven. It has also been suggested that both fort and *vicus* at Malton were victims of the barbarians in AD 367, after which the fort was re-occupied but the walls replaced by earthwork defences. In any case, occupation of the *vicus* contracted and when it

The provinces of Roman Britain. A: in the third century; B: in the fourth century, but omitting the unlocated province of *Valentia*, which may well have been one of those marked but re-named. All boundaries are hypothetical

The Corbridge Lanx, a massive silver dish deposited or lost on the northern frontier in the late Roman period. It was probably the property of a high-ranking official. It was found in 1735 in association with other pieces which have Christian inscriptions

was provided with new defences these cut earlier structures. The new buildings were ramshackle. The entire phase was typical of the Theodosian period and of the use of unskilled labour, recruited by compulsion from the tribal peasantry and working without incentives or skilled overseers.

The markets which were the life-blood of these communities were probably in steep decline. The reduced size of many garrisons and the declining value of the cash-wages reaching the individual soldier pushed down demand for manufactures and services along the frontier. At the same time, government agencies supplied most necessities through taxation in kind and state-run factories. In consequence, there was little room left for entrepreneurs in the northern frontier regions. For the immediate future the route to wealth lay in the taxation privileges available to those in government service and in the possession of large estates. The primary role of towns within this society was administrative – the complex taxation system was presumably town-based and urban markets were the principal source of the gold coinage in which taxpayers were expected to pay at least a proportion of their dues.

The importation of manufactured goods from southern Britain virtually ceased during the second half of the fourth century. Poor quality, cheaper pottery from East Yorkshire dominated those vessels still reaching the Wall garrisons. Farm produce from the south may have no longer travelled beyond the Humber, being diverted to the Saxon Shore. The movement of bulk goods provided a cheap means of transporting pottery, and the dominance of wares from Yorkshire probably reflects the increasing reliance of the *dux* on produce from Yorkshire's grain belt.

By the end of the century this flow of pottery to the Wall garrisons was in rapid decline, and the distribution of Crambeck and Huntcliff-type wares increasingly confined to a relatively small number of sites within the more market-oriented south-east of the region, where they were manufactured. It was here that the Roman pottery industry fought its final and ultimately unsuccessful battle for survival, although the date of its eventual demise is a matter of conjecture: while many would see it as over by 410–20, more optimistic estimates have pushed it towards the middle of the fifth century.

Towns proved more resilient to these pressures than the *vici*, perhaps because they were concentrated in the more romanized parts of the region and housed the growing number of local administrators and bureaucrats whose task it was to oversee the complex system of taxation and registration. Corbridge, Catterick and Carlisle were still occupied in some form at the end of the fourth century and Aldborough has produced a coin sequence which reaches into the 380s. There are some signs of late fourth-century mosaics and house construction in the *colonia* at York, where well-paid bureaucrats and specialists in the movement of luxury goods necessarily congregated, but there is also evidence of abandoned buildings and it may be that the population and the area occupied were both shrinking during the final decades of the century. Even so, excavation has revealed what may have been a late wall protecting the *colonia* along the Ouse, implying that it received attention to its defences comparable with late Roman London. On most sites there has been insufficient recent investigation to comment meaningfully on the later decades of the century, but the impression gained from the shreds of evidence available is one of gradual but not uniform decline.

Several villas were still occupied at the end of the fourth century, if not beyond. The most substantial evidence has come from Langton, near Malton, one of the small number where barbarian raiders in AD 367 have been blamed for destruction levels. Whether or not this is true, coin and pottery evidence signifies a buoyant site economy at the end of the century, and artefacts from this site and that at Beadlam may imply continuing occupation for at least a decade or more thereafter, although the main residence at the latter had already been abandoned. The villa at Welton was similarly still in occupation, and the unusually wide and very deep well at Rudston has provided large quantities of pottery from the last decades of the century, apparently thrown down it when the shaft was in use as a rubbish tip.

Other sites are more likely to have been abandoned or converted to a subsistence basis before the end of the century. At Garstang the main residence was demolished during the fourth century, although another may have been constructed elsewhere on an unexcavated portion of the site. At present there is little evidence that the main residential buildings at Rudston villa were still occupied at the end of the century, despite the late finds from the well. The same might be said of Brantingham, where

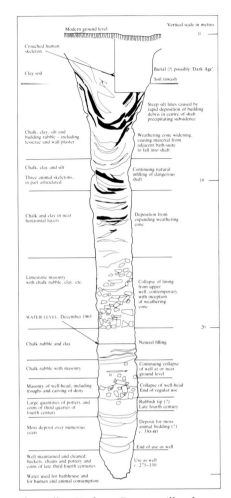

The well at Rudston Roman villa, showing its progressive periods of use and in-filling during the late third, fourth and fifth centuries. (Based on Stead, 1980, figure 16 and pp. 29–30)

abandonment may have occurred a half century earlier, when the harbours of nearby Brough-on-Humber became unusable and the town fell into disuse.

The last decades of the Roman period saw a decline in the incidence of villa-occupation, with no new examples being constructed to replace those which had been abandoned. Among those still in use by *c.* 400, there are signs of major changes in the nature of the occupation, with the abandonment of most features which had been characteristic of a Roman lifestyle. Those few which continued after the collapse of the currency eventually fell into disuse, perhaps at about the same time as the collapse of local ceramic industries, although it is possible that sub-Roman occupation continued for decades but left no artefacts by which to recognize it. As centres of romanized life, villas were an integral part of a market-oriented system of production. This system itself was in decline over the same period, as ever smaller numbers of townsfolk, soldiers and other specialists purchased farm produce. With the market economy in terminal decline, the villa-residence became increasingly difficult to maintain, or keep supplied. Yet, once the sequence of pottery and coin had ended, archaeology offers no clear method of dating abandonment. Gildas's references, *c.* 500, to British monks implies the existence of organized religious communities. Such groups developed on the continent in the private houses of the aristocracy and it is possible that some British villas served the same function in the fifth century.

A Romano-British farmstead adjacent to a probable signal station in Lonsdale

The End of the Roman Diocese

Where garrisons had not been withdrawn, the army remained professional and operative into the last years of the fourth century. Thereafter, the arrival of new coinage ground to a halt as a result of a series of external political and military crises. Pottery had changed little in design over several decades and is unhelpful as a dating mechanism in the new century. As a result, the final phases of occupation in most establishments are no better understood than the villas, and it is difficult to know how the northern army responded to the usurpation and eventual fall of Constantine III (c. 406–10). His authority in Britain was eventually set aside by revolt, but the Emperor Honorius never again exercised sufficient control of the Channel coasts to venture to cross to Britain. The island was, henceforth, to lie outside the immediate governance of the western emperors, although not entirely beyond their influence.

This process had major repercussions throughout Roman Britain, not least in the north. The collapse of the London mint of Constantine III and of imported coinage meant a cessation of what little coin had hitherto reached the northern garrisons and urban bureaucracies. Furthermore, many who had coins in their possession chose to hoard them, so reducing the quantity of coin in circulation. It seems unlikely

A stone wall base, part of a Romano-British field system at Yanwath

that existing stocks enjoyed a long period of use, particularly in the north, where circulation had always been confined to a minority of the population.

The collapse of legitimate government left the provinces of Britain without governors, yet with the internal mechanisms of diocesan and provincial councils and *civitates*, staffed by provincials. Supposing that no new usurpation occurred to an 'empire' consisting solely of the British diocese, effective power devolved upon army commanders and estate owners. This breakdown presumably precipitated the end of deliveries of taxes in kind over long distances.

It has been suggested at this time that some military sites fell to barbarian attack. The most lurid picture of such a catastrophe was painted for the signal-towers at Huntcliff and Goldsborough:

> Plainly the fort was stormed at some period: some of its occupants, whether garrison or refugees, perished by a violent death, and their bodies and other fragments were tossed into the well, which offered a ready grave.
>
> (Hornsby and Stanton, *Journal of Roman Studies*, II, p. 222)

The excavators believed the garrisons to have been the victims of Angles. Although this interpretation is sometimes still credited, the evidence uncovered in the well at Huntcliff and on the internal floors at Goldsborough is, at best, inconclusive, and the reality was probably more mundane. Goldsborough at least was occupied by paid soldiers as late as the reign of Honorius. If the rabbit bones from the floor there were correctly identified, then the tower saw much later use and the skeletons belong to a different millenium. Both sites may have been used in the medieval period, before the eventual collapse of the masonry. There is no evidence of Anglian settlement within a generation of 410 near either site nor any obvious reason to defend or attack an installation which would have become redundant once cooperation with other, larger units was interrupted. This coast was well beyond the reach of Germanic raiders until after their establishment of settlements in East Anglia and the south-east.

By 410, many military installations may already have been abandoned through the withdrawal of their garrisons. At others, the collapse of long-distance supply networks and the administration which organized that supply left soldiers in an impossible situation. Some may have developed short-distance systems of supply and so retained their existing role in some form for a generation or so. The evidence from recent excavations at Birdoswald demonstrates that timber-framed buildings were built above the granaries there after the collapse of the pottery supply, and ovens were built over the furnace floor of the bath-suite of Binchester in the fifth century. Elsewhere, fifth- or sixth-century finds of metalwork, inscriptions or pagan burials may imply some forts remained focal points, their commanders having probably long exercised considerable authority over the communities around them. There may, in other words, have been a sub-Roman phase in the north in which forts played a focal role, and this suggestion receives some support from the frequency with which Roman forts re-emerged as central places, palace sites and early church foundations in the seventh century. The poor quality of most excavations, however, has destroyed the evidence which might have enabled us to evaluate such hypotheses.

For other sites, the collapse of the command structure and the cessation of supply probably brought about the rapid demobilization of whatever military units still remained as their members took to a life of brigandage, sought service in the households of those in control of the agricultural surplus, or were re-absorbed by local communities, among whom many must have had close relatives.

The extent to which the provinces continued is a matter of debate, resolution of which is hampered by a lack of evidence. By *c.* 500, King Maglocunus of Anglesey was exercising 'overkingship' over all those parts of the old western province, that is, Britannia Prima, which were not under, or beyond, Saxon control (as was the upper Thames Valley). Urien's ghostly overkingship in northern Britain in the later sixth century foreshadows the recreation of what amounts to Britannia Secunda under King Æthelfrith of Northumbria and it is possible that a notion that the province should have a central government, tax system and armed forces survived from the Roman period.

The North without Rome

In 410 the region faced immediate dangers. The victims of the Roman system – such as runaway slaves and bankrupts – and the victims of its collapse – unemployed soldiers – may have posed a threat to local security. Raiders from Ireland, Pictland and perhaps even Germany sought out precious and portable goods – clothing, gold, silver, and the

The Traprain Law Treasure, a late fourth- or early fifth-century silver hoard which could have derived either from raiding or from a diplomatic payment

Dumbarton Rock, the defended palace site of the kings of Strathclyde

like – within the erstwhile provinces. A handful of hoards may reflect their activities, although it remains possible that hoards of precious metal, such as that found at Traprain Law, reflect diplomatic gifts from late Roman authorities to barbarian leaders.

The latter also carried off fit young people for the slave markets back home. Among these was a young man called Patrick, later to be the apostle of Ireland. Like the later Vikings, colonization eventually followed in the footsteps of raiding. During the fifth century Irish (Scottish) settlements were coming into existence in western Britain, in Wales and eventually in Argyle, where the Scots established the small kingdom of Dal Riata. Both raids and settlements posed a threat to sub-Roman Britain, which forced some response from local communities.

The nature of that response varied greatly from one region of the north to another, encapsulating within the single province the experience of the entire diocese. Those areas where romanization had made most impact – where towns and villas were concentrated around the provincial capital and bishop's residence at York – showed themselves the least capable of adapting to the new circumstances of the fifth century: the romanized aristocracy were swept away by foreign warriors, who rapidly achieved political dominance. To these communities and their fate we shall return. By contrast, those areas of the north and west where Roman social and economic systems had made least impact proved themselves more capable of the necessary adjustments within a cultural and linguistic climate which was Celtic but also, to an extent, Roman.

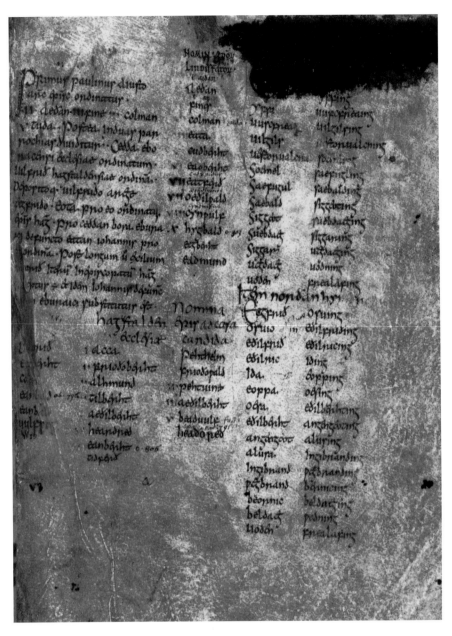

This is the oldest surviving manuscript of the Anglian collection of royal genealogies written between 805 and 814. It contains the names of the kings of Deira, Bernicia, Mercia, Lindsey, East Anglia and Kent. The geneaology of the kings of Deira and the beginning of the Bernician pedigree appear in the extreme right-hand column of the left-hand page

Among the nearer tribes beyond the Wall, where Roman diplomatic influences had been greatest, kingships evolved which had coalesced by the late sixth century into four tribal kingdoms. Like Welsh examples, the king-lists from this region incorporate Roman names, such as Tacitus and Aeternus, perhaps signifying that Roman styles of naming had spread beyond the Empire, although this may have occurred only with the dissemination of Christianity. Given the presence of supervised tribal meeting-places in southern Scotland in the earlier Roman period, such name-borrowing may have been a lengthy process. The king-lists and genealogies of the region are not contemporary evidence but the trend is confirmed by a scatter of Christian memorial stones which convey similar messages, like that at Kirkmadrine which recalls three priests, Ides, Vivetius and Mevonius, and a lost example from Curgie reputed to have named one Ventidius. The tradition of romanized founders may, therefore, have some relevance to actual events during the wreck of the diocese.

In the north and west of the province local society had retained most of the characteristics of tribalism throughout the Roman period. With law under local administration, the indigenous aristocracy were free to revive their own possession of weapons. Local men – perhaps initially men with military experience under Rome – emerged as the leaders of forces which might undertake either offensive or defensive action, recruited from the sons of free tribesmen. There gradually developed a network of competing and competitive local warlordships, each rooted in local kinship groups and gradually shifting from the role of temporary warlordship to petty tribal kingship.

Although Christianity seems to have made little impact within these communities during the late Roman period, the kingdoms of the sixth century were led by Christian kings exercising patronage over the local church. That Christianity should have triumphed during the fifth century among tribal communities who appear to have all but ignored it during the fourth implies that it was imperial authority which provided the blueprint for British kingship. Ecclesiastical patronage was a major plank of late Roman government and the southern Briton, Gildas, witnessed the extent of royal influence in the western British Church in the decades around AD 500.

St Patrick seems to have believed that the Coroticus to whom he addressed his famous letter was a Christian, with influence over ecclesiastical appointments. Both the location and date of this colourful figure are contentious but there is good reason to place Coroticus in western Britain, more probably in Gwynedd than in the north-west, given that he was capable of sending men to Ireland.

Although far less common than they are in Wales, a scatter of inscribed memorial stones mark the burial places of a handful of churchmen and members of the aristocracy in the north, the largest number of which is grouped beyond the boundary of the late Empire, on the Galloway peninsula. One at Kirkmadrine has already been mentioned. At Whithorn, a stone commemorating Latinus (aged thirty-five) and his four-year-old daughter was set up by his grandson Barrovadus in the mid-fifth century, demonstrating that a degree of literacy and a knowledge of the psalms or the Roman offices of the dead survived, or had been re-introduced, in this distant corner of Britain. A stone recording 'the place of St Peter the Apostle', found at the same site, testified to a continuing tradition of literate Celtic Christianity to 600 or beyond. Burial was probably unaccompanied, in traditional Romano-Christian style, and the practice of depositing the dead in stone-lined graves, or cists, was comparatively widespread in the north – following clear Roman precedents, as excavated recently at Lanchester.

Some of the new kingdoms may have been relatively large; a few can certainly be traced to Roman and pre-Roman tribes, as in the case of the Votadini, who re-emerge as the Gododdin of poetic fame in the sixth century. However, group names were probably more volatile than the groups to whom they were applied, and discontinuity in tribal names is not evidence of one population replacing another. Although the continuity of specific communities is beyond proof by such means, it must be significant that almost all the provincial names of early English Northumbria are British in origin, even including Bernica and Deira, the earliest known English kingdoms. The exception is Hatfield in the extreme south, but even there Welsh writings recorded a British name still known in the early ninth century.

A memorial stone at Whithorn recording 'the place of St Peter the Apostle', c. 600

With the collapse of the Roman state, responsibility for law and order necessarily passed to the family, to kinship groups and internal social hierarchies. As society regrouped, it did so on the basis not of artificial institutions imposed from outside, but on the households of the leaders of local communities. The greatest households eventually occupied defended enclosures – as at Bamburgh, Edinburgh, Mote of Mark, Dunbar and Dumbarton Rock (Glasgow) – and gathered about themselves specialists including eulogists, court poets and smiths, as well as warriors and priests. Some of these enclosures were very small, the timber-reinforced stone wall at Mote of Mark, for example, enclosing an area of only 75 × 35 m at most, but all were capable of being defended. Since they do not appear to have been occupied until the sixth century, it may have been the growing threat from Anglo-Saxon warlords which encouraged them to occupy defensive sites. On less precipitous ground, a small number of palisaded areas of high status have also been found, such as those at Yeavering and Doon Hill (East Lothian). Other foci may have remained within Roman walls, as has been postulated at Catterick and at *Campodonum* (Doncaster, see below), although the latter has yielded no evidence of occupation before the 620s.

It remains unclear whether or not the late Roman tax system survived this process of social re-organization. Although opinion is generally hostile to any significant continuity, the highly bureaucratized Roman

Bamburgh Castle, a stately home built during the nineteenth century under the influence of the Gothic revival, utilized the extensive remains of the medieval royal castle on this focal site. The castle in turn shrouds a site of the first rank in early medieval Northumbria

system of taxation in kind had already evolved, by 410, into a form dominated by the estate-owner. The way was open for it to become the customary system of food rents by which Celtic (and eventually English) kings were maintained. To assume that such estate-owners allowed the tax system to fall into abeyance requires that we suppose them to have acted entirely against their own interests. Gildas seems to refer to taxation in kind and compulsory labour markedly similar to that in late Roman Britain. If large-scale earthworks or dykes – such as those which may have protected British Elmet from the Deirans – were being constructed at the behest of British kings, then the latter certainly had the ability to mobilize the labour of the peasant community, whether or not their power to coerce descended directly from Roman systems of labour compulsion. It seems probable that Gildas had in mind British dyke construction when writing his fictional account of the Roman walls, though the work with which he was familiar should be sought in southern Britain.

When did such kingdoms emerge? Warrior bands were clearly already in existence during the later life of St Patrick, whose letter to Coroticus addressed the absent leader of just such a war-band, apparently based in western Britain, but so far attempts to date Patrick's life have not been convincing. At least one generation of such kings had already passed in Wales when Gildas wrote his violent condemnation of them in *c*. 500 and this must remain the earliest evidence of British kingship available to us.

The demands of the ambitious warriors whom such kings grouped around themselves were a spur to undertake warfare, and Gildas, at least, believed that raiding of one British community by another was endemic well before his own generation, that is, by the 460s at the latest. This aristocratic society developed a heroic ethos and a highly competitive ideology focused on the accumulation of wealth and a warlike reputation. The few artefacts which have survived – such as hanging cauldrons, torcs and jewellery – fit easily into a reconstruction of a society of this type.

The existence of such hierarchies presupposes the presence of a still numerous farming population, even though archaeology has not yet identified the settlements or field systems used by these peasants, if these were other than those in use during the late Roman period.

Can we begin to write a detailed history of the north in the fifth and early sixth centuries? For a decade or more, the work of the late Molly Miller and Professor Edward Thompson suggested that this might be the case. It was their belief that Gildas wrote at least part of the historical prologue to his *Ruin of Britain* from a northern perspective. Although this finds some superficial support from the Rhus (Breton) *Life of St Gildas* – which had him sired by a King of Strathclyde – recent re-examination of his *Ruin of Britain* has not confirmed this view. Gildas was a traditionally educated member of the civilian élite of sub-Roman Britain, certainly from within the civil zone. If he can be placed anywhere, internal evidence favours central southern England below the Thames. Errors of fact and of interpretation are so characteristic of Gildas's northern material that it is necessary to set aside the entirety of his information concerning the Picts and their invasions, along with his false ascription of both Roman walls to the decades after the battle of Aquileia (388) and his belief that the deserted Wall forts had been Roman towns. Gildas is not, then, a reliable witness of events in the north at the end of the fourth and during the first half of the fifth centuries, and it is highly improbable that his comments concerning the arrival of the Saxons have anything to do with England above the Humber.

The North and the Anglo-Saxons

The Vale of York and Humber lowlands were severely affected by flooding during the fourth and fifth centuries, which much reduced their value as a habitat for man and covered the plain with water-borne deposits which conceal the bulk of its earlier archaeology. Brough-on-Humber was deserted within the Roman period and the habitable area within York during the fifth century was reduced to the higher ground within the fortress. East of the natural divide formed by the now oft-flooded Vale of York was the most romanized part of the province, focused in the late Roman period on the York–Malton–Bridlington–Brough triangle of the Derwent Valley and the Yorkshire Wolds. Here were concentrated, in their villas, the most civilianized sections of the late Roman provincial élite, at the apex of the most hierarchically organized society in the entire north. Around them were the most commercially organized and well-peopled areas of the province. This was the provincial stronghold of romanized culture in the late fourth and probably the early fifth centuries, and of the episcopal, imperial Church, which we may guess held lands around York. Church writings

Rough Castle, near Falkirk, with its annex; one of the forts on Antonine's Wall

of the early fifth century were consistently hostile to the type of social adjustment being made in the old military zone. Gildas voiced the view of the more extreme wing of the insular Church, criticizing the Welsh warrior kings of his own generation, and his apocalyptic view of the collapse of Britain may have been shared by many of the more romanized gentry, even in distant Yorkshire. To Gildas the several barbarian enemies were no more than tools of a vengeful God whom the British should seek to placate, in the expectation that he would call off his agents.

It was British leaders within the more romanized parts of the country who invited in pagan Saxon warriors to defend them – to take the place of the professional soldiers on whom they had so long relied. The earliest settlers from the Anglian areas of north-west Germany and Denmark (Angeln) were apparently established in what is now East Anglia, between about 420 and 440 and it was probably these whose revolt was described in graphic terms by Gildas. By the 440s, at the latest, Germanic warriors within lowland Britain had wrested control of the heartland of the diocese, bringing with them the material culture of Atlantic Germany and exercising widespread authority on the strength of their military prowess. There is just a hint that even the great Maglocunus of Anglesey recognized the superior power of another king, in which case he was surely a Saxon.

The date at which Germanic settlement occurred in the north is a matter of dispute. The late John Myres suggested that Germanic

RIGHT AND ABOVE: Early Anglo-Saxon cremation urns from Sancton Wold

The well-preserved central section of Hadrian's Wall

OPPOSITE: The Vale of York from the Howardian Hills

auxiliaries were already settling in Yorkshire during the early to mid-fourth century, but there is scant evidence that this occurred outside the military establishments of the region. There is evidence, however, that German soldiers were at times stationed in the north – the Frisians at Housesteads were commemorated both by inscription and by the deposition of their distinctive style of pottery which spread thence along the Wall. On the basis of the equipment buried with them, it is possible to suggest that German officers were interred at Norton, near Malton, and a thin scattering of metalwork and pottery implies that a tiny amount of Germanic material was reaching York, Brough and Malton, if only as souvenirs or as the personal possessions of men drafted in from the Rhine frontier, where Germanic troops made up a large proportion of the élite Roman regiments. However, there is no evidence that German soldiers were present in large numbers in the north or that they made any significant cultural impact on the local community. Germans employed within the Empire tended to become progressively more Roman and it was not until the Empire had begun to collapse that the process was reversed. Finds of pottery made by British potters but decorated in ways reminiscent of Saxon vessels – termed Romano-Saxon pottery – were once thought to indicate the presence of Germanic troops in late Roman employment but recent re-evaluation of these industries has confirmed them to be integral with other styles of late Roman pottery and used by provincials. With the redating of several supposedly late fourth-century cremation urns into the fifth century, evidence for Saxon or Anglian mercenary troops in the decades around 400 has all but evaporated.

When did Anglo-Saxons reach the north? Evidence so far reveals little trace of distinctive Anglo-Saxon material in the region before the mid-fifth century – over a generation after the collapse of the Roman government. There are single objects of early- to mid-fifth-century origin from several sites, including a glass bowl, probably made in the Meuse region, found at The Mount, York, but items such as this may have been heirlooms deposited with Anglian burials a generation later. The earliest group of Anglo-Saxon finds are the early comb and eighteen or so of the early cremation urns which contained the cremated remains of the 454 individuals so far excavated at Sancton. If the latter do not in turn fall foul of new essays in the dating of Anglo-Saxon pottery then they imply that the cemetery there was founded in or marginally before the third quarter of the fifth century, after which it apparently continued without a break to 600 and beyond.

The position of this cemetery, on the Wold edge above an important Roman road junction, has led to suggestions that it was founded by pagan Germanic soldiers stationed near the site for strategic reasons by British authorities. Such hypotheses remain unproven but the small scale and apparent isolation of the initial Anglo-Saxon presence does

An early Anglo-Saxon glass bowl from The Mount, York

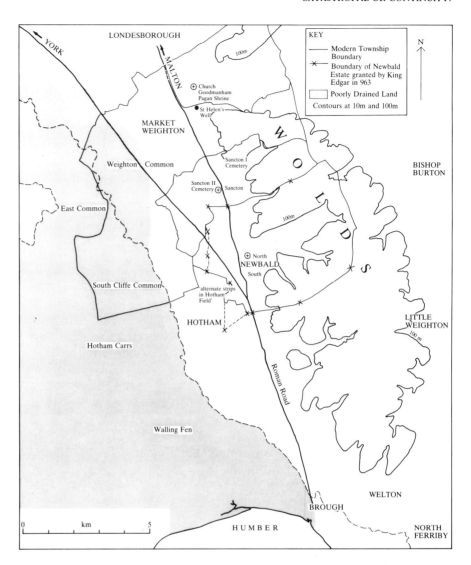

The location of Sancton and Goodmanham

lend some support. However, that British authorities should have employed Saxon warriors after the disastrous experience of Vortigern, the 'proud tyrant', as recounted by Gildas, seems little short of incredible and alternative explanations should be preferred. The cemetery is more likely to reflect the intrusion of an Anglian leader, with a warrior band from Lincolnshire or East Anglia via the Humber crossings, who seized control of the rich Derwent Valley and sited his hall in a strategic location at the focus of what he had acquired. The importance of the pagan shrine at nearby Goodmanham – the principal temple of Anglian Deira by the early seventh century – and the likely proximity of an as yet unidentified royal palace site are both factors consistent with the establishment of the primary Anglo-Saxon settlement in this vicinity.

That they were able to achieve a dominance of the core of *Britannia Inferior* reflects the inability of the still comparatively romanized civilian aristocracy to adapt themselves to the role of a warrior aristocracy. While still in control of local society, through land-ownership, patronage and taxation in kind, that aristocracy was defenceless. This opportunity was probably seized upon by an Anglian war-band whose leader secured control of the core estates and revenues which had supported the Roman aristocracy and Church. Their success sucked in further recruits in search of patronage and that, combined with the rapid production of new generations of warriors from their polygamous marriages, spread their material culture, language and religion across northern England. During the sixth century, Anglo-Saxon cemeteries spread widely in Northumbria, if predominately east of the Pennines. As so far understood, they were concentrated in Deira, in the East Riding, where, counting cemeteries of every kind, about forty-two have been located. The cremation cemeteries at The Mount and Heworth may reflect some late fifth- to early sixth-century settlement in the immediate vicinity of York, but there are only a tiny handful of examples known further west and the Vale of York is marginal to the distribution.

As the Anglian bandwagon gathered pace, similar cemeteries spread up the eastern plain, where only a few have so far revealed more than a handful of graves, the larger examples being at Norton and Darlington in the Tees basin. In Deira, the largest of these new cemeteries contained cremations numbering at least several hundred and Sancton may have contained thousands of burials. However, cremation cemeteries are not common. More contained a mixture of rites or only inhumations, accompanied by a variety of dress fasteners, brooches, weapons and other artefacts of Anglo-Saxon type. The largest inhumation cemetery so far excavated is that at West Heslerton, where 125 graves were identified, although more probably lie beneath the modern road which bisects the cemetery. Like many others, this cemetery was focused on a Bronze Age barrow cemetery. John Mortimer's diggings among the numerous barrows of the region led to his excavation of several similar cemeteries during the nineteenth century, including that at Garton Slack, where he recorded an aligned cemetery with a mixture

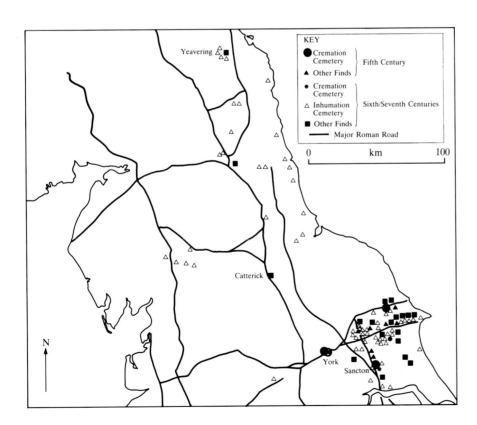

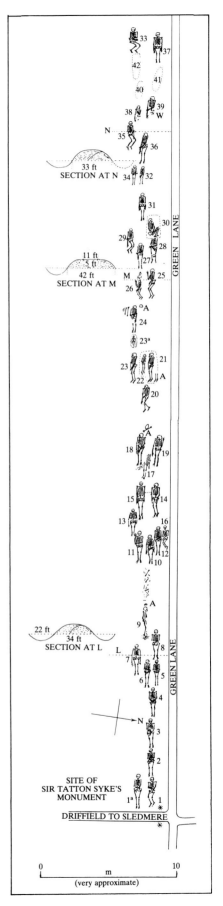

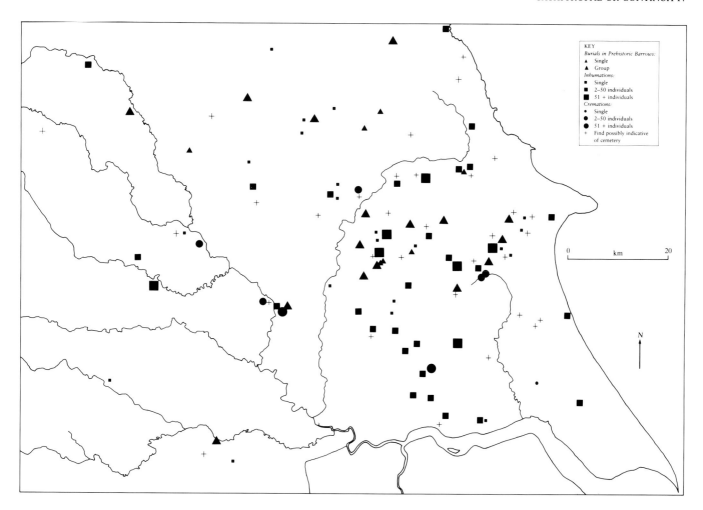

KEY
Burials in Prehistoric Barrows:
▲ Single
▲ Group
Inhumations:
■ Single
■ 2–50 individuals
■ 51 + individuals
Cremations:
• Single
● 2–50 individuals
● 51 + individuals
+ Find possibly indicative
   of cemetery

Anglo-Saxon pagan burials in Deira

OPPOSITE, LEFT: Anglo-Saxon pagan burials in Northumbria; RIGHT: An aligned inhumation cemetery excavated at Garton Slack during the nineteenth century by John Mortimer (after Mortimer, 1905, figure 731)

of flexed and crouched inhumations. Elsewhere Mortimer found numerous well-accoutred Saxon burials under substantial tumuli, many of which had been originally raised in the Bronze Age.

Many burials were isolated examples intruded into prehistoric mounds or linear features. Such individual or very small groups of burials occur in the Crosby Garrett area of Cumbria and in western Northumberland, where some were accompanied by equipment indicative of high status. At Milfield in Northumberland a prehistoric henge attracted a small group of Anglian burials.

In 731 Bede recorded that the Northumbrians were one of the English peoples who were descended from Anglian immigrants from *Angulus* (Angeln, which lies in southern Denmark). However, his comments are better evidence for what was believed in the eighth century than what occurred in the fifth and sixth centuries. The wide variety of burial rites in early Anglo-Saxon Northumbria suggests a more complex background than Bede envisaged. Had the English settlement in Northumbria resulted from direct and massed migration from the Jutland peninsula, one might have expected far greater emphasis on cremation, with a more uniform array of equipment in association. The discrepancy has been interpreted as the result of ethnic and cultural mixing of Germanic peoples on the continent before the migration occurred, but this does not adequately explain several other factors.

At Etton, near Beverley, in English Deira, an inhumation cemetery containing more than fifty graves produced only one pair of tweezers – a level of artefact deposition more commonly experienced in a late Roman, Christian cemetery. In addition, all the bodies had been buried in a crouched position, and similar crouched or flexed burials are common in other Anglo-Saxon cemeteries in the region. Crouched burial was normal practice in the region in the Iron Age and occurs in Roman period burials. The custom is not present on the continent.

In most Anglo-Saxon inhumation cemeteries the principal orientation of the graves approximates to west–east, just as in the late Roman cemeteries from which the rite arguably derives. However, north–south orientation was common in Roman Northumbria, and it may be significant that this occurs widely in Anglo-Saxon cemeteries in the same area. At Saltburn, for example, graves 17 to 40 were laid out in two parallel lines, head to feet on a north–south orientation, and this pattern of 'ribbon' graves re-appears at Yeavering.

An increasing number of Anglo-Saxon cemeteries are now known to have been sited close by hall complexes and, for concentrations of burials, this was probably the norm. There appear to have been two factors influencing the location of burials. Many display signs of having been attracted to a focal point, which might be a ruined villa site (as at Dalton Parlours), a henge (Milfield), a hill-fort (Yeavering) or a prehistoric burial mound (as is normal in eastern Yorkshire). In each instance, those responsible may have been seeking to transfer to themselves whatever traditions of authority or power were represented by the older structure. The siting of Yeavering, for example, was clearly not accidental but neither was it necessarily due to recent British lordship. That the siting of cemeteries within such foci did not originate with the Anglo-Saxons is demonstrated by the Romano-British cemetery within the disused fort of Castleford, which was still in use in the late fourth century.

The number of individual, often well-accoutred graves in pre-existing mounds also excites comment. The suggestion that these represent the burial of warriors who died while campaigning at a distance from their own communities is not an adequate explanation of this particular rite. About eighteen instances are known within the East Riding of Yorkshire, where warriors were probably close to home; elsewhere, many of the mounds used are in obscure locations – as on Crosby Garrett Moor in Cumbria – unlikely to have been handy to a warrior band far from base. The practice is mirrored in the White Peak of Derbyshire, where most, if not all, are individual burials of high status dating to the seventh century. In East Yorkshire a significant number of individual Anglian burials took place alongside prehistoric dykes, some of which were probably estate boundaries in the early medieval period. It seems likely that these burials were of individuals of high social status within the community local to the place of burial. Such individual burials of high status may be examples of boundary burial – a rite known from Irish, Welsh and Anglo-Saxon sources – undertaken so as to protect the rights of inheritance of the kin. Precisely similar boundary burials were a feature of graves of the Arras culture in later prehistory. Like Anglian boundary burials, these were unusually rich, even being accompanied by dismantled chariots. This may, therefore, be another feature of Anglian burial practice which derived from British customs.

The high incidence of 'expensive' grave goods among the comparatively few Anglo-Saxon burials so far discovered in Bernicia may suggest that, outside the Yorkshire Wolds, it was only the military aristocracy who were usually buried with Anglian rites. Professor Leslie Alcock has argued that it was only this aristocracy which was Anglian, taking over the political, military, social and economic arrangements of the local British communities as a going concern, and there is much to commend this view. However, some of the characteristics of the inhumations which have been identified suggest that local British communities had influenced the practice of Anglian burial rites to a greater extent than one might have expected. The inference would seem to be that Bernician burials included persons of British extraction who had 'gone English', as well as genuine incomers and their heirs, who had derived from the more integrated 'English' aristocracy in Deira.

Such an argument might seem to founder when we turn to the place-name evidence. Like other parts of England, the place-names of Northumbria are, ostensibly at least, dominated by Anglo-Saxon and later languages. Although many major rivers retain pre-English names, this is not the case for minor waterways, settlements or estates, and the transfer of place-names from one language to another on this scale has usually been interpreted as incontrovertible evidence of large-scale immigration of English speakers, including persons of low status.

However, arguments about ethnicity on the basis of place-name evidence are insecure in several respects. It is clearly possible for large populations to adopt new languages from a small immigrant group – as occurred in Roman Gaul, for example – provided that enough of the community had sufficient reason to do so. We know very little about the place-names of the pre-English period, since so few can now be recognized, so it is impossible to tell how many have survived in part or been translated into English. The process of sound shift by which British/Latin *Eburacum* became Anglo-Saxon *Eoforwic* ('boar-town'), *Yorvik* and eventually York, may have been comparatively common during the period of language change. Scholars of Bede's generation were keen on folk etymology as a means of explaining the formation of names – Bede's comments on Bamburgh are one instance of what was clearly a widespread if generally spurious scholarly activity. In practice, a surprisingly large number of the small sample of Roman period names have survived in some form: hence the Romano-Celtic element in names such as *Bin*chester, *Man*chester and *Cor*bridge. If the Wall forts be omitted from the sample, on the grounds that many are poorly placed as estate centres, such survivors do represent a high proportion of the Romano-British names known to us within the region.

Attempts to write settlement history from place-name evidence must be suspect. The earliest strata of documents from which place-name evidence can be extracted belongs to the half-century after *c.* 680 – many generations after the English settlement. Place-names are frequently attached to settlements which were not in existence in the sixth century and the substitution of one place-name for another, or the removal of a settlement from one site to another, was probably a comparatively common phenomenon. Given the number of mid- to late Saxon place-names which cannot now be identified on the ground, the possibility of writing the history of the settlement period from place-name evidence seems both remote and fraught with danger.

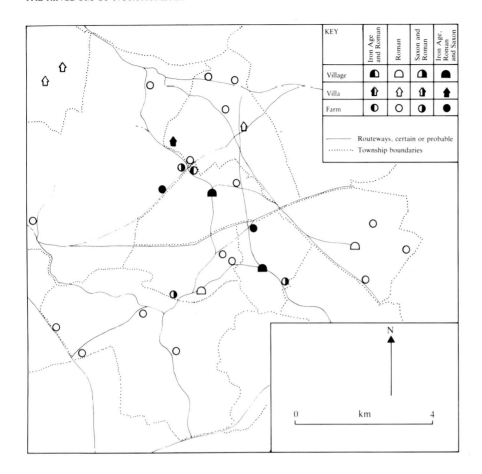

KEY	Iron Age and Roman	Roman	Saxon and Roman	Iron Age, Roman and Saxon
Village	◖	◠	◖	⬤
Villa	⬆	⇧	⬆	⬆
Farm	◖	○	◖	●

———— Routeways, certain or probable
·········· Township boundaries

N

0   km   4

Settlement and routeways on the Yorkshire Wolds: evidence from the Wharram Survey (after Hayfield, 1987, figure 106)

Settlement, Land-use and Continuity

Numerous settlement sites which had been occupied during the Roman period are now long since abandoned. Since the last dating evidence from them is generally Roman pottery, it is normal to assume that abandonment occurred during the fifth century, although in practice aceramic settlement may often have continued for several generations. Another possibility is that Roman pottery remained in use as late as *c.* 450 or even later, and there are some signs that this was the case at Wharram Percy, with Roman pottery continuing until replaced by Anglo-Saxon domestic wares.

There is little sign of a break in occupation at several of the sites now known within the Wharram survey area. There, many sites which had come into occupation during the Roman period failed thereafter, but most settlements which had been in existence in the late pre-Roman period and which survived in use during the Roman period have revealed ceramic evidence of Saxon period occupation. Such was the case at the Roman villa of Wharram Grange, where Saxon pottery came from the outskirts of the Roman site, perhaps implying occupation of ancillary structures or halls comparable to those excavated at several southern villa sites including Barton Court Farm in Oxfordshire. At the North Manor of Wharram Percy, a holloway associated with a Roman villa was clearly out of use before two sunken-featured buildings were constructed over it. An inhumation cemetery, however, has produced evidence of Roman, sub-Roman and Saxon graves, implying that the burial ground remained in use throughout a series of cultural changes. Elsewhere on the site, the upper fills of ditches first cut and used in the Iron Age contained Saxon pottery, implying continuing use of pre-existing ditched and hedged enclosures into the early medieval period.

Similar evidence of continuing settlement activity, albeit within changing patterns, has come from recent and ongoing excavations at West Heslerton. Roman period farms in the Derwent Valley are thought to have been abandoned, perhaps because of a rising water-table, and a large settlement of about seventy timber-framed buildings and sunken-featured structures was built on the valley side and occupied during the late fifth to mid-seventh centuries, before major re-organization occurred. While the sunken-featured buildings common to this and many other sites belong to a tradition which originated in Germany, there is good reason to believe that the post-built hall-type structures which are the normal residences on early Anglo-Saxon settlement sites have their origins in Romano-British building styles. Whether their occupants were indigenous or immigrant is impossible to determine, although the material culture of this and similar sites was certainly Anglo-Saxon. The territory occupied by this community was divided during prehistory by a series of substantial dykes and the 'Anglian' settlement seems to represent the last phase during which this system of banks and ditches remained in commission.

Despite the decline in the number of sites producing evidence of occupation in the fifth and sixth centuries, the drop in population was

Inglewood Forest viewed from Stock-dalewath, looking east. The Pennines form the backdrop. The forest was enclosed by Act of Parliament in 1819

probably more relative than absolute. In several areas it is certain that the pattern of Roman period land-use survived into the mid-Saxon period with little change. In south and east Durham widespread agriculture continued, with hemp retained as a crop throughout the period. There seems little likelihood of extensive reforestation of the Yorkshire Wolds, if the term *wald* was coined to describe pasture with isolated stands of woodland. The Lake District attained its most open aspect in the late Roman and early post-Roman periods, with an upsurge of agricultural activity. Elsewhere there is site-specific evidence of the continuity of land-use, as at Carle Moor near Laverton (North Yorkshire), and for continuing use of prehistoric or Roman boundary systems, as at Wharram Percy and West Heslerton. Among the upland pollen diagrams there is some evidence of a recession in agricultural activity during the period, with regeneration of woodland, but this is characteristic only of the more fragile ecosystems of the region, where local communities may have been severely affected by increased rainfall, and even here signs of recession are neither universal nor synchronous. If a relative decline in the demand for land during the fifth and sixth centuries led to the abandonment of some terrain utilized during the Roman period, it should surely attract little surprise.

Several lowland areas had been left as woodland throughout the Roman period – such has been demonstrated at Neasham Fen, Teesdale, and may be inferred for Inglewood in Cumbria and the Lyme of the upper Mersey basin. Elsewhere there may have been some increase

Bronze hanging bowl with three bird-shaped escutcheons (mounts), probably of Celtic workmanship but found in a seventh-century burial mound at Hawnby, N. Yorkshire

Glass claw-beaker made in the Rhineland, *c.* 500, found with an Anglo-Saxon burial of high status at Castle Eden, Co. Durham

in the extent of woodland pasture and some overall decrease in cultivation, as smaller populations adjusted to changes in the demands placed upon them by the social hierarchy, but the palaeobotanical evidence does imply a widespread continuity in the use of land.

The fifth century saw the demise of the Roman system in the north, and its replacement with a warrior-centred society. In areas where romanization had made little headway, these warriors were local men gathered around indigenous tribal leaders who saw themselves as the heirs of Rome and adopted Christianity.

In the south-east corner of the region, a more thoroughly romanized and Christianized aristocracy was less adept in making this transition and was vulnerable to the predatory pagan Germanic warriors who had established themselves by the 440s in East Anglia and were pushing into Lincolnshire. Anglo-Saxon warriors probably forced an entry to the Derwent Valley and established themselves as a land-controlling aristocracy. In consequence, Germanic material culture, language and ideologies became entrenched in this corner of the region in the second half of the fifth century and spread thence into other parts of the eastern plain early in the sixth, by conquest. The extent to which this involved mass-migration is now debated, although a core of immigrants must have been responsible for the initial introduction of the Anglo-Saxon culture. Much of the subsequent spread may have been through patronage and cultural borrowing, as ambitious individuals of indigenous extraction chose to adapt themselves to Anglian culture in order to secure access to the patronage of the kings.

This community established itself in the cultural and political heartland of the Roman province, and its wealth, vitality and consequent military advantages probably encouraged many of the low-status, indigenous population to embrace the Anglo-Saxon culture and language. The result was a period of rapid transition between the fifth and the seventh centuries, during which 'Englishness' spread widely, perhaps being transmitted in part through social hierarchies and systems of patronage from immigrant aristocracies to the mass of the indigenous peasantry. Even Deira was probably populated very largely by Britons and there can be little doubt that Bernicia contained no more than a tiny minority of immigrant stock. Bede clearly believed himself to be an Angle by blood and one cannot doubt his membership of an English culture and society. It is likely, however, that he, his kin and compatriots were descendants also of the very British he so openly despised.

By the early sixth century, the pagan and Anglicizing Deirans between the Vale of York and the North Sea were confronting Celtic, Christian aristocracies to the west and north. The critical issue of the next half-century was whether the Celtic or Anglo-Saxon language and culture would prevail. The matter was decided in a contest between rival kings who were themselves competing not over such abstract issues but for patronage, renders, booty, honour and glory in a heroic world far distant from the Roman province from which they had ultimately sprung. In such a contest, the advantage lay with those who could command the resources of the provincial heartland, the grain basket of *Britannia Secunda* and what was probably still the densest and most productive farming population of the north.

CHAPTER 3

The English Take-over

Historical Sources and their Interpretation

The third quarter of the sixth century is a watershed in the availability of historical sources for the north: earlier, there is nothing which even approaches historicity, leaving the incautious to convert the careers of characters from literature, such as Arthur and Cunedda, into an historical account; afterwards there is a thin trickle of manuscript sources which, even if most were only assembled in their existing form centuries later, at least hold out the possibility that they incorporate material which dates from this period. These written materials stem from both British and English sources, between which there was clearly considerable interchange – witness Bede's reliance on Gildas and the use made by the author of the *History of the Britons* (*Historia Brittonum*) of English genealogies. Unlike the English, the British clergy were literate throughout the fifth and sixth centuries, so that there is some potential for the survival of written material from an early date.

Writing in the first third of the eighth century, Bede thought of Ida as the founder of the Bernician dynasty but offered little detail for the history of his own people before the reign of Æthelfrith (killed *c.* 616), whose exploits seem to have reached Bede via epic poetry of the *Beowulf* kind. British literature purports to deal with events a generation or more earlier than Æthelfrith.

There are huge problems in using these sources, and recent histories have varied dramatically in the degree to which writers have been prepared to accept as historical, material quarried from works composed in the middle centuries of the Middle Ages. These problems are best illustrated by a brief examination of the *History of the Britons*. During the medieval period this work was credited to Nennius, a Welsh priest in the patronage of that Elvodug who encouraged the Welsh Church to accept the Roman method of calculating Easter and who, according to the *Annales Cambriae* (*The Welsh Annals*), died, as Bishop of Bangor, in 809. However, his authorship has been placed in doubt by the researches of David Dumville, who has argued that it is an anonymous work composed at the court of Gwynedd in 829–30. It bears the imprint of efforts by Welsh scholars to use and systematize a rag-bag of material from a great variety of sources. The actual composition was by no means free of political pressures. The result is a work of literature with propogandist properties. It contains a certain amount of material which may have derived from earlier written sources but the process of the transmission of the northern material within it is not understood. It can not be accepted at face value.

The earliest northern episode within the *History* is an account of the establishment of Hengest's son and nephew with troops in the north 'around the wall (*murus*) which is called Wall (*Guaul*)', by Hengest and Vortigern. It subsequently describes their expedition around Pictland to waste the Orkneys and their occupation of many districts beyond the sea of the *Frenessici* (unlocated but perhaps Frisians, so the northern reaches of the Channel), as far as the borders of the Picts (*HB*, 38). The tale does not fall foul of the few facts concerning the arrival of the English to be found in the work of Gildas and was probably developed by writers familiar with it, whether at first- or second-hand. Since the place-names are English, it is unlikely to represent an early British tradition. The theme probably derives from attempts to tie the foundation of English Bernicia into the dominant group of otherwise southern English foundation myths, associated with Hengest and Vortigern. The result is a Bernicia already stretching from Edinburgh to south of the Wall established within the lifetime of the putative founders of the first English kingdom in the fifth century. This is utterly implausible and smacks of history being rewritten, probably in association with the rise of the Bernician kings in the seventh century, when men like Oswald and Oswiu had every reason to commission or encourage bogus traditions which would re-inforce their 'overkingship' of the south by suggesting that their own northern realm was established by the same tight family group who were believed responsible for the first Saxon kingdom in Britain. This material is clearly not historical, even if it is instructive concerning the later development of a Northumbrian foundation myth.

The *History of the Britons* returns to events in the north in chapters 57 and 61–5, although Welsh material was interwoven from chapter 62 onwards, where the opportunity was taken to advertise the famous claim that Cunedda, reputed hammer of the Irish and founder of numerous Welsh dynasties, had derived from Manaw Gododdin – the name survives in Clackmannan(shire), on the northern shores of the Firth of Forth. Treatment of King Ida is little more convincing. The Bernician king was credited with an implausible twelve sons of one queen as well as sons by concubines, and Æthelfrith, 'the Artful', seven sons. Such numbers imply that this version of sixth-century history owes a large debt to later Christian scholarship: the twelve sons of Ida recall Christ's apostles, while seven was the commonest number in the Old Testament. Again, these look like later embellishments of the foundation story of the Bernician royal house.

More reliably, the *History* offers a Welsh perspective on the wars between themselves (and Mercia) and Northumbria during the seventh century. The specifically northern material was drawn from both English and British sources. The collection of genealogies (57–61, 63) covers five of the English kingdoms and derives from an English collection of the very early ninth century, compiled possibly in Mercia but more probably in Northumbria. To it the author added a gloss from

A	DEIRA	B	BERNICIA
Vespasian B. vi (The order is reversed in the original)	*History of the Britons*, 61	*Vespasian* B, vi (The order is reversed in the original)	*History of the Britons*, 57
Uoden Frealifing	Woden	Uoden Frealifing	Woden
Uegdæg Uodning	begat Bældeg	Beldæg Wodning	begat Beldeg
Siggar Uegdæging	Brond begat Siggar	Beornic Beldæging	
Suebdæg Siggaring	(begat Swebdeg)	Wegbrand Bernicing	begat Gechbrond
Siggeot Suebdæging	(begat Sigegeat)	Ingibrand Wegbranding	
Sæbald Siggeoting	begat Sebald	Alusa Ingibranding	begat Aluson
Sæfugel Sæbalding	begat Zegulf	Angengeot Alusing	begat Inguec
Soemel Sæfugling	begat Soemil	Ethilberht Angengeoting	begat Ædilrith
	He first separated Deur from Birneich	Œsa Ethilberhting	begat Œssa
	Soemil begat Sgerthing	Eoppa Œsing	begat Eobba
Uestorualcna Soemling	(begat Westerfalca)	Ida Eopping	begat Ida
Uilgils Uestorualcning	begat Giulglis		Ida had twelve sons whose names are Adda, Ædldric, Decdric, Edric, Deothere, Osmer, and one queen Beornoch (who was their mother and six sons from his concubines. . . .)
Uuscfrea Uilgisling	begat Usfrean		
Yffi Uufcfreaing	begat Iffi	Ethilric Iding	Ealric
Ælle Yffing	begat Ulli (Ælle)	Ethilfrith Ethilricing	Ealdric begat Ælfret (Æthelfrith),
Edwine Ælling	(begat) Ædgum (Edwin)		He had seven sons, named Anfrid (Eanfrith), Osgald (Oswald), Osbiu (Oswiu), Osgudu, Oslapf, Offa.
	(begat) Osfirth and Eadfirth	Osuio Ethilfrithing	Oswiu
		Ecgfrith Osuing	begat Alcfrith, Ælfwin and Ecgfrith

other sources. The remainder of his material was predominantly Northumbrian, since only the Bernician and Deiran lists are expanded, and the later kings from Æthelfrith (reigned *c.* 592–616) to Ecgfrith (died 685) – and the Mercian Penda, who was well known to the Welsh – were each accorded a thumbnail outline of selected features of the reign (63–5). Some of these, such as Æthelfrith's grant of Bamburgh to his queen and its renaming, apparently derive from Bede's *History of the English Church*.

To this English material the author of the *History* added information originating in northern British sources, which may have been entirely literary in form, and which focuses on British kingdoms in what was, by then, Bernicia. It therefore pre-dates the rapid expansion of that kingdom under Æthelfrith and his successors. No British information concerning Yorkshire but pre-dating Deira has survived, which appears to confirm that this was by far the earlier of the two English kingdoms.

The information which purports to be the oldest is confined to the earlier generations of the two English royal genealogies. Both descend from Woden, the most popular divine ancestor of the English dynasties in Britain. In the earliest surviving version of the Anglian genealogies, the Deiran contains fourteen names including that of Woden (*U[u]oden*), ending with that of Edwin King of Northumbria, *c.* 616–33. To this number, the *History* added a further two names,

A: The genealogy of the Deiran royal house. B: The genealogy of the Bernician royal house inserting Brand as Woden's grandson, and Swærta, in the ninth generation from the god, bringing the total to sixteen – although the reasons for these interpolations are obscure. This genealogy probably originated at the court of Oswiu or one of his descendants, given that his sons were Edwin's grandsons and that the kings of the collateral line of Edwin's cousin, who were rivals of the Bernician royal family, were omitted. There can not, however, be much doubt that Edwin, overlord of all England (626–33), would have had at his court eulogists capable of reciting an impressive genealogy and this may be the ultimate origin of the surviving list. If we were to accept it at its face value, the length would imply that the Deiran royal house was already in place in the mid-fifth century – as archaeology would seem to confirm – but, in practice, the majority of its entries need be no more than window-dressing inserted into a list compiled for reasons of prestige in the early seventh century.

The author of the *History* added a gloss against the name Soemil, recording that 'he first separated Deira from Bernicia'. Given that the earlier English kingdom was Deira, not Bernicia, and that it was the latter, rather than the former, which is likely to have broken away, this interpolation may derive from the Bernician supremacy after 635. Bernician kings would probably have favoured interpolations into the genealogy of their erstwhile rivals which back-dated the primacy of Bernicia. The sweeping alliteration of the central sections of this genealogy look contrived. 'Ælle, son of Yffi', the penultimate king named, is the earliest of the Deiran line of whose existence we can be sure. The take-over by Æthelfrith appears to be the horizon of historicity for Deira in Bede's works as well as the *History*.

The Bernician genealogy is significantly shorter than the Deiran, signifying either that its mythical origins were later, or, if preferred, that Woden was much older when he begat its earliest mortal representative. The quantity of information which the *History* appended to King Ida, variously the eleventh or ninth name listed, suggests that the history of Bernicia emerges in some form in about 550, a generation or two earlier than that of Deira. Bede looked back on Ida, whom he credited with a reign of an improbable twelve years starting in 547, as the founder of the royal house of Northumbria. The *History* also notes that it was Ida who joined Din Guaire (later Bamburgh) to Bernicia. Ida's prominence in northern legend implies that he was remembered in song as a warrior king, and the conquest of Northumberland would have been an appropriate success around which heroic lays could have been woven. If so, numerical allusions to Christ may have seemed appropriate to the court poets responsible for the transmission of this material in the seventh and eighth centuries.

Politics and Geography

The earliest name of the English settlers in northern England remains a matter of controversy. It has been suggested that the *Humbrenses* were Anglian immigrants settling in southern Yorkshire and northern Lincolnshire, those in the former eventually being distinguished by the prefix *Northan*. The Anglian genealogies distinguish the Deirans as *Northan hymbra* and the Bernicians as *northanhymbrorum*, and it has been further suggested that the prefix originated as a description of Bernicia, not Deira. However, Bede thought it necessary to define his

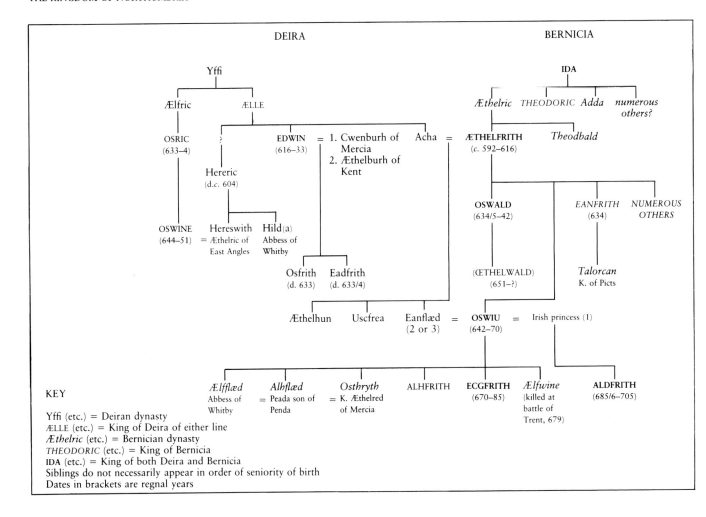

Family tree of the Northumbrian kings in the seventh century

use of the term as applying to 'all those peoples who live to the north of the river Humber' (*EH*, I, 15), and it may, therefore, be no more than a group name which originated after the union of the region under one dynasty in the seventh century. The case for the *Humbrenses* rests on Ecgfrith's title – *rex Humbronensium* – recorded in the preamble of the Council of Hatfield (in 680), but this signifies no more than that he still retained the kingship of at least one of the provinces south of the Humber (certainly Hatfield and probably Lindsey) which had first been usurped by Edwin between 626 and 633. In the anonymous *Life of Gregory the Great*, written *c.* 680–704 at Whitby, Edwin was described as 'of the Humbrenses'. The *Humbrenses* were, therefore, an artificial creation of the seventh century, by kings in search of a title appropriate to the peoples under their control. The stem of the river name is British, not English, so that as an early English 'people' name it can not have predated their arrival in the area. Although there can be no doubt that the Angles of Deira were from the same, ultimately immigrant stock as those of Lindsey and East Anglia, the entire concept of an early 'Humber-folk' is without foundation.

If we can separate the two sixth-century English kingdoms of Bernicia and Deira from the confusions in which they are ensnared in the *History*, we can begin to establish their respective geographies. Neither name is English in origin, and both presumably emerged from British precursors. The *History* (61) provides British versions – *Deur* and *Bernech*. Bede referred not to geographical units but to peoples – the *Deiri* and *Bernicii*

– but even these necessitate some notion of territories.

Of the two, Deira is the easier to define. There is every reason to believe that its eastern boundary coincided with the North Sea, and its southern with the Humber. East of the Wolds was the 'Wood of the Deirans', around Beverley. The North York Moors provide the obvious natural frontier to the north, although Deira certainly stretched to the Tees in the later Anglo-Saxon period. York was the site of Edwin's baptism at the hands of Paulinus in 627, and was then within Deira although probably still marginal to it. Edwin also had a palace at Catterick. If the Aberford Dykes are relevant to the geography of Elmet (see below), then these presumably represent an attempt to delimit the territorial power of Deiran kings at one or more periods before the absorption of that kingdom into English Northumbria, *c.* 626–30. The frequently-drowned landscape of the Vale of York was probably peripheral to Deira on its western side.

The survival of the British name implies that the Anglo-Saxon kingdom emerged from a pre-existing British polity. Deira approximates to the tribal territory of the Parisi, although that name is not evidenced any later than the second century and may have decayed or been replaced even within the Roman period. The later name may derive from the British *daru–* or *deru–*, an 'oak', in which case the name is cognate with the River Derwent (and with the Romano-British name of Malton (*Derventio*) which derived from it), where late or even sub-Roman activity was certainly present. If so, the Deirans are the people of the Derwent Valley.

This finds support in the identification of their principal shrine at Goodmanham (*EH*, II, 14) and the primacy and large size of the cremation cemetery at neighbouring Sancton, both sited where the valley meets the Wolds. King Edwin was at a royal residence by the Derwent celebrating the pagan festival of Easter when an attempt was made to assassinate him in 625 (*EH*, II, 9). It was, therefore, close by the shrine. If this were the primary royal residence of the Deiran monarchy it was probably also the site at which Edwin's famous conference concerning conversion occurred and from which Coifi rode out to desecrate the temple complex at Goodmanham. It would be natural for the estate focus of this area to lie within the route corridor between the Wolds and the valley, much in the same way as did the West Heslerton Anglian settlement. That this lost palace should be sought in the immediate vicinity of Sancton village is implied by the presence of the largest, earliest and longest utilized of the pagan cemeteries of Deira on Sancton Wold and the location of a second burial ground in the vicinity of the church, in which were interments using various rites which belong to the late sixth and seventh centuries. The identification may be re-inforced by the presence of the element 'king' in two field names within the township, the medieval 'Kuniggesholm' and the more recent 'King's Hill'.

If this palace were destroyed by Cadwallon of Gwynedd in 634, then it may have been replaced quite soon after by a new complex sited slightly further south and even closer to the Roman road junction, at Newbald ('new building'). The link between the large (thirty-hide) Newbald estate and the Northumbrian monarchy was severed as late as 963, when it was granted by King Edgar to his representative, Earl Gunnar. In 1066 the estate was still large and in the hands of another royal appointee, the archbishop, and Gunnar may have obtained it only in order to give it to the Church.

The Derwent Valley

Early sixth-century Bernicia is far more problematical than Deira. If the author of the *History* was correct in attributing the capture of Bamburgh to Ida of Bernicia in the middle of the century, then the core of the kingdom cannot have lain in Northumberland north of the Coquet. Nor was it either north or west of Bamburgh. A cruciform brooch dating to *c.* 500 from Corbridge implies some early contact with that area and this may be an indication of the date of its initial conquest. The importance, agricultural potential and size of the seventh-century royal estate of Hexhamshire and the focal role of Corbridge in the Roman period may imply that this area was the focus of an early sub-Roman kingdom originating from those *Corionototae* mentioned in a Roman cavalry commander's dedication found at Hexham (*Roman Inscriptions of Britain*, vol. 1, no. 1142). The likeliest origin of an English kingdom founded from Deira must lie in Cleveland, where the recently excavated cemetery at Norton reflects the presence of a pagan Anglian community with close ties to the south. If so, the capture and retention of Bamburgh signified a late stage in the expansion of the territory available to Bernician kings.

Ida is portrayed as a powerful warrior king who brought all the north under his own protection. He was, therefore, probably an 'overking'. The several individuals named as rulers of the Bernicians after Ida may imply the break up of his 'overkingship' at his death, with several dynasties ruling separate kingdoms descended ultimately from British lordships, in which case the re-unification of English Bernicia was another achievement of King Æthelfrith during the 590s.

During the later sixth century the northern and western neighbours of the Bernicians were still British kingdoms, although it is extremely difficult to reconstruct the majority of those whose dynasties later succumbed to the expansion of Bernicia. The author of the *History of the Britons* (62) recorded that Outigern fought bravely against the English nation, juxtaposing him with Ida. The name is certainly British and the form is early. He may have been an opponent of Ida but there can be no certainty that Outigern was even a northerner.

Similar problems attend a series of entries in the *Annales Cambriae*. Under the year 573, its author recorded 'the battle of Arfderydd between the sons of Eliffer and Gwenddolau son of Ceidio; in which battle Gwenddolau fell'. The sons of Eliffer were identified as Gwrgi and Peredur in the *Annals* in 580, the year of their deaths. Arfderydd may be Arthuret, on the border between England and Scotland near Carlisle, and the personal name Gwenddolau may be the root of the place-name Carwinley near by, but neither attribution is certain. If they are correct, the principals were probably the rulers of whatever sub-Roman kingdoms had emerged in the territories of the Novantae of Galloway, the Selgovae of the valleys of Dumfriesshire, and Rheged.

The latter is known from the extant poetry of Taliesin as one of two kingdoms associated with a great hero, Urien, whose exploits were recorded in Welsh literature. Although there is now little confidence that the poems attributed to this late sixth-century writer have survived without substantial later alteration (they may even have been written significantly later), one identifies the presence of a royal estate of Urien at Llwyfenydd, which should probably be identified as the valley of the Lyvennet, a tributary of the Eden running through Crosby Ravensworth. This detail relating to a minor river name is unlikely to be a later invention. It seems probable that the mysterious Rheged was broadly coterminus with the Romano-British Carvetii in the Solway

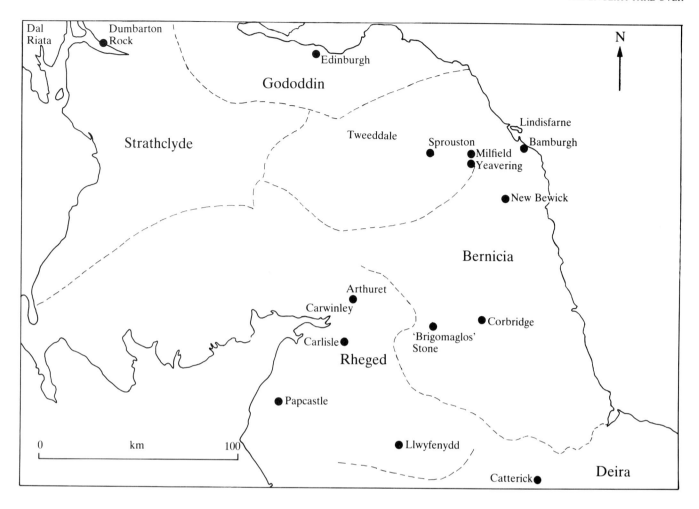

Northern Northumbria in the sixth century

lowlands and that Urien's patronage was centred on the Eden Valley, in which case the presence of belligerent pagan neighbours in Teesdale would have been a matter of considerable concern to him. His portrayal in Welsh poetry as ruler of *Catraeth* (Catterick) is implausible and probably reflects the influence of the *Gododdin* poems. The preservation of Urien's memory may owe much to the feud between Welsh and Northumbrian kings during the seventh century, which encouraged Welsh poets to applaud the heroic qualities of an earlier British king at war with the northern Angles. Urien was depicted in the *History* as a British 'overking', exercising leadership in war over the British kings of the north, comparable with that exercised throughout much of Wales by Cadwallon and other Kings of Gwynedd.

To the north was the long-lived British kingdom of Strathclyde. The people here, like the Deiri, took their name from a river valley and had probably developed from a pre-existing British tribe – the Dumnonii of Roman Scotland, whose territory extended in the second century from the watershed of the Southern Uplands to the Trossachs. The principal centre was Alt Clut – *Dum*barton – the English form of the name apparently retaining the Roman period tribal name. Gododdin – the Votadini of the Roman period – probably occupied the bulk of the remainder of Scotland below the Firth of Forth, although the name was later restricted to the northern marches of their territory. Etin (Edinburgh), Mynyddog's palace site, where Irish annals recorded a siege in 638, was presumably its principal stronghold.

Concerning the central Pennines there is no literary evidence. Whether the Setantii of the Fylde, for example, survived as a kingdom into the sixth century we have no way of knowing. In southern Lancashire, Makerfield is a name with Welsh origins attached to a district of some size which may have originated as a kingdom. It has been suggested that the Pabo, whose son, Dunod, died in 595, should be associated with Papcastle in Cumbria. The best candidate for a Dark Age kingdom is the British-named Craven. Although no dynastic information has survived, this name was attached to a wide area during the later Middle Ages, stetching from the Ribble valley and Dentdale across the Yorkshire Dales. The core of it was a wapentake in 'Domesday Book', to which outlying manors in Cartmel were attached, implying that Craven may once have stretched as far as Lancashire north of the Sands.

South of Craven was Elmet, a kingdom which survived under British control a generation later than Rheged and Craven. There is a comparative wealth of references to Elmet, which appears in the primary list of the Tribal Hidage (arguably written in the autumn of

Elmet and its neighbours. A tentative reconstruction of an early seventh-century British kingdom.

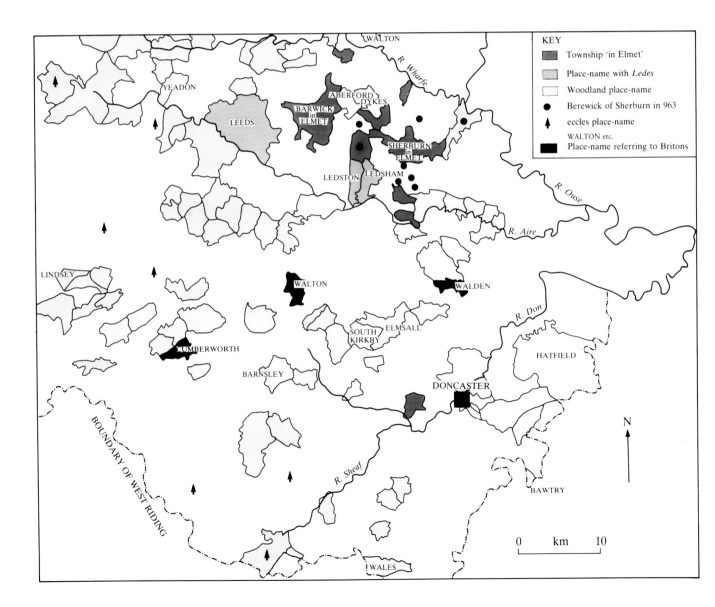

Limestone (karst) scenery: Wharfedale in November

625), in the *History of the Britons*, the *Annales Cambriae* and in Bede's *Ecclesiastical History* (II, 14) and also in a group of medieval place-names between the Rivers Wharfe and Don. Given the prominence accorded Edwin's suppression of the last British king, Ceretic (probably wrongly dated in the *Annales Cambriae* to 616), its kings would seem to be the rulers or overlords of all territories in southern Northumbria still in British hands after the conquests of Æthelfrith. If the place-name evidence pinpoints the core kingdom, that would seem to lie between the River Don and Wharfedale, sharing its western boundary with the region named by Bede as *Loidis* (Leeds), but the territories for which Ceretic paid tribute of 600 hides to Edwin could have included *Loidis*, Yeadon and Makerfield.

The geography is confused by the problems surrounding Edwin's palace at *Campodonum*. This name has been equated with the *Camboduno* which appears in Route II of the *Antonine Itinerary* but the Tadcaster–Manchester section of this road is corrupt and the twenty Roman miles apparently separating a site of this name from Tadcaster does not equate with any known Roman settlement. Attempts to identify *Camboduno* with Leeds, only thirteen miles from Tadcaster, are not convincing. If the name is not entirely garbled in the *Antonine Itinerary*, which is a distinct possibility, then it should relate to a fort in the vicinity of Cleckheaton.

The equation of *Campodonum* with *Cambodunum* may be mistaken. The more reliable reference is that of Bede:

Nevertheless, in *Campodonum*, where there was also a royal residence [i.e. as well as at Catterick, just mentioned] he built a basilica, which afterwards the pagans, by whom Edwin the king was killed, burnt along with the whole residence. As a replacement for it later kings built their palace in the region [*regio*] which is called Leeds [*Loidis*]. However, the altar, which was made of stones, survived the fire and it survives even now in the monastery of the very reverend abbot and priest Thrydwulf, which is in the wood of Elmet.

The tension in this passage between Leeds and *Campodonum* demonstrates that the latter lay outside the former. *Campodonum* translates as 'the Field (of) *Donum*' and should be identified with Doncaster (Roman *Danum*), perhaps in the form of one of the 'field' names which are still common in the vicinity (such as Austerfield, Hatfield and Sheffield).

King Edwin travelled frequently between Deira, Bernicia and Lindsey and his palaces on the Roman road network at Catterick and Doncaster probably served these needs. Doncaster was on the borders of Hatfield and Elmet, and was therefore convenient for his oversight of both, but a most improbable site for the earlier palace of Ceretic. The heavy altar stones from Doncaster are unlikely to have travelled far, implying that the wood of Elmet was close to Doncaster. The township names derived from woodland elements which stretch from the two Elmsalls via Barnsley to the Pennines at Lindsey may reflect its extent, in which case the kingdom name might be reflected in *Elm*sley, even though this is quite easily explained as descending from the Old English tree name 'elm'. One might even hazard a guess that the monastery to which Bede referred lay at South Kirby – 'church-settlement' in the Viking Age.

The boundary of Elmet further west may have been the Sheaf, a river name which, like Mersey, derives from an Old English word meaning boundary. This would be the frontier with the 'Peak dwellers' of the Tribal Hidage, later incorporated into Mercia. If the defensive site at Carl Wark is of Dark Age date, then it was presumably constructed by one side or another to police the watershed between the valleys of the Derwent and the Sheaf. Its proximity to Dore, the later meeting-place between southern and northern kings, may be significant.

The main grouping of settlements 'in-Elmet' was further north, between the Aire and the Wharfe, where they congregated on the rich farmland of the magnesian limestone ridge around the A1 (Dere Street). Sherburn-in-Elmet was, in 1066, a vast estate held by the archbishop, which had been in royal hands in the tenth century and this is the best candidate for Ceretic's palace site. The suffix appears to distinguish these settlements not so much from Deira, from which it was clearly delineated by the Wharfe, as from neighbouring *Loidis*, the district name which survives in Ledston and Ledsham, also on the Ridge. *Loidis* would seem to be centred on the Aire Valley and was probably also in origin a separate lordship. The battle of *Winwæd* was fought in the same *regio* in 655 (*EH*, III, 24) and Bede regularly used this term for early kingdoms. His description of events in 633–5 implies that eighth-century Northumbrians thought of Elmet and Leeds as being linked together and these links arguably date back to Ceretic in the 620s. A Roman-period inscription from Ledston may record the *Latenses*, who could be the precursors of British Leeds – but the reading is disputed. The district of Leeds was probably delimited to the south by a string of woodland township names and by Yeadon to the west. It

The parish church of Sherburn-in-Elmet. This hilltop site is one candidate for the 'capital' of Elmet

was, therefore, very small and just one of several British lordships subject to Ceretic, most of which we cannot even name.

Elmet, therefore, may have been both a specific territory and the title of a dynasty deriving from it, exercising 'overkingship' or even direct rule of some neighbouring territories. These may have extended as far as Makerfield and the Irish Sea. The region of Leeds should be included but the extent of Ceretic's power northwards is no more than guess-work. Craven was probably already under English rule by 616, so Craven's southern frontiers were probably the northern limit of Ceretic's influence. The presence of Elmet in the initial list of peoples in the Tribal Hidage who are ordered in a clockwise circuit around Mercia may imply that Elmet was tributary to Cearl of Mercia before c. 615.

A complex series of dykes exists at and around Aberford and it is possible that the north-facing South Dyke was constructed as a defence for Elmet. The Reedgate Dyke, an east-facing earthwork across the Roman road west from Tadcaster may also be relevant. If the east-facing Grim's ditch, only 6.4 km east of Leeds, is also of this period, it may have defended Leeds from Elmet at some time in the sixth century. However, the south-west-facing Rein dyke is medieval and the Becca Banks and the Ridge earthworks are more likely to have been con-structed by Northumbrian kings against Mercia than by the rulers of Elmet. The origin of the various dyke systems of Northumbria are obscured by a lack of even near contemporary written evidence but several, including the Dane's Dyke on Flamborough Head, could belong to the sixth or seventh centuries.

One further people or kingship merits a mention. This is *Haethfeld-laṇde* – Hatfield. Unlike the petty kingdoms north of the Humber, this name is of English origin, although a British name – Meicen – survived in Welsh literature. In the Tribal Hidage, 'Hatfield land' was coupled with Lindsey as a single kingship and the difference in size implies that the former were the minor partner in this relationship. Lindsey was the subject of a brutal contest between Mercian and Northumbrian kings during the seventh century and the issue was resolved in favour of the Mercians only after Ecgfrith's death at Nechtanesmere (685). Reconstruction of the power politics of the period implies that it was here, not at Hatfield in Hertfordshire, that Archbishop Theodore held his synod *c.* 680 (see chapter 4) and this again reflects its border situation. Hatfield was eventually incorporated in the West Riding, so it was retained by the Northumbrian kings, but the confusion of boundaries in this vicinity in 1066 (and still pre-1974) between the West Riding, Nottinghamshire and Lincolnshire reflects its marginal location.

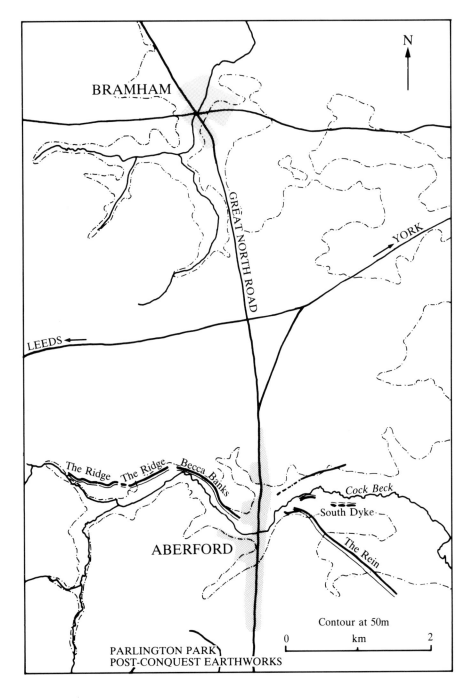

The dykes at and around Aberford

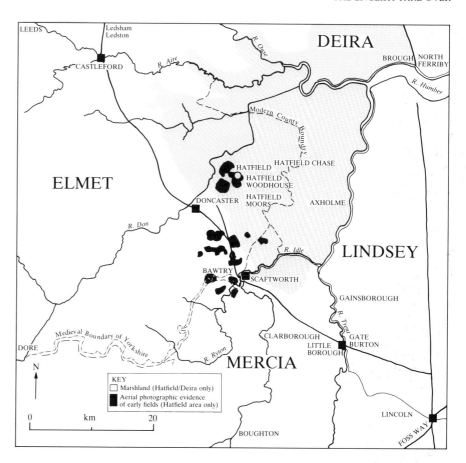

Hatfield, a petty kingdom in the Trent/
Ouse fenlands

Recent fieldwork in the Fens and parts of western Lindsey has
recovered ceramic evidence of early to mid-Anglo-Saxon occupation in
very similar terrain. Crop marks of field-systems have been identified
from the air west and south of Hatfield. Although these are characteristic of Iron Age/Roman period activity, parallels in East Anglia and Kent
suggest these may have continued in use into the early Middle Ages and
this area, now largely under the plough, is an obvious candidate for the
sort of treatment accorded the Fens. The royal centre was probably at
Hatfield itself and its use for a synod in 680 (if it was here) implies that
this was maintained throughout the period. Edwin was killed in the
immediate vicinity, if not at the actual palace site.

Hatfield was probably not, therefore, part of any of the Northumbrian
kingships in the sixth century, but eventually became attached to it as the
only remnant of the interests of Kings Æthelfrith and Edwin below the
Don which Ecgfrith's successors (after 685) were able to defend.

This brief examination of the geography of the early kingdoms has
underlined several important facts. One is the paucity of the information that has reached us and the consequent difficulties in establishing
the names, dynasties and whereabouts of many of those kingdoms. A
second fact is that, despite this paucity, the degree of continuity of the
principal cores of pre-English society and even of names from the local
tribes (as known in the second century) to the Dark Age kingdoms is
sufficient to encourage the expectation that if more were known then
the extent of that continuity would be even greater. Long-lived kinships,
local group identity and social hierarchies certainly underlie
several, if not all, sixth-century polities. Thirdly, there was a widespread

abandonment of those foci which were peculiarly Roman – rather than native – in inception. York, the erstwhile focus of provincial and military authority, appears to have become marginalized in the fifth century. Its economic, social and governmental functions gone, it had no role to perform in the new tribal configuration since it was isolated by environmental catastrophe from the core territories of the Derwent Valley and the Jurassic ridge. In this respect, its fortunes matched those of London, similarly abandoned in the fifth and sixth centuries. Aldborough likewise appears to have declined into insignificance, perhaps underlining the artificiality of the *civitas* of the Brigantes in its final, Roman form. The late fourth-, fifth-, sixth- and even early seventh-century focus was at Catterick, far closer to Stanwick, the centre of the Brigantes on the eve of the Roman conquest, and a palace site survived here into the ninth century.

There may be an important message in these patterns. Where Roman policies had merely stabilised existing tribal geography, that geography displayed a tenacious capacity for survival into the late sixth century, and was then absorbed into the Northumbrian state. Where Roman soldiers and administrators had tampered with that geography or had established pan-tribal or entirely artificial patterns of settlement or organization – as at many fort sites – then the post-Roman return to tribalism led to an abandonment of those settlement patterns which were without a role within the local tribal system and its economic base, reverting to patterns more relevant to the Iron Age. Continuity was substantial but nowhere total, with specifically Roman sites and territories the most vulnerable to abandonment.

Lastly, the various kingships of what was to eventually become Northumbria were highly interactive. It is possible to point towards shadowy 'overkings', both British and English, from the mid- to late sixth century, providing leadership to the warriors of several peoples and presumably drawing tribute from them. The basic building blocks of these groupings were extremely small and it was only those with access to the resources of several who could hope to achieve a degree of autonomy. Successful kings were already ousting their less powerful neighbours – hence the expansion of Bernicia and suppression of Elmet. This type of expansion was probably a powerful factor in the creation of new names, as those with which dynasties were originally associated became progressively less appropriate to the bundle of kingships held. Such pressures probably brought into existence names like Rheged. They were certainly responsible for the Northumbrians, which, in the form used by Bede, was appropriate only to the aftermath of Nechtanesmere, in 685.

Warfare

The petty kingships of the decades around 570 were organized for war. Indeed, warfare was the principal stimulus which had enabled the dynasties to emerge. English and British warriors used a broadly comparable range of weapons and, presumably therefore, of tactics. Although cremation burials do not generally contain weapons, Anglo-Saxon inhumations suggest that the military classes of pagan Northumbria were equipped with swords, or more commonly spears, and might carry shields and a certain amount of defensive armour. Some of these weapons were clearly of the highest quality: the pattern-welded sword

Accompanied inhumations at the sixth-century cemetery at Norton, Teeside. ABOVE: Grave 120, a male burial with an iron spear and wooden bucket; OPPOSITE: Grave 69, a male burial in flexed position with iron spear

found at Acklam Wold and dating to *c.* 600, for example, was the product of a complex process of manufacture, the purpose of which was largely ornamentation. Warfare was the role of an aristocratic élite who monopolized land-ownership and political influence in both societies and who maintained complex relationships one with another both inside and beyond tribal frontiers.

For a comparable picture of British society, we are heavily dependent on the *Gododdin* poetry. This corpus of literature has survived in a single thirteenth-century text, now stored at Cardiff (South Glamorgan County Library, MS 2.81). It comprises a series of eulogies to Celtic warriors, who, where identifiable, were placed in a northern British context, with special links with King Mynyddog the Wealthy of Edinburgh (*Din Eidyn*), and with Catterick (*Catraeth*), around which several battles appear to have been fought. The individual praise poems are highly formalized, with numerous recurring phrases and a standardized structure, extolling the bonds existing between lord and warrior and heroic qualities. The reward of excellence was fame (as in pagan English society) and eulogy played a vital role in this process. Although they are phrased in a Christian context, they contain much which derived from a pagan past, particularly in the idioms used to identify heroic excellence and the powerful animal-similes:

Wearing a brooch, in the front rank, armed in the war cry, a powerful man in combat before the day of his death, a captain charging forwards before armies; there fell five times fifty before his blades, of the Deirans and Bernicians there fell a hundred score, they were annihilated in one hour. He would sooner wind up food for wolves than attend a wedding, sooner be carrion for the raven than go to the altar, sooner his blood poured over the ground than he should have due burial, in return for mead in the hall among the war-bands. Hyfaidd the tall shall be honoured as long as there is a bard.

(*Gododdin*, A5, adapted from the translation by K.H. Jackson, 1969).

How and why this corpus reached Wales and was preserved there is unclear but it should perhaps be associated with the struggle between Cadwallon of Gwynedd and Edwin, 'overking' of all Britain, early in the 630s, when Cadwallon attempted to revive British lordship and the British Church in the north (see chapter 5). As such, a collection of praise poetry focused on northern British heroism in earlier conflicts with the Angles of Deira, in particular, would have had an important role in rekindling the martial ardour of the northern Britons against Edwin's dynasty. Cadwallon's death in battle in 634/5 and the siege of Edinburgh in 638 probably ended the dream of a northern British revival. The focal role of Mynyddog and Edinburgh imply that it was to the Lothians that Cadwallon looked for northern British allies in 633–4/5 and it was probably from that part of the Forth lowlands

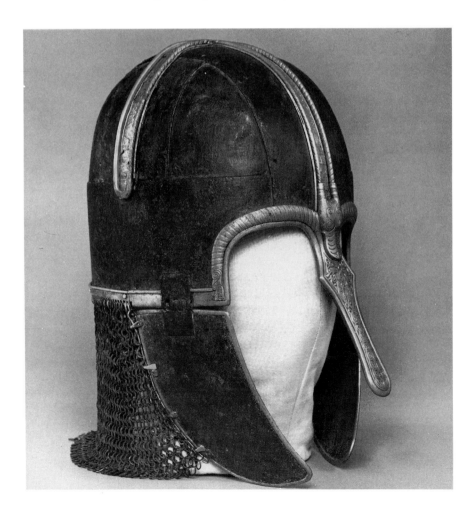

The York helmet was discovered on the Coppergate site, preserved in a wooden lined shaft. It was found carefully positioned in the shaft, along with a spearhead. The decoration and inscription on the helmet date it to the second half of the eighth century

Edinburgh Castle. A sixth- and early seventh-century British palace site

known as Gododdin that the corpus was transmitted to Gwynedd, as the name suggests.

The context of the contents is approximately a century earlier than this. Catterick had only recently been lost to the English — and with it the Tees Valley — and it was still possible to envisage direct conflict between Votadinian warrior bands based in the Lothians and Angles in Yorkshire on a common frontier. English Bernicia barely existed.

Although analysis of this corpus is probably still in its infancy, it is possible to extract a certain amount of incidental information to lay beside the much fuller archaeological evidence from the Anglian areas. This literary evidence suggests that sixth-century British warriors would normally be equipped much as were their English opponents. The warriors described had spears and swords and some were protected by mail-shirts and shields. Neither the *Gododdin* nor Anglo-Saxon inhumations suggest that helmets were commonly worn by either side; Anglo-Saxon helmets are scarce in archaeological deposits throughout England. There have been suggestions that the Bernicians, at least, copied their Celtic neighbours in using cavalry but this seems improbable. British warriors were certainly often mounted, but it is clear that much, if not all, of their fighting was on foot, and they were probably mounted infantry, not fighting from horseback except in the pursuit of a defeated enemy. Eddi's description of Ecgfrith's campaign against the Picts refers similarly to mounted infantry (*Life of Wilfrid*, 19), placed on horseback for speed of advance rather than as a method of fighting. There is no reason to think that the army which Ecgfrith led soon after

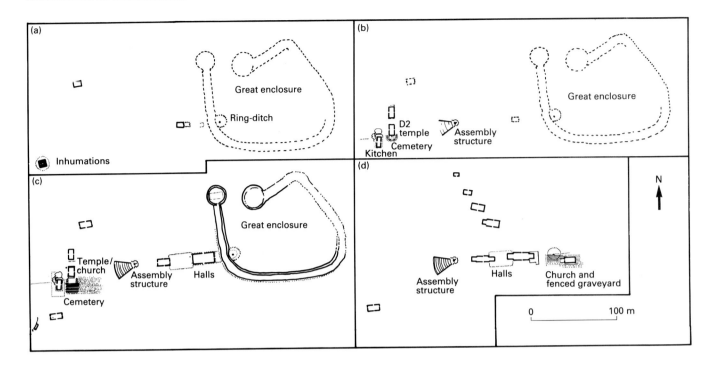

Successive palace complexes at Yeavering in the Till Valley in the sixth and seventh centuries

against the Mercians was other than an infantry force (ibid., 20), although it is worth noting that mounted soldiers predominate on the Aberlemno symbol stone (p. 138).

What emerges forcibly from the *Gododdin* are the close parallels between Anglo-Saxon and British society. Both produced literature which extolled the reciprocal services linking lord and warrior and concentrated almost exclusively on intensely secular ideals. In neither instance is there any evidence that the armed forces might ever consist of the nation in arms. Instead, the warriors of both were full-timers attendant on the king, drawn from a warrior class, membership of which was hereditary. The institution of king, household and war-band was the central organ of the kingdom, indeed the only organ, excepting that of the Church, of which we are now aware. From a very different vantage point, the *Gododdin* identifies the same social structure as that headed by the Welsh 'tyrants' in the *De Excidio* of Gildas and these two quite different forms of literature were not far from being contemporary in subject matter, if not in actual composition.

The similarities between Britons and English are very evident. There may, however, have been significant differences, particularly in the paths by which these two communities reached similar positions. Anglo-Saxon society stemmed from a militarily self-sufficient society on the continent and the central bond between military leader and warrior was imported ready-made into Britain, where it fuelled the great land-grab in which the English kingships came into being. This is not to suggest that it was impervious to change, but in this crucial respect it needed little alteration.

In England, the Saxons were slow to adopt fortifications and it is noticeable that where new sites were adopted for settlements of the very highest status in the core territories of English Northumbria they were barely defended, if at all. Such were the open palace sites at Yeavering, Milfield or 'by the Derwent'. The palace site at Yeavering was repeatedly destroyed and rebuilt during the wars of the early seventh century, until the decision was made to replace it with the palace at Milfield.

A sunken-featured building under excavation at New Bewick

Recent excavation has confirmed the presence of *Grubenhaüser* or 'sunken-featured buildings' at New Bewick (Northumberland) and comparable marks have been identified from the air at Sprouston, Thirlings, Milfield and Yeavering, as well as further north, inside the Scottish borders. It is clear that such Anglian settlements were being established in the course of the sixth and seventh centuries in what was rapidly becoming the focus of the Bernician kingdom. At Sprouston, in the Tweed Valley, a palace complex was complimented by an Anglo-Saxon cemetery in a manner very reminiscent of Yeavering. Such sites were focal points for a wide range of governmental, religious and ritual activities.

The status of the residents of such sites remains a matter of speculation. There has been an unfortunate tendency in recent years to unquestioningly interpret early groups of halls and sunken-featured buildings – such as that so expertly excavated at West Stow in Suffolk – as Anglo-Saxon farms, hamlets or even villages. However, the hall was the characteristic building of the warrior classes, where a king or thegn would preside over his household and companions. Lesser timber-framed structures may have been the private chambers of the élite, as evidenced in *Beowulf* and the Cyneheard/Cynewulf episode in the *Anglo-Saxon Chronicle* (757). The sunken-featured buildings which are generally the only other type of structure present were described long before by Tacitus as primarily for the storage of grain and their presence implies an in-flow of renders in need of storage against the winter. The absence of equipment and buildings associated more directly with farming, the close association of such complexes with

A reconstruction of a sunken-featured building at West Stow, Suffolk

well-accoutred graves and the profligate abandonment of artefacts on such sites all imply that the settlements so far discovered should be viewed less as the residences of incoming farmers than as those of an Anglian warrior élite, supported by renders drawn from large estates. While the several palace sites were royal residences, lesser complexes such as New Bewick probably housed warriors – thegns – in receipt of land grants from the king, not farmers.

A replica Saxon hall under construction at West Stow

The derivation of British kingship and its military capacity was very different, emerging from a period of adjustment after long generations when soldiering was the preserve of a professional army. British kings borrowed the notion of defensive households, either from their Celtic neighbours or from the late Empire. Such foci were dissimilar to the large hill-forts of the pre-Roman period, being much smaller defensive enclosures, often in several courtyards and built on extremely steep hilltops. These 'citadel'-type hill-forts, or *urbes* ('cities') as Bede was to call them, were high-status dwellings with governmental functions, within a fortification. In the British period such sites were important centres of manufacture, particularly of smithing, as was identified archaeologically at Mote of Mark, perhaps in order to produce the high-status goods necessary for the reward of service, diplomatic gifts and tribute payment. In the *Gododdin*, Edinburgh was described in a similar vein, 'Eidyn of many goldsmiths'. Within a society in which the vast majority apparently had no access to the types of artefact identifiable by archaeology, the few artisans worked at or close by the aristocratic households from which their commissions emanated. The economic system had closer parallels with that of the Bronze Age than of the Roman period.

Trial excavation at Bamburgh has illuminated the history of one such site. Occupation began before the Roman Conquest and continued during parts at least of the Roman occupation. Occupation associated with 'native' pottery but later than the third century was probably defensive in character and this was sealed by massive deposits of charcoal, possibly associated with Anglo-Saxon pottery, laid down before the seventh century. It is tempting to see this sequence as evidence for successive occupation of a focal site by British and Anglo-Saxon kings during the sixth century.

As the northern British kingdoms were conquered by English kings, so these British citadels were taken over, retaining their functions as centres of government and of the collection of food renders under the supervision of an English royal reeve. Within the old Roman province, such sites included romanized walled settlements which had probably been pressed into service as palace sites, as at Catterick and Lincoln. Beyond the Wall, they were predominantly of native inception, and Northumbria's northern provinces were initially focused on a series of hilltop sites and British fortresses, such as Doon Hill, Edinburgh, Stirling and Dunbar. It was just such a site in northern Northumbria which the author of the *History of the Britons* had in mind when he recalled that Oswiu of Northumbria was forced to hand over his treasure in the *urbs* of 'Iudeu' to Penda of Mercia, who distributed it among his Welsh allies.

Both British and English warriors passed across tribal or kingship boundaries in their search for patrons with the reputation for success and the wealth to enable them to be generous lords. There is no evidence that English warriors took service with British kings, nor vice versa, although English royals certainly sought a refuge in exile among their Celtic neighbours and would presumably have fought for them in that capacity, if called upon. The barrier of language apparently divided the Anglian and British warriorclasses, although refugees clearly learnt the language of their hosts.

The contest between British and English kings for dominance in the north depended on the war-bands each could sustain. The forces available to a successful king would comprise his own household warriors and those of other members of his own tribal aristocracy who owed him service – his landholding thegns. Beside these would fight the warriors of those neighbouring kings who had acknowledged his superiority. The underlying agricultural wealth of the eastern plain – particularly Deira – favoured the English kings whose larger renders could support more numerous war-bands. It was the Bernician dynasty which made most of the later running, perhaps because its territories lay on the interface between the English and British, and so had more opportunity to lay tribute on weaker neighbours. Those war-bands could be constantly replenished with young hopefuls of high status but inadequate income, whose path to fortune lay in obtaining the patronage of a generous and grateful lord. Welsh stories concerning Ida's family imply that the pagan English aristocracy were polygamous, in which case they had a tendency to produce a surfeit of recruits suitable for service as warriors under royal patronage. Their capacity to accept far higher casualty rates than the British aristocracy probably gave English kings another crucial edge over their British and Christian neighbours.

The chronology of the Conquest can be outlined thus: the Derwent Valley probably fell to Anglian warriors in the third quarter of the fifth century, so bringing English Deira into being. This rich corner of the north apparently absorbed the expansionist tendencies of the Anglian warrior classes for the remainder of the century, after which they expanded by successful warfare northwards into Teesdale, so bringing English Bernicia into being. This was initially retained as a part of the same kingship but eventually became much larger, perhaps by the same type of opportunistic land seizures as the Normans later perpetrated in Wales. These broke away from Deiran control. Ida was credited with the conquest of Bamburgh in the mid-sixth century, by which time English kings probably controlled the Wear and Tyne Valleys. Ida presumably established an 'overkingship' of all Bernicia, perhaps evicting various rivals in the process, before his conquest of Deira. His 'overkingship' lapsed with his own death and the north broke up once more into several competing kingships.

The *History* recalls that four British kings fought against Theodoric, Ida's son (note the pretentious name, meaning 'King-king', given him by Ida). Urien is identified in poetic sources as ruler of Rheged. He was acknowledged as the foremost in military skill and so was probably the 'overking' of the remaining British lordships of the north. Those named were Rhydderch Hen, identifiable from genealogical sources in Strath-

Fragments of clay moulds used for making jewellery at Mote of Mark, Dumfriesshire (courtesy of David Longley and Lloyd Laing)

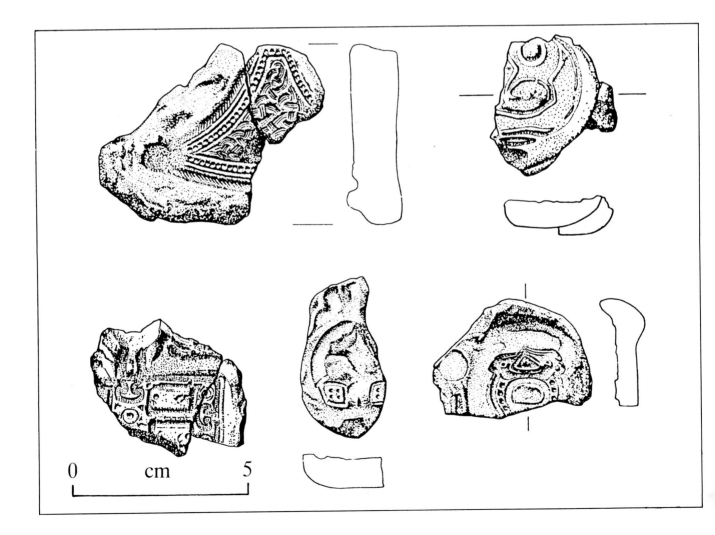

0   cm   5

clyde, Gwallawg (Elmet) and the mysterious Morcant (of Gododdin?). Since they temporarily bottled-up Theodoric on Lindisfarne, Urien appears to have taken advantage of the collapse of Ida's 'overkingship' to attack his heir, but the British effort failed when Morcant had Urien assassinated. With his leadership removed, the common British front appears to have failed and this effort proved to be the last challenge to English expansionism launched by a British king based in the north.

Further English aggression followed under Æthelfrith, who was remembered in the eighth century as a king 'fortissimus et gloriae cupidissimus' ('very powerful and most eager for glory', EH, I, 34), as the conqueror of great swathes of British territory and as the victor of the battle of Degsastan, c. 603, when he overthrew Aidan, king of Scottish Dal Riata. In c. 604 he usurped the crown of Deira. The result was not a unified state but a collection of peoples over whom Æthelfrith was variously king or 'overking'. Northumbria began as a bundle of kingships and it was long to exhibit this characteristic, with a slow rationalization to just two, the most successful English kingdoms of Deira and Bernicia.

The Nature of the Conquest

Bede compared Æthelfrith to Saul, scourge of the Philistines, and recorded that: 'No leader or king had made more land tributary to the English people or habitable [by them], the natives having been exterminated or subjugated' (EH I, 34). The venerable historian believed that he and his contemporaries in Northumbria descended from English stock and wrote accordingly, using this biblical parallel with an Old Testament king to substantiate his belief that, although pagan, Æthelfrith was God's agent. However, there is little real likelihood of there ever having been mass destruction of the entire British population, only that of the royal and aristocratic classes. The victory of the English occurred rapidly, Northumbria coming into existence in the period c. 550–640, and to suggest that the peoples of the tribal British kingdoms could have been replaced wholesale by waves of settlers in their tens of thousands from the core of Deira or Bernicia is to create problems of demography which are insurmountable. Æthelfrith was known to the writer of the History of the Britons by the nickname Flesaurs, 'the Artful Dodger', which is hardly an epithet which a Welsh writer would have attached to a warrior-king responsible for the wholesale extermination of his own people.

The process of English conquest probably took several forms. Some British dynasties came early to an accommodation with the English and survived for several generations, at a price which included the loss of independence, and perhaps some territorial concessions. Strathclyde was the ultimate British survivor but the Lothians probably survived under British kingship to 638 and Elmet to c. 616–30. Such kings were tribute-paying, hence Elmet's inclusion in the Tribal Hidage.

In no case is there any good evidence for the destruction or flight of the bulk of the indigenous population. Redundant British aristocracies were clearly forced out but what evidence there is implies that the British farming population remained and became assimilated into the new English polity. The best evidence is comparatively late, belonging to the reign of King Ecgfrith, but there is no reason to think it atypical. In the 670s, at the dedicatory ceremony of Ripon, St Wilfrid enumerated the holy places which the British clergy had vacated, fleeing from 'our' hostile sword, and mentioned by name lands around the Ribble, Yeadon, Dent and Catlow as newly granted to his monastery. The flight of the British clergy testifies to their fear of ill-treatment and displacement as a consequence of the feud between the English and British Churches, probably during the supremacy of Bishop Paulinus. We are left with the distinct impression that their parishioners would have stayed on under the new regime, and would have been expected so to do. When Cuthbert was granted the Cartmel peninsula by the same King Ecgfrith, all its Britons were included in his title deeds.

Unfarmed land was of little use to the new owners, be they the monasteries and minsters of the post-conversion period, or the advisors and warriors of earlier kings, both pagan and Christian. What the Northumbrian kings dispensed was not land for their followers to cultivate but estates measured in hide or household units, the renders from which had hitherto supported British kings, churchmen and warriors. The expansion of English Northumbria was more an exercise in patronage than of direct colonization.

Barring late name formations of the Viking Age or beyond, Northumbrian place-names are as characteristically of English formation as those of any other part of England and it seems probable that something close to a total replacement of place-names occurred in the sixth, seventh and eighth centuries. Setting aside only the major river names, there is little difference between the earliest English areas and those which were conquered in the late sixth or seventh centuries. With specific groups excepted, the pre-Scandinavian place-names of Elmet or Lancashire are almost as heavily dominated by English formations as those of Deira or, for that matter, of East Anglia. As English kings, warriors and administrators fastened their talons upon British estates, so an increasing number of the inhabitants chose to learn the language of their new masters, English rapidly driving out the British language, and English place-names eventually replacing the vast number of pre-existing names, leaving only certain categories of names – such as major rivers, hills and key central places – largely unaltered. The differences between regions where river names were largely replaced and those where they survived arguably reflect not the ethnicity of the early medieval community but the degree of contact with English-speaking households of high status. Grants of peripheral estates beyond the Pennines to non-resident religious institutions sited in Deira or Bernicia had less impact on local names than occurred in the core territories where those institutions were situated. Additionally, estates which entered English hands only after the writing of charters became commonplace would naturally tend to suffer less from changes to important boundary features, including rivers and hills, than other regions.

The survival of place-names using the element *ecles* (borrowed from Latin via the Primitive Welsh ancestor of Modern Welsh *eglwys*, 'church') is generally accepted as an indicator of pre-existing British churches. Given the near wholesale replacement of British place-names throughout Northumbria in the Anglo-Saxon period, the survival of names with *ecles* appears eccentric and probably owes much to the interest of Anglian or Scottish bishops in defending the rights of their own churches to properties and church sites 'inherited' from a British past.

Such names are entirely absent from English Deira and the Tyne – Wear core of Bernicia where paganism probably took deep root in the sixth century. A single example on the Tees (Egglescliffe) may imply the survival of Christianity on the boundary of the two early pagan kingdoms near Catterick of *Gododdin* fame. Another in the Tweed Valley (Eccles, *c.* 8 km from the large Anglo-Saxon site at Sprouston), one in northern Cumbria (Eaglesfield, near Cockermouth) and a thin scattering in Dumfries and Galloway may have similar connotations there. Beside these few surviviors, there has either been a large-scale loss of Christian sites or widespread name substitution. A handful of possible candidates carry names indicative of the presence of Britons – such as Walton-on-the-Hill (Merseyside) – and speculation concerning links between circular churchyards and the Celtic origins of churches may imply that many medieval church sites in the north-west and particularly in Cumbria owe their origins to British Christianity. However, such hypotheses remain as yet unproven.

By far the largest concentration of *ecles* place-names is in West Yorkshire and Lancashire. In both, the survival of British kings until the reign of King Edwin protected Christianity until the latter's conversion and consequent persecution of Celtic Christianity. Within Elmet, numerous names with *ecles* have been postulated, although all those which are major names are compounds – Eccleshill, Ecclesfield, Eccleshall, Exley, Exley Head, Ecclesden – and three survive only as field names. In Elmet, but more markedly on the western plain, the distribution of *ecles* place-names is far from random and seems to relate to territorial divisions – or shires – which are known to have existed by the late Saxon and early post-Conquest periods. The distribution of one *ecles* place-name per territorial hundred throughout most of southern Lancashire implies that these tenth-century divisions were based on earlier territorial units which date back to before the English takeover. Some of these had been subdivided: Makerfield, in southern Lancashire, certainly contained Newton Hundred and almost certainly Warrington, but the location of Eccleston in the far west of this territory may suggest that it also originally included the Domesday Hundred of West Derby, the *caput* of which was close by. The mother church of Hallamshire (Sheffield area) was at Ecclesfield in the medieval period. Such churches seem to have been constructed within an estate system which was characteristic of much of Northumbria. The shire acted as the interface between the farming population and lordship, and the shire church served what were presumably scattered communities within the shire territory. The churches were probably staffed by small groups of clergy, much in the same way that later Anglo-Saxon minsters were to be. The transmission from the British to the English periods of the religious and secular organization of western Northumbria displays signs of an impressive degree of continuity.

By the mid- to late Saxon period, the presence of communities which were still identifiable as British (or Welsh) was so uncommon that their identity found its way into place-name formation, with the use of the English term *walh* to distinguish them. Such names are not common, occurring in the two Walworths of southern Durham and Walton (the name for two communities in Lancashire and one each Cumbria, in West Yorkshire), but not in the core English territory of Deira or in the Tyne Valley. However, some instances could derive from personal names. Names derived from *Brettas* or *Bretar* may imply that some local groups were still distinguishable as British during the period of Scandinavian influence on place-naming, and these occur in the same areas.

Estates, Land Management and Land-use

Beneath these military, political and cultural changes, the bulk of the population was probably engaged in food production comparatively unhindered by the doings of the social élite to whom they paid a large part of the surplus. With archaeology rarely able to distinguish the presence of sectors of the community which are not diagnostically Anglo-Saxon, and which did not use quantities of Anglo-Saxon pottery, both the identification and interpretation of settlement sites of the sixth and seventh century are deeply flawed and entirely slanted towards the highest ranks of local society.

Despite this shortfall, it is clear that farming activity continued through the expansion of English Northumbria in most areas, if at times on a level which was somewhat reduced from the Roman period. The most dramatic reduction in activity has been identified in the Wear Valley, where one pollen core evidenced a near total reforestation, yet the growing of hemp continued unabated on the magnesian limestone of southern Durham.

Several references in the earliest lives of the Northumbrian saints – eighth-century writings but looking back to the seventh century – suggest that men were not averse to hunting and eating wild animals, such as seals, salmon, boar and deer. St Cuthbert was reputed to have overnighted in early winter in what was almost certainly a hut or a shieling used by shepherds, where he discovered and ate a lunch clearly belonging to someone else. The uplands of southern Scotland and northern England lent themselves to use as summer grazings. References to the 'Wood of Elmet' and 'Wood of Deira' may in each case imply a large expanse of grazing, common to the herds of all or a large proportion of the kingdom, suggesting an economy which was tribal in extent. Cattle were probably the most important livestock in the north throughout the period. Certainly, the early seventh-century deposits at Yeavering were overwhelmingly dominated by cattle bones, but these were not necessarily directly related to the range of stock grazed locally. Even so, the survival of Welsh systems of livestock rentals into

A sunken-featured building under excavation at West Heslerton, N. Yorkshire

Timber-framed buildings at West Heslerton

post-Conquest Lancashire – the *horngeld* – probably reflects the pre-English origin of estate revenues in a landscape in which the right to pasture cattle was one regularly used to extract renders. Woollen cloth and leather were the raw materials from which clothing and many other products were made.

The farming population formed the basis without whose surplus the warrior classes would have been unable to function, and they seem to have been organized in estate systems which operated on two levels: in one respect, the estate was a unit within which individual farmers were able to exercise customary rights of access to the resources they needed; in another, it provided the apparatus by which surplus produce was transferred to the élite.

Although the core of any estate was the permanent homes of its occupiers and the land which they cultivated, estates did not need to be discrete territories but could be made up of rights to land for various purposes, which might have included relatively distant pastures, woodland or other types of land.

Bede and his audience were familiar with the notion of an English system of land measurement based on a notional family holding. Although Bede translated this into Latin, it is almost certainly the system of hidage, based on the *hid* or household. The approximate parity of land tenure from one holding to another reflects the need to establish a bench-mark for households of free status. The lowest rank

General vew across the Anglian settlement at West Heslerton

of the free English community was that of the *ceorl* and the hide seems to be a unit of value attached to the minimum renders deemed sufficient for the maintenance of a household of this status. That an estate valued at only a single hide was far more than the lands of a peasant farmer is demonstrated by Bishop Aidan's grant of a hide of land on the bank of the Wear to the royal-born St Hilda and her companions, who were necessarily supported by a surplus deriving from the labours of peasants or slaves (*EH*, IV, 23).

The multi-hide estates (approximately ten to forty in number) regularly granted by seventh-century kings for the foundation of monasteries imply that most warriors receiving land-grants from English kings could expect far more than a single hide. Thus if the estate was retained by the family, subsequent generations could sub-divide the family holding and establish a group of halls with their attendant storage facilities – sunken-featured buildings – of the kind found at Milfield and now under excavation at Heslerton. Such need not be hamlets or villages of farmers. Many may have been centres of consumption of high status, resourced by large landholdings worked by a British labour force who remain, to date, archaeologically uni-dentified, just as do the farming population of contemporary Dal Riata, Strathclyde and Wales.

CHAPTER 4

Politics and the Conversion

English Paganism

The Angles were pagan – their religion deriving ultimately from continental Germany in the fifth century. Many sub-Roman communities in the Deiran countryside were probably still practising Romano-Celtic paganism when they came under the influence of Germanic intruders in the fifth century. These religions may have fused but neither history nor archaeology have yet offered the means to assess the process. The *Gododdin* poetry implies that it was Christian British warriors who disputed English control of the old northern province in the sixth century but this perspective may owe more to the Christianity of those who assembled this corpus of praise poetry in Wales than of those whom it ostensibly described in northern Britain, as previously discussed.

Our knowledge of Anglo-Saxon paganism is minimal. Neither Bede nor other Christian writers wrote extensively or objectively on the subject, and we are left with the calendar in Bede's *Concerning the Organization of Time* (written *c.* 725), passing references in the *Ecclesiastical History* (completed in 731), other non-contemporary literary asides and archaeological evidence as the basis upon which to evaluate Northumbrian paganism.

The Anglian kings had acquired some priestly functions during the settlement period. As protectors, they personified the fortunes of their people. The eighth-century royal genealogies traced back the Deiran and Bernician dynasties to Woden, the warrior god paralleled by Mercury in the Roman pantheon (see Tacitus, *Germania*, IX) – hence Wednesday in English and *mercredi* in French. His special attributes lay in communication, exchange and trickery. These qualities were well suited to the ideological and moral outlook of opportunistic warriors as reflected in the nickname accorded Æthelfrith, the 'Artful Dodger'.

Although the precise site remains unlocated, Bede described an enclosed group of pagan altars at Goodmanham. The northern Angles

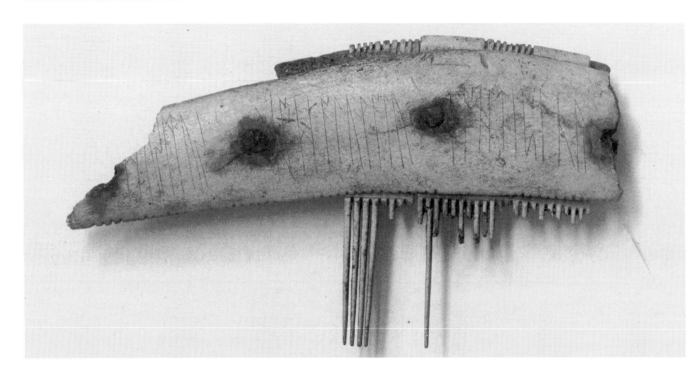

may, therefore, have sacrificed to gods other than Woden. Pope Boniface's letter to King Eadwine implies that he believed the king to worship carved images or idols, in the plural, and he was probably tolerably well-informed by the Italian missionaries in England.

As Gildas noted, the Anglo-Saxons used divination extensively in decision-making. The auspiciousness of an enterprise was determined by the use of augury, the mechanics of which were described by both Tacitus and Procopius. Amulets and spells were probably the normal method of guarding against misfortune or ill health and occur widely in pagan cemeteries and in runes on artefacts, such as swords, which were potential life-savers. Charms and sacrifices were also relevant to the fecundity of man and beast. Gregory's letter to Mellitus (quoted by Bede) implies that religious activity in England followed a recurring annual cycle of feasts, festivals and public sacrifices at major temple sites. The pagan calendar named months with reference both to religion and the farming cycle. English paganism was a religion of warriors but with its roots in the farming calendar of north Germany.

The most detailed literary description of a priest is Bede's (*EH*, II, 13) of Coifi, described as *primus pontificum* ('chief of the priests'). He was portrayed as the last chief priest of Deira, who defied the taboos surrounding his own person by receiving arms from the king and riding a stallion from the site of the conference to the enclosures surrounding the idols at Goodmanham, which he profaned by casting a spear. He then had his followers set fire to the entire complex.

Coifi denied the efficacy of paganism because it brought him no tangible benefits – particularly the favour of the king. The immediacy of divine power and the extent to which the gods were expected to intervene in human affairs on behalf of worshippers were recurring themes on both sides of the religious divide during this period and the *Ecclesiastical History* was written, in part, to illustrate the superior potency of the Christian God in precisely this respect.

This bone comb was found in 1867, near the site of the Whitby monastery. The inscription, in Latin and Old English, is in Anglo-Saxon runic characters. Several of the letters are damaged and the end of the text breaks off in the middle of a personal name. The inscription reads:

'd/[æ]usmæus   godaluwalu   d/oh/el lipæcy–' (My God, God Almighty help Cy–)

There is much in this description — the taboos, the enclosed pagan idols and altars, the destruction of the complex by fire and the name of the principal pagan priest — which suggests that Bede was drawing on reliable historical traditions surrounding Edwin's conversion, even if the conversations were entirely reconstructed. Such could have come down to him via the long-lived James the Deacon, Paulinus's only known indigenous assistant.

There is no reason to think English paganism was an organized religious system beyond the limits of the tribal community and its kingship, although its myth- and story-based beliefs appear to have been broadly consistent across England and north Germany. Each English kingdom, each *regio* or *provincia* in the Latin texts, probably had a temple as a religious focus, just as it had a dynasty whose role was to provide leadership in war. The taboos which Bede mentioned isolated priest and king from one another within Deira. Such priesthood may have been hereditary. Their role may descend from the priests encountered in the *Germania* of Tacitus, who also dispensed capital punishment and were, therefore, judges as well as priests, but their aegis was only as extensive as the people and kingship for whom they provided religious functions of a public nature. If Coifi had any influence outside Deira it was only as a consequence of Edwin's 'overkingship' of neighbouring kingdoms.

The only Anglo-Saxon temple site so far excavated in England is that at Yeavering (Northumberland) in Bernicia. There, one of the several well-built, early seventh-century timber-framed halls, measuring approximately 11.7 × 6 m internally, was reconstructed on the same site and to very similar dimensions after destruction by fire. A pit within it was entirely filled with animal bones, almost all of which were the skulls of oxen, and it was suggested that these may once have been piled up well above ground level. The presence of an ancillary building with a hearth and evidence of butchery implies that these skulls were from sacrifices which were otherwise consumed in feasting, the head alone being reserved for the god. The marks of successive stake- or bough-built huts outside the temple recall the advice given by Pope Gregory to Abbot Mellitus, by letter (*EH*, I, 30). The extended inhumation cemetery with which this complex was associated has parallels among the Anglian cemeteries of Deira but the layout has as much in common with Christian cemeteries, and the scarcity of accompanying artefacts may imply that it contained the graves of a local community of very mixed origins. The cultural status of the temple remains uncertain, particularly given its proximity to a defensive palisade of a type associated more normally with British than English construction. It was probably connected with the palace complex of Ida's dynasty until the reign of King Æthelfrith, who may have been responsible for the assembly building close by. Yeavering provides much-needed confirmation of the existence of the temples referred to by Bede.

Place-names provide little assistance. Examples containing the names of Germanic deities or Anglo-Saxon words for shrine or temple occur throughout south-eastern England but are elusive in the north, where neither of the two certain temple sites now carry diagnostic names. Although new instances are still being identified in the south, the discrepancy between south and north is unlikely to change. The absence of pagan place-names from even eastern Northumbria suggests that they were replaced after the conversion. Bede implied that Goodmanham was a recently formed place-name. Yeavering was, in origin, the

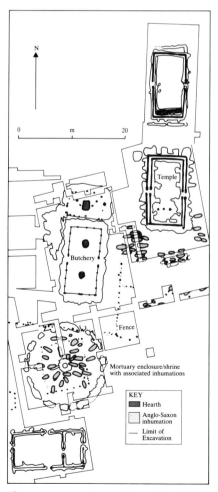

The pagan temple at Yeavering (after Hope-Taylor, 1977)

KEY
- ■ Hearth
- □ Anglo-Saxon inhumation
- — Limit of Excavation

N

0   m   20

Temple

Butchery

Fence

Mortuary enclosure/shrine with associated inhumations

name of the hill-fort rather than the palace complex and the early abandonment of the latter militated against it being given an English name. Bede clearly believed the renaming of places was commonplace: he explained 'Bamburgh' by reference to Æthelfrith's queen and noted that the estate near Catterick on which James the Deacon dwelt for thirty years or more was known by his name. If so, the estate arguably acquired the name after 664, when James the Deacon's pro-Roman stance was suddenly vindicated, but before he died in the 670s or 680s. Since no such name now exists it was presumably renamed thereafter. Such examples of successive renaming have fundamental implications for the chronology of Northumbria's place-names but provide little evidence for the prevalence of paganism.

While it seems probable that many of the more important early medieval churches replaced pagan shrines or temples (as at Goodmanham, perhaps), in no instance has this yet been demonstrated archaeologically. At Yeavering, the building identified by the excavator as a church was constructed on another part of the site, 200 m from the building which he believed to be a temple. If such distances were commonplace, excavation under and around a medieval church would need to be very extensive to test the presence of a pre-Christian religious site. Even so, the commonplace siting of early churches next to water or on hilltops may imply that some situations were successively used for pagan and then Christian worship.

The British aristocracy who were displaced or 'anglicized' by the expanding English kingships of the early seventh century were Christian, and Christianity had probably by then permeated down through rural British society, mixing perhaps with local Celtic paganism among the farming community, to create a popular and localized, cult-based religion. Outside of the rarely diagnostic cemetery sites, known principally in southern Scotland and Northumberland but also, perhaps, at Winwick in southern Lancashire, there is little archaeological evidence pertaining to British Christianity in the decades around 600.

A pagan aristocracy practising distinctive rites of burial had little opportunity to make an impact in western Northumbria. Only in those (unnamed) areas where Æthelfrith imposed himself as king between c. 592 and 603 can we expect to find the graves of Anglian warriors granted estates in the newly conquered territories. Such are almost entirely absent in West Yorkshire and southern Lancashire, where British kingship survived until displaced by Edwin, but occur as a thin scattering of aristocratic burials in the limestone terrain around Kirkby Stephen (Cumbria) with several poorly provenanced possibilities in Amounderness. Other parts of the west were little affected by English paganism, and Christian worship clearly survived where British kings were tributary to pagan Angles.

Æthelfrith and the 'Overkingship' of Northumbria

Stories of the heroic achievements of the pagan King Æthelfrith were circulating in Bernicia late enough for Bede to hear them. Those which he used centred on the battles of *Degsastan* and Chester and he added to them material culled from the church-derived stories surrounding

OPPOSITE: The medieval church at Goodmanham. If seventh-century churchmen followed Pope Gregory's advice in this instance, the church may stand on the site of the principal pagan shrine of the Deiri, which was destroyed by Coifi, the chief priest, in the winter of 626/7. St Helen's Well in the same township offers one alternative site for the pagan temple

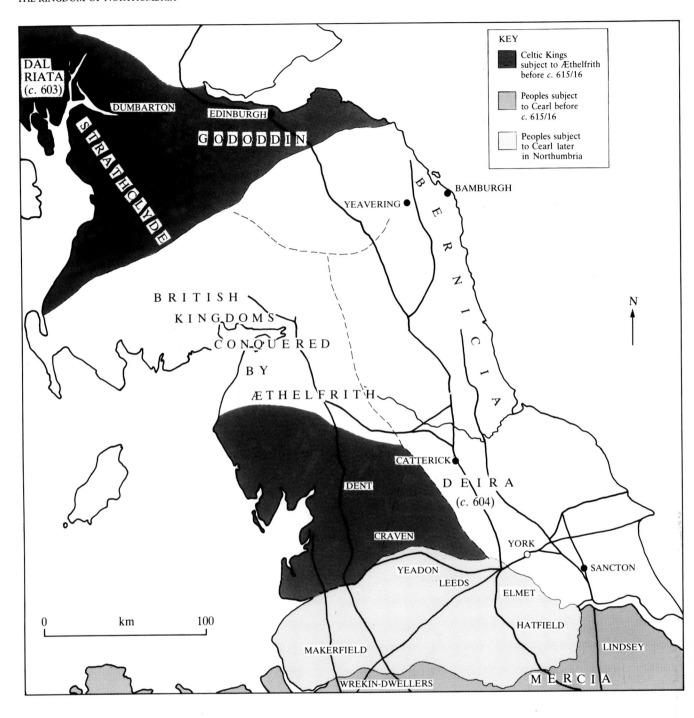

A very tentative reconstruction of the territory ruled by King Æthelfrith before c. 615

Edwin, Æthelfrith's rival and younger contemporary. The history of Northumbria in this period has been told many times before, but the importance of Æthelfrith, his sons and Edwin (his brother-in-law) to the Christian conversion and the foundation of Northumbria is so great that a relatively detailed analysis is warranted.

To Bede, Æthelfrith was 'a very powerful king, most desirous of renown', comparable in his opinion to Saul of Old Testament fame and from whom would spring the first Christian kings of Bernicia. He was a king from a mould now best portrayed in *Beowulf*:

who ravaged the British nation more than any previous English leader [in Northumbria] . . . For no one placed more under tribute or extended his rule over more of their land, killing or enslaving the inhabitants, he made them tributary to the English people or habitable by them.

(*EH*, II, 9)

Æthelfrith was an extremely successful warrior-king who subjugated the neighbouring British kingdoms of the north. Independent corroboration of his achievements derives indirectly from the Tribal Hidage (discussed below). Bede's description is capable of a variety of interpretations and he clearly believed, however erroneously, that the British race was exterminated throughout Northumbria. His language differs little, however, from that used to describe Edwin's assault on the West Saxons in 626 and talk of extermination should clearly not be taken too literally. Æthelfrith, then, dispossessed some of the British kings of the north, usurping the renders which they had been wont to receive and using his increased patronage to reward warriors in his service, to some of whom he granted estates in the newly sequestrated territories. The principal casualties of this process were the landholding classes of Celtic society, the kings, aristocracy and Church, leaving the render-producing peasantry in place. Where this occurred was not recorded by Bede, but it was presumably in areas with a common border with Bernicia, as it then was. The scarcity of *ecles* place-names in Cumbria, Dumfries and Galloway, Craven and Tweeddale may suggest that his conquests carried pagan warriors into these areas in the late sixth-century, taking his own direct exercise of kingship to the west coast and into southern Scotland. Bernicia was later to include all these areas and it seems likely that Æthelfrith was the first to expand the Bernician kingship into most of the areas it was to eventually encompass, barring only the conquest of Gododdin and Fife by his sons.

Bede's account suggests that other British kingships were left *in situ* under Æthelfrith's protection. Such kings probably sought his protection before they were attacked, accepting tributary status and the loss of autonomy in military affairs as the price of immunity. That the expansion of his power caused alarm in Dal Riata implies that his 'overkingship' extended as far north as Strathclyde and Lothian. Æthelfrith's destruction of the Scottish army of King Aidan at *Degsastan* (*c*. 603) suggests that he was able thereafter to exact tribute from Dal Riata. The death of his brother Theobald in this battle would have given Æthelfrith an added incentive to exact a high *wergild* (compare Ecgfrith's stance after the battle of Trent: *EH*, IV, 21).

Through his success in war, Æthelfrith created a much enlarged kingship. He was king of a half-dozen or so separate territories, several of which were only in the first throes of 'anglicization', having hitherto been subject to British kings. Around this core under his own direct rule were kingdoms under Celtic kings, who would march with him when he went to war and pay him annual tribute, perhaps in a public ceremony held in the magnificent auditorium constructed at Yeavering Palace. In its origins Northumbria was, therefore, an 'overkingship', within which the direct kingship of the dominant dynasty was extended by usurpation. The durability of the structure Æthelfrith had created was yet to be tested.

Soon after his victory at *Degsastan*, Æthelfrith repeated his policy of usurping neighbouring kingships by acquiring Deira (*c*. 604), taking over the renders of that large and rich territory for himself. He quelled

any local hostility by marrying Edwin's sister. By so doing he offered a sop to the Deiran aristocracy by providing them with a sympathetic and influential, but militarily ineffective, royal patron. Whether the young Edwin was King of Deira in 604, or an *ætheling* ('royal prince') is unclear. His father Ælle had been king but the *Anglo-Saxon Chronicle* suggests that the otherwise unknown Æthelric was ruler of Deira in between. If this extremely late and unverifiable reign has any substance, Æthelric may have been a tributary king imposed on Deira by Æthelfrith, whose dramatic rise to power in the north might be expected to have had implications for Deira even before 604. Alternatively, this very late source may merely have confused the two dynasties, since Æthelfrith's father was named Æthelric.

Secure in the north and at the head of a powerful war-band, Æthelfrith is next seen attacking his southern neighbours. His victory at Chester against a British army, *c.* 615, was recounted in the *Ecclesiastical History* (II, 2). The reasons for the inclusion of this episode by Bede are historically spurious but his comments are none the less revealing. The incident finds support in British sources. Æthelfrith's expedition may have been spurred by the attitude of King Cearl of the Mercians who had taken Edwin under his own protection and given him his daughter in marriage. Cearl's independence of action implies that he was tributary neither to Æthelfrith nor to Æthelberht of Kent, at this stage the 'overking' of the south from the Severn to East Anglia,

Chester, the hub of the Roman road network in the north-west Midlands. The battle was presumably close by

POLITICS AND THE CONVERSION

and analysis of the Tribal Hidage implies that he himself may have been a tribute-taking king in the Midlands and Wales. Such a sign of favour to Edwin involved recognition of his claims to Deira, although Bede (whose suppression of information concerning Mercian initiatives is notorious) had nothing to report of Cearl's status or his possible participation at the battle of Chester.

The latter conflict was another triumph for King Æthelfrith, and its repercussions seem to have brought down his Mercian opponent, who was replaced by Penda's family, with Northumbrian support (*HB*, 65). Edwin fled to the protection of Rædwald of East Anglia, a powerful king then only just emerging from the protection of Æthelberht of Kent at the latter's death in February 616. Æthelfrith's victory at Chester and the dynastic revolution in Mercia probably brought all the northern Midlands under his protection, his 'overkingship' henceforth marching with that of Æthelberht. If the first sixteen peoples of the Tribal Hidage (see below) should be seen as Æthelfrith's southern tributaries at the end of his life, then the king of the *Westerne* (the King of Gwynedd) had also sought his protection after Chester. Between about 615 and 616, Æthelfrith was the overlord of more kings, more peoples and more territory than any other king in Britain.

Having chased Edwin out of Mercia, Æthelfrith set about extracting him from East Anglia. Bede's incorporation of these events into an extended and semi-hagiographical account of Edwin's conversion has provided us with graphic details of the threat he posed to Rædwald. Prompted by his wife and by the opportunities offered by his own protector's death early in 616, Rædwald gathered his forces and succeeded in surprising and overpowering Æthelfrith as he awaited the return of his envoys. That the battle was fought in Mercian territory on the bank of the Idle provides important confirmation of Æthelfrith's 'overkingship' of Mercia. The battle was, perhaps, fought at or in the vicinity of the Roman fort at Scaftworth, where the Roman road from the south-east crosses the Idle into Yorkshire at Bawtry.

With his death in battle the fragility of Æthelfrith's Bernician supremacy was exposed. All had depended on the reputation, the prowess and the retinue of the king himself. With them in tatters, his young sons could achieve nothing against Rædwald, whose hostility was probably intensified by the death of his own son Rægenhere in the battle. They fled northwards into exile beyond Northumbria with 'a great following of noble youths'.

So passed the true founding father of Bernicia and Northumbria, from whose reign stem many of the major issues which were to dominate dynastic politics for a century. Not least of these was the savage competition between Northumbrian and Mercian dynasties for the dominance of the centre of England, a dominance which carried with it a powerful claim to the general 'overkingship' of all Britain.

The Rise of Edwin

Rædwald's victory over such a redoubtable opponent catapulted him, in turn, into the 'overkingship' of the south, a role recently voided by the death of Æthelberht of Kent. His preoccupations elsewhere probably encouraged Rædwald to delegate the north and its rule to his protégé, Edwin. The latter replaced Æthelfrith in all respects, as king of an enlarged Bernicia as well as Deira and as 'overking' of his Celtic

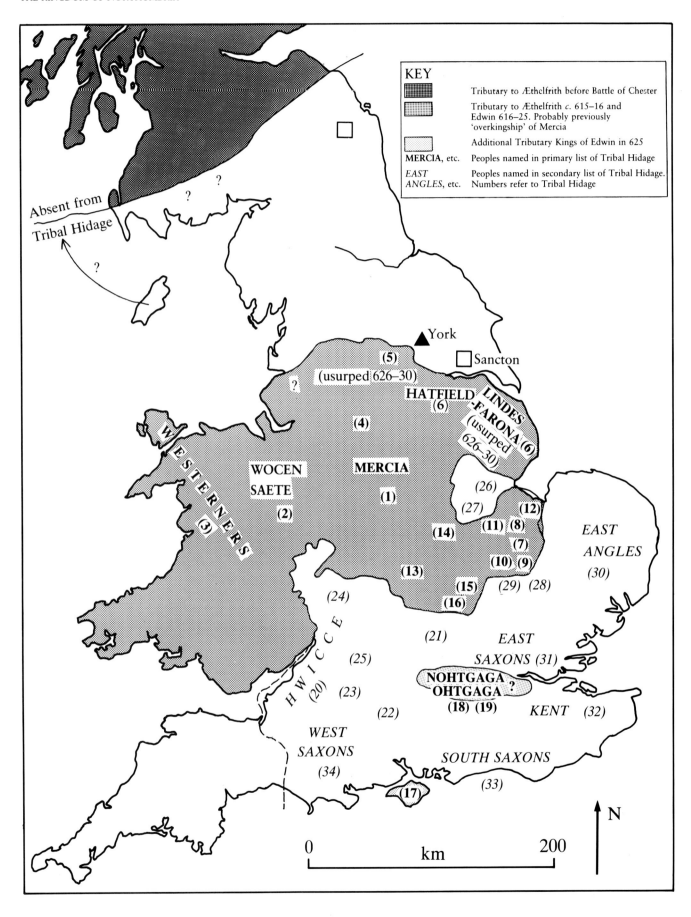

KEY

Tributary to Æthelfrith before Battle of Chester

Tributary to Æthelfrith c. 615–16 and Edwin 616–25. Probably previously 'overkingship' of Mercia

Additional Tributary Kings of Edwin in 625

MERCIA, etc.   Peoples named in primary list of Tribal Hidage

EAST ANGLES, etc.   Peoples named in secondary list of Tribal Hidage. Numbers refer to Tribal Hidage

Absent from Tribal Hidage

? ?

?

▲York

☐Sancton

(5)
(usurped 626–30)
?

HATFIELD (6)
LINDESFARONA (6)
(usurped 626–30)

(4)

WOCEN SAETE (2)

MERCIA (1)

WESTERNERS (3)

(26)
(27)

(12)
(11) (8)
(14)
(7)
(10) (9)
(13)
(29) (28)

EAST ANGLES (30)

(15)
(16)

(24)

(21)

EAST SAXONS (31)

HWICCE

(25)

(20) (23)

(22)

NOHTGAGA OHTGAGA ?
(18) (19)

KENT (32)

WEST SAXONS (34)

SOUTH SAXONS (33)

(17)

N

0   km   200

neighbours. Edwin's northern supremacy was initially subject to the protection of King Rædwald. The latter therefore became the first English king in history to extract tribute from all of what had been Roman Britain.

That edifice survived only until the death of Rædwald, *c.* 624–5, leaving the still untried Edwin supreme in the north but exposed to the rise of a less sympathetic 'overking' in southern Britain. In an undated but important battle probably fought at this stage, Cuichelm of the West Saxons defeated the East Saxons. His rise towards general supremacy was a major threat to Edwin, who countered by sending envoys to Eadbald of Kent, at this stage the only Christian king in England. During the summer of 625, Edwin contracted a marital alliance in Kent, made a series of half-promises concerning his own conversion and accepted Bishop Paulinus into his household. The despatch of a bishop implies that this was seen at Canterbury as a full-blown mission.

Paulinus was consecrated on 21 July 625 and the wedding party probably returned north immediately thereafter. At Canterbury, Edwin's agents (or the king himself if he made the journey) had probably come into contact with several of the dependants of the Kentish dynasty, including the King of Wight, who was particularly fearful of the ambitions of the West Saxons. These kings may have requested and obtained Edwin's protection.

It was arguably this interference in the deep south which antagonised the West Saxon king. As Edwin held public court at Easter 626, in his palace by the Derwent, an agent sent by Cuichelm attempted to assassinate him. In the fracas the king was wounded and two of his thegns slain in his defence, one of whom, Lilla, was accounted by Bede Edwin's 'dearest thegn' (*EH*, II, 9). Edwin was under a heavy obligation to avenge such an attack but was himself inexperienced in war and seems to have been far from confident of his ability to prosecute a successful campaign at such a distance against a king with a proven military reputation.

The Deiran king was portrayed by Bede as an indecisive man of weak character whom Paulinus found little difficulty in persuading to his own viewpoint. The latter used the opportune circumstance of the queen's safe delivery of her first-born, Eanfled, to persuade the king to switch his allegiance to the Christian God. Edwin committed himself to Christianity provided only that he was granted victory over Cuichelm.

In the campaign which ensued Edwin was overwhelmingly successful against the West Saxons. This, the only clear military success of his career, catapulted Edwin in turn into the role of 'overking' of all Britain. His victory enabled him to impose a punitive tribute on Wessex, and the remainder of the kings of southern England sought the protection of the victor.

The account of Edwin and his conversion is the fullest and least stereotyped of all Bede's pen-portraits of royalty (*EH*, II, 9–17, 20) and, in part, it can be confirmed and amplified by reference to the sole-surviving fiscal document of pre-Viking England, commonly known as the 'Tribal Hidage'. This document, often ascribed to any one of several later Mercian kings, survives only in an early eleventh-century transcript of unknown provenance, but recent re-examination of it has suggested that it was written by Paulinus on behalf of King Edwin. The full list consists of a primary group of twenty peoples under nineteen

OPPOSITE: The 'overkingship' of the Northumbrian kings, 615–33

115

A sword hilt of Anglo-Saxon workmanship found in Cumbria, decorated with garnet-inlaid gold plates

headings or kingships, apparently written soon after Paulinus' arrival in Deira following the royal wedding in the summer of 625. The list was then extended by the addition of a further fifteen names arguably following Edwin's triumphant return from Wessex in 626.

The tribal names are largely in the possessive (genetive) case, followed by the tribute for which they were responsible, in hides. The syntax requires the addition of a subject in each case, which logically should read 'tribute'. So, for example, 'the tribute of the *Wocensæte* (Wrekin-dwellers), 7,000 hides' would be the proper extended reading of the second entry. The abbreviated nature of the document is entirely understandable when it is remembered that it was written by Paulinus for his own eyes alone, since he was the only man who could read at Edwin's court. It is, therefore, a list of kings identified by the peoples over whom they ruled and the annual tribute owed by them to Edwin, at whose court 'by the Derwent' they were presumably expected to deliver it in person at a great annual ceremony, perhaps in *Blodmonath* (November). Such tribute was presumably paid in valuable horses, precious metals and items of skilled workmanship (see *HB*, 65, and *Beowulf* for parallels).

Bede's description of Edwin's supremacy assists in the interpretation of the list. The nineteen kingships of the first part are headed by the chief menace to any northern king, Mercia, now ruled by a dynasty put in place by Æthelfrith and so bitterly hostile to Edwin and his half-Mercian first family. 'The original Mercia' heads the list, expressly shorn of recent acquisitions among neighbouring kingships, and with a heavy tribute of 30,000 hides. The bulk of the remainder were peoples of the Midlands but the appearance of Elmet may imply that Elmet had, prior to 615–16, paid tribute to Cearl of Mercia in return for protection. Reference to the 'westerners' should be understood as pertaining to the Celtic peoples of the west. Bede recorded Edwin's supremacy over all the Britons (*EH*, II, 9), particularly Anglesey and Man. Given the leading role of Cadwallon, 'King of the Britons', in the coup against Edwin in 633, it seems probable that he was a subordinate 'overking' within the Irish Sea Basin who was personally responsible to Edwin for the tribute of all the Welsh in Wales and perhaps other British regions.

The Tribal Hidage

[After British Library, MS Harley 3271, f. 6v. rendered into modern forms where possible and with some additions to the punctuation. Additions are bracketed.]

Primary List
(1)	Mercian lands is thirty thousand hides that is the area first called Mercia.	(30,000)
(2)	Wrekin dwellers is seven thousand hides.	(7,000)
(3)	Westerners the same.	(7,000)
(4)	Peak dwellers twelve hundred hides.	(1,200)
(5)	Elmet dwellers six hundred hides.	(600)
(6)	Lindsey-folk seven thousand hides with Hatfield (Haethfeldlande).	(7,000)
(7)	South Gyrwa six hundred hides.	(600)
(8)	North Gyrwa six hundred hides.	(600)
(9)	East Wixna three hundred hides.	(300)
(10)	West Wixna six hundred hides.	(600)
(11)	Spalda six hundred hides.	(600)
(12)	Wigesta nine hundred hides.	(900)
(13)	Herefinna twelve hundred hides.	(1,200)
(14)	Sweord ora three hundred hides.	(300)
(15)	Gifla three hundred hides.	(300)
(16)	Hicca three hundred hides.	(300)
(17)	Wight spear(men) six hundred hides.	(600)
(18)	Noxgaga five thousand hides.	(5,000)
(19)	Ohtgaga two thousand hides.	(2,000)
	That is six and sixty thousand hides and one hundred hides	(66,100)

Secondary List
(20)	Hwicce seven thousand hides.	(900)
(21)	Chiltern dwellers four thousand hides.	(4,000)
(22)	Hendrica three thousand hides and five hundred hides.	(3,500)
(23)	Unecu'n'g(a)ga twelve hundred hides.	(1,200)
(24)	Arrow dwellers six hundred hides.	(600)
(25)	Faerpinga three hundred hides.*	(300)
(26)	Bilmiga six hundred hides.	(600)
(27)	Widerigga the same.	(600)
(28)	East Willa six hundred hides.	(600)
(29)	West Willa six hundred hides.	(600)
(30)	East Angles thirty thousand hides.	(30,000)
(31)	East Saxons seven thousand hides.	(7,000)
(32)	Kent defenders fifteen thousand hides.	(15,000)
(33)	South Saxons seven thousand hides.	(7,000)
(34)	West Saxons one hundred thousand hides.	(100,000)
	This all two hundred thousand and two and forty thousand hides and seven hundred hides	(242,700)
	Corrected:	(244,100)

The text of the Tribal Hidage (various terms have been translated and names rendered into modern usage where such exist, but based on Dumville (ed.), 1989)

[* In the left hand margin: '(i)s in Middle Anglia Faerpinga', a comment which probably derives from *EH*, III, 21 and so was a late addition to the text.]

117

To these were appended in 626 all the peoples of southern Britain, including Edwin's own brother-in-law, Eadbald of Kent and his erstwhile protector's dangerously powerful heir, Eorpwald, as well as his defeated enemies, the West Saxons, whose punitive tribute of 100,000 hides, the last entry, has caused historians many problems.

The purpose of the Tribal Hidage was presumably to act as a check-list at the annual payment of tribute. This must have been a brilliant ceremony, at which the subordinate kings were either present in person or at least represented by their near kin. They came laden with rich gifts to the value specified in hides and the more favoured of them would have received valuable gifts in return. This grand occasion probably took place, initially at least, at Edwin's principal palace site in Deira, 'by the Derwent' – the river from which his people took their name. The location of what must have been a palace complex of unusual size and complexity remains unidentified but, as argued in chapters two and three, it should probably be sought near Sancton. It was probably here, too, that Edwin held the great debate as to whether or not to convert to Christianity, as reconstructed by Bede (*EH*, II, 13). From it, Coifi most probably rode out to desecrate the pagan shrines at neighbouring Goodmanham, a short ride along the Roman road. This lost palace was, from 626 to 633, the focus of all Britain below the Tees.

Edwin's 'overkingship' of the northern Celtic kingdoms and the Isle of Man does not feature in the Tribal Hidage. It seems possible that these dependencies of Edwin as King of Bernicia were kept separate. The magnificent timber auditorium at Yeavering (Edwin's principal Bernician palace) would have continued to provide an appropriate setting for the reception of tribute from the northern kings, who would otherwise have had to ride the length of Edwin's territories to attend upon their superior, to the detriment of his people. Its design is reminiscent of Roman theatres and may owe something to Roman

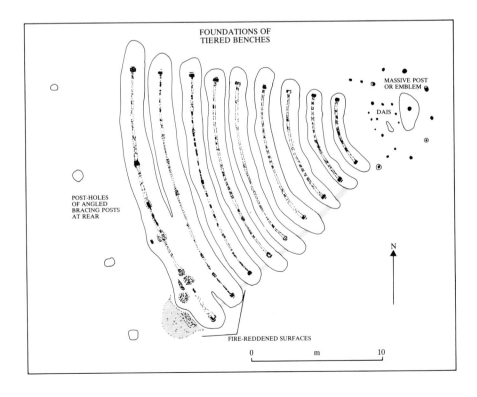

The 'theatre' or auditorium at Yeavering (after Hope-Taylor, 1977)

prototypes, which may still have been standing at Brough-on-Humber, Chester and York. King Æthelberht of Kent probably made a similar use of the Roman theatre at Canterbury.

Edwin and the Conversion

In order to clinch his marriage alliance with Kent in 625, Edwin made a series of conditional promises concerning his own conversion to Christianity. In his eyes (and those of Bede) these conditions were fulfilled by his victory over the West Saxons in 626, and his elevation to a general 'overkingship', the responsibility for which he conceded to the Christian God. Bede surrounded his conversion with premonitions of a kind more normally to be found in the lives of the saints (particularly *EH*, II, 12) but he did recall the great conference chaired by Edwin at which his 'noblest friends and advisors' concurred with his decision to convert (ibid. II, 13). Bede used this opportunity to place several of his own most persuasive arguments into the mouths of pagans, so that the detail he offered is probably apocryphal, but he did grace it with perhaps the most effective rhetorical allegory to be found in the *Ecclesiastical History*. One of those present was said to have argued:

> So, oh king, when we compare the present life of men on earth with that which to us is uncertain, it seems to me like the swift flight of a single sparrow through the great hall where you are resting during the briefest days of the year with your leading thegns and your councillors. A comforting hearth at the centre is heating the hall but outside, all about, are furious storms of winter rain or snow. A sparrow coming in through the doorway flies around quickly but will soon depart through the other.
>
> (*EH*, II, 14)

The reasoning is Christian but the image of a court immured in the hall in inclement, yule-time weather was universal and the flight of the sparrow must have been a commonplace occurrence with which Bede's own audience would have instantly identified.

The first Northumbrian to be baptised was the infant Eanfled, born to Edwin and Æthelburh during the crisis of Easter 626, and she was reportedly accompanied by the apostolically correct, twelve attendants (*EH*, II, 9), twelve days after Whitsun (*HB*, 63). Her role was as a hostage to fate for the king. Edwin's own baptism took place at York and Bede suggested that the Deirans shared in the ceremony *en masse*. The author of the *History of the Britons* (63) appropriately gave the number accompanying him as 12,000 during a marathon ceremony lasting, equally appropriately, forty days. Such numbers were heavily influenced by the number systems of the Bible and are not trustworthy, but thereafter the king threw his full weight behind Paulinus and mass conversions occurred in the River Glen below Yeavering in Bernicia (for thirty-six days) and in the Swale at Catterick, near the frontier of the two English kingdoms and therefore accessible to individuals from both.

Paulinus clearly obtained greater influence over Edwin than had Augustine over Æthelberht of Kent and seems to have been his most important advisor from 626 to 633. A letter to the king from Pope Honorius (written in 634 and so undelivered) contained nothing but

praise for his sponsorship of Christianity. He was enabled to fulfil Pope Gregory's design to establish a northern archdiocese at York, although Paulinus' pallium seems not to have reached him before his flight back to Kent in 633 and no suffragan bishops had then been consecrated. It was the establishment of the diocese there which began the slow process of reviving Roman *Eburacum* from the decay into which it had fallen during the intervening period and, although the process was interrupted for a generation thereafter, it was Edwin, Paulinus and Pope Honorius who laid the foundations of the archdiocese.

Paulinus had been part of the mission at Canterbury and, although not necessarily present himself, was familiar with the rebuff which Augustine had received from the British clergy at Augustine's Oak. His rise to a position of influence within Edwin's court offered him a golden opportunity to strike at the British Church and its heresies and it was probably this which provided the stimulus for Edwin's expulsion of King Ceretic from Elmet, *c.* 626. The *ecles* place-names of West Yorkshire and southern Lancashire imply the retention of Christian worship under direct English rule and this contrasts with those parts of the Celtic north already placed under direct pagan authority by Æthelfrith. It was probably this event to which Wilfrid's biographer referred when describing the rich gifts of land made to Ripon by the Northumbrian kings:

Lady's Well, Holystone, is reputed to have historical associations with St Ninian. The well is said also to be the site at which Christian converts were baptized by Paulinus in the seventh century

120

... he went on to enumerate holy places in various parts of the country which the British clergy, fleeing from our hostile sword, had deserted

(*Life of Wilfrid*, XVII)

Their flight had already occurred before the donation of these places and their cure of souls to Ripon, probably when Edwin's support gave Paulinus the means to evict a member of the clergy whom he considered heretical and schismatic. The sword in this instance was surely that of St Peter and not that of an English pagan king.

There was otherwise nothing unusual about Edwin's usurpation of Elmet. Æthelfrith had taken over several kingdoms and the West Saxon and Mercian dynasties were actively pursuing comparable policies whenever the balance of power allowed. Edwin either expelled or downgraded the King of Lindsey and Hatfield and usurped the kingship of that region, perhaps largely in an attempt to secure the strategic lines of communication between Deira and his friends in East Anglia and Kent, so outflanking Mercia. He may, alternatively, have been influenced by the presence of British Christians at Lincoln, where archaeological evidence suggests continuing Christian burial rites from the fifth to the seventh centuries. In both Edwin's new acquisitions he encouraged Paulinus to spread the Roman Christian message. The first

The excavated remains of the early Saxon church of St Paul-in-the-Baile at Lincoln

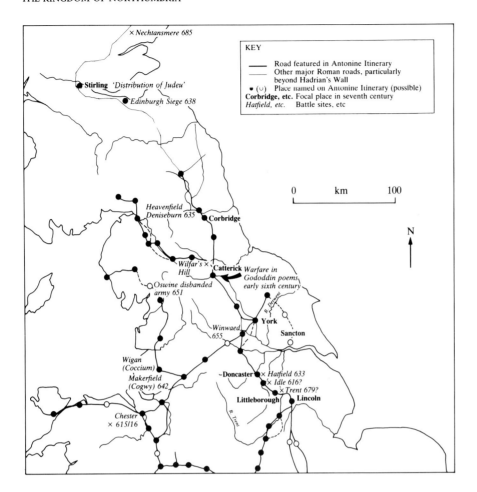

Seventh-century battle sites and the Roman road system. The fact that the battle sites lie so close to the roads confirms the impression gained from Bede's description of Edwin's watering-places along the major roads, that early Anglo-Saxon kings had a considerable interest in the Roman road system

converts in Lindsey were the family of Blaecca, the reeve in charge of Lincoln, who was a nominee of Edwin and quite possibly a Deiran. It was he who had a stone church built in the old Roman town. Another was constructed at *Campodonum* (probably Doncaster). Roman masonry provided the materials from which such structures could be built without the need to cut stone afresh.

What was Edwin's perception of the religion which he espoused for the last seven years of his life? In Paulinus he had an Italian missionary who had a profound knowledge of the Gospels and of the teachings of Christianity. Yet he was almost alone in his mission, his only known Northumbrian acolyte, James, having only attained the rank of deacon by 633. There were then no churches in Bernicia and neither Edwin nor Paulinus apparently spent much time there. Only single examples existed in Deira (York), Lindsey (Lincoln) and among the small kingdoms between (*Campodonum*), and these could only be used for divine service when a priest was present. The bishop was generally resident within one of the several royal courts, and often moved around the kingdom with the king himself. He was probably the sole priest in Northumbria, so Roman Christian worship was largely confined to the royal household.

There are close parallels between this first phase of Christianity in Northumbria and the paganism it replaced. The priests of both were associated specifically with the public face of religion – great annual festivals such as Christmas (the first day of the pagan calendar) and Easter (the festival of Eostre) passing virtually unchanged from one religion to the other. The role of both lay primarily in matters of state and in the collective welfare of the people as personified in their king. Private worship and sacrifice necessarily remained the business of the head of the household and there can be little doubt that most of those going through mass conversion continued traditional pagan practices in the privacy of their own homes.

We should not forget that Edwin and his councillors were considering their situation from a pagan viewpoint when they elected to convert to Christianity. Their expectations of the role the new religion would fulfil were fundamentally pagan. Edwin's commitment to Christianity hinged on his victory in battle over the West Saxons. In his own mind, he had matched Christ against their pagan protector (probably Woden) and his overwhelming victory demonstrated the potency of the Christian God in war. Such was surely the most persuasive argument by far at the council meeting where the Deirans adopted Christianity, notwithstanding Bede's version of this conversation.

There were, however, further significant advantages for Edwin to gain from Christianity. His kingship had evolved from an institution operating within a limited social and geographical ambit, the foci of which were the Deiran royal dynasty and the shrine at Goodmanham. Before the takeover of neighbouring communities by their kings, Deira and Bernicia had both been societies in which government was face-to-face, with easy access by the regional gentry and aristocracy to their king.

Æthelfrith's expansion of the Bernician kingship required the rapid evolution of political structures capable of contending with the problems posed by a peripatetic individual ruling over numerous, quite separate, political communities. The proliferation of royal households in Northumbria during the seventh century provided a number of focal points and this facilitated access to royal patronage for local aristocrats like the young Wilfrid, who approached Oswiu's queen in search of a sponsor. Some subject kings retained local patronage which fed into the central hierarchy, but they were under a variety of cultural and economic pressures from above and vulnerable to sudden ejection, whether they were men from local dynasties or men appointed by the Northumbrian kings. By 633 it seems unlikely that any British kings still existed in the north between the Humber–Mersey and the Southern Uplands–Cheviots.

Their own successes created increasing tensions around Æthelfrith and Edwin and forced them to become ever more mobile, in order to serve the social, economic and judicial functions of kingship over as wide an area as possible. The problems of multiple kingship lay behind Edwin's construction of palace sites on the main Roman roads and on important boundaries between once very separate peoples (as at Catterick and Doncaster), where he would be accessible to as wide a cross-section as possible of the Northumbrian nobility. Problems of access to the king encouraged both Bernicians and Deirans over the next few generations to prefer a king of their own native dynasty, who could be relied upon to share their interests and prejudices and spend the bulk of his time inside the kingdom of which he was a native, to their advantage.

With Edwin's elevation to supremacy over all England these problems were massively accentuated. His espousal of Christianity may have been, in part, a response to his unprecedented problems of government. Even before his own baptism, Edwin was arguably exploiting the literacy of Paulinus in the interests of his own administration – the Tribal Hidage may be the only administrative document surviving from any pagan government in Britain. The hierarchical structure, centralized organization and monotheism of the Church were all attractive to a warrior-king wrestling with unprecedented problems of adminstration.

One of the primary problems facing a centralizing regime such as Edwin's was the entrenched position of paganism within tribal society. Coifi was in some senses independent of Edwin, and his influence could be detrimental to royal authority. Among tributary tribes local shrines probably played a major role in the survival of local or regional separatism and a sense of social identity. Certainly the spread of Christianity was to be a political matter, with Edwin and Eadbald of Kent sponsoring it within their own lands and successfully persuading Rædwald's successor, Eorpwald, to convert. His complacency was not shared by the East Angles, who had not forgotten the supremacy of his heathern father, Rædwald, and the king was soon assassinated by a pagan. His kingdom apostatized. The continuing paganism of Mercia was as much a statement of opposition to the Kings of Northumbria and their allies as a matter of religious conviction. Throughout the seventh century, wars were to be fought both on earth and in heaven. Edwin's perceptions of the political and religious issues confronting him were inseparable.

Despite the glowing terms in which Bede described the Northumbrian conversion under Edwin, he was the first to recognize its superficiality and underlying fragility. When Edwin was killed by Cadwallon and Penda, on 12 October 633 at Hatfield (according to Bede; the *Annales Cambriae* named the site of the battle as *Meicen* and date it to the kalends of January, 630), the Northumbrian Church was only six years old, and Christianity little more than a clone of the public face of paganism. James the Deacon was left to tend the few, beleaguered and marginalized believers and the partly built church at York.

Edwin owed his death to several factors: the inadequacy of the intelligence reaching him from North Wales and Mercia was due largely to his failure to place missions in these areas, yet it was probably Paulinus' treatment of the British Church in the north that had so enraged Cadwallon, the most powerful Welsh king then living. Cadwallon had been besieged off Anglesey and Edwin, as 'overking' of all the parties involved, presumably played a direct part in this action. The Welsh king's dynastic interests were, therefore, as much at stake as his religious sensibilities. Cadwallon was joined in revolt by Edwin's Mercian enemies led by the *ætheling* Penda, a son of Pybba but not then in power.

The topography of Hatfield suggests that Edwin was trapped by superior forces which had come upon him from the west, between the mosses and carrs of Thorn Waste and Hatfield Common, and the River Don, miles away from the fords to safety across the latter around Doncaster. Perhaps he was breaking a journey at his palace there, with only his household thegns around him. The timing may imply that he was returning from Lindsey to Yorkshire for the annual tribute-taking ceremony, in which case his passage through this vicinity could have been predicted by his enemies. His son, the half-Mercian Osfrith, was killed in front of him and another was taken and later put to death by Penda. Edwin's direct descendants never regained his throne, excepting the female line, the children of his second marriage being escorted to Kent by Paulinus, whose baggage arguably included the Tribal Hidage.

Hatfield Chase, looking towards Hatfield. This area is slightly higher than Hatfield Moors but there is no escape from it to the north without crossing wet fenland

Æthelfrith's Heirs: Politics and the Scottish Church

Bede's description of the crisis of October 633 implies that Cadwallon and Penda had very different objectives. While Penda set about establishing himself as king in Mercia, Cadwallon probably returned to Wales for the winter, then marched into Northumbria in 634, where he defeated and killed Osric, Edwin's cousin. He briefly became ruler of Deira, when he broke the latter's siege of a *municipium* – a walled Roman town (York perhaps?) – and remained there in control of all Northumbria for an entire year. Bede's description of these events is highly prejudiced against the Welsh Christian whom he described as an 'impious man' who 'laid it waste with the ferocity of a tyrant' (*EH*, III, 1).

Had it been merely his intention to replace Edwin as 'overking', Cadwallon would surely have negotiated a settlement in the north and returned to North Wales far earlier. Bede's comments imply that he was attempting something of greater moment, probably the resuscitation of British kingship and of the British Church in the north, to achieve which would have necessitated a longer stay. Although his death in battle destroyed whatever initiative he had set in motion, a revival of the Celtic north was surely not at this stage an impossibility. Elmet had

The church of Heavenfield, marking the site where Oswald was reputed to have set up his cross before the battle of *Denisesburn*

125

presumably still a population virtually untouched by 'anglicization' and in the British territories usurped by Æthelfrith there must still have been many who remembered and preferred the British dynasties which he had displaced. Even in the core of Bernicia and Deira, the bulk of the population was presumably Celtic and the British language not yet entirely abandoned. Beyond were the British kingdoms based on Edinburgh and Dumbarton, their dynasties and aristocracies still intact. Cadwallon's destruction of the palace sites of English Northumbria (identified archaeologically at Yeavering) was part of a carefully considered attempt to eradicate English lordship in the north and reverse the processes of acculturation in a substantial part of England.

Bede had little sympathy for either Osric (Edwin's cousin) or Eanfrith (Æthelfrith's eldest son), both of whom abandoned the Christianity into which they had been variously baptized in favour of paganism. Their apostasy may have been offensive to Bede but in both instances it demonstrates the ideological realities within Edwin's Northumbria, where Christianity had made only the most superficial impact. Discre-

Iona, the mother church and monastery of the Scots in Britain and of their missions to Pictland and Northumbria. The monastic *vallum* is clearly visible in the foreground

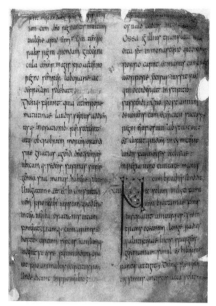

Bede's account of the miracles of St Oswald, from *The Ecclesiastical History of the English People*. Bede's work, completed in 731, has proved an invaluable source of information on the development of the Northumbrian Church during the seventh and early eighth centuries (British Library, Cotton MS Tiberius A. XIV., f. 84)

dited by the disaster at Hatfield and bereft of both its royal patron and its episcopal leadership, the new religion was swept aside and both kings sought to utilize the social cohesion offered by the paganism traditional to their respective kingdoms.

According to Bede's timetable, Osric was killed in the summer of 634 and Eanfrith put to death a full year later, taken by treachery when he had attended a conference accompanied by only twelve picked men (note Bede's allusion to Christ once more). In neither case had Woden protected them and the Bernician and Deiran communities must have been in a quandary concerning which god they should next propitiate to find success in war.

The problem was solved for them by Eanfrith's younger brother, Oswald. While in exile (616–35), Æthelfrith's several sons and their numerous adherents had diplomatically accepted baptism at the hands of the Scottish churchmen among whom they had found a refuge. With his brother dead by treachery but his friends untried in battle, Oswald led these men and whomsoever of the Bernicians he could attract to his banner into battle against Cadwallon, whom he encountered close by Dere Street, near Hadrian's Wall. Oswald is reported to have made great play of the protection of the God of the Scottish Christians, setting up his cross at Heavenfield before defeating and killing Cadwallon at the battle of *Denisesburn*, near Hexham. The monks of the minster at Hexham were later to honour the putative site of Oswald's cross with a church.

Like Edwin, Oswald had submitted his god to the ultimate test on the field of battle and had been granted victory. The contest was one which Northumbrian apologists later developed into a miracle equivalent to David's defeat of Goliath. Thereafter, Oswald proved himself a committed patron of the Scottish Church, sending to Iona for a bishop whose preaching he himself habitually translated for his fellow countrymen. As king he provided land and political support to the Scottish priests and monks who flocked into Northumbria.

The Christianity which they brought with them was an offshoot of British Christianity, taken to Ireland by St Patrick and other missionaries and thence to the Scots of Dalriada and the Picts, in northern Britain, largely by St Columba (died *c.* 597), the founder of Iona. Perhaps under the influence of Irish kinship systems, the monastery at Iona had diverged from Roman practice and had evolved an independent system of authority, with theology and ecclesiastical custom overseen by the senior monks and abbot of Iona, rather than a bishop. Long isolation had also led to significant differences between the customs of the Irish Church and that of Rome, often because of changes in the latter, and among these the attention of seventh- and eighth-century commentators focused on conflicting methods of dating Easter.

It was this Church which Oswald introduced to Northumbria during the 630s, establishing a bishopric on Lindisfarne, as near a clone of Iona's island location as possible. The monastic community established there was of the Scottish type and initially staffed by Scots. The choice of bishop was clearly crucial. Bede reported that the first returned home with stories of the obstinacy and barbarity of the English, and headway was only possible when Aidan was appointed (*EH*, III, 5), for whose humility and commitment to poverty Bede had nothing but praise. Indeed, there is an implicit contrast within Bede's work between the pride and wealth of the senior clergy of his own day and the apostolic simplicity of the Scottish mission.

In King Oswald, the Northumbrian Church found its first royal martyr and saint, and Bede recorded at length the miracles with which the site of his death and his corporal remains were associated. His cult rapidly became widespread, founded on the dispersal of various parts of his anatomy to the churches of his palaces, his arm, for example, being carried to Bamburgh, where it was venerated as a relic. His body was eventually exhumed and reburied at Bardney in Lindsey by his niece, Osthryth, then Queen of the Mercians, despite the opposition of the monks to a king whose rule in their 'province' was resented as that of an outsider.

His death in battle against the Mercians on 5 August 642 was less of a blow to Northumbrian Christianity than Edwin's death had been, since his brother Oswiu continued his religious and dynastic policies with considerable success during a reign which lasted twenty-eight years. It was this period which finally gave permanence and substance to the conversion of Northumbria.

Oswald was king in Bernicia, Deira and Lindsey but his 'over-kingship' was less secure than that of Edwin. Adomnan, writing at Iona late in the seventh century, wrote of him as 'overking' of all Britain, but Scottish writers are likely to have clothed this adopted son in the best apparel possible. Stray finds of Anglo-Saxon metalwork on the palace

This statue of St Aidan, by Kathleen O. Parbury, stands outside the ruins of Lindisfarne Priory. It was unveiled in summer 1958. Lindisfarne Castle is in the background

sites of the Scots probably arrived as gifts to kings who were fellow communicants in the Scottish Church during the reigns of Æthelfrith's children. That Bede included his name among his short list of 'over-kings' does, however, imply that Oswald was universally recognized as supreme in the immediate aftermath of his defeat of Cadwallon.

South of the Humber, Oswald's preference for a heretical Church and his replacement of Edwin's dynasty meant that he could not expect support from Kent, where his predecessor's second family and bishop had found succour. Oswald substituted Edwin's Kentish alliance for one with Wessex, Edwin's principal enemies, and he attended the baptism of King Cynigils there (*EH*, III, 7). That this was a baptism into the Gallic and Roman Church implies that Oswald's superiority was minimal and their alliance not far from equal.

Whether or not this was the case, it proved ineffective. Cynigil's heir was apparently pressurized by the Mercians to marry Penda's sister and was then dispossessed when he put her aside. Although the chronology of these events is obscure, it seems clear that Oswald was unable to retain control of the south in the face of Penda's rise to power and the Mercians and their Welsh allies found it a simple matter to cut his communications with Wessex on the Foss Way. Mercian armies were henceforth to include contingents led by numerous tributary kings, both Welsh and English. Against Penda's southern and western 'over-kingship' Oswald had only the lesser resources of the northern 'over-kingship' as that was constituted before the battle of Chester, with the probable addition of Elmet, Hatfield and Lindsey. It was arguably their central location and their long-sustained and mutually supportive relationship with the Welsh kings that were the crucial factors in Mercia's supremacy.

The rivalry of these two warrior-kings came to a head at *Maserfelth*. Although Oswestry was long proposed as the site of this battle, the identification has recently been challenged. Makerfield in Lancashire is the obvious alternative, in which case *Cogwy* in the *Annales Cambriae* is *Coccium* – Roman Wigan. If this reconstruction is correct, Oswald 'Brightblade' (as he was known in Wales) died confronting a Mercian-led invasion of Northumbria via the Roman crossings of the Mersey near Warrington.

Oswald's support for Scottish Christianity had served him well. The focus of his power lay in Bernicia. It was thence that his companions in exile had come and there too that he established an episcopacy with religious authority throughout his kingdoms. His Scottish brand of Christianity served to distinguish his Bernicia-centred kingship from the Deira-centred rule of his maternal uncle, King Edwin, the Christian Welsh whom he had defeated and the pagan Mercians by whom he was eventually killed.

After the disaster of *Maserfelth*, Deira once again broke away from Bernicia under its own king, although there appears to have been no disruption of the Northumbrian Church, both kings continuing to patronize Bishop Aidan and his Scottish clergy. Their unity on religious matters belied their political differences. The scale of his victory at *Maserfelth* and incidental references in the *Ecclesiastical History* to his subsequent campaigns in Bernicia imply that Penda had successfully detached Lindsey and southern Northumbria (the core of Deira in Yorkshire, Elmet and perhaps southern Lancashire) from Oswald's successor, placing them under Oswine, son of the apostate Osric, Edwin's cousin, whom Cadwallon had killed in 634. Tensions between the two Northumbrian kings probably reflected this wider context.

OPPOSITE: The mother church of the Scottish mission in Northumbria was founded at Lindisfarne, close by Oswald's principal centre at Bamburgh, on a site as closely resembling Iona as it was possible to achieve

Perhaps because of his tribute-paying status, Oswine was unable to match his rival's military power and, without support from Mercia, the Deiran king backed down from a military confrontation on the frontier near Catterick in the summer of 651, disbanding his army and seeking safety in hiding. Although his passivity attracted high praise from Bede (*EH*, III, 14), his craven behaviour was entirely at odds with the heroic ideals of contemporary society and unacceptable to his own aristocracy, who had perhaps discovered that the overlordship of Penda was less palatable than the kingship of Æthelfrith's sons. One of their number betrayed Oswine to Oswiu and he was subsequently murdered at Gilling. Although this crime clearly shocked Northumbrian opinion and necessitated the foundation of the monastery of Gilling in expiation, it enabled Oswiu to place his nephew, Oswald's son, Œthelwald, in Deira as a client-king, and gave him control of all Northumbria, with the option of pursuing expansionary policies beyond. Oswine was buried safely out of harm's way in Bernicia, at Tynemouth, but even there a cult rapidly became established.

Oswiu's contest with Penda of Mercia continued and the Northumbrians were at times under great pressure from their southern neighbours. Oswiu renewed the Kentish alliance of Edwin, marrying the latter's half-Kentish daughter, who had found refuge at the Kentish court, as his second or even his third bride, and this probably gained him some support against the Mercians. Ideology clearly played a part in their struggle, Penda and the bulk of the Mercians remaining pagan until his death, but Oswiu took every opportunity to spread Scottish Christianity among the southern English and so tie other dynasties to his own fortunes. Bede recalled that Sigberht of the East Saxons was a frequent visitor to Oswiu's court, and he and his supporters were baptized by Finan, Aidan's successor as Bishop of Lindisfarne, at the royal settlement of Wall, in Hexhamshire in the heartland of Bernicia. His most notable coup was the conversion of Penda's son, Peada, king of the artificial Middle Anglia, whose marriage to Oswiu's daughter was accompanied by his baptism, also at Wall, in 653. When he returned home he was accompanied by four priests from Northumbria, three of whom were English (including Cedd) and one Scottish, but the absence of a bishop implies their subordination to one of Oswiu's own bishops, probably in Lindsey. The movement of such priests provided Oswiu with valuable intelligence. Cedd's frequent visits to Deira and his familiarity with Œthelwald were recorded by Bede in his description of the foundation of Lastingham Monastery, 'in steep and remote mountains which seemed more suited to the dens of robbers and wild beasts than to the homes of men' (*EH*, III, 23).

Oswiu's fortunes hung by a thread in the 650s. War with Mercia brought him to the brink of disaster. Both Bede and the author of *The History of the Britons* recorded that he was forced to offer a vast treasure to Penda and the Welsh as the price of peace, although they do not agree as to the outcome of this episode. With his son Ecgfrith a hostage in Mercia, his nephew once more recognizing the superiority of Penda, and many British and southern English kings swelling the ranks of his enemies, Oswiu finally met Penda in battle at the 'River *Winwaed*' (*EH*, III, 24), near Leeds (or at the 'River *Gaius*': *HB*, 64), on 15 November 655. The Welsh abandoned Penda and Oswiu comprehensively defeated his opponents, killing most of their leaders, including Penda himself.

The Gilling sword, dating from the late ninth century, is a two-edged iron sword with an elaborate hilt encircled by five decorated silver bands. It can be compared with Viking swords found in Norway

OPPOSITE: Bernician patronage of the Scottish Church

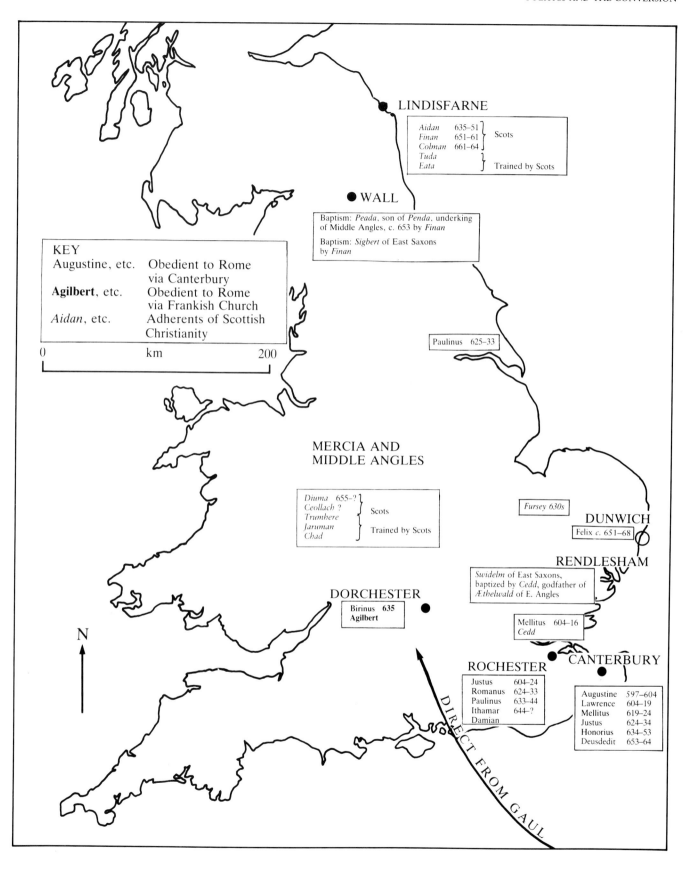

LINDISFARNE

Aidan	635–51	Scots
Finan	651–61	
Colman	661–64	
Tuda		Trained by Scots
Eata		

● **WALL**

Baptism: *Peada*, son of *Penda*, underking of Middle Angles, c. 653 by *Finan*

Baptism: *Sigbert* of East Saxons by *Finan*

KEY

Augustine, etc.	Obedient to Rome via Canterbury
Agilbert, etc.	Obedient to Rome via Frankish Church
Aidan, etc.	Adherents of Scottish Christianity

0   km   200

Paulinus 625–33

MERCIA AND MIDDLE ANGLES

Diuma	655–?	Scots
Ceollach	?	
Trumhere		
Jaruman		Trained by Scots
Chad		

Fursey 630s

DUNWICH

Felix c. 651–68

RENDLESHAM

Swidelm of East Saxons, baptized by *Cedd*, godfather of *Æthelwald* of E. Angles

Mellitus 604–16
Cedd

DORCHESTER

Birinus **635**
Agilbert

ROCHESTER

Justus	604–24
Romanus	624–33
Paulinus	633–44
Ithamar	644–?
Damian	

CANTERBURY

Augustine	597–604
Lawrence	604–19
Mellitus	619–24
Justus	624–34
Honorius	634–53
Deusdedit	653–64

N

DIRECT FROM GAUL

The death of Penda left Oswiu in a dominant position. He established Penda's son Peada – his own Christian son-in-law – in Mercia south of the Trent and ruled northern Mercia himself. However, Peada was assassinated soon after and, in 658, the southern Mercians rebelled against Oswiu's attempts to impose his own direct rule there, under another of Penda's young sons, Wulfhere. An entry for the same year in the *Welsh Annals* records that Oswiu waged war against Mercia's Welsh sympathizers. It seems clear that Oswiu was attempting to chastise both parties to the Mercian–Welsh alliance.

That the Mercian revolt was not followed by a reversion to paganism implies that Wulfhere initially recognized Oswiu's supremacy. The administrative advantages of Christianity must have been the envy of the Mercian establishment and the success of the outnumbered Oswiu in battle in 655 was probably decisive in persuading the Mercians to adhere to his religion. As bishops of Mercia, Lindsey and the Middle Angles, the Scots Diuma and Ceollach were followed, after Whitby, by Trumhere, Abbot of Gilling, all of whom owed their positions to the Northumbrian king.

Church, Patronage and Politics

Edwin's conversion was achieved at minimal expense. The Scottish Church was similarly established by Oswald and Oswiu without excessive cost to themselves, despite its heavy reliance on royal

Lastingham, a monastery founded by St Cedd in 'steep and remote mountains infested with robbers and the dens of wild beasts'. The earliest fabric in the present church, particularly its crypt, belongs to the refoundation of the community which began in 1078

patronage. Aidan was initially granted Lindisfarne, conveniently close to royal Bamburgh and an island which duplicated the site of the mother monastery at Iona. There followed a number of small grants of land, to match the reported gifts of horses, plate and foodstuff to the bishop. A handful of monasteries were established over the next two decades but many depended on an income from land sufficient to support only a single warrior or *ceorl*. Desperate for divine aid against Penda in 655, Oswiu dedicated his daughter as a nun and estates sufficient for the foundation of twelve monasteries, if God might give him victory. The result was twelve estates of ten hides apiece, six in Bernicia and six in Deira. Similarly, the monastic sepulchre of Oswiu, his queen and their abbess daughter at Whitby were initially founded on a single estate of ten hides. Such politically inspired donations were the beginning of an accelerating flow of royal resources to the arbiters of divine pleasure.

Other churches were established within important estates, many of them royal, as, for example, that which we should assume to have existed at Wall, but churches were clearly few and far between even in the 650s. The best putative example so far excavated – at Yeavering – was a timber-framed hall of typical indigenous type, the raw materials and constructional skills for which were available locally. The buildings discovered at Tynemouth and Dacre are closely comparable in kind,

Lindisfarne Priory as it is today. The present ruins are of the Benedictine re-foundation in the eleventh century on the site of the Saxon monastery destroyed by the Danes

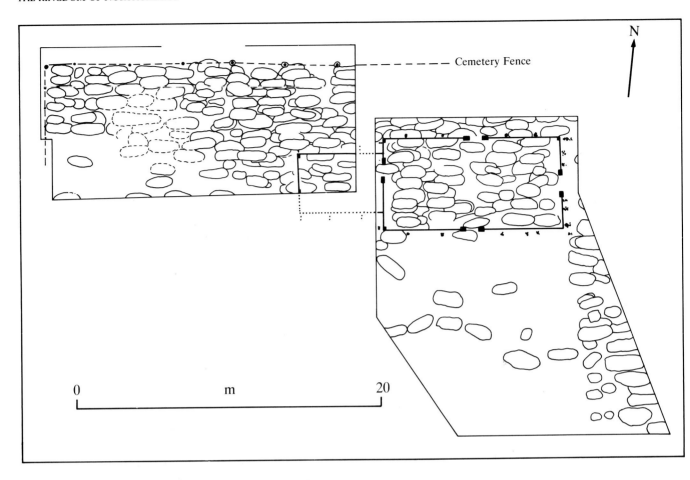

N

Cemetery Fence

0   m   20

A timber-framed, hall-type building at Yeavering which was the focus of a large and oriented inhumation cemetery of the early seventh century. The excavator interpreted this building as a church (after Hope-Taylor, 1977)

although neither is likely to have been as early as this and those at Tynemouth probably did not include a church. Bede described Bishop Finan's construction of an episcopal church on Lindisfarne which was clearly of the same kind, built of hewn oak and thatched with reeds in a manner which Bede explained as 'Scottish' (*EH*, III, 25), but would then equally have been 'English'. In this respect, the churches of the period 633–64 contrast with those begun by King Edwin in stone, the architecture of which proclaimed their debt to the Kentish Church. Of the latter, Oswald was reputed to have completed Edwin's principal church, at York, but whether in stone or timber is not recorded. On balance the presence of skilled masons in Northumbria before 664 seems extremely unlikely.

This economical religious regime came to an end during the 660s. Partisans of the Roman Church had survived in Northumbria, headed by James the Deacon, and they were patronized anew by Oswiu's queen, Eanfled, King Edwin's daughter, raised at the court of her kinsmen in Kent as a Roman Christian. Prince Alhfrith had strong links in southern Britain and followed his mother in patronizing the youthful Wilfrid, whose search for training in the service of the Church had taken him to Gaul and Rome. Alhfrith was sub-king of Deira late in Oswiu's reign, and pursued a religious policy which was strongly influenced by his mother and by Deiran sensibilities. He reversed his earlier patronage of Scottish monks, reclaiming from them an estate of forty hides at Ripon and giving it instead to Wilfrid for a community of the Roman persuasion.

The Whitby seal. The seal was found in the 'kitchen-midden' of Whitby Abbey in 1874 and dates from around 660. The only Archdeacon Boniface, the name imprinted on the seal, known to have had connections with Whitby held office from 654 to 685. The seal may have been used to verify the credentials of Agatho (papal representative at the Synod of Whitby in 664) and the decree sent from Rome to the Abbess Hilda in reply to her appeal against St Wilfrid

Ripon Cathedral: a detail of the crypt

Divisions of this scale on religious policy were unacceptable to the king and the matter was resolved at the famous synod held at St Hilda's monastery at Whitby, convened and chaired by King Oswiu in the presence of his son. Also present were Bishop Colman and the clergy of the Scottish Church in Northumbria and the Frankish Bishop Agilbert and priest Agatho, St Wilfrid, James the Deacon and other supporters of the Roman cause. As reported by both Bede and Eddi, the principal bone of contention was the computation of Easter, an issue which was addressed by Bishop Colman and Wilfrid, but the final decision by King Oswiu was conditioned by the comparative seniority and authority of St Peter over St Columba.

This arbitrary royal decision implies that the Synod of Whitby was as much a political as an ecclesiastical event. Oswiu's position in southern Britain had deteriorated in consequence of the revival of Mercia under Wulfhere. Oswiu had married his son Ecgfrith to an East Anglian princess in the late 650s and his synod implies that he was seeking to re-activate his own alliance with Kent. The deaths of King Earconberht of Kent and Archbishop Deusdedit in 664 offered an opportunity for an outsider to intervene in the appointment of the next archbishop, and Oswiu's reunion of the English Churches under Canterbury enabled him to capitalize on this role, entirely wrongfooting Wulfhere of Mercia.

Oswiu's abandonment of Scottish Christianity had obvious repercussions. For the future, he could rely on the wholehearted support of the archbishop of all England in his confrontation with the Mercians. Even a rank outsider like Archbishop Theodore saw fit to honour that obligation throughout the 670s and his partisan support contributed significantly to Ecgfrith's successes.

Whatever the thinking which lay behind it, the result of the Synod of Whitby was the utter discomfiture of the Scottish party, whose leader, Colman, resigned the see of Lindisfarne. Few, if any, native Scots remained and some of the English clergy of their persuasion departed with them. Others, such as Cedd and Tuda, proved more pliable and accepted promotion to the positions that had been vacated. The bulk of the Northumbrian clergy of the late seventh century owed their training to the Scottish Church and clearly retained much sympathy for many of its traditions. There was widespread ignorance of the teachings of the Roman Church for a generation or more thereafter.

The obvious corollary of the Synod of Whitby was the rapid advancement of the Romanist party and their preferred ecclesiastical structures. The see of York was revived, initially as the Bishopric of Deira, and Wilfrid, spokesman of the Romanist view at Whitby, was appointed to it. He departed for Gaul in search of canonical consecration but stayed away too long and found on his return that the less fastidious Chad had been ordained to the see by the West Saxon bishop acting in conjunction with two British bishops. Wilfrid busied himself introducing continental artisans to construct the new basilican church at Ripon, as well as the choralists who were to train Northumbrian monks in Gregorian chants. When he obtained York he set about the reconstruction of Paulinus' poorly finished stone church. His status as the best qualified member of the triumphant Roman Church brought Wilfrid a plethora of estates, both in Northumbria and Mercia, while his troubled career was later to find him converting the pagans of Sussex and Frisia.

It was probably the grant of Hexhamshire to Wilfrid which brought him into conflict with the royal house. This came at the hands of Queen

Æthilthryth, the East Anglian wife of Ecgfrith, Oswiu's son and successor. The monastic church which he raised there was clearly exceptional, although of it all only the Merovingian-inspired crypt has survived:

The remains of the abbey at Whitby which replaced the original Saxon structure

> the great depth of the foundations, the crypts of beautifully dressed stone, the vast structure supported by columns of various styles and with numerous side-aisles, the walls of remarkable height and length, the many winding passages and spiral staircases leading up and down . . . we have never heard of its like this side of the Alps.
>
> (*Life of Wilfrid*, XXII)

However, the virgin queen retired to a nunnery and her successor, Iurminburgh, wanted the return of the royal dower lands. Her hostility gave the bishop's critics a royal patron. Bishop Wilfrid was driven into exile in 678 and was never again to enjoy the full fruits of the massive grants he had received. He spent substantial parts of the remainder of his life abroad, where he strenuously canvassed the papacy and other authorities for his re-instatement. He was briefly imprisoned by King Ecgfrith, yet, when he died in 709, he left more portable wealth and wider estates than would have been the lot of many kings.

Wilfrid's career was both exceptional and contentious, not least in the different treatment he was accorded by his biographer and apologist and the Venerable Bede. However, his career does illustrate the rising

Relief of a running horse at Hexham, possibly part of a frieze from the early Saxon church

Stained glass at St Paul's Church, Jarrow. The window was made in the monastery workshop in 681, and was originally used in the refectory. It has remained unaltered since that date and is the oldest stained glass in Europe

tide of land-grants to the Church for the foundation of ever more numerous and ambitious churches and monasteries. Others were almost as well supported: among them the much travelled Benedict Biscop, founder of Monkwearmouth and Bede's own monastery at Jarrow. The result was a rash of stone building-work, with masons, sculptors, floorers, glaziers and lead-workers imported from abroad at great expense. Their work is still to be seen in the surviving churches at Jarrow, Monkwearmouth, Escomb and Ledsham.

By the 670s the flow of both land and portable wealth to the Church was probably sufficient to impair the capacity of kings to reward the service of their warriors, non-clerical advisors and lieutenants. The transfer of entire shires to monasteries such as Hexham, Lindisfarne and Monkwearmouth meant that the richest lands of eastern Bernicia were in clerical hands. By the reign of King Ecgfrith vast estates in the

Eddius's account of the foundation of Hexham Abbey by Wilfrid. Eddius Stephanus was a Kentish priest who came to Northumbria with Wilfrid, probably in about 669. He became a monk at Ripon, and was closely linked with Wilfrid for the next four years. Eddius provides valuable details of Wilfrid's building activities at York, Ripon and Hexham. The manuscript is one of only two known copies and dates from the eleventh century (British Library, Cotton MS Vespasian D. VI., f. 90)

Pictish and Northumbrian warriors are depicted on this seventh-century Pictish symbol stone at Aberlemno, near Forfar. The stone stands just six miles from the battlefield of Nechtansmere and is believed to portray the Pictish victory there of 20 May 685. The Anglian warriors of Northumbria are portrayed wearing helmets with long nose-guards, similar to that found at York (see p. 92); the Picts are bare-headed

Pennines and further west were being granted *in toto* to churchmen like Wilfrid and Cuthbert.

This transfer of royal capital to monastic hands had important implications for the ability of kings to reward service. Unlike their grants to their warriors, these grants seem to have been treated as heritable, rather than reverting to the Crown at the death of the holder. Monasteries established a corporate identity which made them secure from royal rights such as heriots and military service. By the latter part of his life, Bede was commenting adversely on the practice of royal thegns converting land obtained from the kings into monasteries over which they then presided as hereditary abbots. Inheritance of ecclesiastical position was widespread – Benedict Biscop had to expressly rule out the practice at his own death and Wilfrid was succeeded by a near relative as abbot at Ripon.

In these circumstances, the Northumbrian monarchy became far less robust than hitherto and proved for the future less capable of revival after military defeat. It depended heavily on the tribute which flowed in during the reign of Oswiu and his son. King Ecgfrith (670–85) responded vigorously and successfully to a rebellion among the Picts over whom Oswiu had extended English control, and then defeated an invasion by Wulfhere at the head of a southern army (*c.* 673). Wilfrid's

An early Anglo-Saxon cross at Warden, near Hexham

biographer stated that Ecgfrith levied tribute on Mercia. If so, Ecgfrith was probably 'overking' of all the south. When Wulfhere died (675), the same author claimed that Ecgfrith ruled peacefully over a wider kingdom. The implication must be that he took this opportunity to regain Lindsey.

Wulfhere's successor, Ethelred, once more undermined Ecgfrith's supremacy, reducing Kent in 676. The south secured, he attacked Ecgfrith in 679. Since the ensuing battle occurred on the banks of the Trent, the Mercian attack was probably launched against Lindsey, in which case it may have occured in the vicinity of Littleborough, on the boundary of medieval Lincolnshire and Nottinghamshire. In a bloody battle Ecgfrith's brother and potential heir was killed but the Mercians seem to have been in no condition to follow up their success. A peace was negotiated between the kings by Archbishop Theodore which gave Ecgfrith a royal *wergild* for his brother and seems to have left him Lindsey while acknowledging Ethelred's superiority over the south.

It was shortly after this battle that Theodore presided over the Synod of Hatfield. In 673 King Ecgfrith travelled to Hertford to oversee Archbishop Theodore's first synod and it was probably no coincidence that he defeated the Mercians and placed them under tribute at about this time. The decision was then made to hold similar synods each year at *Clovesho* – an unidentified site but presumably one well placed for the Roman road system in the same general vicinity as Hertford, where Ecgfrith would have been keen to demonstrate his capacity to provide protection to an all-England synod. By 676 Ecgfrith's superiority was once more waning but the partnership between Ecgfrith and Theodore was still close and mutually supportive.

Whether or not the annual synods continued in the late 670s is unrecorded but it seems unlikely. In 680 the road south was closed to Ecgfrith by the Mercian supremacy and it was probably not Hatfield in Hertfordshire to which Bede referred but that Hatfield (or Heathfield) under Ecgfrith's control on the borders of Deira, Mercia and Lindsey to which he had already referred. It was Ecgfrith's name which led the list of kings included in the preamble, implying that he was present and acting as protector of the synod, followed by Ethelred of Mercia and Ecgfrith's principal sympathizers in the south, Ealdwulf of East Anglia and Hlothere of Kent (*EH*, IV, 17).

Theodore used the synod to suppress heresy (by implication Scottish Christianity). Having witnessed this, his royal ally may have felt himself to be justified in a crusade against the Scottish Christians of the far north, where he probably thought to expand his father's supremacy and conquests. In 684 he sent an army into Ireland which brought back hostages and so presumably promises of tribute. In 685 Ecgfrith led his warriors in person against the Picts beyond the Tay, only to be killed and his army destroyed at Nechtanesmere, near Forfar. With Ecgfrith died Northumbrian pretentions to the 'overkingship' of all Britain. Weakened by the over-generous disposal of land to the Church and consistently thwarted by Mercian dominance of the Midlands, his successors were unable to re-establish the military reputation of their ancestors. Hitherto, Bernician and Deiran kings had operated an extensive protectorate over their Celtic neighbours, exacting from them tribute and troops. In the aftermath, Britons, Scots and Picts broke away and were never again to be consistently brought to heel. Northumbrian claims to the 'overkingship' of even northern Britain died with Ecgfrith on a fateful field near Strathmore on 20 May 685.

CHAPTER 5

A Christian Kingdom: Northumbria 685–867

The rich crop of near-contemporary saints' lives and Bede's writings – particularly the *Ecclesiastical History* completed in 731 – render Northumbrian history in the early decades of this period better evidenced than that of any other English community prior to King Alfred. Thereafter, contemporary textual material amounts to little more than a handful of letters. The *Continuation of Bede* is brief and late, although this and several even later literary sources all seem to have utilized Northumbrian annals not now extant. Beyond 802 even derivative writings are woefully thin and of dubious historicity. Although the regnal sequence is supported in broad outline by numismatic evidence, the precise chronology of individual kings and bishops becomes a matter of conjecture in the ninth century.

Politics and Power

The Northumbria ruled over by Aldfrith – the scholar-prince who was illegitimate half-brother and successor to Ecgfrith – was smaller than hitherto. In 680, the year after the great battle by the Trent, the exiled Bishop Wilfrid addressed the Council of Rome, claiming that he represented the Britons, Scots and Picts, as well as the Angles, in the northern parts of Britain, Ireland and the islands. Such claims reflect the pretensions of King Ecgfrith to extensive control over his Celtic neighbours, in support of which he sent forces into Ireland in 684 and himself led his troops to destruction in 685 in as yet unconquered Pictish territory beyond the Tay.

In the aftermath of his death in battle, Wilfrid's claims could never again look even remotely realistic. The Picts of Fife, the Scots of Dal Riata and the British kings of Strathclyde all re-asserted their independence. The English bishop for the Pictish territories, at Abercorn, was forced to flee and the see was never to be re-established. The Picts seem

The crucifixion scene carved on this plaque at Penrith depicts Christ, with two angels above and the figures of the spear-bearer, Longinus (left), and Stephanus (right) below. This combination of figures, with the crossless crucifixion and cup-shaped sponge, does not appear in any other sculptural form in Northumbria, and the Durham Gospels is the only manuscript that offers a similar combination (see p. 157)

to have taken the fight to the Bernicians, killing Brihtred (or Berht, probably a sub-king in the Lothians) in 698 and fighting against Beorhtfrith (probably of the same family) in the vicinity of Falkirk in 710–11. Aldfrith is not credited with any military achievements, although he may have detached the Scots from alliance with the Picts by returning to his old friend Adomnan of Iona the prisoners taken by his brother's army in Ireland. Bede did portray him as an 'overking' so he presumably retained some clients among his neighbours and he passed this position to the next generation but the death of his son and heir, Osred, 'south of the borders' in 716 may have been at the hands of Pictish or British opponents. It was not until the reign of Eadberht (737–58) that we have any evidence of renewed Northumbrian aggression in the north: while the king and his army were fighting the Picts (in 740), Æthelberht of Mercia wasted part of Northumbria; in 750 he was reputed to have added the Plain of Kyle (Ayrshire) and other unspecified regions to his kingdom, presumably from Strathclyde; in 756, in alliance with the Picts, he brought the Britons there to terms but was disastrously defeated on 4 August, presumably when retiring south without Pictish support.

There are signs that a *rapprochement* occurred between the Picts and Northumbrians during the eighth century. The Picts followed Northumbria in adopting the Roman method of calculating Easter, and expelled representatives of the Columban Church, even before Iona itself followed suit in 716, having sought and followed the advice of Ceolfrith, Abbot of Monkwearmouth and Jarrow, on these issues. By the middle of the century at least one of the several dynasties competing for the Crown in Northumbria was favourable to a Pictish alliance and

Stirling Castle, the probable site of a royal *burh* or defended palace site in the seventh and eighth centuries

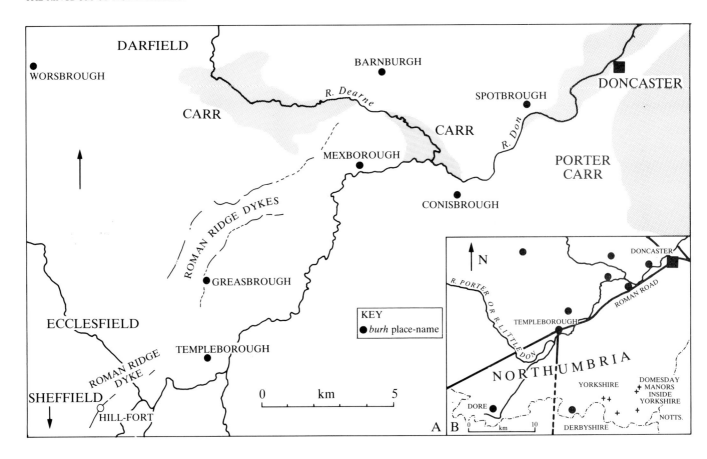

The Roman Ridge dykes. A: dykes and lowlying wetlands; B: Roman roads and the southern boundary of medieval Yorkshire

several defeated kings took refuge there – as did, for example, King Alhred, *c.* 774.

In retrospect, alliance with the southern Picts seems justified. In the 840s, Scottish kings established lordships north of the Forth. Whether or not the Picts received English assistance (as later Scottish sources were to claim), there followed a series of invasions of the Lothians and Tweeddale, and Scottish kings rapidly established a degree of political control over Strathclyde. For the future, Northumbrian leaders were to be confronted by far more powerful northern neighbours, whose menace was to grow during the late ninth and tenth centuries. The Pictish alliance was ultimately a failure but it may have long postponed these dangerous developments.

There is no evidence that the northern boundaries of the kingdom were ever fortified. Individual defended palace sites – such as Stirling, Dunbar and Edinburgh – probably provided bases from which conflicts occurred in the open field in the central Scottish lowlands, and particularly around the defended palace site of the British kings at Dumbarton. The north was probably left in the hands of hereditary royal reeves and shadowy underkings. In contrast, Northumbrian kings seem to have created a deep, defensive frontier system to the south against their powerful Mercian neighbours. This can be traced between the Pennines and the vicinity of Doncaster – around which the Don, Aire, Ouse and Humber and their widespread fens provided an adequate defence against a large force. Man-made defences consisted of two elements. The Roman Ridge survives as a dyke which shadows the river Don within 4 km of its northern bank, from the Sheffield suburbs as far as the River Dearne. Furnished with a ditch up to approximately 10 m across, it must have been a formidable boundary which may have

The southern line of the Roman Ridge at the intersection of the B6090 and the A633 south of Swinton

The Nico Ditch at Melling playing fields. The derelict condition of this monument encapsulates the problems of identifying and managing early medieval monuments in an urban setting

been supplemented by a short second linear feature, known as the Bar Dyke, on Broomhead Moor; in addition, an unusual concentration of *burh* place-names in the same vicinity (eight are identifiable from Kexborough to Conisbrough) may imply a range of defended sites. The entire complex was perhaps based on Doncaster. It has already been suggested that this was the *Campodonum* where Edwin had a palace and Bede implied that another existed there by the time of writing his *Ecclesiastical History*, (II, 14). It was a site of some strategic consequence defending the lowest fords across the river, and its destruction by fire in 764 was sufficiently important to be noted in whatever annals formed the basis of the later *History of the Kings*. Finds of Northumbrian coins at Moses Seat (North and South Anston) and Pot Ridings Wood, close to the boundary between medieval Yorkshire and Derbyshire, may indicate further high-status interest in defensible sites even south of the Don.

This defensive cordon is undated but fits easiest into a late eighth- or early ninth-century context. It may be mirrored west of the Pennines by the Nico Ditch in southern Manchester, the *magna fossa* of *c.* 1150, equipped with a ditch on the south side and likewise set back from the actual frontier with Mercia (on the Mersey) and so also well inside Northumbrian territory. One might have expected a similar barrier at Warrington but none has so far been identified. The entire system implies a degree of central planning and a government capable of mobilizing a considerable workforce.

For the year 829, the West Saxon compilers of the *Anglo-Saxon Chronicle* retrospectively recorded a meeting between Ecgberht of Wessex – briefly ruler of Mercia – and an unnamed Northumbrian king (it was Eanred) at Dore (South Yorkshire). If this meeting occurred at or near the frontier, then that presumably approximated in this area to the medieval shire boundaries. Until evidence is presented to the contrary, it seems likely that the southern boundary of Yorkshire approximated

The Nico Ditch, Roman roads and low-lying wetlands

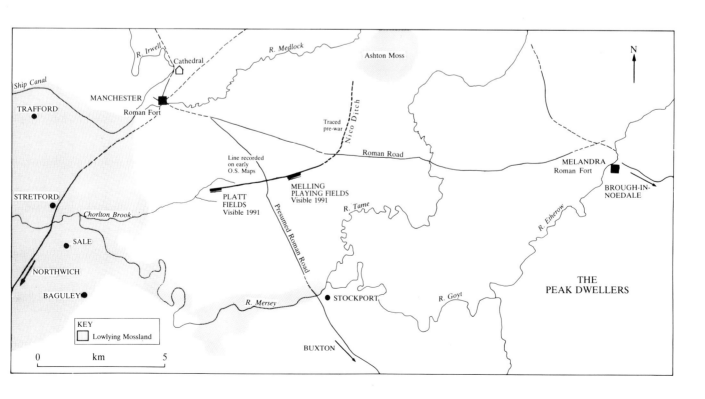

to the frontier of Northumbria throughout its length, with the defensive system set back from it to minimize the danger of surprise attack.

If Dore was the regular meeting-place between Northumbrian and Mercian kings, its location clearly favoured the Mercians, operating from palaces in Staffordshire and Derbyshire, rather than the Northumbrian kings for whom the site was characterized by its comparative inaccessibility – again reflecting the implicit superiority of Mercian kings over their northern neighbours.

Only a single attack on Mercia by a Northumbrian king is recorded for the entire period (by Eardwulf in 801) and that was in reaction to interference in Northumbrian affairs and ended inconclusively. If they were faced by an impressive defensive system, it is not surprising that attacks on Northumbria were barely more frequent. Mercian kings were heavily committed in the west and south and were probably generally content that their northern frontier should be quiet, although King Offa certainly interested himself in dynastic conflicts among the Northumbrians and may have attempted to reduce the kingdom to client status. The Roman Ridge dyke on the east bank of the Idle at Scaftworth was probably a Mercian defence of the river crossings into the Northumbrian province of Hatfield but is more likely to have been constructed in the seventh century than later.

Northumbria was smaller in extent than hitherto and its kings contented themselves with less ambitious external policies. However, within increasingly fixed borders there is no more than the occasional suggestion of military interference from outside, despite the Viking raids which began in 793. In this respect, at least, Northumbria looks to have been comparatively peaceful throughout the period.

Dynasty and Faction

A single dynasty governed Northumbria continuously from 634 until 716, when Osred was slain at the tender age of twenty after an eleven-year reign. The ability of his household in 705 to fight off a challenge from another candidate and mount a regency says much for

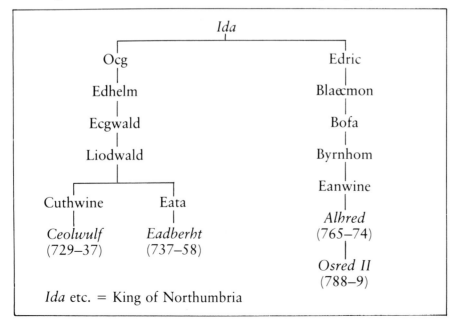

The 'official' genealogy of three of the competing Northumbrian dynasties in the eighth century

A decorated initial from the Durham Gospels. (Durham, Cathedral Library, MS A. II. 16, f. 34v)

the residual durability of the patronage system associated with the dynasty. His premature death was a disaster and the dynasty, although King Osric (c. 718–29) was probably a member of the same, thereafter lost its hold on the throne. Henceforth the kingship was to be a matter of dispute between several families, whose respective claims to royal descent were already contentious, with challenges coming from as many as four dynasties within any one generation.

Despite numerous judicious murders and the frequent, forcible suppression of armed rebellion, few subsequent kings were able to marshal sufficient resources to establish a new dynasty for more than one or two generations – and this despite occasional abdications in order to allow the succession of a preselected relative at a time which might be considered opportune. This strategy was adopted by the unusually successful Eadberht in 758 in favour of his son, only to see him murdered by his own household within the year.

Regicide, assassination, civil war, burnings, forcible tonsuring, exile – all were familiar elsewhere in Anglo-Saxon England. What separates the Northumbrian kings from their neighbours is the apparent normality of these methods of disposing of kings and their rivals. The rate at which these incidents occurred was high throughout all but the earliest decades of this period. It may help to tabulate what is known of these events (remembering always that the chronology is no more than approximate, particularly after 802):

685–705   Aldfrith (illegitimate brother of Ecgfrith and son of Oswiu): died

705–16   Osred (young son of Aldfrith): slain (by the Picts?)

716–18   Coenred: fate unknown

718–29   Osric: died appointing Ceolwulf to succeed him

729–37   Ceolwulf (brother of Coenred, the *Gloriosissimus Rex* to whom Bede dedicated his *Ecclesiastical History* in 731): captured and forcibly tonsured in 732 but regained power until 737 when he abdicated, perhaps under pressure from Eadberht

737–58   Eadberht (cousin of Ceolwulf): abdicated

758–9   Oswulf (son of Eadberht): murdered by his own household

759–65   Æthelwald Moll: deprived

765–74   Alhred (married daughter of Oswulf): exiled

774–9   Ethelred (a child, son of Æthelwald): driven out

779–88   Ælfwald (related to Oswulf): assassinated

788–9   Osred II (a youth, son of Alhred): expelled

789–96   Ethelred: resumed reign, assassinated

796   Osbald: twenty-seven-day reign, exiled

796–806   Eardwulf: survived murder attempt, 790, expelled, restored by continental allies 808–c. 811–12

806–8   Ælfwald II: died

808–11/12 Eardwulf: deposed

811–40   Eanred: died

840–4   Ethelred II (son of Eanred): expelled

844   Rædwulf: killed by Vikings

844–8   Ethelred (second reign): killed

848–66   Osberht: expelled

866–7   Ælle (rival and possibly brother of Osberht): killed with Osberht in battle of York.

The statistics make grim reading: kings were on sixteen occasions succeeded by candidates from outside their own close family circles and only four times by a close relative who was their preferred heir. Three of those had reigned for the unusually long period of twenty years or more and so were more likely to have adult sons (although Aldfrith's heir was still a child). Children were certainly appointed, perhaps as compromise candidates, but their tenure of the throne was generally brief. Given the pressures to select a competent adult, the rapid turnover of the kingship made it inevitable that more than a single family would be involved but this goes no way to explaining the failure of the heirs of long-established kings like Eanred or Eadberht to retain the throne.

An extract from Bede's letter to Ecgberht of York. Written on 5 November 734, a copy of this letter is included in a manuscript written at Durham Cathedral priory in the twelfth century. The letter makes reference to the state of the Northumbrian Church, Bede urging Ecgberht to obtain support from King Ceolwulf for major reforms (British Library, Harley MS 4688, f. 93b)

The successive and worsening crises which befell the Crown suggest that there was an underlying shift in the power structure within Northumbrian society that created circumstances in which only an exceptionally able or lucky individual might hold the throne for any period, and made an unchallenged succession extremely unlikely. Regional aristocracies and sub-kings already existed in the seventh century and many of them could at least lay claim to royal blood from one dynasty or another, although any high ambitions were held in check by the superior power and prestige of Oswiu's line. However, the position of the latter was undermined during the last third of the seventh century by several factors which, in combination, left the kingship severely weakened.

Oswiu and his children began the transfer of vast amounts of land from direct royal control into the hands of the Church, which, collectively, came to control a large slice of what had been royal land – particularly in the richer and more productive territories east of the Pennines. So long as kings retained tight control of the principal appointments in the Church, they probably kept the necessary degree of interest in these lands and the revenues and political power which they represented. However, the career of Bishop Wilfrid demonstrated the dangers of alienating vast estates to a man whose commitment to the dynasty and its policies was less than total, and tensions clearly occurred between the ambitions of kings and even those churchmen who were loyal to them – as between Ecgfrith and St Cuthbert over the northern campaigns.

The most successful of the dynasties to follow Oswiu's was that of Eadberht and this may have been largely because the latter's brother, as Archbishop of York, controlled ecclesiastical patronage and policies. Other kings were saddled with clerics like Bishop Wilfrid, or Archbishop Eanbald, *c.* 800, who had been appointed by their predecessors and opponents, wielded considerable political influence and even retained numerous soldiers. Instability in the tenure of the Crown was a natural consequence.

In a letter written in 734 to Bishop Ecgberht, Bede argued that the permanent alienation of royal estates for the founding of private monasteries would deprive young warriors of the lands they might otherwise have expected as their reward for loyal service to the king. He feared they would either remain in the royal household and indulge in various vices or go abroad in search of wealthier patrons. His fears seem to have been borne out. At several points the royal household played an unsavoury but critical role in the selection and deselection of kings. Other warriors may well have departed for better rewarded service abroad, as many local churchmen were to do. Eadberht excepted, no Northumbrian king of the period is known to have conducted more than a single campaign outside his own frontiers and few had a following sufficient to deter other warlords from rebelling. In Anglo-Saxon kingship, success tended to breed success, as young men flocked to join the retinue of a generous king with a proven military reputation. By contrast, the Northumbrian kings depended heavily on the goodwill of other members of the aristocracy – both lay and clerical – to provide military and political support in times of crisis. There are signs that the Northumbrian aristocracy was collectively able to select and deselect kings and its members may have sold their support dearly in a constantly shifting system of factional alliances.

imago aquilae-

The eagle symbol of St John is one of only two surviving fragments from a gospel book produced at the Lindisfarne *scriptorium* in the late seventh to early eighth century (Cambridge, Corpus Christi College, MS 1978, f. 1)

The comparative poverty of the kings forced ambitious young men to look elsewhere for opportunity. Within Northumbria, alternatives were offered by the regional aristocracy and the Church. The result was a plethora of small patronage systems in competition with one another, the goal of each being control of royal patronage. Many candidates for the throne may well represent such regional patronage systems. The focus of support for several kings lay in Deira and it is possible that their advancement reflected re-emergence of the old contest between the Deiran and Bernician aristocracies for the control of Northumbria.

To a limited extent, the geography of these dynastic factions can be reconstructed from royal burials and from the political attitudes of particular monasteries. The *History of the Kings* recounts the dramatic action taken by King Eadberht against Lindisfarne in 750, removing Bishop Cynewulf as a prisoner to Bamburgh and besieging the Church of St Peter until King Aldfrith's son, Offa, although almost dead from hunger, could be dragged from sanctuary there, 'although innocent'. There can be little doubt where the sympathies of the Lindisfarne community or the unknown chronicler lay and this crisis must place in doubt the willingness with which Eadberht's cousin, Ceolwulf, had relinquished the throne and retired to this same monastery. On 23 September 788 King Ælfwald was buried at St Andrew's, Hexham, and a church was founded at the place of his murder, dedicated to St Cuthbert (the principal Bernician ecclesiastical saint) and St Oswald (the principal Bernician royal saint, whose victory at *Denisesburn* was the basis of specially close links with Hexham). Ælfwold's killer, Sicga, was buried at Lindisfarne in 793, demonstrating the contrary policies of the two great Bernician monasteries.

Kings regularly used pre-emptive murder and military confrontation to face-down their challengers, and several assassinated leaders were subsequently revenged by loyal retainers. However, there are signs that various kings attempted more positive steps. In 762 Æthelwald married at Catterick. Although it was reputedly (perhaps significantly) burnt by Eanred in 769, Æthelwald's son, Ethelred, chose the same site for his own wedding to King Offa's daughter in 792. This selection of a border settlement – and the unusual detail in which these two events were reported – may reflect attempts to unite the political communities of both Bernicia and Deira by a dynasty the focal influence of which unusually lay in the latter, and which was pursuing traditional Deiran interests south of its own borders. Acts by members of the dynasty recall the apparent significance of this royal site under the regimes of Edwin and his immediate successors.

Several kings constructed marital alliances with other powerful dynasties, thus forging factions which were more broadly based. Hence King Alhred's marriage to the daughter of Oswulf (Eadberht's son and heir) probably purchased him the support of that powerful family by sharing royal patronage with them. Eadberht's line and its allies were the most successful lineage for three-quarters of a century, with blood links to Ælfwald I and Osred and perhaps even Osbald and Ælfwald II. Other kings sought to mobilize foreign support through marriage. On 29 September 792 King Ethelred, opponent of the dynasties linked to Eadberht, married Ælfflæd, daughter of Offa, the great Mercian king. His opponent, King Eardwulf (the king credited with an invasion of Mercia), married into the Carolingian royal family – the only western European house of greater prestige than that of Mercia – and this alliance eventually bore fruit: in 808 a Frankish annal recorded Eardwulf's arrival at Charlemagne's court and his subsequent re-instatement to the Northumbrian throne by the envoys of the Pope and the Emperor. This alliance implies a diplomatic rivalry between Charles and the Mercians, whose Northumbrian ally or client had been killed in 796, and demonstrates that Northumbria was far from isolated in these years from the greater European political stage. However, the foreign support for neither king was sufficient to enable him to die a natural death or pass on the throne to his heir.

Church and Society

The Synod of Whitby inaugurated a wave of change in the Northumbrian Church. Shorn of its primacy within the Scottish tradition,

At Hackthorpe various fragments of Anglo-Saxon stone crosses have been combined to form a single monument

Lindisfarne lost its pre-eminence as the religious centre of all Northumbria, gradually giving way to the authority of York and the intellectual leadership of the several Romanist houses founded by Benedict Biscop and Bishop Wilfrid, although the island see retained a focal role in Bernicia. The synod allowed the authority of the southern archbishops into Northumbria. It was an alliance between King Ecgfrith and Theodore (Archbishop of Canterbury, 668–90) which broke Bishop Wilfrid's domination of the Northumbrian Church in 678. Theodore's willingness to abet the king even against papal pressure owes much to the political alliance which existed between them.

Theodore's plans to increase the number of northern sees was clearly stated at Hertford in 673 but postponed probably due to resistance from Wilfrid. With the latter in exile, three were established in 678 at York, Lindisfarne and Hexham, to add to the short-lived see based on Abercorn for territories recently conquered from the Picts. A further addition was made early in the eighth century, at *Candida Casa* – Whithorn – where Bede recorded that the number of believers (presumably meaning in Roman as opposed to Celtic Christianity) had recently increased sufficiently to justify the appointment of Pecthelm as its first bishop. With the loss of Abercorn in 685, this disposition stabilized under the overall jurisdiction of the Canterbury archbishops. The synod at Hatfield (680) was a triumph for Theodore and the Roman Church, with all those present confirming their rejection of heresy – and so the Scottish Church. However, Northumbrian leverage in the south collapsed in 685, leaving the Northumbrian Church under the jurisdiction of southern archbishops over whom Northumbrian kings had little or no influence and whose appointment was increasingly to be controlled by Mercian kings. Bishop Acca attended the Mercian-dominated Council of *Clovesho* in 716 as the sole Northumbrian representative. This unpromising situation was effectively ended by King Eadberht, who re-activated the Gregorian plan for a northern archdiocese (but not for twelve bishops) in favour of his brother, Ecgberht, Bishop of York, who acquired the pallium from the papacy in 745. Henceforth, the Northumbrian Church enjoyed autonomy from Canterbury, with its own councils separate from those of its southern neighbour.

Although the Northumbrian Church was episcopal in structure, it is difficult to overestimate the extent and influence of monasticism within it. All five of the diocesan churches were monasteries – and those at Lindisfarne, Hexham and perhaps Abercorn were primarily monastic. That at Whithorn was believed in the eighth century to owe its origins to an earlier episcopal centre of British Christianity dating from a time when that was still part of the wider Western Church, Ninian being represented as a Rome-educated associate of St Martin. Recent excavations have confirmed activity on the site during the later fifth and sixth centuries but whether or not the physical remains uncovered constituted a Celtic monastery or a secular settlement of high status remains a matter of interpretation. The claims of its early bishops for St Ninian should not be given too much credence.

Monasticism was equally an important element in the Augustinian Church, pushing into Northumbria during the late seventh century. In the north its role was massively reinforced by the prevalence of Scottish traditions, within which monastic institutions were paramount.

Outside the main centres, church sites were still few when Bede died, particularly in the hillier and less-populated areas, and probably remained so throughout the period. Kings, bishops, abbots, abbesses and

Part of the cross base at Auckland St Andrew

The interior of the church at Escomb. The chancel nave was reconstructed from material taken from the ruins of the nearby Roman fort at Binchester

the secular aristocracy established churches, often at or convenient to existing centres of administration and jurisdiction. In consequence, the pastoral care emanating from them was heavily influenced by existing estate structure. Such territories or estates appear to have been large, often encompassing numerous communities scattered in farms and hamlets over a wide area, subordinated to a single focus for purposes of tenure and jurisdiction. As a result the density of new church sites remained comparatively low, with, for example, just a handful at or close to the foci of the great estates or shires of Gainford, Staindrop, Auckland/Escomb, Chester-le-Street and, perhaps, Lanchester.

What there were tended to house groups of minster clergy living a communal life. Such communities had some or all of the characteristics of monasteries and it is difficult to make a clear division between, on the one hand, groups of clergy and, on the other, monks following a rule based on that of the Benedictines, as introduced from Gaul. Such focal churches performed many of the functions of the pagan temples of the sixth and seventh centuries and their comparative scarcity may owe much to existing religious attitudes within society. In the pagan view, private sacrifice would normally be performed by the head of the household, as in the case of King Edwin (as portrayed by Bede, *EH*, II, 9). Only public sacrifice and divination required a priesthood. The immediate effect of the conversion to Christianity was felt in the public sphere. Many households may have retained pagan practices for private matters as late as the Viking Age.

Churches were often constructed on or close by Roman ruins (for example, at Corbridge and Wall), perhaps to enable masons to re-use good building stone, although the prevalence of sixth-century pagan burials on such sites may imply that some already had a religious

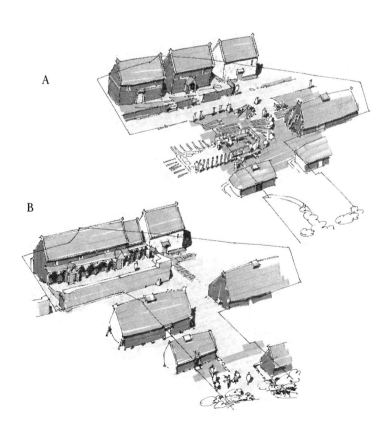

Whithorn. A: two small timber churches and a mortuary chapel overlook the rest of the settlement under construction, *c.* 700; B: a large timber church and mortuary chapel overlook the timber-built settlement, *c.* 800 (courtesy of Dave Pollock and the Whithorn Archaeological Trust)

significance. Many churches were not primarily congregational, although it is possible to pack large numbers into a church as small as the average Manx *keeill*: the primary role of the small church was to provide protection for the altar. There are references to several constructed for commemorative purposes; others were associated with the saints and may have functioned as the foci of pilgrimages. Many monasteries constructed retreats, resulting in the grouping of early stone churches in particular areas, although that described by Bede in the vicinity of Hexham as an 'isolated house surrounded by open woodland and a dyke' seems to have lacked one (*EH*, V, 2). Others were chapels associated with monastic cells, such as that on Farne.

In his last years Bede made several references to the growing popularity of the religious life among his contemporaries. Notice has already been directed towards his letter to Ecgberht in 734, in which he argued that the possessions of unworthy monasteries established so as to escape obligations to the Crown should be seized and used to support new dioceses. In the concluding words of his *Ecclesiastical History* (V, 23) he noted that:

> many of the Northumbrians, both noble and simple, together with their children, have laid aside their weapons, preferring to receive the tonsure and take monastic vows rather than study the arts of war. What the result of this will be the future will show.

The foundations of a *keeill* (an estate chapel or small church), one of several in the cemetery at Maughold on the Isle of Man. Many early Anglo-Saxon churches were no larger

St Cuthbert's Chapel, the Farne Islands. The masonry now standing is medieval and later

The Lord's Prayer, as depicted on the earliest surviving illuminated manuscript from Northumbria, a seventh-century gospel book. The volume was probably written before the Whitby Synod (664) and is an example of the decorating of gospels which peaked at Lindisfarne in about 700. The script itself shows a strong Irish influence (Durham, Cathedral Library, MS A. II. 10, f. 3v)

The tomb reputed to be that of the Venerable Bede in the Galilee Chapel, Durham Cathedral

This suggests that such issues had been on his mind for some time. Eadberht and his brother, Archbishop Ecgberht, seem to have followed Bede's advice in part, taking control of at least three monasteries but, instead of establishing new bishops, granting them to a leading nobleman – a deed which triggered a protest from Rome in 757–8.

The impact on the military capability of Northumbrian kings aside, it is difficult to assess the danger to the Church posed by such private monasteries. Except for Monkwearmouth and Jarrow, which were protected by papal privileges, the Northumbrian monasteries were subject to the jurisdiction of the bishops and their oversight provided a barrier of some sort to gross immorality, even if the Northumbrian Church was chronically short of sees. That private monasteries were heritable does little to distinguish them from other foundations. In the Scottish tradition, monastic authority regularly descended within specific families. Nor was the Roman Church ever free of nepotism – even the great Wilfrid established a relative as abbot at Ripon and disposed of his monasteries and portable wealth to his followers by testament and Alcuin inherited a small monastery. Within the first few generations, Bede's own community was subject to different standards of behaviour but it was exceptional in this respect. Elsewhere, family-centred and dynastic pressures were commonplace without this necessarily affecting the religious performance of an institution. Of far greater importance seems to have been the internal regime and tradition of a monastic house. The dynamism of a few great houses, already established in the seventh century, was maintained well into the ninth, when *scriptoria* remained operative at York and within the community of St Cuthbert. In contrast, many small private houses may never have even sought to attain similar standards of literacy, architecture or asceticism, the better of them concerning themselves predominantly with the cure of souls.

Seventh-century Christianity had been adopted with enthusiasm by kings and intellectuals but had offered little to the bulk of the farming population. In the process of its triumph during the conversion period, Christianity was necessarily adaptive to the conservative cultural perspectives of local communities. The religious beliefs and practices of many a *ceorl* or even an *ealdorman* in the eighth or ninth century probably differed little from those of his pagan ancestors. Archbishop Theodore (died 690) established penances for those sacrificing to demons, using pagan rites of healing or cleansing after a death, charms and divination, thus demonstrating that private paganism was still widespread during Bede's youth. For Christianity to become more than a veneer, the Church needed to invest in widespread missionary activity and in a more localized, parochial organization.

There was obviously much interchange between the higher ranks of the secular community and the Church: indeed, the two must be seen as alternative manifestations of a single and integral society. For many experienced political figures, like the long-lived King Ceolwulf, entry to a religious community offered the best chance of a long and comfortable life with the expectation of salvation at the end of it. Under the year 799, the *History of the Kings* recorded the death of Osbald, 'once *ealdorman* and patrician, and for a short time king, then indeed abbot', who was buried at York. Many such nobles brought significant wealth with them into the Church, as did King Ceolwulf in 737 to Lindisfarne.

Leadership of the Church seems to have been the preserve of the aristocracy even from the late seventh century and, despite occasional isolated cases of imprisonment or deprivation, the chances of a long life were good. A bishop or one of the wealthier abbots enjoyed an affluent existence, with substantial influence in local and regional affairs and the support of a large retinue. Clerical marriage may have been common-place but tonsure seems to have excluded an aristocrat from the kingship.

The majority of Northumbrians were always outside the ranks of the clergy and the less aristocratic of them are the least well represented in the written and archaeological records. There were substantial tensions between clerical and secular ambitions, lifestyles and culture – as Bede recognized when he recounted the story of a prophecy by Bishop Aidan concerning the pious Prince Oswine of Deira:

> I know that the king will not live for long; for I have never previously witnessed a humble king. I believe that he will shortly be taken from us, because this nation is not worthy of such a king.
>
> (*EH*, III, 14)

Although King Aldfrith was well educated, his early experience of the intellectual life among the Scottish monks was the exception among secular leaders, most of whom were probably as illiterate as the poor. Although heroic literature was in circulation in Northumbria in the eighth century (witness the details concerning the battle of Chester which Bede borrowed from such a source), secular literature was rarely copied in monastic *scriptoria*. The vast bulk of the material which must have entertained the households of Northumbria's kings has been lost without trace, yet it was literature of this kind which nurtured the heroic ideals underlying the dynastic blood feuds and the revenge killings of the period.

In many respects, Northumbria was a deeply traditional society, even though its *mores* are rarely accessible to us. Late in 793 Alcuin (at the Carolingian court from before 792 until his death in 804) wrote to King Ethelred asserting that the sack of Lindisfarne by the Vikings was a direct consequence of the fornication, adultery, incest, avarice, robbery and luxurious habits that characterized his court, and attacked the personal appearance of the secular élite – specifically styles of wearing the hair and beard – on the grounds that they too closely resembled styles used by the pagans. A papal visitation led by the Bishop of Ostia in 796 pronounced itself dissatisfied with several Northumbrian customs, including the use of lots in lawsuits (presumably a traditional practice unchanged since the pagan past), the eating and mutilation of horses and the wearing of garments 'according to the fashion of the gentiles'. 'Gentiles' was a term normally applied at this date to pagans of any kind and was to become synonymous with Vikings but the context implies that the legate had in mind Germanic styles. The legate referred additionally to pagan practices, suggesting that he was by no means convinced that pagan sacrifices were no longer being offered by sections of the Northumbrian population. Alcuin's subsequent letter to Bishop Higebald of Lindisfarne expressed his hostility to secular attitudes and behaviour within the monastic community, particularly censoring story-telling at table. One has only to contrast the work of Caedmon, the Whitby cowherd-poet, with *Beowulf* to recognize the disapproval of the secular literature which characterized the greater houses. Yet it was impossible entirely to exclude secular attitudes and pastimes from the monasteries – hence the games of chance identified by excavation at Hartlepool.

Caedmon's hymn, transcribed in the Northumbrian dialect of Old English in a copy of Bede's *Ecclesiastical History*. Bede tells the story of how Caedmon, a cowherd attached to the monastery at Whitby, was inspired by a dream to compose the first vernacular religious poetry (Cambridge University Library, MS Kk. 5. 16, f. 128v)

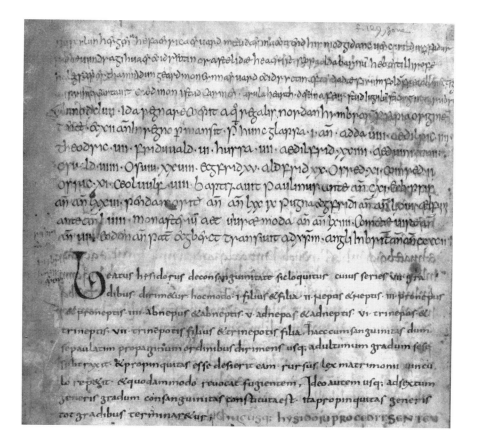

A detail from the *Codex Amiatinus*, written at Monkwearmouth/Jarrow before 718 (Florence, Biblioteca Medicea-Laurenziana, MS Amiatino 1, f. iv)

Monastic Culture

The eighth century – and particularly the first half of it – has justly been described as the golden age of Northumbrian monasticism. The monasticism of the Scottish Church had been eremitic and ascetic. In the 670s, Wilfrid and Benedict Biscop introduced Benedictine monasticism, with its emphasis on discipline, communal activities, choral music and intellectualism – all derived from the Frankish Church and particularly from Lérins. The subsequent integration of these two traditions resulted in a cultural achievement of unique richness. In Bede and Alcuin the Northumbrian Church provided two of Europe's most distinguished medieval scholars and teachers, yet they were only the front-runners among a number of intellectuals, associated with the most productive *scriptoria* in the Western Church. Northumbrian churchmen travelled widely in Celtic lands and their missions to pagan Germany were crucial to the conversion effort there for over a century. Their activities long maintained close contacts with the Frankish Church and court, to the ultimate benefit of both parties.

These scholarly and missionary achievements were centred in a handful of the larger monasteries – principally St Peter's at York, Monkwearmouth and Jarrow, Ripon, Hexham and Lindisfarne. The triumph of the Roman Church at Whitby led to a spate of European books into Northumbria, where they provided the models for local copying. The *Codex Amiatinus* is one of three new copies of the Bible commissioned by Abbot Ceolfrid of Monkwearmouth/Jarrow (690–716) which, had his death at Langres *en route* not prevented him, he had intended to present to the Pope. This was the work of nine monks

using a spectrum of scripts but predominantly the continental uncial, which kept close to the style of the prototype, preferring discrete and unobtrusive initials and rapidly resuming normal scripts thereafter.

The *scriptorium* of Monkwearmouth/Jarrow was peculiar for the long-continued purity of the Roman tradition but it was placed under growing pressure by rising demands for its products, both from England and the continent, in particular for editions of the works of Bede. Bishop Boniface was writing to Northumbria for his works in 746–7 and the Carolingian Bishop Lul a quarter-century later. By 746 the *scriptorium* had bowed to the pressure of work and adopted the far faster insular miniscule script which, in four separate hands, can still be seen in the Leningrad copy of Bede's *Ecclesiastical History*.

A full-page miniature of the crucifixion from the Durham Gospels, probably created at Lindisfarne during the late seventh or early eighth century (Durham, Cathedral Library, MS A. II. 17, f. 38³v)

OPPOSITE: This page from the *Codex Amiatinus* shows the scribe Ezra. The Bible was one of three made for Ceolfrith, Abbot of Wearmouth/Jarrow. In 716 Ceolfrith took the manuscript with him on a final journey to Rome, intending to present it to the pope, but he died *en route* (Florence, Biblioteca Medicea-Laurenziana, MS Amiatino 1, f. v)

Other *scriptoria* were less conservative and soon developed techniques of decoration characterized by large and illuminated initials, first lines and first pages distinguished by different scripts, ornamented margins and the use of full-page illustrations. A variety of patterns were adopted and entire pages often featured the symbol associated with the evangelist whose work followed, to serve as place-markers. The Lindisfarne Gospels, based on a southern Italian original, were produced in around 700, lavishly illustrated and written in the stately insular majuscule normally reserved for such de luxe Bibles, and are the most disciplined of these luxury volumes. The Durham Gospels are likely also to have been a product of the Lindisfarne *scriptorium* and the Echternach Gospels were probably a Northumbrian work of this period, too, although it is not a simple matter to distinguish Northumbrian works from derivatives. The styles were extensively exported – both by the flow of books back to Frankia, Brittany and Germany, and by the substantial influence of the Northumbrian Church among the Irish and Picts. The surviving carpet page in the Lichfield Gospels betrays strong similarities to the work of Eadfrith in the Lindisfarne Gospels, although it need not have been produced in the same *scriptorium*. At Iona Northumbrian influences met and mingled with existing Scottish traditions of scholarship and a large library was available to its monks in the eighth century, when they or some neighbouring Pictish or Scottish house were probably responsible for the Book of Kells. This volume betrays strong Northumbrian influence

The front panel of the Franks Casket, a decorated box made of whale-bone, showing the Adoration of the Magi (right) juxtaposed with the adventures of Wayland the Smith, a popular figure of pagan mythology (left)

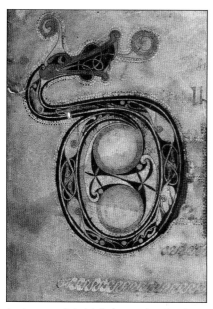

A decorated initial from the Durham Gospels (Durham, Cathedral Library MS A. II. 17, f. 38⁴

and particularly close parallels with a series of manuscripts from Lindisfarne – in origin itself, of course, a daughter house of Iona.

The vigorous output of Northumbrian scholars and copyists in the eighth century is reflected in the comparatively large numbers of manuscripts which have survived the Viking Age and all that followed, and are now housed in collections as far afield as Paris, St Omer, Würzburg, Utrecht, Dublin and Leningrad, as well as in at least five insular libraries. The leading monasteries had fine collections of books, perhaps the largest of which was at York. Alcuin cited a long list of these in his epic poem and they included a range of commentaries by Church Fathers, works by grammarians, poetry and some classical prose which, in combination, might be regarded as one of the foremost libraries of western Europe. Other monastic *sciptoria* were probably less well founded but Æthelwulf's poem from the early decades of the eighth century, written in an unidentified Northumbrian monastery, demonstrates his knowledge of the works of several of the ancients.

The magnificent products of these monastic *sciptoria* were matched by artistic achievements in other media. Foremost among these were metalworking, the manufacture and arrangement of coloured glass, work with textiles and the carving of both stone and wood. Little evidence for many of these skills survives – the less robust materials and the more portable objects being vulnerable to a variety of destructive pressures. The so-called Franks Casket is a rare example of early

This pectoral cross from St Cuthbert's coffin was probably buried with the saint in 687 or at his enshrinement in 698. It was manufactured in Northumbria in the seventh century and, showing signs of use, was possibly worn by Cuthbert during his lifetime

eighth-century relief carving of whalebone, depicting scenes from both Christian and pagan mythology, which is often ascribed to Northumbria and which has recently been claimed for Ripon. A silver hanging bowl found in the eighth-century St Ninian's Isle treasure probably derived from Northumbria and the Ormside bowl, with its inhabited vine-scroll decoration, was certainly a product of the region, made *c*. 800. Otherwise local metalworking is best seen in the cross from St Cuthbert's coffin.

The same context provides a rare instance of chisel-decorated timber. Cuthbert died on 20 March 687 and was buried in a stone coffin beneath the floor of St Peter's, Lindisfarne, but his tomb was opened on the anniversary of his burial in 698 and his incorrupt body transferred to a light chest made from six oak planks – the coffin which is today on view in Durham Cathedral. This coffin was inscribed with the figure of Christ, the symbols of the four evangelists, various archangels, the twelve apostles and the virgin holding a Christchild (identified by runes). The effect was not intended to be decorative but to invoke the protection of the individuals represented, using a minimal number of lines, the design being based on Italian or Byzantine miniatures similar to those used as models for illustrations in the Lindisfarne Gospels and Book of Kells.

By far the most widespread and numerous relics of the period are carvings in stone. The tradition of stone carving was imported from Frankia in the 670s and its earliest use was as an adjunct to masonry construction – used to dramatic effect for the first time after Whitby at

Cuthbert was enshrined in this decorated wooden coffin in 698, twelve years after his original burial, and it soon became the focus for the cult of the saint. The fragments shown here, from one of the sides, depict four of the apostles

The 'hunter', a human figure set in an inhabited vinescroll, found at St Paul's, Jarrow

The bishop's throne, known as the 'Frith Stool', at Hexham

Ripon (begun in 671), Hexham (673), Monkwearmouth (674), York and Jarrow (682–5). The monastic churches and even other buildings at Hexham, Jarrow, Monkwearmouth and Whitby were ornamented with lathe-turned balusters and a wide variety of friezes, often featuring plant-scrolls inhabited by human figures and a variety of animals.

Stone church fittings have also been identified at many other sites, such as Hart and Greatham: the daily cycle of religious observance necessitated accurate knowledge of the time and sundials are a common feature, still *in situ* on the wall of Escomb Church and on the south face of the Bewcastle Cross, but often later re-used – as in the later medieval church porch at Old Bylands. Stone was also used for the manufacture of furniture. There are vestiges of what may have been stone writing tables at Jarrow and Kirkby Stephen and the bishop's throne or 'Frith Stool' has survived at Hexham, formed from four sandstone blocks, the elevations and the tops of the arms decorated with a restrained, incised ornament.

The skills of the sculptor were also harnessed to the need to mark and distinguish Christian burials. Stone coffins were being manufactured for the corporal remains of the religious élite by the later seventh century and lesser members of the monastic communities could expect grave markers, decorated simply with a cross or bearing an inscription commemorating the name of the individual, sometimes accompanied by an injunction to pray for the soul of the departed.

In these highly literate communities incised lettering was used for a variety of purposes. The oldest surviving church dedication in England (though moved from its original position in the north wall in 1783) is that of Jarrow, dated to Sunday 23 April 685 and – as behoves such a Romanist institution – prefixed by a chi-rho monogram. The crude scratched cross situated behind the pulpit at Escomb may be a commoner relic of the dedicatory service but lettering occurs on a wide variety of other monuments, including several of the free-standing stone crosses (for example, Ruthwell, where runes were used), which are the most sophisticated products of these monastic workshops.

Free-standing stone crosses were first made in Northumbria in the first half of the eighth century. The origins of this type of monument are obscure. There was a tradition of cross-carved slabs within the Celtic Church and Northumbrian sculpture of this period occurs at several

RIGHT: The seventh- or eighth-century church of Escomb viewed from the south. The corners are reinforced by massive quoins. The original windows are visible in the wall of the knave above the porch and medieval window. ABOVE: The dedication cross behind the pulpit at Escomb Church

W.G. Collingwood's drawing of the complex and highly geometric vine ornamentation on Acca's Cross (*c.* 740), Hexham Abbey (Collingwood, 1927, p. 31)

sites where these were extant (such as the Hirsel, Coldstream, and Addingham). However, these monuments were no more than one of several influences on Northumbrian sculptors. The more important prototypes were probably metal or ivory miniatures imported from the Mediterranean, which were then translated (and massively enlarged) into the medium of stone for the first time in Northumbria. Early examples, which were either the work of continental craftsmen or based directly on imported prototypes, are Acca's Cross at Hexham and a comparable piece at Lowther (Cumbria). The technique spread rapidly thence throughout England and to Ireland, Scotland and the Isle of Man, where local sculptors developed their own preferred styles and decorations – with the development of the ring-headed cross and decorative spirals particularly favoured by Irish patrons.

Most examples were carved in sandstone, the height varying upwards to 3–4 m. Many were probably painted but little pigment has survived. Crosses, fragments thereof and related carved stones are the most widespread archaeological relics of the period, occurring sometimes in marked concentrations, particularly at monastic sites known to us from literary sources. Many other sites of churches or monasteries are evidenced solely by fragments of carved stone or even substantive crosses – as at Bewcastle. Such evidence goes some way to rectifying the imbalance in the literary record between the west and east sides of the Pennines.

The dedication stone at St Paul's Church, Jarrow. The inscription reads: 'The dedication of the church of St Paul on the ninth of the kalends of May [i.e. 23 April] in the fifteenth year of King Ecgfrith [685] and the fourth year of Ceolfrith, abbot, and with God's help the founder of this church'

LEFT: Biblical scenes on the west face of the Bewcastle cross. The carver apparently used the same models for these scenes as were used at Ruthwell. The top figure is John the Baptist, then Christ treading on the beasts, with St John and his eagle below a memorial inscription in runes, all apparently of the early eighth century; RIGHT: The south face of the Bewcastle cross: geometric interlace and an intricate vine decorate a masterpiece of eighth-century ecclesiastical sculpture, although the sculptor seems to have been more familiar with hops or clematis than grape-vines

Free-standing crosses may have served a variety of functions. A schematic monastic plan in the eighth-century Irish Book of Mulling portrays a rampart-enclosed monastic precinct within which were several crosses and churches. The retrospectively named St John's Cross at Iona is an eighth-century example of just such a cross within a monastic precinct. Northumbrian monasteries were similarly enclosed and some contained paired or grouped churches, or a church and separate baptistry – as at Hexham and Jarrow – so it seems probable that crosses were distributed within Northumbrian religious precincts in a similar fashion. As such they were presumably intended to encourage meditation and private prayer.

Keynote scenes from the Bible occur on numerous examples. Among the commonest is the crucifixion but other biblical episodes and miracles are illustrated, particularly on the more complex crosses such as those at Ruthwell and Bewcastle, and the fragmentary Rothbury example. These include the flight into Egypt, the raising of Lazarus and Christ healing the blind man. Such scenes would have been meaningless to an audience which lacked a good working knowledge of the Bible. The excellent condition of several examples may imply that they were housed indoors – perhaps in the church.

The iconography of the finest examples is extremely sophisticated. Juxtaposed crucifixion and annunciation scenes on the south face of the

OPPOSITE, LEFT: The seventh- to eighth-century church at Jarrow, later adapted as the chancel of the medieval church. The tower is pre-Conquest; RIGHT: The eighth-century cross at Ruthwell, Nithsdale, has been reconstructed within the parish church. The inhabited vinescroll at the side is surrounded by a runic inscription in Old English from the early Christian poem 'The Dream of the Rood', in which the cross of the crucifixion relates its grief. The central panel shown here, on the back of the cross, depicts Mary Magdalene washing Christ's feet

Monkwearmouth Priory, from an engraving of 1779

Ruthwell Cross, and a series of panels centred on the figure of St John the Baptist holding the *Agnus Dei* there and on the Bewcastle Cross, can be associated with the form of the mass after the liturgical innovations of Pope Sergius (686–701). Such monuments could only have been executed by highly trained craftsmen, who were probably attached to particular schools associated with the great monasteries. Only churchmen sensitive to biblical exposition and European innovations in the litany are likely to have commissioned them. The bulk of pre-Viking sculpture was probably the work of small numbers of craftsmen in the permanent employ of the Church. The uniformity of the work they produced implies that the churchmen who employed them travelled extensively within the province and hired the craftsman whose work had already impressed them elsewhere.

The skills of the mason were in strong demand in other spheres in the eighth century. Bishop Acca was credited with the completion of the magnificent church at Hexham and much work at Monkwearmouth and Jarrow was probably delayed until this period. Excavation at Hartlepool has revealed that the boundary complex there was slighted *c.* 700 and the numerous small timber buildings, used variously as workshops and living quarters, were refurbished or entirely replaced over the next quarter-century with buildings constructed on stone footings. Similar replacement of timber with stone-founded buildings has been identified at Whithorn and postulated for

165

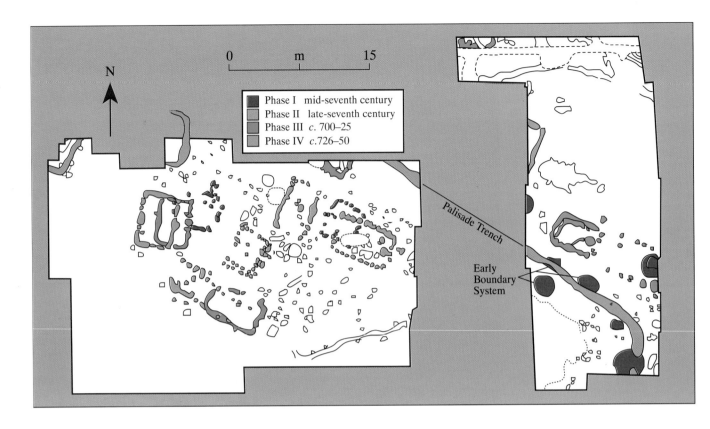

Whitby. The more durable stone-founded or stone-constructed buildings revealed by excavations became the norm on the major monastic sites but elsewhere churches and monastic buildings continued to be constructed in the local vernacular tradition, often in timber.

Excavations on the Anglo-Saxon monastery at Hartlepool (simplified after Daniels, 1988)

Coinage and the Economy

Barring such exotic finds as the handful of seventh-century gold coins from York, the first Northumbrian coinage was the silver penny (*sceatta*) of King Aldfrith. Nationwide deterioration in the silver content of coinage was locally reversed by Eadberht (737–58), whose silver pennies were struck with the king's head on one side and either a prancing animal or the archbishop's name on the reverse. Minting continued thereafter, with the names of the coiner replacing the prancing animal in the 780s, but Northumbrian kings did not adopt the new standards established by King Offa and appear to have been faced by a shortfall in the supply of silver. Local lead deposits may have yielded silver during the eighth century but, if so, exploitation can only have been at modest levels. A high proportion of the silver in circulation arguably derived from occasional large inflows as tribute in the seventh century – the pagan cemeteries of the region have produced so little that

Sceattas (silver pennies) of the eighth century

166

This collection of coins includes a penny of Cnut, the Danish king of York, *c.* 900–5, which displays an elaborated cross symbol, and a coin of Anlaf Cununc – Olaf Guthfrithson who re-established Norwegian rule in York after Æthelstan's death (with bird symbol). The coin-die bears the obverse of a penny of 'St Peter' (Sword type), and dates from *c.* 925. The strip of lead, a trial or record piece, dates from 955 and shows details of a penny of Eadwig by the moneyer Frothric. All the pieces were discovered in and around York.

it seems unlikely that there were large quantities of precious metals present before the reign of Edwin.

In the final decades of the eighth century the region suffered from a net outflow of silver which caused shortages. These problems may have been exacerbated by the hoarding of plate and silver coins by a Church that was both rich and, perhaps, tax-exempt. The collapse of the silver coinage in the 790s coincided with antagonism between King Eardwulf of Northumbria and Offa of Mercia and may have been the result of tribute payments to this powerful neighbour by Eardwulf or his immediate predecessor. It also coincided with the first recorded Viking attacks, which may have exacerbated the problem, but, of the two, Offa was the more capable of draining the north of silver if he was able to establish a political superiority over its kings.

Whatever the cause of this crisis, coining was resumed early in the ninth century with the continuous production by a well-staffed mint of a prolific coinage but one in which the silver content was rapidly reduced, from *c.* 40–60 per cent to 8–20 per cent during the reign of Eanred. Under Ethelred the coinage consisted of *c.* 90–8 per cent brass, with only small residues of silver, which may have been reduced still further during the brief reign of Rædwulf. It is these debased pennies which are generally known as *stycas*. Silver was in part replaced by zinc, perhaps also from mines in the Pennines. The coinage was once again reformed by King Osberht with the replacement of the zinc alloy by bronze with a high tin content but the silver content never recovered and large numbers of coins derivative of those of Osberht may imply that royal control of minting was in decline before the end of his reign.

Coins in circulation in the ninth century may have numbered hundreds of thousands. The only mint so far identified was at York and it seems unlikely that coins were being struck elsewhere, despite speculation that another mint may have operated in Bernicia. From the 740s onwards archbishops played an important role in minting but no other ecclesiastical figures seem to have been involved, as one might have expected had there been a mint, for example, at Hexham. By the 740s very few foreign coins were being deposited in the region,

Stycas of the ninth century

Fishergate: the excavation of a pre-Viking trading site outside the city walls at York

implying a high degree of royal control over the exchange of different currencies, occurring largely at York. Very few Northumbrian coins have been found outside the region, the few escapes being along the east coast.

The largest hoard yet found and the earliest deposited was of around eight thousand ninth-century coins in a bronze bucket buried in the monastic precinct at Hexham in the later 840s. This hoard is of exceptional size but its location is characteristic – a high proportion of coins coming from royal and monastic sites, among which the royal mausoleum at Whitby is prominent. This distribution may reflect the centres at which coins were used in large quantities – as a convenient means of saving for land purchase, for transactions between different sections of the élite and for taxation. Coins have not been found elsewhere in the small numbers which might represent the settlements of farmers or the lesser aristocracy, and the extent to which these sectors of society regularly used the royal currency other than as a medium of taxation is unclear. There are signs that the circulation of coinage was slower in Bernicia than in Deira, where find-spots are more common, but secondary concentrations of finds have been identified in Tynedale and the Tweed Valley. The coastal distribution west of the Pennines may imply that the principal coin-users in the west were merchants using the beach trading-sites which have been identified at Meols and Whithorn, or the excise men who oversaw their activities.

The Humber provided the main route by which foreign trade entered Northumbria. In the decades around 700, coin finds suggest that this was centred on a *wic* at North Ferriby – where estuarine traffic met the cross-Humber ferry which eventually gave the two Ferribys their names. This may have been established in the third quarter of the seventh century, if it is properly identified as 'King Ecgfrith's town', and implies a notable resurrection of late Iron Age patterns of trade. By *c.* 750 the principal focus had shifted to the royal and archiepiscopal site of York, where stray coin finds and new excavations have revealed a trading site on the right bank of the Ouse in the vicinity of the River Fosse. Here we should envisage the community of Frisian merchants at York in the 780s, mentioned in the *Life of St Liudger*.

Residual pottery found in Viking Age deposits at Coppergate has much enlarged the quantity of pre-Viking Age pottery known from York and illustrates the types of wares in use at this time, with wheel-made cooking vessels and spouted pitchers of Ipswich and Ipswich-type ware and handmade Maxey-type vessels being imported. These imports reflect the east-coast trade routes connecting York with the east Midlands, East Anglia and the south-east (and thence the continent) and York probably acted as an entrepôt for such goods, which have been found in small quantities at Beverley and Wharram Percy. Coppergate also produced small quantities of handmade 'Anglian'-type wares in clearly standardized forms which probably reflect the emergence of a local industry but the absence of such vessels from eighth- and ninth-century occupation sites explored elsewhere in York implies that this production was no earlier than the mid-ninth century, after which it gave way to the vessels characteristic of the Viking period.

Elsewhere there is little evidence for direct contact between Northumbrian ports and the outside world. Several prominent monasteries on both sides of the country were sited close to good harbours (for example, Whitby, Carlisle, Tynemouth and Hexham) and this may have been intentional, allowing churchmen to travel by sea and to extract revenues from commerce. Excavations at Whitby have identified a series of coins from the Rhineland and south-east England but, as

Whitby Abbey from the south, engraved from a drawing of 1772

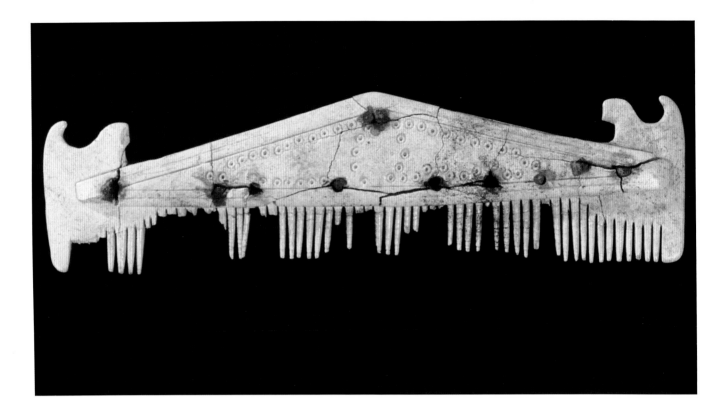

A pre-Viking bone comb from Wharram Percy

the sepulchre of Oswiu's dynasty, the site is exceptional in its close links with the kings of the early eighth century and has produced an unusual profusion of artefacts made of silver. When, in 716, Abbot Ceolfrith retired from Monkwearmouth and Jarrow and set out for Rome, he travelled first on horseback to the mouth of the Humber (North Ferriby, perhaps?), whence he took passage in a coastal ship which, 'before it touched the coast of Gaul, was brought to land in three provinces'. Almost certainly, therefore, he crossed on the Narrow Seas. He sailed on 4 July and reached Gaul only on 12 August. This was probably the normal route taken by seamen and their passengers travelling between Northumbria and the continent: the Frisian, Liudger, may have used the same route on his way to study under Alcuin at York and these same ships probably brought east-coast pottery into York.

Away from the palaces, the monasteries and the principal markets, it is difficult to catch more than a glimpse of the lives of ordinary men. Finds from Wharram Percy could be diagnostic of either an aristocratic or a private monastic establishment. Excavation of one of the homesteads (toft 10) revealed the post-holes of timber-framed buildings associated with thousands of pottery sherds, a smith's workshop, slag, and a coin of the early eighth century, not far from a similar site in the North Manor area which produced another coin, imported Frankish pottery and a bone comb of good quality. Between the two sites were found traces of manufacturing in copper-alloy. A cross fragment of c. 800 and associated burials imply that the church site was already performing some religious functions by this stage.

Literary evidence is anecdotal but serves to confirm the practice of seasonal pasturing, with livestock grazed on upland pastures in the summer in the keeping of shepherds residing in shielings. In Northumberland many settlements were widely scattered, and a bishop and his retinue might find themselves having to carry tents with them and construct temporary shelters of branches for the night. There is no evidence that nucleated villages had made an appearance by this period, the earliest known in the region coming into existence in the late eleventh or twelfth centuries.

Information on diet enshrined in literary works suggests that bread was made from a variety of grains and that joints of many different types of meat were eaten, even dolphin, by monks who used swine lard to grease their leather boots. Excavations at Hartlepool yielded evidence of the butchery of sheep and cattle alongside the consumption of various fruits and coastal fish.

Whether it is valid to describe Northumbria in the eighth and ninth centuries as a prosperous society must remain a matter of opinion. Views will depend in part on the sector of society under discussion. Alcuin's comments clearly imply a royal court which enjoyed a degree of affluence but the Northumbrian peasantry were poor by comparison with their southern counterparts, with low productivity per unit of labour, and of area, providing little opportunity to enter the cash economy or exchange an agricultural surplus for manufactured goods. In consequence there is little evidence of a commercial infrastructure in the hinterland, the few needs of these communities being satisfied by itinerant traders or simple *wic* sites and by barter. There is no evidence of the growing demand for regular 'week-work' which was arguably beginning to emerge in southern England during the ninth century, nor of the nucleation of farms into villages. If the heavy plough and large ox-team were coming into use in Northumbria, it was within a traditional pattern of settlement and land-use characterized by dispersed settlements, comparatively low levels of population and a high incidence of grazing land which enabled large numbers of beasts to be pastured without limiting the spread of better agricultural equipment.

The wealthiest monasteries were the possessors of large estates from which they drew off profits sufficient to enable large bodies of monks to live a life free of agricultural labour and to build and maintain comfortable stone buildings. Their abbots and bishops had accumulated considerable portable wealth and were active as patrons of several branches of art and architecture. Somewhat different arts were patronized by a secular aristocracy whose culture was more obviously a compromise between the pagan past and a Christian present. Over all sectors there presided a monarchy resourced by its control of ecclesiastical patronage, of estates and of a tax system which is little understood but which was based on the hide.

The collapse of the Northumbrian currency before 800 and the minting of a coinage without any significant silver content in the ninth century imply that the Crown lacked the precious metals that were consistently available to southern English kings. Yet the need to maintain taxation necessitated that coining continued up to the reign of Osberht with every sign that royal and archiepiscopal authorities were in control of the procedure. If the coinage was then in some confusion, this is more likely to reflect the savage contemporary dilution of precious metal in Frankish and southern English coins, to the value of which the Northumbrian *stycas* were presumably tied. There seems little reason to doubt that the kingship survived the savage dynastic warfare of the period in comparatively good health.

Since the 790s Church and State had come under intermittent piratical attack from a new direction – from the sea. In 867 an unusually large force of these pirates, or Vikings, would bring the Christian and English leadership of Northumbria to a brutal end, and their subsequent settlement in southern Northumbria was to be one of the most decisive political and cultural events in the history of the north, which ushered in the Viking Age.

This extract from the *Anglo-Saxon Chronicle* details the year 793 (see opposite). The author wrote in terms which express his own view of the Viking raids as a judgement of God. The sack of Lindisfarne was presaged by portents manifested through inclement weather and a great famine. The chronicler's words recall epic scenes from the Old Testament, in which God afflicted the transgressions of his people, the Israelites (British Library, Cotton MS Domitian A. VIII., f. 49v)

CHAPTER 6

The Viking Age

The sun and moon that appear above the cross on this late Saxon grave-marker at Lindisfarne could be a reference to the Day of Judgement. Alcuin interpreted the Scandinavian raids as a judgement of God

The late ninth-century author of the *Anglo-Saxon Chronicle* wrote of the distant Northumbria of 793 that:

> There were excessive whirlwinds, lightning storms and fiery dragons were witnessed flying in the sky. These portents were followed by great hunger and, shortly after in the same year, the ravaging of heathen men destroyed God's church at Lindisfarne.

Such a sea-borne attack was something unknown in Northumbria since the initial arrival of Anglian warriors and even they most probably came overland to the Humber. The earliest known Viking atrocity in England, the murder of a West Saxon royal reeve, had occurred only four years before. The hit-and-run raid on Lindisfarne was probably the work of Norse rather than Danish warriors, straying from their accustomed haunts in the Faroes and Orkneys down the North Sea coast of Britain in search of easy loot. It is the first recorded instance of a Scandinavian raid on Northumbria and heralded the opening of the Viking Age.

Since 792 Alcuin had been at the court of Charlemagne and so was free to vent his frustration on the Northumbrian authorities. He (and presumably his royal patron) took this opportunity to blame the deplorable morals of King Ethelred of Northumbria, the son-in-law of the Mercian Offa, for what was widely viewed as a visitation of divine wrath and he commiserated with Bishop Higebald of Lindisfarne:

> ... the pagans desecrated the sanctuaries of God, and poured out the blood of saints around the altar, laid waste the house of our hope, trampled on the bodies of saints in the temple of God, like dung in the street. What can we say except lament in our soul with you before Christ's altar, and say: 'Spare, O Lord, spare thy people, and give not thine inheritance to the Gentiles, lest the pagan say, "Where is the God of the Christians"?' What assurance is there for the churches of Britain, if St Cuthbert, with so great a number of saints, defends not his own?'
> (Trans. D. Whitelock, 1954)

The coastline at Lindisfarne, looking past the castle towards the priory and modern-day village

The problem was, indeed, a substantial one and Northumbria's saints proved somewhat backward in coming forward in this crisis. The 'E' version of the *Anglo-Saxon Chronicle* records that Monkwearmouth and Jarrow were attacked in the following year and Roger of Wendover may have been using lost northern annals when describing the destruction of Hartness and Tynemouth in 800. The evidence of burning revealed by excavation at Monkwearmouth and Jarrow is certainly consistent with this chronology and the flames were hot enough at the latter to melt window glass. Both sites were temporarily abandoned at approximately this date.

Alcuin urged the monks at Lindisfarne to model their lives upon those of the saints and so deflect the wrath of God, but in reality there was little he, they or the king could do to protect the island church. The coastal locations of many of Northumbria's richest monasteries left them vulnerable to piratical raids. Soon after, the Lindisfarne community removed to the greater security of Norham-on-Tweed. The archdiocesan minster, monastery, school and library at York were safe within Roman walls. The 'Anglian Tower' and a rebuilt section of the north-west wall of the Roman fortress predates the Viking seizure of York. Although Alcuin himself directed attention to York's Roman walls in a lengthy Latin poem, it is not improbable that the new work was commissioned by archbishops made nervous by Viking attacks on other Northumbrian monasteries. Whether or not this is the case, the walls did not ultimately save York Minster. Indeed, the defensible

OPPOSITE: David as worshipper. This is one of three original whole-page miniatures (only two survive) in Cassiodorus' eighth-century psalter, *Commentary on the Psalms*. It depicts King David playing his harp. The second remaining page shows David as warrior. The book may well have been produced during or shortly after Bede's lifetime (Durham, Cathedral Library, MS B. II. 30, f. 81v)

174

nature of the site was what ultimately attracted the Danish invaders. Unless the Durham manuscript of Cassiodorus' *Commentary on the Psalms* is a unique relic, nothing of that exceptional library survived the Viking Age. Other monastic communities disappeared more or less dramatically during the ninth century or reverted to a less rigorous rule, surviving only as small communities of secular canons or single benefices. Even so, a monastery as vulnerable to coastal attack as Heversham seems to have survived into the tenth century in the lee of the Furness peninsula and it is difficult to distinguish between the general silence of the sources and the destruction of religious houses.

The Vikings should not be held accountable for the whole of this decline but their responsibility was far from negligible. The lack of substantial market centres and the general dispersal of population in Northumbria meant that the major churches presented attractive targets for piratical raids and the Vikings were not deterred by respect for Christianity. Churches may even have been targeted by pagans keen to undermine the morale of their opponents. Alcuin was not alone in recognizing the danger posed by such attacks to the Christian faith. Under stress there was a danger that the English would follow the example set by many Irishmen and abandon Christianity in favour of the pagan gods of their persecutors.

The role of the Vikings in western Europe has been under the microscope ever since the revision pioneered by Peter Sawyer. Professor Sawyer questioned the credibility of the clerical victims of Viking

The carving of armed men on the reverse of the grave-marker at Lindisfarne illustrated on p. 173 may represent a Scandinavian raid such as the one that took place in 793.

The Anglian Tower, an internal tower on the west side of the fortress at York, which was constructed when repairs were carried out on a collapsed section of the wall after the end of the Roman period, but before the Viking Age

Pagan Scandinavian mythology provides the subject matter for decoration a cross fragment found and now preserved at Kirk Michael, Isle of Man. The stone fragment is mounted in wood which seeks to continue the outline of the cross

attacks regarding the numbers of Scandinavians involved and the entirely negative descriptions of them, preferring to emphasize instead the more positive aspects of their contribution as colonizers, merchants, artisans and seafarers. The result has been a series of influential studies of various aspects of the Viking phenomenon which have treated them and their culture in a far more sympathetic light.

At the last, attitudes towards the Vikings will depend on the viewpoint of the commentator. From the perspective of the insular community, their sudden and savage depredations ended in destitution, mutilation, death, ransoming or enslavement and sale overseas, the fate which befell the youths captured at Lindisfarne in 793 and perhaps also those brought back to Dublin from Strathclyde, Scotland and Northumbria by the Norse in 871. Such raids injected an extra risk into lives already beset by the threat of harvest failure, disease, accident, enslavement for debt and the blood feud. To argue that the skills shown by Scandinavians in trading, manufacturing and colonization in any respect compensated for their aggression, terrorism and looting is little short of offensive, irrespective of the scale on which that occurred. When an Irish cleric recorded that, 'The Norwegian king, Gothfraid, died of a sudden hideous disease. Thus it pleased God,' he was voicing not just clerical opinion but that of any victim of the Vikings.

This is not to underestimate the forces which lay behind Viking expansion. Eighth- and ninth-century Scandinavia was a mass of pagan communities in the process of rapid social and political change, within which the élite practised polygamy. Successively larger generations were born to the free, warrior classes, who shared the status and aspirations of their parents but had only poor prospects of an adequate inheritance. It was not coincidental that the Viking threat receded within a few generations of their conversion, once Christian priests had suppressed polygamy and stigmatized illegitimacy. The Viking onslaught was fuelled by the same expansion of the élite that underlay the success of Anglo-Saxon warriors twenty generations earlier. In the ninth and tenth centuries well-born young men without prospects at home were forced out into the world, primarily as mercenaries and raiders. Their principal purpose in the early generations appears to have been to amass sufficient resources to enable them individually to return home. Scandinavian armies often dispersed after a particularly lucrative success.

This pattern of behaviour can be traced throughout the Viking Age, as late as the expeditions of Sweyn against England. It was, however, complicated by growing land shortage and inflated land prices in the north, which resulted in the colonization of other parts of Europe.

During the late eighth and early ninth centuries, Norse raiders wreaked havoc among the monastic houses in Ireland and began the settlement of the Orkneys and Western Isles as a staging post. The monastic community on Iona withdrew to Kells in 807 in search of greater security, although the island retained a Christian presence throughout the ninth century. A large Norse fleet under Turgeis was operating off Ireland from 839. Dublin (*Ath-cliath*) was established in 841, followed by further coastal strongholds in the next few years. The Scandinavian domination of the Irish Sea had begun.

A Northumbrian king, Rædwulf, was killed by the Vikings c. 844. Whether those responsible were Norse or Danish is unclear but Northumbria's long coastline made it more vulnerable than any of the other English kingdoms to forces operating from Ireland and several of its neighbours were severely affected, with the Isle of Man, for example, being drawn into the Norse world during the ninth century. A Saxon victory over the Norsemen was recorded in the *Fragmentary Irish Annals* for 851 and may well have occurred in Northumbria, since the several battles known to have been fought in southern England by West Saxons and Mercians in that year were against Danish armies.

Perhaps encouraged by this defeat of their rivals, a Danish fleet wrested control of Dublin from the Norse in 851 but, despite a series of bloody engagements, Danish control proved transitory and Dublin was ruled by Olaf, son of the King of Norway, from 853 until he returned home as king in 871. Olaf was credited with raids against Scotland (*Alba*), Northumbria and Strathclyde, and his successor – his erstwhile ally, Ivar, King of Limerick (died 873) – was termed King of the Norse in both Ireland and Britain, implying a political and military 'overkingship' of the Viking settlements and war-bands throughout the Irish Sea basin. Thereafter, the flow of warriors from Norway probably slackened, with many diverted to the colonization of Iceland. Over the next four decades the Norse on the Irish coast launched fewer and less spectacular raids against their neighbours than hitherto, although Scandinavian forces remained active in wars fought within Ireland.

Northumbria and the Danes

Excepting only the adventure at Dublin in 851, Danish fleets generally preferred to attack western Europe via the continental coast, only crossing to Britain once they had reached the Narrow Seas. Northumbria was comparatively distant and Frankia, Wessex and Mercia took the brunt of the Danish raids during the mid-ninth century. This was to change when the Great Danish Army, which had long been based in the Low Countries, crossed over to England in 866 and overwintered in East Anglia. It was here, on the coastal trading route to York, that the Danes seem to have learnt of the civil war currently underway in Northumbria. The Danes were habitually opportunistic (note, for example, their descent on Winchester *c*. 860, at the death of King Æthelbald). They were also now present in force. The Great Danish Army was not a band of raiders but an army capable of wresting from indigenous kings control of government and taxation in the coin-rich world of Anglo-Saxon England. This army, in 866–7, must have been numbered in thousands, even as many as around ten thousand men.

In the summer of 867 the Danes secured horses and rode northwards, crossing the Humber estuary and seizing York. The *Anglo-Saxon Chronicle* was written only a quarter of a century after the event and its description of the campaign is probably accurate:

> And not until late in the year did they [the two rival Northumbrian claimants to the throne] unite sufficiently to fight the raiding host; and nevertheless they collected a large force and attacked the enemy in York, and broke into the city; and some of them got inside, and an immense slaughter was made of the Northumbrians, some inside and some outside, and both kings were killed, and the survivors made peace with the enemy.

In the *History of the Church of Durham* the Danish seizure of York is dated 1 November and the battle the following 21 March. The battle of York was a disaster for Northumbria more extreme than even those of 633–4 or 685 and it presaged the collapse of the Anglo-Saxon state.

The Danes imposed a client-king on Northumbria to act as a tax collector on their own behalf. There was probably no shortage of royal claimants from the mutually antagonistic royal dynasties prepared to take on the role. The Danes returned to York from the south in 869 for a full year before achieving the conquest of the East Angles in 870 and the Mercians in 874. The author of the *History of the Kings* recorded that the Northumbrians ejected King Ecgberht and Archbishop Wulfhere in 872, in favour of King Ricsige but, in Deira at least, the uprising was suppressed by the Danes.

For the year 875 the West Saxon chronicler recorded that the army split and Healfdene led one part into the north. He over-wintered on the Tyne, imposed his rule on Bernicia, and demonstrated his power by raiding among the Picts and Britons of Strathclyde. In 876 the same chronicler recorded that 'Healfdene shared out the land of the Northumbrians, and they proceeded to plough and support themselves.' Such were the origins of the Viking kingdom of York.

The *Chronicle* account is brief in the extreme but it is sufficient to tell us something about this crucial event. Healfdene's campaigns in the far north imply that he understood the need to control both of the two ancient parts of the kingdom and to impress the formidable nature of his own power on Northumbria's northern neighbours. If anything were likely to thaw the hostility of the surviving Northumbrian aristocracy to his usurpation, it was surely the re-establishment of Northumbrian supremacy and the renewal of the inward flow of tribute.

His thrust northwards was probably what drove the ex-Lindisfarne community at Norham to take flight into western Bernicia. For several of those years in exile (later accounts offer the suspiciously common number of seven) they carried with them relics which included the head of St Oswald and the coffined remains of St Cuthbert, the latter being the greatest Christian talisman to survive the Viking invasions in all Northumbria. Their journey was in later years to become the centrepiece of the histories written at Durham.

The *History of the Church of Durham* places Healfdene's residence at Tynemouth, where he was able to marshal both his army and his fleet. The prominent and already embanked monastic promontory was an important focus of local landownership and government and lent itself to use as a defensible military camp of the kind favoured by the Vikings in Britain. At York, Healfdene had already occupied a defensive site with similar facilities and Tynemouth – the burial place of the saintly King Oswine – had been a wealthy place of pilgrimage before the Viking depredations. Whether it had been reoccupied after the sack of 800 is unclear, but if so Healfdene presumably finished it. The demise of the diocese of Hexham suggests that the abbey there was also a casualty of this campaign.

The most contentious issue remains Healfdene's final settlement of his army. This was described in the *Anglo-Saxon Chronicle* (written *c.* 892) in terms explicit of an apportionment of peasant holdings. The chronicler was distant from this event and it may be significant that his

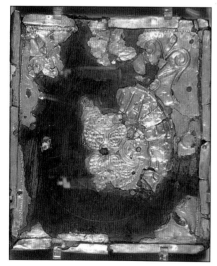

A portable altar found in St Cuthbert's tomb along with other relics. The original altar was made of wood; inscriptions on it resemble the Lindisfarne Gospels and date the original altar to the end of the seventh century. The silver casing was added at a later date when the altar was enshrined as a relic

description of the Danish settlements in Mercia (877) and East Anglia (880) omitted comparable references to their supporting themselves by ploughing. Description of the northern Danish army at York as yokels may be no more than a calculated slur on them by a chronicler writing for King Alfred, in whose eyes the Danes at York were, in the 890s, the most dangerous of the insular Scandinavian lordships. It seems most unlikely that the triumphant Healfdene conferred peasant farms on his followers. More probably, they were established as the new estate-owning élite, with a large group retained in and around York itself as an inflated retinue to guarantee Healfdene's own kingship. The organization of the territory dependent on the royal centre into three 'ridings' probably dates to this period and implies a division of the warriors available to the York kings into three 'shifts', comparable to the division of the West Saxon army credited by Asser to Alfred. If so, the Kings of York would have been able to campaign on a continuous basis, accompanied by a third of the military classes. The notion of a Viking peasant influx into Northumbria or eastern Mercia is a modern myth which has long caused unnecessary complications in ninth- and tenth-century history. Viking ships held a complement of thirty to sixty warrior-oarsmen with little room for passengers. There is no evidence whatsoever that large numbers of peasants bought passage from Scandinavia to England. Incoming women were probably fewer than the men.

Healfdene's reign was extremely brief. His fate is obscure: he was probably killed in Ireland attempting to establish his rule over Dublin. If not, his death occurred on a sea-borne raid against South Wales and

Tynemouth Monastery: the remains of the medieval monastery and a post-medieval cemetery now obscure the site of an important pre-Conquest monastery on a coastal promontory

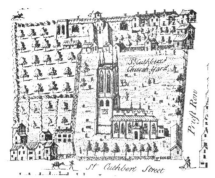

St Cuthbert's Church, Wells, from William Simes's *Plan of the City of Wells*, 1735

Devon (in 877). In either case, his death was a consequence of military defeat, itself likely to have been a blow to his nascent kingship and its military resources. In the aftermath, his successors at York failed to maintain the unity which he had imposed upon the north by force.

Whether or not it had survived Healfdene's attacks, a 'Saxon' kingship in Northumbria re-emerged in the late ninth century in the persons, successively, of Ecgberht II and Eadwulf (died 913), based on Bamburgh. This dynasty retained contact (perhaps even alliance) with other English leaders in Wessex and Mercia, where an interest in the northern Saxons is evidenced by a series of church dedications to Northumbrian saints, as at Wells (Somerset). Their control of north-eastern Bernicia went unchallenged for the remainder of the century by the Yorkshire Danes, whose attention was, for the moment, to be directed to English Mercia.

In the far north-west, the Kings of Strathclyde secured control of Cumberland (as it was henceforth to be called), expanding their

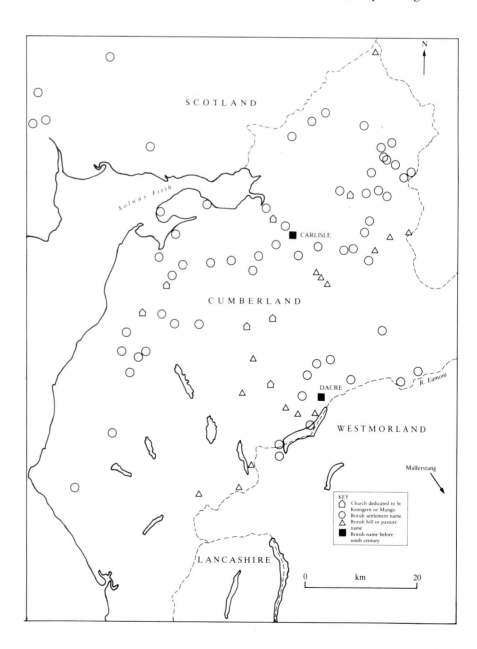

British place-names and dedications to St Kentigern (or Mungo) in north-west Northumbria

181

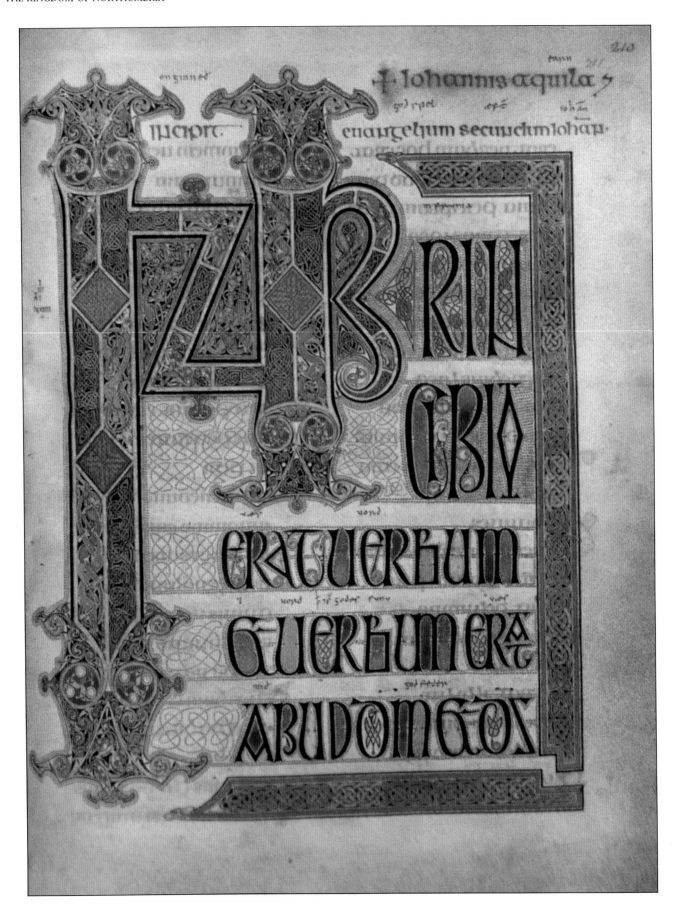

influence down to the Eamont river, where King Athelstan met the kings of both Strathclyde and the Scots on 12 July 927. The chronology of this advance is obscure and it may have been more a phenomenon of the early tenth than the late ninth century. Whether it was resisted or encouraged by the Bernicians is also unknown but the latter is a possibility, the English aristocracy perhaps preferring the protection and patronage of a well-known, Christian neighbour to the Scandinavian powers. The process has left behind a scattering of British place-names and dedications to St Kentigern (or Mungo) in what had been for three centuries a region of Northumbria.

Perhaps the least likely success of this shake-out was the establishment of the community of St Cuthbert at Chester-le-Street. Post-Conquest accounts of this event centre on an intervention in the affairs of Danish York by St Cuthbert through the agency of Eadred, Abbot of Carlisle, then leader of the Lindisfarne community in exile (*History of the Kings*, 884). As it stands, this account is unhistorical but it does provide a version of the sort of political settlement which must have occurred in southern Bernicia. An agreement between the King of York and Egbert of English Northumbria was necessary before the Northern Army could pursue an active role in southern England and there are other signs of reconciliation between the Danes and English Northumbrians during this period, including the resurrection of the mint at York. Given the Christian symbolism of the Cnut coinage, it seems likely that the archbishop was also reconciled to the Danish kings at this stage. What the Durham tradition provides is, therefore, a propagandist and hagiographical view of a real political settlement.

The solution adopted beyond the Tees was to establish the Lindisfarne community at the ancient minster church of Chester-le-Street, with substantial landholdings. This focus of institutional lordship would eventually become the episcopal County Palatine of Durham. For the moment, it provided a buffer between the two Northumbrian kingdoms. In the insular context, this solution to a frontier problem was unique but parallels exist on the continent, where ecclesiastical princes were not uncommon. Henceforth, the influence of the Danish kings would be confined to Deira.

By the 880s, therefore, Northumbria had ceased to exist as a single political and cultural province. The most important fracture was between the ancient kingdoms of Bernicia and Deira, with English control of the former contrasting with Danish kingship in the latter. Both these lordships were centred east of the Pennines but both retained territory on the western plain, southern and central Lancashire being an integral part of the kingdom of York.

That kingdom was founded from the south and allied itself with the Danish lordships in East Anglia and eastern Mercia. In an exceptionally full account of what were probably contemporary events, the Anglo-Saxon chronicler recorded that forces from the Northern Army joined with Danes from East Anglia in 893 for a series of campaigns against West Saxon and Mercian territories which culminated in the battle of Buttington and the first siege of Chester. From Chester they ravaged in Wales then returned to East Anglia via Northumbria 'so that the English army could not reach them'. Their return was presumably via the Mersey crossings into southern Lancashire, since that was the sole frontier shared by English Mercia and Danish Northumbria. Those crossings were not to be forgotten by either side.

OPPOSITE: The beginning of St John's Gospel from the Lindisfarne Gospels, perhaps the most outstanding example of early medieval book illumination. No expense was spared in its production, the highest quality vellum and ink together with approximately forty different pigments being used. The colophon informs us that the manuscript was written in honour of God and of Saint Cuthbert and that the scribe was Eadfrith, who was installed as Bishop of Lindisfarne in 698. A priest named Aldred added the interlinear translation of the Latin text into Old English, while the manuscript was in the keeping of the community of St Cuthbert at Chester-le-Street (British Library, Cotton MS Nero D. IV., f. 211)

Both Northumbria and East Anglia gained new Danish recruits in 896 from a disintegrating raiding force and sent out sea-borne raids to harass the West Saxon coasts, but the Danes in England had lost the initiative to King Alfred, whose stalwart defence had caused this last great Danish host to disband. The military situation drifted towards a temporary stalemate. Danish attempts to profit from a disputed West Saxon succession in 900 were brought to nought by the death of their candidate in 903 and the Peace of Tiddingford in 906 brought hostilities to a close. The Danish ambition to take over every English throne had failed and Wessex remained the most powerful single kingdom in England. At the same time, other Viking forces in Ireland were experiencing even greater reversals of fortune and were arriving in considerable disarray on the western coasts of Britain.

York and Dublin

Against the year 901 *The Annals of Ulster* recorded the:

> Expulsion of the Gentiles from Ireland, from the fortress of Ath-cliath [Dublin] ... where they left a great number of their ships, and escaped half-dead, after having been wounded and broken

The fragmentary *Irish Annals* place this event in 903 but whatever its precise date it was a matter of considerable significance. The survivors of this battle fled to various shores of the Irish Sea, presumably being followed there by the communities of the other, smaller Norse strongholds in Ireland. The subsequent career of one such fleet under Ingimund was described in considerable detail by an Irish chronicler. Repulsed from North Wales by King Cadell, he sought and obtained permission of Queen Æthelflæd of Mercia to settle and was probably granted lands on the Wirral 'near Chester'. Subsequently:

> What resulted was that when he saw the wealthy city, and the choice lands around it, he yearned to possess them. Ingimund came then to the chieftains of the Norwegians and Danes; he was complaining bitterly before them, and said they were not well off unless they had good lands, and that they all ought to go and seize Chester and possess it with its wealth and lands.

The Irish scribe clearly envisaged Ingimund's appeal to the Norse and Danish leaders as a single event, occurring where both could be found together. It has recently been suggested that such conditions pertained in the Ribble estuary, where a *hold* (equivalent to an English 'high-reeve', perhaps the eponymous Agmund of Amounderness) represented the authority of the King of York at a site which he may have placed at the disposal of the Irish Norse gathered around Ivar II (killed 904) and his brother Ragnald. Chester was 'restored' in 907 and the subsequent attack on it was a collaborative effort by Danes, Norse and ex-patriot Irish forces. Their failure may have resulted in Norse and Irish survivors being settled under Danish authority in western Lancashire, resulting in place-names such as Croxteth and Toxteth, beside the more normally Danish Derby and Ormskirk.

The central panel on the cross-shaft fragment at Nunburnholme depicts the Virgin and Child. Other figures include wyverns and perching birds on the shoulders of a large figure, although the latter two are defaced

The Cuerdale Hoard, the largest Viking Age hoard found in western Europe, deposited on the banks of the Ribble, c. 905

The association between the Irish Norse and the Ribble estuary was illuminated by the discovery in 1840, on the banks of the river at Cuerdale, of the largest hoard of Viking Age silver ever found in western Europe. The principal components were approximately 1,300 items of hack silver and bullion bars of characteristic Irish extraction, alongside about seven thousand silver coins. The latter included Arabic, Frankish and Anglo-Saxon issues but the bulk had been newly minted at York. Deposited within a year or two of 905, the hoard does imply a degree of cooperation between Danish York and the Irish Norse. The latter made it their business over the next decade to attack only the rivals of the Northern Army – the Scots, Strathclyde and the 'northern Saxons' of Bernicia, where the death of King Eadwulf in 913 was the signal for a Scandinavian invasion (in 914). According to an apparently well-informed Irish source, this was undertaken jointly by Danes and Norwegians, and similar joint enterprises were alluded to in the vicinity of the Clyde in 913. In Irish eyes, at least, the Irish Norse in exile and the Danes of Yorkshire were in close alliance.

Given the brutal wars between them for control of Dublin a half-century earlier, this alliance may appear surprising but it was probably a political and military necessity. Irish sources noted a military alliance forged by Æthelflæd of Mercia with the northern Celtic kings which can only have been aimed at the Vikings. Edward the Elder of Wessex and his sister were preparing to take the offensive against the Scandinavian lordships in Britain and intermarriage between the leaders of the Dublin Norse and the Great Danish Army had occurred a generation earlier.

In the early years the Northern Army was the senior partner in this alliance, playing host to the Norse, but its very independence was under increasing threat. English armies ravaged the territory of the York kings in 909, probably invading southern Lancashire across the Mersey, and Æthelweard recorded that they were forced to accept the superiority of the now fatally sick King Ethelred of Mercia. Their response the following summer was to invade and ravage Mercia but they were decisively defeated at Tettenhall in the West Midlands, among the dead being two kings, two earls and eight other leaders, including Agmund the *hold*. The Northern Army was never again to take the initiative against the English.

In contrast, the Norse in exile maintained their momentum. They chased the English aristocracy out of Cumbria, forcing the Abbot of Heversham and others to seek new homes under the patronage of the St Cuthbert community. They defeated an Irish fleet off the Northumbrian coast in 912 and a rival Norse fleet off Man the following year. The arrival in Ireland of a Viking fleet from Brittany via unsuccessful raids on Wessex and Wales brought Ragnald much needed reinforcements and both he and his cousin Sihtric (or Sigtryggr) returned to Ireland. The latter remained there to regain Dublin, perhaps *c.* 917 but Irish sources differ as to the date of this event. Ragnald, another cousin Gothfrith and the bulk of the Breton Norse returned to Britain and attacked and defeated the English Bernicians, establishing Ragnald temporarily as the ruler of Bernicia. Scandinavian rulers once more seemed capable of acquiring control of all Northumbria.

Norse and Saxon

Ragnald's policies in southern Bernicia were less conciliatory towards existing interests than those pursued by the Danish kings. His confiscation of large territories in the lowlands of County Durham from the community of St Cuthbert was long remembered there. Ragnald gave these estates to his protégés, Scule and Onlafball, and their warriors, although English tenure survived in the poor hill country to the west. For a Norse king eager to conciliate the Danish community and so inclined to respect their landed interests, such inroads into ecclesiastical lands were the only way to reward his own followers.

The sudden collapse of the southern Danelaw seems to have taken Ragnald by surprise. Æthelflæd reinforced the Mersey frontier in 914–15 with *burhs* at Eddisbury and Runcorn but it was the storming of Derby by her troops in 917 which began the rout. The Danes at Leicester submitted to her without a fight in 918 and the Northern Army was negotiating for Æthelflæd's protection when she died at Tamworth on 12 June.

Although her daughter held the Crown for a further year, Æthelflæd's death ended the political and military independence of Mercia. This did not assist the Danes. Instead, her formidable brother imposed his own overlordship on Mercia, and its dependants then usurped the

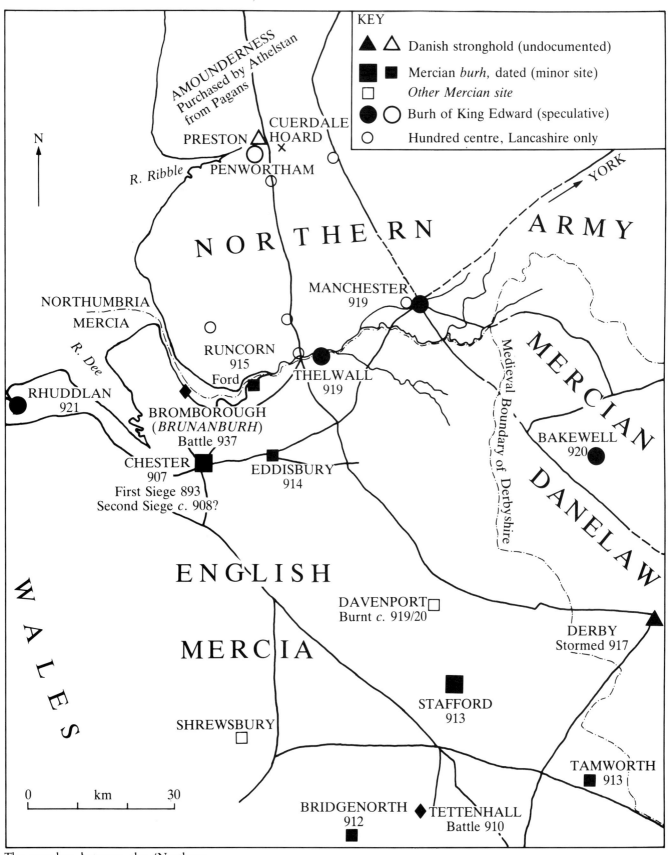

The marches between the 'Northern Army', based at York, and English Mercia

Mercian Crown, taking over the Mercian forces and reducing the last free Scandinavian stronghold south of the Humber, at Nottingham. There was every likelihood that the isolated Danish lordship of York would submit. In what was probably little more than an exercise in damage limitation, Ragnald marched south from Bernicia and seized York, thus at the eleventh hour combining the limited military resources of the last two insular Scandinavian armies and seeking to stem the tide of Edward's conquests on Northumbria's southern frontier.

The response from Edward was swift, with the construction of *burhs* at Thelwall and Manchester 'in Northumbria' in the winter of 919 and further activity in and around the Mercian Danelaw to follow. If Ragnald were to be successful in his policy of confrontation he needed to attain approximate equality with the military resources of his opponent. Without outside assistance, this meant that he had to raise the Mercian Danelaw against Edward. It was presumably on this errand that Sihtric, from Dublin, raided English Mercia (probably from the Mersey frontier) and razed Davenport – perhaps a market at the manor of that name near Congleton, Cheshire, on the very frontier of the Danelaw. The Mercian Danes, however, remained quiet. They probably judged Edward the likely victor and their disinclination to revolt against him doomed the Norse strategy. In 920 all the northern kings including Ragnald recognized the supremacy of King Edward and sought his protection.

Both sides gained limited objectives from the submission. For Edward it ended the confrontation and left him free to consolidate his new territories, both English and Danish. For Ragnald and the other northern rulers it represented recognition of their rights as territorial lords by a king whose power was now superior to their own, severally or in combination. It was presumably at this stage that Ealdred recovered the kingdom of Bamburgh, lost to Ragnald through the battles at Corbridge, and the St Cuthbert community may have regained their Durham estates.

It seems likely that Ragnald paid an even higher price for peace than this would imply. The *burh* at Manchester already represented a threatening encroachment on Northumbrian territory from south of the Mersey and it was probably at this stage that southern Lancashire (between Ribble and Mersey) was extracted from the kingdom of York and placed under the control of Edward as King of Mercia. Its hundredal organization, hidation, assimilation into the diocese of Lichfield and its peculiar name all imply that it came into southern English hands. Of no particular value in terms of its tax revenues, this moss-ridden frontier region was of considerable strategic significance and brought Edward oversight of the Ribble estuary – crucial to links between Dublin and York. It has been suggested that an undocumented Edwardian *burh* underlies the Norman castle of Penwortham.

The accord of 920 was no more than a temporary truce between two parties, neither of whom would have felt bound by its terms had an opportunity arisen to press their own advantage. Neither of the principals lived long enough to break it but Ragnald's successor, his cousin Sihtric, does seem to have raised the northern Danelaw on Edward's death in 924, if only because coins portraying motifs identical with those from York were issued by the mint at Lincoln. Sihtric and Athelstan established an accord in 926 but this was

The ruined Viking Age chapel or church of St Patrick at Heysham

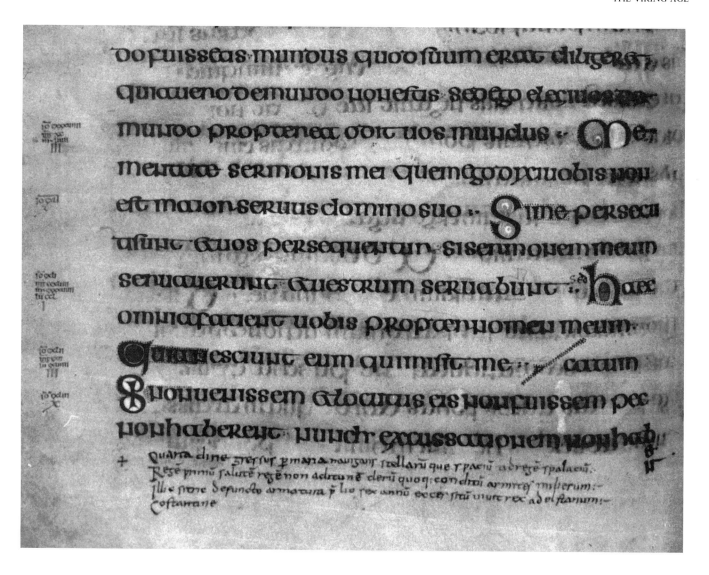

The Durham Gospels was originally created on Lindisfarne but was preserved by the community of St Cuthbert when they fled the island. At the foot of this page a scribe added in 927, when the community was settled at Chester-le-Street, an abbreviated version of a poem in praise of King Athelstan, heralding 'this united England' (Durham, Cathedral Library, MS A. II. 17, f. 31v)

largely on English terms. The marriage between King Sihtric and Athelstan's sister was a Christian ceremony at royal Tamworth in Mercia under Athelstan's tutelage and can only reflect Sihtric's recognition of his superiority. Sihtric's rejection of his wife and Christianity the following year constituted a re-opening of the conflict but his death soon after provided the English king with the opportunity he needed. In 927 Athelstan 'succeeded to the kingdom of the Northumbrians'.

This bland statement by a southern chronicler disguises a usurpation more blatant even than that perpetrated by Edward the Elder in Mercia. In both instances their sole blood relationship was through the queen, a link identical with that between Harold and Edward the Confessor in 1066, but whereas the West Saxon and Mercian kingdoms had been in close political association for generations, the usurpation of 927 was unprecedented. Northumbria had normally been independent of the southern 'overkings' of the eighth and ninth centuries, despite King Offa and the enthusiasm with which West Saxon chroniclers wrote up the fleeting achievements of King Ecgberht. Under its own kings and archbishops, Northumbria had retained a strong sense of its own distinctiveness.

Northumbrians of all persuasions and ethnic origins viewed the events of 927 with outrage. Athelstan was resisted by the house of Bamburgh as King of English Northumbria and by Sihtric's ill-prepared heir, Gothfrith, who was expelled by Athelstan from Strathclyde (whence he had been raiding northern Ireland). With their individual efforts swept aside, the northern rulers had little option but to accept Athelstan's acquisition of the kingdom of York – ancient Deira and Elmet, as well as those areas west of the Pennines attached to it by the Norse – and Ealdred of Bamburgh, Constantine of the Scots and Owain of Strathclyde recognized his superiority and 'renounced idolatry'. The meeting occurred on 12 July near the boundary between the Kingdom of York and Strathclyde, probably at the ancient monastic church site at Dacre, where a unique group of four tenth-century stone bears still stand as sentinels around a much later church.

An embroidered stole was presented to the shrine of St Cuthbert at Chester-le-Street by King Æthelstan in 934. The detail shown depicts the prophet Joel

One of the four stone bears which stand sentinel around the church at Dacre

OPPOSITE: The frontispiece of Bede's *Life of St Cuthbert*, copied at Winchester in the tenth century, showing Athelstan's gift of it to St Cuthbert's shrine at Chester-le-Street in 937 (Cambridge, Corpus Christi College, MS 183, f. 1v)

W.G. Collingwood's high quality line drawings of the Giant's Thumb, a free-standing sandstone cross of the tenth or eleventh centuries, at Penrith (Collingwood, 1927, p. 146)

The roof of this hogback from Heysham has clear *tegulae* and the side wall features, amongst other characters, a human with arms up-raised, a quadruped and a carnivorous animal, all somewhat crudely carved

Within his new territory, Athelstan did what he could to reconcile the aristocracy to his kingship. He gave rich gifts to the minsters of Beverley, St Cuthbert and York, so reinforcing his image as the champion of Christianity versus the pagan Norse. He further consolidated his father's control of Lancashire by purchasing Amounderness from its pagan lords and conferring it on the Archbishop of York, his most powerful lieutenant in the region, and he maintained the mint at York, producing a coinage which advertised his commitment to Christianity with a representation of a church or shrine.

His rule was, however, fundamentally that of an outsider and much resented. His overwhelming military power posed a threat so great that the Celtic kingdoms of the far north were encouraged to re-align themselves with the Dublin Norse.

Athelstan ravaged Constantine's Scotland in 934 but was unsuccessful in detaching him from his allies. Olaf (or Anlaff) Guthfrithson of Dublin married Constantine's daughter and the allies brought their plans to fruition in 937 with a joint invasion of Northumbria. They appear to have anticipated a welcome within Deira and there is certainly no record of opposition to them there.

Although 'Florence of Worcester' recorded Olaf's landing in the Humber, his account may have been influenced by the much later arrivals of Danish forces and of Harald Hardrada there (in 993 and 1066 respectively). The Humber is an implausible point of access to Northumbria for a fleet from Dublin. The Ribble was a far more likely landfall. Constantine probably joined Olaf in Lancashire after a journey overland from Strathclyde, marching thence south with him for the expected trial of strength with the English in north-west Mercia. The battle of *Brunanburh* was a dramatic encounter, the epic qualities of which were captured by several Anglo-Saxon authors. Although the battle site is a matter of dispute, the place-name is cognate with Bromborough in Cheshire and this estuarine plain is the most plausible battlefield so far offered. The result was a crushing victory for Athelstan and his brother. As an English chronicler boasted:

> Then the Norsemen, the sorry survivors from the spears, put out in their studded ships on to Ding's mere, to make for Dublin across the deep water, back to Ireland humbled at heart. Also the two brothers, king and *ætheling*, returned together to their own country, the land of the West Saxons, exulting in battle. They left behind them the dusky-coated one, the black raven with its horned beak, to share the corpses, and the dun-coated white-tailed eagle, the greedy war-hawk, to enjoy the carrion, and that great beast, the wolf of the forest.

Yet for all the poet's praises, when Athelstan died, Olaf was able to make himself King of York (939–41). The ease with which he overran Northumbria and the Mercian Danelaw implies that his reception in 937 had been more welcoming and his defeat less damaging than Saxon writers were prepared to admit. Only after the storming of Tamworth and a siege of Leicester did Olaf recognize the loss of the five boroughs to King Edmund. The terms acknowledged his kingship of York but he was required to convert and concede superiority to Edmund. In subsequent years Edmund's lieutenants suppressed the Norse kingship of Sihtric II (son of Sihtric I: ?941–2) and he himself ravaged Strathclyde, detaching it from the Norse alliance by conferring it on King Malcolm of Scotland, of whose subservience West Saxon kings were henceforth to be more confident.

Edmund's assassination provided renewed opportunity for Northumbrian rebellion but his heir, Eadred, once more reduced the north in 946. The Northumbrians retained separatist ambitions sufficient to elect Eric Blood-axe as their king in 948 but, despite a limited victory, lost their nerve in the ensuing campaign and bought peace. Another Dublin–Norse candidate was briefly recognized at York in 952 but, in what appears to have been a last attempt to secure significant outside aid against the West Saxon kings, Eric was re-instated, only to be killed on Stainmore in 954 as the Northumbrians were once more brought to heel. This proved their last throw and the southern Northumbrians bowed to the pressure exerted on them by successive West Saxon monarchs and henceforth fell into line with the southern kingdoms, recognizing the line of Cerdic as kings.

The simple long panel from York Minster is occupied by a large human figure flanked by two smaller figures, who are sitting holding a rectangular panel in front of the larger figure. The figure may represent the risen Christ

Culture and Ethnicity

In no part of mainland Britain were Scandinavian cultural influences so widespread and profound as in the Viking Age kingdom of York. There alone was 'Scandinavianization' allied to deep-rooted political separatism and only there, too, was the initial Danish influence reinforced by Norse kings and their warriors during a period which lasted (if somewhat intermittently) over eighty years. Scandinavian words and syntax became enshrined in the place-names and even the field names of Yorkshire, Lancashire and Cumbria; runic inscriptions occur throughout the period and those at Pennington and Conishead Priory imply the long survival of spoken Scandinavian in Norman England. A dialect derived from Norse survived far longer in the hill country of Cumbria and parts of the Dales; motifs, sculptural forms and decoration characteristic of the Viking world are a common reminder of the period.

BELOW, RIGHT: A typical carving of the Viking Age in the Irish Sea area, this wheel-headed cross at Maughold, Isle of Man, is decorated with knotwork, swirls and animals, all in shallow relief; LEFT: Runic inscription on a fragmentary cross-shaft in Jurby church, Isle of Man

The 'warrior's tomb', Gosforth. Processions of warriors, with spears and shields, can be seen on this hogback tomb dating from the early tenth century. One end of this tomb is carved with a figure thought to be carrying a book and a staff. It was initially believed, however, that the items in question were a shield and an axe, and hence the name of the 'warrior tomb' was devised

Yet the number of immigrants is unlikely ever to have amounted to a high proportion of the regional population. Despite the deaths in battle, sales into slavery and general disorder, the pre-existing gene pool of Northumbria surely continued as dominant. The relationship between culture and ethnicity is one of the most complex issues of the period.

The Viking impact on Northumbrian culture was strongest in those regions where significant numbers of Viking warriors were granted (or otherwise acquired) estates. The rulers of the core of English Bernicia were successful in the long term in keeping out both warriors and Scandinavian cultural influences. None of the characteristically Scandinavian types of stone sculpture, for example, are to be found in Northumberland. The dissemination of Scandinavian culture and language occurred, therefore, through a social hierarchy headed by Scandinavian kings, via the warrior gentry and aristocracy who were the principal beneficiaries of their patronage.

Healfdene's assumption of the kingship of Northumbria was accompanied by a general settlement of his army which was probably far closer in style to the Norman settlement of southern Britain than that parodied by the West Saxon chronicler. If the place-name evidence reflects this process of estate-seizure and re-allocation, it must be significant that typically Danish '-by' names are concentrated in lowland Yorkshire within a single day's ride of the city of York. The distribution reaches as far north as the valley of the Tees but no further. A substantial influx of Scandinavian personal names is also represented, particularly in the type of place-name known as a 'Grimston' hybrid, formed from an Anglo-Saxon generic such as '-ton' or '-ham' to which a Scandinavian personal name or other element (such as 'kirk') has become attached.

Interpretation of the place-name evidence has tended to lend itself to an interpretation centred on the settlement of numerous peasant farmers. There are, however, other factors which need to be given consideration when reviewing the spread of Scandinavian place-naming, which is only a late chapter in a complex history of renaming already identifiable in the seventh century. Prominent among these factors is the disestablishment of the Church. Richly endowed monasteries and minsters were important landowners in Yorkshire before 867 but far less so in the tenth century. The Viking conquest apparently transferred erstwhile Church property (both movable and immovable) into secular hands. Although it survived, the archdiocese of York emerged from the Viking settlements impoverished, implying the loss of most of its estates. Ripon aside, the monasteries of Yorkshire lost their

Viking Northumbria: place-names attached to civil townships which derive from Scandinavian languages

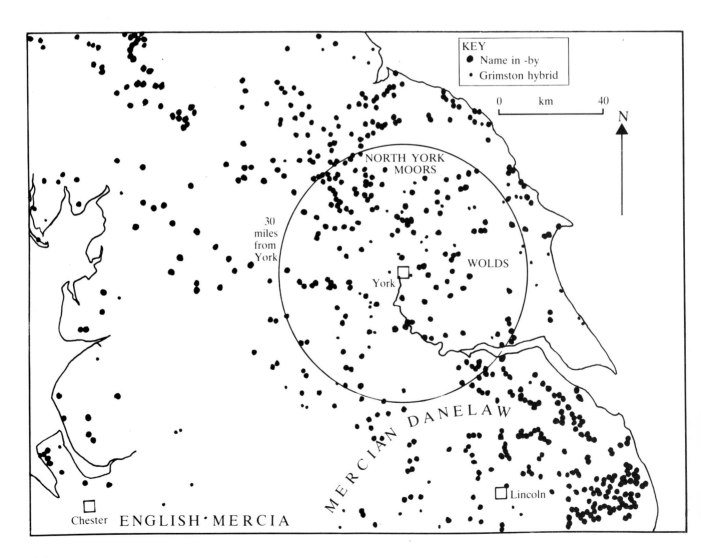

Two Viking Age relief figures from cross-shafts at Sockburn. RIGHT: A warrior armed with sword and spear and equipped with a helmet; LEFT: A warrior equipped with helmet and spear

A hammer-headed cross at Addingham, of a type common in areas of Northumbria open to Norse influence from the Irish Sea

lands. When Ragnald dispossessed the St Cuthbert community in large parts of County Durham, he was arguably following a well-established procedure for rewarding and settling Scandinavian warriors. The precedents that he followed were surely those set by the Danish Kings of York.

The passage of ecclesiastical estates into the hands of a new Viking gentry necessitated the fragmentation of many large and integrated estate systems into smaller manors or farms attached to individual households. Sub-division required major changes to the organization of renders, with tribute collection giving way to a more intensive and localized manorial economy. There came into existence the plethora of small manors which were to be such an important component of Yorkshire in the Domesday survey. Since such units were novel, many presumably had no pre-existing place-names appropriate to their new boundaries. In other instances the opportunity to rename was, perhaps, too good to pass by, the new name serving to advertise the status and cultural perspectives of the new owner.

It is unlikely to be an accident that Hiberno-Norse place-names in southern and eastern Cumbria cluster in the vicinity of the erstwhile monasteries at Heversham and Dacre (but only south of the Eamont), in areas where English and Danish names were otherwise dominant. The situation at Whithorn is precisely comparable, implying that here, too, Viking warriors displaced the clergy from their estates.

This disestablishment of the Church was a fundamental element of the Viking Age which the grants to northern churches by subsequent English kings were unable to reverse. It coincided with the loss of half of the northern dioceses. The history of the St Cuthbert community was so extraordinary that it should be considered entirely unrepresentative, although it may be significant that its new-found estates included those hitherto owned by other religious houses.

In these circumstances, areas of patronage which had been exclusively ecclesiastical fell into the hands of a local aristocracy newly enriched by the spoils of conquest. One such area was the employment of the masons and sculptors whose services had hitherto been monopolized by the Church. In place of the religious symbolism of the pre-Viking Age there emerged an art form of lower relief but far richer in motifs and antecedents. This industry rapidly abandoned the artistic unity which was so characteristic before 867, increasingly fragmenting into local schools of craftsmen working on local commissions, with little evidence of contact with their neighbours.

The pre-existing art forms of standing crosses, decorated slabs and grave covers continued to dominate production but the new patrons expected very different ornamentation. Warriors acquainted with Ireland or Man commissioned the types of monuments with which they had been familiar there, with the result that wheel-crosses and their derivatives, such as hammer-headed crosses, became fashionable, particularly in western Northumbria. Another characteristic of the period is the replacement of the conservative, stylized and somewhat classical pre-Viking decoration with heavily stylized animals and flamboyant, abstract patterns reminiscent of the decoration of Viking Age brooches and weapons. This process was not universal, for more disciplined and typically ecclesiastical pieces continued to be produced by some schools probably for Church patrons, as at Stonegrave, Leeds and several sites in and around York itself. However, churchmen were probably now only a small minority of the patrons offering commissions.

A shallow relief carving on the face of a 'hogback' fragment at Sockburn depicting two warriors mounted on ponies or horses equipped with reigns, with their long tails knotted to keep them away from the ground

Elsewhere, a warrior aristocracy expected to see representations of themselves or their kind fully accoutred in arms, and the depiction thereof became a widespread subject for relief carving, featuring prominently in the Tees Valley and North Yorkshire. This style is conspicuous on the numerous pieces surviving at Sockburn, where a fragmentary hogback tombstone is decorated with a naturalistic relief featuring men on horseback. Similar motifs abound in Man, as on the cross-shafts in Maughold churchyard, although the latter are generally interpreted as representations of figures from pagan mythology.

The resulting artistic achievement was quite distinct from Scandinavian, Irish or Anglian antecedents but drew heavily on each in creating a new 'Anglo-Scandinavian' art which was all but unique to the Viking Age kingdom of York. Motifs borrowed direct from pagan mythology were commonplace: the figure of Thor fishing for the world serpent at Gosforth is mirrored by the bound and horned 'devil' at Kirkby Stephen; several scenes depicting the battle of Ragnarok can be found in Man; numerous depictions of Sigurd are apparent in Northumbria (as at Heysham and Halton, Lancashire), and again in Man.

This cocktail of pagan and Christian symbolism is best explained as the work of artisans working within a continuing Anglian tradition with its roots in the Christian past, producing commissions for an aristocracy heavily influenced by Scandinavian culture. That aristocracy was experiencing a gradual shift from paganism and polytheism towards Christianity and monotheism. Sculptors were able to combine

The 'ship-burial' at Balladoole, Isle of Man. The pattern of nails found during war-time excavations suggested to the excavators that this Viking grave lay within a ship. When the excavation was back-filled, stones were arranged in the shape of the ship below

fundamentally Christian monuments with decoration featuring a wealth of Celtic and pagan motifs. The result was a sculptural renaissance of exceptional vigour, with a substantial output, the finest products of which display considerable artistic skills.

In northern parts of the Isle of Man numerous burial mounds were heaped over furnished Viking graves and what may have been a ship-burial was excavated during the last war at Balladoole, south of Ronaldsway. On Man, therefore, a Scandinavian aristocracy conformed to traditions deriving from Scandinavia but they were none the less open to Christian ideas. Their burials occurred in existing Christian cemeteries and their use of stone for grave markers was British, not Scandinavian, in origin.

On the mainland such men were rarely buried under barrows in an ostentatiously pagan style, although exceptions do occur in areas more open to western influences, as at Heskett in Cumbria. Elsewhere burials accompanied with appropriate weapons and other grave goods occurred in pre-existing graveyards. Such is the likeliest origin of the decorated silver bowl found in the cemetery at Ormside, Cumbria, in the shadow of a fine late Saxon church. At York, two of the small group of burials excavated at St Mary Bishophill Junior were accompanied by grave goods, deposited, on coin evidence, *c.* 920. The coinage minted at York for King Cnut (*c.* 895–905) made prominent use of the Christian cross in a fashion which must imply a firm accord with the Christian community and its archbishop. A similar coinage of approximately the same date bears the name of the otherwise unattested 'King Sievert'. The St Peter coinage, so called after its obverse

The Ormside bowl, a decorated silver bowl of pre-Viking date and probably made in Northumbria. It was buried in the churchyard at Ormside, presumably with a Viking Age inhumation

Mound covering a warrior burial of the Viking Age in the cemetery of Jurby, Isle of Man. A second mound can be seen on the horizon

legend which abbreviates the Latin *Sancti Petri Moneta* – 'St Peter's money' – was probably an archiepiscopal issue of *c.* 905–19, after which Norse kings adapted the form by adding symbols which advertised their own paganism. The common occurrence of the hammer of Thor beside the St Peter motif on the coinage of Sihtric I epitomizes the political message being broadcast by a Norse king keen to unite Northumbrian opinion behind his own kingship against the West Saxons.

King Guthfrith, the second Danish king known to us, was buried in York Minster, the most important religious site within the city where his power was centred. Many members of the Scandinavian aristocracy clearly followed his example, both there and at the churches nearest their own estates and within their own patronage. Such men might be equipped and buried with typically Anglian weapons, as was an inhumation of the late ninth century at Wabley (Yorkshire). Men like the Manx residents Melbrigdi (at St Michael) and Aleif Ljotolfsson (Ballaugh) raised crosses for their own souls or those of the departed and these were but two in a steady stream of sculpted stones, the survivors of which far outnumber those of the pre-Viking Age, on the same sites and more besides. The ideological stance of even the Norse leadership was hybrid and the Scandianavian warriors were prepared from the earliest period of settlement to make important concessions to the Christianity to which they eventually conformed.

Perhaps the most significant departure from pre-existing forms of sculpture was the hogbacked tombstone. This was an insular category of monument, almost precisely limited in distribution to the kingdom of York but including the late additions to that realm in southern and central Cumbria. Based on the reliquaries of Viking Ireland and censors of Anglo-Saxon England, these massive slabs stood on edge, with both

Coins of Viking Age York, including a silver penny which combines the symbolism of St Peter with that of Thor's hammer

The 'saint's tomb' at Gosforth is decorated with two deeply incised monsters on each side and a dragonesque beast in interlace on the pitch of the roof

faces sculpted, often into the likeness of a house. The more ornate examples have bears' heads at the extremities, tegellation on the roof and relief decoration of the walls, the emphasis being on interlace and zoomorphic designs. Such slabs are invariably found on church sites and they were probably erected lengthways over graves, but the style is distinctly un-Christian, perhaps implying that either the individual being buried, or those doing the burying, were pagans. Among the finest are those at Gosforth, a site which benefited from the presence of an exceptionally talented sculptor whose work is best known in the slender free-standing cross there. The most impressive group now on display, however, is of eleven examples excavated during renovations from the foundations of Brompton Church. Comparable groups in varying states of decay are extant at Sockburn, Penrith and at Lowther, on one of which is a representation of a Viking longship in shallow relief. The concentration of hogbacks in areas where Norse kings were free to exercise patronage, such as Teesdale and Cumbria, implies that they were particularly favoured by the followers of the Norse kings and their descendants.

Speculation concerning the ethnicity of those responsible for such monuments poses unanswerable questions. In the first generations of the several Viking settlements, paganism was presumably very largely the preserve of the incomers but this could have changed rapidly as Northumbrians were more generally attracted by the culture of the élite, elements of which probably found echoes in deep-rooted attitudes already present. For an ambitious Deiran, conformity to the culture and language system of the Scandinavian kings at York offered significant advantages, and merchants and artisans supplying the court were necessarily encouraged to produce the goods it demanded. The same could be said for those in contact with any Viking household. The Viking kings presided over a mixed community, the two halves of which are hopelessly confused by the marriages which occurred between them.

An undated Northumbrian *wergild* list, written early in the eleventh

Three of the eleven hogbacks preserved [at] Brompton Church. The foremost has prominent, muzzled end beasts and the [sid]e is decorated with a geometric design [of] trapezoidal panels containing inter[lace]

century, probably preserves much from the era of Viking kings. The compensations and status groups within it were expressed in Northumbrian terms (king, *ealdorman*, archbishop, *ætheling*, thegn, *ceorl*, *gesith* and so forth), with occassional parallels between Anglian and Scandinavian terms, such as the *hold* and 'high reeve'. Although it was probably written by or for Archbishop Wulfstan II, this document provides a backdrop appropriate to the career of the first Archbishop Wulfstan. Himself an appointee of the West Saxon kings deriving from the Mercian Danelaw, Wulfstan I's support for Northumbrian separatism under Scandinavian kings led to his incarceration by King Eadred in 952. Even if his attitudes were shaped by concern for the autonomy of his own archiepiscopacy, it is difficult to imagine a more powerful demonstration of the values shared by both Scandinavian and English, pagan and Christian. York valued its autonomy and long sought an alternative to the usurpation of Cerdic's descendants.

Economy and Society

The disestablishment of the Christian Church and the transfer of its lands to a Scandinavian or 'Scandinavianizing' gentry had major repercussions for Northumbrian society and its use of the agrarian surplus, now focused on secular as opposed to clerical households (see p. 171). That the rural community had access to the same range of tools

Detail from a hogback of *c.* 900 at Sockburn showing one of several beasts impeded by ropes, possibly part of a salvation scene

The Viking Age cross at Gosforth. This is probably the finest single piece of stone carving of the Viking Age now extant in Northumbria, dating from the first half of the tenth century

as in southern Britain would seem to be demonstrated by the large hoard of iron equipment, including scythe blades, axe-heads and a pick-axe, deposited at Hurbuck (County Durham) in the late ninth or early tenth century. Additionally, the period witnessed a series of important developments, particularly in coinage and urban life.

The settlement of part of the Danish army under one of its foremost leaders brought to Northumbria a large quantity of silver which derived from other parts of Britain and western Europe. Thereafter repeated raids by warriors from the Northern Army were presumably expected to bring back more silver and other transportable goods of value. Danish leaders did not habitually mint coins themselves, normally using those of their neighbours or weighing out bullion but, perhaps at the instigation of the archbishop, the Danish rulers of Northumbria began minting during the 890s. With these silver pennies, Northumbria at last came into line with southern Britain and Frankia, after a period of approximately a century of nonconformity during which the necessary silver was apparently unavailable to its rulers.

Although the Cnut coinage is comparatively widespread and numerous, by far the largest group was found at Cuerdale. This hoard also illustrates the second influx of Viking Age silver to the region, brought in as bullion and hack-silver by the Irish Norse in the early years of the tenth century. If much of this bullion stayed in Northumbria to be

A detail from the south face of the Gosforth cross, depicting a horseman sometimes interpreted as the god Odin, with bridle and downturned spear, with a mythical beast below, which may be Mímir

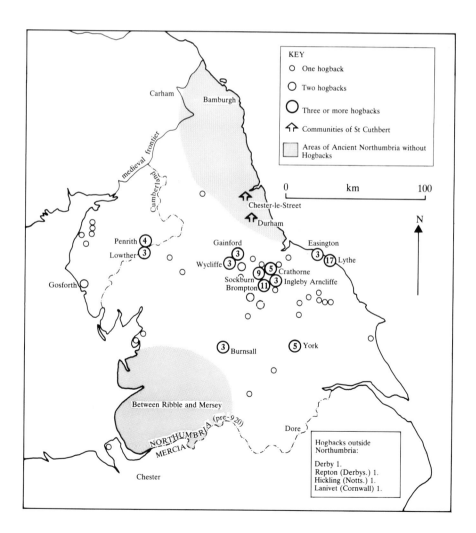

The distribution of hogbacks in Northumbria

Hoard of iron tools from Hurbuck, *c.* 900

re-utilized and circulated there as coin or ornament, then this second injection may have significantly enlarged the quantity of silver available to the Viking kings for coining and for the exercise of patronage.

The Viking kings monopolized this influx of silver. The Saxon kings at Bamburgh had no such resource and are not thought even to have continued the styca coinage of the pre-Viking Age. This is a powerful argument against the existence of a Bernician mint in the earlier ninth century. Viking silver is represented by a large number of finds, including mixed hoards, such as the silver Viking-style jewellery, hack-silver and coins deposited *c.* 920 at Goldsborough and the several silver thistle brooches of vast size found on Newbiggin Moor, Orton Scar and in the vicinity of Penrith, in Cumbria.

The renewal of a silver coinage stemmed, therefore, from political rather than economic events, just as had its demise in the late eighth century (see chapter five). Although there were periods when only low-weight coins were minted (as in the swordless St Peter coinage), the York mint survived the various political changes of the following half-century without breaks in production of more than a very temporary nature.

The coinage apart, the principal economic development of the period was the surge in urban activity at York. Viking Jorvik is justly considered one of the most important archaeological sites in Britain and only here have there been found structures comparable to those dating from the refoundation of the Viking stronghold at Dublin in *c.* 917. The work of the York Archaeological Trust has done much to make the city's development intelligible, through a series of well-publicized excavations and the prompt publication of reports thereon.

Viking Age York rose within the protection of a defensive cordon which included the north-west and north-east sides of the Roman fortress wall and earth ramparts which were refurbished at this stage with a clay bank. South-west of the Ouse, the deposition of Anglian artefacts in the eighth and ninth centuries intensified in the Viking

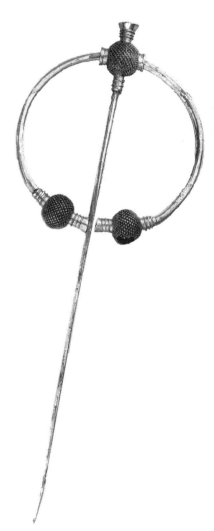

Massive silver thistle brooch found on Newbiggin Moor

Age, when burials occurred in the cemetery of St Mary Bishophill Junior and carved stones ornamented the church. The medieval street system owes little to that of Roman York and the substantial Old Scandinavian element in the street names may imply that it was laid out in the tenth century. Only at this stage does it become certain that the Roman bridge over the Ouse was abandoned. The settlement density in the old *colonia* was increasing, with new church foundations during the century, and nearly a hundred sites have so far provided archaeological evidence of Anglo-Scandinavian activity. Although little of this has been observed in structural form, four rectangular timber-framed buildings excavated in Skeldergate provided Carbon[14] evidence of construction under the Viking kings or within the century thereafter.

Excavations on the Lloyd's Bank and Pavement sites north-east of the Ouse provided similar evidence of structures. At the latter, eleven successive timber buildings began before *c*. 850 and continued into the eleventh century, and finds from several sites are indicative of settlement and crafts which included the manufacture of shoes and other leather goods, jet and amber working, spinning and weaving. It is, however, the Coppergate excavations which provide the most comprehensive evidence for buildings and crafts in Viking Jorvik.

This fragment of a cross-shaft from St Mary Bishophill Junior shows two standing figures dressed in shin-length gowns. The left-hand figure carries a horn on his belt while the figure on the right has a short sword

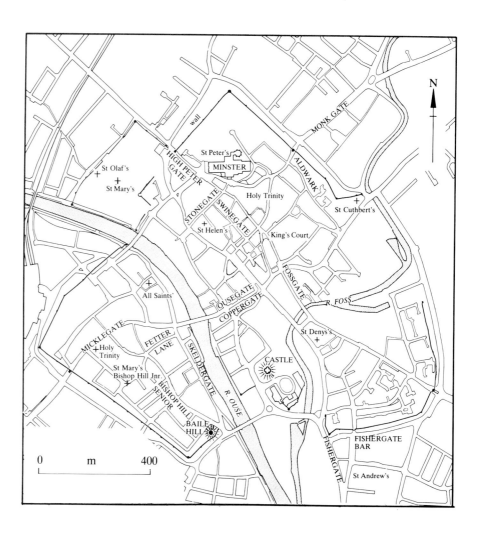

Viking Age York. The modern road plan s simplified

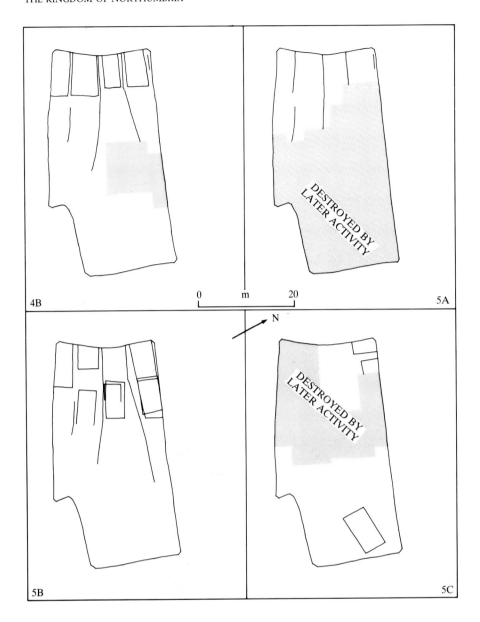

0   m   20

N

4B

5A

5B

5C

Coppergate, the excavations. Phasing is taken from the reports by the York Archaeological Trust. 4B: early tenth century; 5A: mid-tenth century; 5B: c. 970–1000; 5C: early eleventh century

The approximately 1,000 m² excavation at 16–22 Coppergate lies on a spur of land between the Ouse and Foss on which both construction and burial had taken place in the Roman period. Thereafter the site received a thick layer of silt from flooding, into which a scatter of pits and other features were dug, predominantly in the eighth century, from one of which came a helmet and spearhead. Before the Viking seizure of 867 glass-making was also present, but more intensive activity stems from the Viking Age, with initial division of the site soon after the conquest. It was not until the 930s (phase 4B) that four recognizable tenements were defined by wattle fences, the lines of which were to change little over the next thousand years. Each enclosure contained structures built of wattles supported on posts, their gable-ends to the street, behind which long rear yards were used for a variety of purposes, including the disposal of rubbish. These structures were used for crafts of several kinds.

Two adjacent tenements ('C' and 'D') seem to have housed coiners or die-cutters, from whose activities survive a die for a sword St Peter penny of Sihtric I's reign, a trial piece of the coiner Regnald, who worked for King Athelstan *c.* 928–39, and a damaged coin die of Athelstan. These activities continued at least until the reign of Eadwig (955–?9). Other finds of pottery crucibles and metallic waste suggest that gold, silver, iron, lead and copper-alloy were all being worked on site by craftsmen who habitually manufactured metal products in several media, including the coins and dies for which the site has become famous.

The dramatic evidence of an upturn in urban activity in tenth-century York and many other English towns has generally been interpreted as trade-led, with the upsurge of activity being stimulated in this instance by:

> the seafaring enterprises of the new inhabitants, who voyaged far and wide bringing back exotic luxury goods such as animal furs and skins, ivory and silk for sale in York. In the export field, the city's prosperity may well have owed much to the woollen industry.
>
> (Hall *et al.*, *1000 Years of York*, p. 11)

Early tenth-century wattle-built structures, excavated at Coppergate, York

but such interpretations may be somewhat optimistic and owe rather too much to the ongoing search for positive aspects of the Viking impact.

What distinguishes York in the Viking Age from its Anglian predecessor is not so much the special enterprise of its inhabitants (which is not measurable) but the wealth, size and permanence of its consumers. It is a characteristic of Anglo-Saxon descriptions of the Danelaw that Scandinavian leaders and their large retinues, even armies, were perceived as stationed permanently within the strongholds from which they took their names. York, the stronghold which eventually gave its name to the shire, was the best example of this phenomenon, housing the most powerful and wealthy dynasties in Scandinavian Britain.

Unlike the English kings who preceded them, the Viking kings had no responsibilities in County Durham, Northumberland, Lothian, or on the shores of the Solway to draw them away from York. Except when leading their troops, they had, therefore, little reason to leave York for any period of time. Unlike their predecessors, they minted silver coins to an internationally recognized standard, which enabled their merchants to engage more effectively in trade outside the region and encouraged foreign merchants to bring their goods to the marts of York. The finds of foreign coins at York imply that they were less careful to collect the coins of their neighbours entering York than were the West Saxon kings and they may have imposed fewer restrictions on merchants generally. Their own coinage was probably primarily a medium of taxation and the tax-take of the Viking kings would have

Objects of amber found in excavations at York

maintained the circulation of their coins, as well as their own comparative wealth, until much of it was paid over to southern kings in tax or tribute during the tenth century.

Their presence and that of the warriors on whom they lavished their patronage resurrected the Roman practice of recycling the agricultural surplus through the urban households of the landholding nobility. The palace of the king, situated probably at *Conungsgurtha* ('King's Court') on the site of the Roman east gatehouse, was the engine which drove the demand for goods within the city and that demand was lubricated by the large amounts of silver with which the Vikings had arrived. Their purchasing power and taste for exotica attracted merchants. Artisans settled within the city so as to manufacture as close as possible to market. They, in turn, recycled their profits into consumption in a spiral of economic activity which fed through to the suppliers of bulk goods and necessities, like agricultural produce and woollen clothing.

High-value goods aimed at wealthy consumers certainly dominated the imports identifiable through archaeology. Amber, jewellery and whetstones came across the sea from Norway and the shores of the Baltic and these same routes brought oils, fats and animal hides from the Arctic. Pottery, ivory and silks came from the Mediterranean, and

York: a view from the south across the city towards the minster

jewellery, pottery and quern-stones from the Rhineland. York clearly maintained close contacts with Ireland and the Scandinavian colonies of northern Scotland, though whether these were predominantly trading or social is unclear.

In terms of the pottery in use, York remained comparatively insular. At Coppergate, locally manufactured wares had a virtual monopoly in the late ninth and early tenth centuries and retained a dominance during the period *c.* 930–75 but alongside an increasing influx of wares from the Mercian Danelaw and further afield. Pottery does not travel well, so manufacture close to a major market made good commercial sense. However, local dominance was threatened by the mid-century by the importation of good-quality glazed wares from outside the region. Local artisans could offer no immediate response to these.

To place responsibility for the economic boom at York on exports such as woollens is to ignore the sudden inception of this phase of the city's history. Recent examination of the bones from Coppergate suggest that, besides a few meals of golden plover and red deer, the local diet was dominated by beef rather than mutton or lamb, with dairy produce coming in from outside the town, probably through regular markets. Pigs, fowl and geese were, perhaps, kept in the city and eels caught close by but there is no indication of the mutton which provided such a large part of the diet at Lincoln in the tenth century. Yorkshire was to be cattle country until the twelfth century, at least, as it had been since the Roman period.

Nor did other sites in Northumbria experience the same sort of urban renaissance witnessed at York. Coin finds are scarce excepting only the hoards which represent the wealth of individuals. With the exception of the coastal trading site at Meols, only Whithorn has produced evidence of trading activity in the whole of western Northumbria but the bulk of this belongs to the eleventh century. Pottery, known as York 'd' ware, found at Thwing, York and Beverley, probably derives from a kiln in East Yorkshire, suggesting that, in the richest part of the hinterland, a degree of market activity was present. However, this seems to have been restricted in scope and may have been short-lived. Outside York, no sites certainly had markets active in the early tenth century. The regional economy away from York and the East Riding remained entrenched in a cycle of subsistence, in which the élite consumed the agricultural surplus, with little market penetration other than via the households of the aristocracy. Markets were typically on or near frontiers (as at Stockport, on the Mersey frontier, and perhaps Winwick and Berwick). The result was a low level of mercantile activity and a material culture that was impoverished by contrast with eastern and southern England. With so few artefacts, settlements are hard to identify.

It is difficult to overemphasize the role of the court of the Viking kings at York and its impact on the culture and prosperity of that erstwhile ecclesiastical city. The city community probably played a leading role in the political uncertainties of the mid-tenth century and their nervousness of West Saxon rule may have been due in part to fears of economic disaster under non-resident kings. That an abrupt recession did not coincide with the demise of the Viking kingship is an indication that the final settlement of this thorny political issue guaranteed the interests of the city, its merchants and its artisans. So did the kingdom of York – the first, the oldest and the greatest Viking kingdom in Britain – succumb to West Saxon rule.

CHAPTER 7

Northumbria and England: 954–1054

Politics, Culture and Community

In 954 the *Eoforwicingas* – the 'York-folk' – recognized the inevitability of southern kingship, withdrew their support from Eric Bloodaxe for the last time and made the best deal they could. It is only at this stage that it is possible to start speaking of England, in place of the West Saxons, Mercians and Northumbrians, and it must be significant that the term emerges within the half-century following this event.

With the question of military supremacy at York decided in their favour, the West Saxon kings could afford to compromise over the political settlement. There can be little doubt that local customs were respected and law-making left in the hands of the local aristocracy, as in the Mercian Danelaw. This guaranteed existing rights over property. Local autonomy in legislation was confirmed by King Edgar in the 960s and probably lasted into the next century.

Our understanding of the role of the kings in Yorkshire depends heavily on eleventh-century evidence but there seems little reason not to backdate several prerogatives to 954, such as their right to various royal pleas and the heriots of important thegns. The kings certainly exercised stringent control of the York mint, which enjoyed favourable treatment under all kings bar Ethelred, as a centre of die-cutting as well as striking.

English kings rarely visited the north or spent more time there than absolutely necessary, preferring to leave its government in the hands of royal lieutenants, *ealdormen* (later earls) and the archbishops. These *ealdormen* were generally selected either from the house of Bamburgh (Osulf, Uhtred) or from south of the Humber (Oslac, Ælfhelm) and care was taken to avoid power becoming attached to any one family. Since York could only be governed effectively by men with local resources, royal estates were placed in the hands of the earls, leaving eleventh-century kings with very few manors between the Humber and the Tees.

Coin of King Edgar minted at York

The house of Bamburgh shared the hostility of Alfred's descendants to the Vikings but their commitments beyond the Tees and antagonism towards them at York may have encouraged the kings to appoint Mercians to the earldom of York, although neither Oslac (exiled in 975 at Edgar's death) nor Ælfhelm (murdered in 1006) ultimately retained royal confidence.

The earls probably occupied the palace complex at York and provided war-lordship and secular patronage within the old kingdom, retaining household soldiers much as the kings had done. The archbishops also played an important role in administration – there are signs that Wulfstan II at least was active as a judge – but York probably retained a good deal of self-government, the local merchants and the territorial aristocracy of the region forming a closed political establishment led by men of the rank of *hold* or 'high reeve'. Such men spoke a dialect which was unintelligible to southerners, peppered with Scandinavian words, sound-changes and mannerisms. They paid taxes assessed on the carucate, counted their money after a Scandinavian duodecimal system of *ora* and met in local wapentake courts rather than hundreds. Under their patronage the culture of the Viking Age lived on until the Norman Conquest. The 'gate' street-names of York, Stamford Bridge and elsewhere are just one type of relic of the period. The three Ridings also survived the English Conquest and, indeed, the following millennium, only to fall victim to another southern government in 1974.

After his unwelcome show of independence, Wulfstan I was imprisoned, then probably 'retired' south to political extinction at Dorchester in 954 (the *Chronicle* account is ambiguous). It was in that diocese that he was buried at Oundle in 956. Archbishops were

The Gainford cross-shaft fragments exemplify the Scandinavian influence apparent in the early tenth century. The three figures carrying books are carved in an Anglo-Scandinavian style, possibly copied from the cross at Auckland St Andrew. If the bird is attacking a serpent and the beast at the foot of the carving is the wolf Fenrir, then this is a clear illustration of Scandinavian mythology

This fragment of a cross-head at Durham dates from the eleventh century. The centre-piece features the cross and the Lamb of Christ

henceforth recruited from the Mercian Danelaw, whence clerics could be expected to share something of the cultural and linguistic background of the Yorkshiremen while drawing on a longer tradition of Christianity.

During the next quarter-century, the Danelaw embraced monastic reformation. A small number of estates in Yorkshire were granted to the nearest reformed houses at Ramsey and Peterborough. The northern archdiocese was granted by King Edgar to St Oswald, one of the leaders of this movement, but there were to be no new monasteries in the north, probably because of the poverty of the see. That York was, henceforth, generally held in plurality with Worcester implies that its revenues were deemed inadequate to support the dignity of an archbishop but the practice fell foul of the reformed papacy during the eleventh century and was discontinued.

At York, the households of the earl and archbishop and perhaps many others of Yorkshire's landed aristocracy served to preserve the focal role of the town in the administration and economy of the region. There were few other settlements with any of the characteristics of towns in Northumbria, the most obvious of the latter being Pocklington, Penwortham, Bridlington, Tanshelf (all modest Domesday *burhs*) and Durham.

The kings may have offered the Northumbrians tax concessions. In southern Lancashire, Domesday Book equated six carucates with a single hide, implying that the area was taxed very lightly. Whether this was standard across Northumbria or peculiar to a region which had arguably become detached in 920 is unclear, but there are signs that the administration of Northumbria was subsidized from the south. Insufficient charter evidence has survived for Yorkshire to be confident of the general tax status. The archbishop's great lordship of Sherburn-in-Elmet was assessed at ninety-six carucates in 1086 but only thirty-four hides in 963 when granted by the king to a certain Æslac (but this hidation was clearly incomplete). The 1086 carucage of Newbald (twenty-eight carucates and two bovates) approximates to the hidage (thirty *cassati*) when granted by King Edgar to Earl Gunnar in 963. On balance, the treatment of *Inter Ripam aet Mersham* was probably unique. Elsewhere a carucate was probably equivalent to the Old English hide.

Attempts were made, therefore, to treat Yorkshire as an ordinary part of the kingdom of England but its size, the scarcity of royal assets, its distinctive culture and its recent autonomy always made it something of a cuckoo in the English nest. The local community was neutralized rather than won over and the process of integration had barely begun before the second Viking Age opened once more the prospect of Scandinavian kingship in England. That York's lack of sympathy for union with England was no mere anachronism has recently been highlighted:

> The idea of backwoods northerners being so impertinent as not to appreciate the splendid unity offered them by the West Saxon Kings . . . is . . . as unpalatable to some historians as the picture of William the Bastard making mistakes is to others.
> (Kapelle, *The Norman Conquest of the North*, p. 3)

Northumbria's separatism was deep, old and not so easily set-aside as that of Mercia.

The political changes of the mid-century had little impact on the economy or demography of York itself, which remained prosperous and dynamic, retaining existing links in the Scandinavian world. The mint was, or had already been, re-activated by King Eadwig, from whose coiners a lead trial-piece was discovered in recent excavations. York's mint was to be one of the most continuously active and vigorous in late Anglo-Saxon England, with coins struck here and at Chester particularly common among finds of late English coinage in Scandinavia. These exported coins suggest a trade deficit with York's northern trading partners.

Archaeologically, there is no significant break between the Viking kingdom of York and the Norman Conquest. Finds from various city-centre sites imply that numerous trades, such as bone comb manufacture, textiles (including linen, wool and silk), shoe-making, leather work and ironwork, were characteristic throughout. Attempts to divide the pottery into distinctive period groups have been refined no further than the recognition of a broad classification of material of *c.* 850–1100 as section II, dominated numerically by late Saxon grey wares, with a sub-division (III, 1000, or more probably 950 to 1075, based on the analysis of a rubbish pit excavated in Bishophill and confirmed by work on finds from Coppergate. In phase III large

The foundations of the late Saxon church of St Helen's on the Walls, York

The semi-basement buildings at Coppergate under excavation

quantities of Stamford and other east Mercian wares were used at York alongside a small range of continental imports.

At Coppergate, the buildings along the road frontage were reconstructed *c.* 970–80 with semi-basements featuring massive horizontal oak beams acting as retaining walls supported by closely spaced posts. These were residential buildings occupied by artisans working in jet, amber, and perhaps silk, and turning wood. During the early eleventh century, these buildings were augmented by the construction behind them of a post-founded rectangular building (8.4 × 4.6 m), protected by a storm-water gulley and thought to have been a warehouse associated with the nearby waterfront. Comparable tenements have been found fronting Micklegate, Skeldergate and Fetter Lane. In all respects, York's merchants and artisans appear to have thrived throughout the period. York, therefore, had achieved the necessary critical mass during the first Viking Age to maintain momentum as an urban centre even without the catalyst of a silver-rich royal court. Yet it was probably still the urban establishments of the earl, the archbishop, archdiocesan clergy and the principal leaders of the local community that provided the engine of an urban economy which proved impossible to duplicate elsewhere in the north without their presence.

The Church

This impression of economic well-being is confirmed by renewed commitment to church building, perhaps to be associated with the energies of Archbishop Oswald (972–92). The earlier tenth-century graveyard at St Mary Bishophill was augmented by the construction of the church, the layout of which was influenced by upstanding Roman material, some of which was quarried for the building fabric. St Helen's-on-the-Walls was similarly shown by excavation to have been constructed in the later tenth century, directly on Roman mosaics, and concentrations of fragments at St Deny's, All Saint's, Pavement, St Sampson's and St Crux all imply churches on these sites. While late Anglo-Saxon York did not rival London in respect of urban churches, it was the scene of considerable church building, most of which was probably funded by its wealthier householders.

There are similar signs of church-building in the countryside. St Martin's at Wharram Percy probably began in the second half of the tenth century as a timber church which was replaced in the eleventh century by a two-celled stone church, on lines best seen today at Escomb or Ledsham. It was this second phase which was associated

Vertical view from the tower of St Martin's Church, Wharram Percy, during excavation. The foundations of the first stone church are clearly visible and a small number of post-holes may imply an earlier church built in timber, although later medieval burials under the church floor have seriously eroded the earliest evidence

The entrance of the early Anglo-Saxon church at Ledsham, which originally opened into a two-storey porch. This was extended upwards to make a tower in the later Saxon period. The decorative surround was replaced in the Victorian period

OPPOSITE: Norton Church, an impressive salient crossing church, probably built in the eleventh century

with burials in the cemetery covered by limestone slabs. Elsewhere, there was considerable investment in stone churches, from *c*. 990 through to the Norman period, to augment those which had survived the Viking onslaught. The distribution of these buildings was not uniform. The St Cuthbert community was responsible for several on estates in their possession – including Staindrop and the important salient crossing church at Norton (Cleveland) – while secular patrons were responsible for others in the eastern lowlands, such as St Gregory's, Kirkdale, where a building date of 1055–65 is confirmed by an inscription on the sundial. The eleventh-century iron work which embellishes the door of Stillingfleet Church is even more evocative of the patronage of a 'Scandinavianized' aristocracy. Several churches, such as Wharram-le-Street, hitherto assigned to Norman work-manship, have recently been re-categorized as buildings originating in the late Saxon period and the number of late pre-Conquest towers still standing is impressive – as at Ovingham, Newburn, Billingham, Kirk Hammerton and Appleton-le-Street. Barring only the two churches at Heysham, the ruinous St Patrick's and St Peter's, there are no examples of pre-Conquest masonry surviving in Lancashire and barely any in Cumbria, suggesting that building in timber continued in western Northumbria into the post-Conquest period, as it did in Cheshire. To place this in context, the eleventh-century St Andrew's Church on

The sundial at Kirkdale is located inside the porch above the south doorway of the nave. It is divided into three panels; the sundial itself and two inscription panels. The Latin inscription translates: 'Orm the son of Gamel bought St Gregory's minster when it was utterly ruined and collapsed and he had it rebuilt from the foundations [in honour of] Christ and St Gregory in the days of King Edward and in the days of Earl Tostig'

The iron hinges and other fittings of the church door at Stillingfleet were fashioned in the eleventh century in a style reminiscent of Viking Age stone work. Figures reminiscent of Adam and Eve (top left) are juxtaposed with a dragon-ship, dragon-headed hinges and interlace

Fishergate, York, was also constructed in timber, and if so important a church as Chester-le-Street was only rebuilt in stone in the 1050s, the prevalence of timber churches in the poorer west is hardly surprising. Notwithstanding this, the quantity of pre-Conquest churches which do survive in the eastern lowlands implies that there, at least, the medieval parish system was now coming into being.

Although most of these churches were arguably small and staffed by single priests, there were concerted efforts to bolster the communal life at St John's Beverley, Durham and York itself. Attempts to convert Durham to a monastery were fiercely resisted by the canons but a succession of conscientious and able archbishops set about constructing dormitories and refectories at St John's and York (and Southwark in Nottinghamshire. in the southern quarter of the archdiocese) to enable the secular canons to conform more closely to the Lotharingian style of communal life then coming into vogue in England. However, progress was slow and the buildings were only completed at the personal expense of Archbishop Ealdred (1060–9). Athelstan had made efforts to add to the lands and income of these communities and his example was followed by King Cnut. Several earls certainly granted estates to the St Cuthbert community but the major churches probably lost far more to the senior aristocracy in lapsed tenancies and sequestration than they

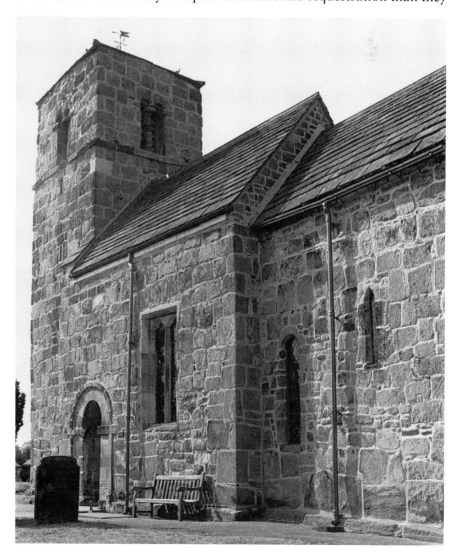

ABOVE: The late pre-Conquest church tower at Billingham; RIGHT: Kirk Hammerton boasts a fine pre-Conquest tower and church. The church was retained as the south aisle of the larger medieval church

were to gain. Archbishop Oswald recorded the estates lost by his church in the recent past, some of which had been purchased by Archbishop Oscytel at considerable personal expense. It seems clear that tenure of the northern archdiocese could be a daunting financial commitment.

Excepting only those implanted into it at the highest level, the later Northumbrian Church appears to have been intellectually undistinguished and most of its personnel were probably poorly educated and little acquainted with continental reforming pressures. Wulfstan II, the 'wolf' of the famous sermon to the English and an active law-writer under Ethelred and Cnut, was a capable outsider placed at the head of the northern archdiocese. It was he who attempted to bring the Northumbrian Church into line with recent thinking further south, framing the 'Law of the Northumbrian Priests' as a guide to his staff. That a Bishop of Durham should have fathered and recognized a daughter of rank sufficient to marry into the house of Bamburgh demonstrates that clerical marriage was commonplace and widely acceptable. However, the forfeit of Helperby to Archbishop Oscytel 'because two brothers had one wife' does imply that flagrant violations of ecclesiastical law could be disciplined.

The gulf between the personal religion of the handful of southern churchmen and the intellectual environment in which they found themselves remained to the end of the period. The northern archbishops preferred to be buried not in York Minster but in the new monasteries of the East Midlands from which most had originated.

These rock-cut graves at Heysham have been associated with the ruined Viking Age chapel or estate church of St Patrick. The separate sockets at the head of several probably held memorial stones

OPPOSITE: The disinterment of St Cuthbert from a twelfth-century copy of Bede's *Life of St Cuthbert* (British Library, Add. MS 39943, f. 77)

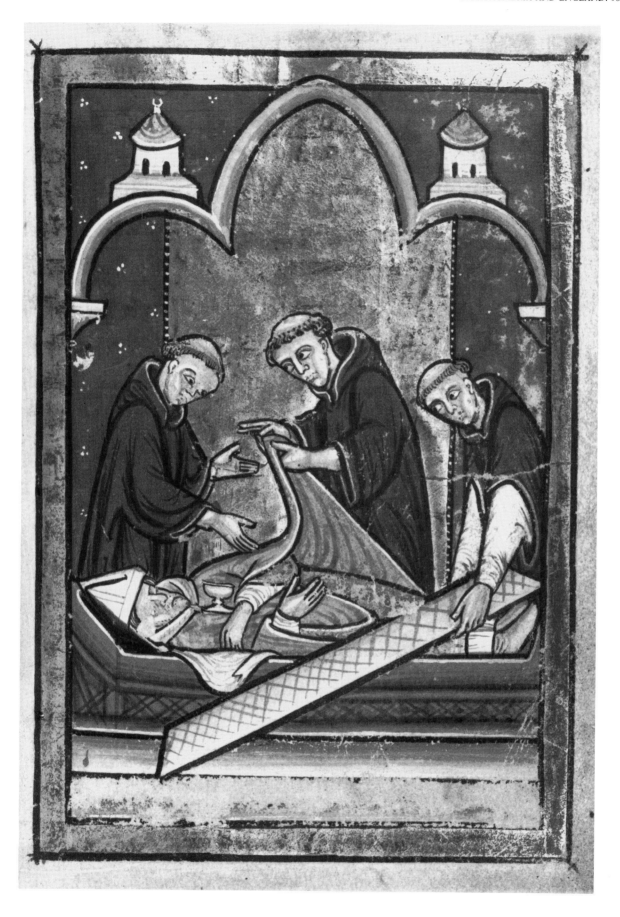

A characteristic of the reforming monasteries was their enthusiasm for the cults of the saints. This was not a new phenomenon for the monasteries of the age of Bede had fostered numerous cults. The late Saxon period saw the 'export' of several important northern saints to southern houses. King Oswald was exhumed from Bardney (Lindsey) and removed to Gloucester as early as 909 and this was followed by Wilfrid's removal to Canterbury, Benedict Biscop's from Monkwearmouth to Thorney, Patrick and Aidan to Glastonbury and Oswald's right arm from Bamburgh to Peterborough. Eleventh-century York was without major relics but Beverley had St John and Whalley claimed St Tuda. Durham eventually had St Cuthbert when, on returning from Ripon, Yorkshire, where they had sought temporary refuge from 'pirates' (almost certainly Vikings), the canons of the community of St Cuthbert decided to occupy a new and more defensible site on a great bluff in a loop of the River Wear. A sacrist there early in the eleventh century collected numerous other northern relics from Tyningham, Hexham, Tynemouth and Jarrow. These became a stockpile of powerful talismen which were of relevance to the territorial claims of the community. The coincidence of this outbreak of relic-hunting with the second Viking Age implies that the canons expected their trophies to provide real assistance against the Danes. Durham's relics made it the foremost centre of pilgrimage in the north, to the financial advantage of the community, but Beverley and Whalley may also have featured in this respect.

Shallow relief of a figure attended by snakes on a Viking Age cross at Whalley. St Patrick may be intended

An aerial view of the city of Durham

The Second Viking Age

The formidable military resources and preparedness of Edward the Elder's sons and grandsons deterred fleets from the Scandinavian homeland from attacking England while also controlling the lesser Viking kingships of the Irish Sea. Edgar's premature death in 975, aged only thirty-two, brought his son Edward, still only a youth, to the throne and enabled his opponents to react against the reformed wing of the Church. There ensued a muddled and regionalized struggle for power in England in which some elements of the senior aristocracy (particularly in eastern Mercia and East Anglia) lent their support to the monks while others (particularly Ælfhere in western Mercia) attacked them. In 978 King Edward was murdered, apparently by the enemies of monasticism, and his even younger half-brother, Ethelred II, succeeded to the throne of the English in the following year.

The power vacuum at the centre and the disarray in the regions were not lost on Viking observers. In 980 Southampton was attacked by a small fleet and Cheshire was ravaged by 'a northern naval force' – presumably Norse ships based in Scandinavia or the Isles. Although the main pressure was to come from the Danes, attacks from the west were to be significant over the next quarter-century. Ethelred's long reign was not to end until 1016 and, although it was not quite the dismal succession of disasters portrayed retrospectively by the Anglo-Saxon chroniclers, it was dominated by Viking attacks and culminated in Danish seizure of the throne itself.

Northumbria was rapidly embroiled in the conflicts. The vehemently pro-monastic 'C' version of the *Chronicle* recorded that Oslac, the Earl of Yorkshire, was driven into exile in 975,

> over the heaving waves, the bath of the gannet, the turmoil of waters, home of the whale; a grey-haired man, wise and eloquent, he was shorn of his lands.

He was, therefore, presumably a partisan of monasticism. The origins of the next earl, Thored, are obscure but Archbishop Oswald died in 992 and was replaced by the Abbot of Peterborough, so the earl was at least able to work with a reformer. Thored was responsible for contributions from Yorkshire to the defence of the North Sea coast against the Danes and appointed joint-leader of the great fleet assembled in 992 at London to attack the Vikings at sea. Despite his leadership of a contingent of Anglo-Danes, it was his co-commander, *Ealdorman* Ælfric of western Mercia, whose treachery was blamed for their failure and Thored's forces appear never to have come to grips with the enemy.

Confidence in the English cause remained high until 991, the year of the disaster at Maldon and the first Danegeld. Although it has been suggested that this was a turning-point, Thored was still able to raise Yorkshire for Ethelred in 992, implying that opinion there still anticipated an English victory. All this was to change in 993, when a large Danish army crossed direct to eastern Scotland and attacked the north-eastern coasts of England, sacking Bamburgh, where they captured much booty. Thereafter the fleet came into the Humber and ravaged the coastal regions on both sides of the estuary. The large force raised to oppose them refused battle and took to flight. In the opinion of one post-Conquest commentator, 'Florence of Worcester',

One of the two Viking Age crosses in the churchyard at Whalley

the treachery of the English leaders was due to there 'being Danes on the father's side'. His reasoning was probably deductive but the episode certainly smacks of treachery, with a secret agreement reached between leaders from Yorkshire and Lincolnshire and the Danes. Henceforth the Yorkshiremen stood aside, sending no aid to Ethelred, their territory apparently immune from Danish attack. With Sweyn of Denmark increasingly set on the English throne, his cultivation of this pocket of sympathetic opinion is entirely understandable. Not until 1013 did Sweyn return to the region and then only to receive the immediate surrender of Yorkshire and the Mercian Danelaw.

Ethelred's conflicts with the Danes left his northern sympathizers in remote Bernicia vulnerable to attack. Bishop Ealdhun's decision to move the community of St Cuthbert to Ripon, then Durham, was taken to avoid 'pirates'. Although the move was subsequently shrouded in miracles and manifestations of Cuthbert's wishes, it was a rational response to troubled times. The new site soon proved its worth, withstanding a siege by the Scots in 1006. Earl Ælfhelm of Yorkshire was murdered by Ethelred during the course of this year, so no help could be expected from Yorkshire. The elderly Earl of Bamburgh left it to his son, Uhtred, the bishop's son-in-law, to gather an army, defeat the Scots and relieve Durham. Delighted with the result, Ethelred made Uhtred Earl of both Bamburgh and Yorkshire.

A cross-head found in the foundations of the chapter house at Durham. This eleventh-century scene features the crucifixion, with Christ attended by Longinus and the sponge-bearer, with figures bearing crosses and books on the two lateral arms of the cross-head and the eagle of St John on the vertical arm

Uhtred's career was covered at length in a late eleventh-century tract, *Concerning the Siege of Durham*. He was probably the most committed of Ethelred's earls in the latter years of his reign and was rewarded with the hand of the king's daughter in marriage (his third wife). He allied himself with one Styr at York who was opposed to the pro-Danish attitudes of other leading citizens and forged an alliance of sorts with the senior churchmen of the region. However, his rule was in defiance of the majority opinion in Yorkshire and was heavily dependent on the fortunes of the English monarchy. He was unable to resist Sweyn in 1013 but resumed his support for Ethelred as soon as that was practicable, campaigning with Edmund Ironside in north-west Mercia in 1016. Yet the temporary interment of Sweyn's body at York in 1014 was probably an accurate indication of opinion there. Cnut occupied Yorkshire in 1016 and allowed Uhtred's enemies to assassinate him at Wighill.

With Uhtred's death, attempts to rule Yorkshire in the interests of the West Saxon dynasty through the Bernician earls lapsed. His murder threw Northumbria beyond the Tees into revolt against Cnut, with dire consequences. Yorkshire was entrusted by Cnut successively to one of his principal lieutenants, the Norwegian Eric of Hlathir, then Carl, *hold* of York and son of Uhtred's murderer, and lastly Siward, a man of obscure origin but a Viking to the core. For the first time in three-quarters of a century, southern Northumbria was subject to a king with

The present-day Bamburgh Castle overlooking the North Sea

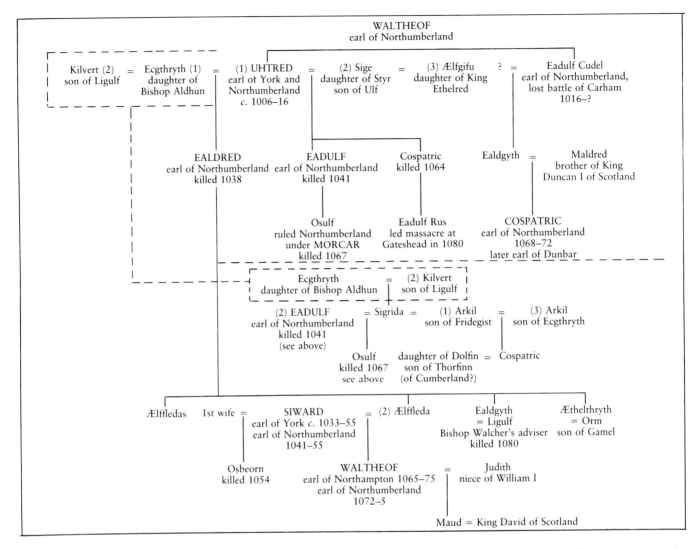

Family tree of the House of Bamburgh

whose lordship they could easily identify. Cnut was an infrequent visitor to the north and his policy of delegating royal power to a handful of great men reduced the gap which separated the Earl of York from the status of a king. The reign was understandably a period of prosperity at York, where the architect of much of Cnut's legislation, Wulfstan II, was enthroned as the northern archbishop.

Bamburgh and the Rise of Scotland

Beyond the Tees, Bernicia was treated far more like a client-kingship than an integral part of England. The earldom descended within the house of Bamburgh with little interference and the kings had no lands, *burhs* or mints in the region. There is little evidence that they could even expect to receive tribute from it, although some was probably owed. Nor were the Bishops of Chester-le-Street (then Durham) appointed from outside until Siward forced his own candidate upon the community. That Uhtred's first wife took the veil there implies the presence of a nunnery of sorts in the early eleventh century but the principal institution was a community of secular canons, whose resistance to the monastic reformation probably owed much to their determination to retain their own customs and privileges.

Southern Northumbria could be said to be shired in the sense understood by the West Saxons, even if the shire of York was nothing but the old kingdom divided into three. Like the Mercian Danelaw, these were subdivided into wapentakes. No such re-organization occurred beyond the Tees or in Lancashire beyond Amounderness, where the traditional shires or ancient sub-divisions of Northumbria survived, although there are signs that northern Northumbria followed the Viking areas in adopting the carucate as a unit of assessment and of estate measurement, abandoning the Old English hide.

The protection from Scots, Cumbrians and Vikings afforded by their subordination to the English kings was probably adequate recompense for the loss of a royal title which West Saxon chroniclers had withheld since 867. Such protection was sorely needed during the later Anglo-Saxon period, when the house of Bamburgh was faced by a growing threat from the north.

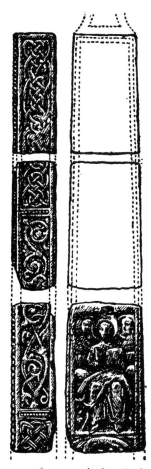

Fragments of a cross-shaft at Easby, NW Yorkshire. The figure-of-eight patterns in the upper section also occur at Thornhill in work dating from not later than the ninth century. The plait, scroll work and ambitious figure-carving imply that the Easby cross was produced when this style of working was at its height (Collingwood, 1927, p. 43)

A fragment from Jedburgh Abbey. Dating from the early ninth century, this decorated fragment probably formed part of a panel or screen. The ornate decoration includes plants and fantastic animals

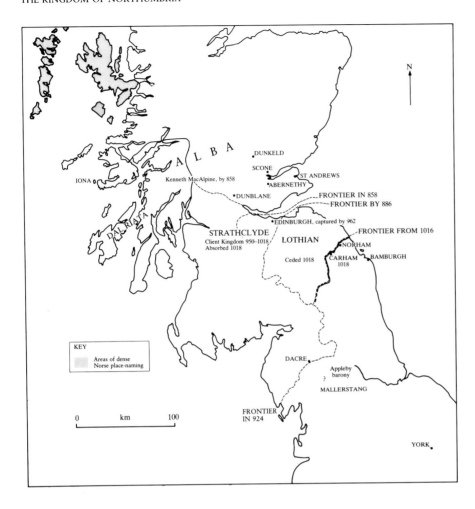

The rise of Scotland

Scotland

Pictish history is perhaps the most obscure of any part of Britain during the early Middle Ages. After a period of military success in the early to mid-eighth century, the Picts lost control of Dal Riata and their coastlands were settled by Vikings in the decades around 800. The Norse defeated a Pictish army 'almost without number' at Fortriu and killed King Eoganan *c.* 839, whose death was the last of a Pictish king to be recorded in Irish annals. A spate of short-lived and undistinguished successors were displaced in obscure circumstances by Kenneth MacAlpine of Dal Riata (died 858), who was named as the King of Scone and credited with a rule in Pictland of eight years. His opportunistic conquests created Alba, a new Scots-led and 'Scotticized' kingdom based in Angus. By 943 the religious focus of the new kingdom had shifted from Dunkeld to St Andrew's, a reformed house of the 'Culdee' order of the Columban Church.

The momentum of this militarily successful dynasty enabled it to attract significant numbers of warriors. Kenneth was reputed to have led six expeditions into Lothian and King Indulf (954–62) captured Edinburgh. With the kingdom of Northumbria riven by the Vikings and Scottish pressure on Strathclyde and the Lothians, Scandinavian intervention in the region declined and it was only the northward expansion of West Saxon military power which checked the Scottish kings. Edward the Elder's pacification of the north was followed by

A Pictish symbol stone at Abernethy, Fife

Athelstan's, whose meeting with the northern kings occurred on the very borders of Strathclyde, at Dacre in Cumbria. To counter the rising tide of West Saxon 'overkingship' Constantine of Scotland allied himself with the Dublin Norse and led his forces to defeat at *Brunanburh*. Thereafter, a series of compromises with Athelstan's successors led to a re-alignment, with English acceptance of Scottish overlordship in Strathclyde (ancient Cumbria) in return for cooperation against the Vikings and respect for the territories of Bamburgh.

The meeting of the northern kings with King Edgar at Chester in 974 illustrates this relationship. 'Florence of Worcester' may have been quoting a near contemporary chronicle when he recalled that eight sub-kings,

namely Kenneth, King of the Scots, Malcolm, King of the Cumbrians, Maccus, king of many islands, and five others, Dufnal, Siferth, Hywel, Jacob and Juchil met him as he commanded, and swore they would be faithful to him and be his allies by land and sea. And on a certain day he went on board a boat with them and, with them at the oars and himself taking the helm, he steered it with skill on the River Dee from the palace to the Minster of St John the Baptist. . . .

The palace was probably at Farndon where Edward the Elder had died and St John's lies on the riverside immediately outside Chester's walls.

Tynwald, the parliament site of the Isle of Man. Constructed on part of a prehistoric burial mound, this was a Viking Age meeting-place of a type which place-name evidence suggests was present in parts of Northumbria during the same period

This was an unparalleled demonstration of English supremacy, backed up by a fleet against which they were powerless. That Kenneth headed the list underlies his importance and it was his nominee who answered for Strathclyde.

It was the revival of Scandinavian attacks on England that provided the opportunity for renewed Scottish and Cumbrian encroachment on the north, probably in alliance with the Irish Sea Norse. In response to this second front Ethelred attacked Strathclyde and Man in 1000. Malcolm II's raid deep into Bernicia and his siege of Durham in 1006 may have been an attempt at conquest, taking advantage of Ethelred's preoccupation with Danish attacks. The long-lived and very capable Malcolm (1005–34) commanded a lengthy frontier which wandered down the centre of Britain from the Clyde – Forth isthmus to the Eamont river, or even beyond. His ultimate ambition was probably the conquest of all of ancient Bernicia, so bringing his frontier to the line of the Rivers Tees and Ribble. The assassination of Uhtred and the consequent break in relations between Cnut and the northerners provided him with an opportunity. Malcolm invaded Tweeddale and heavily defeated Earl Eadulf Cudel, Uhtred's brother, who was forced to cede the Lothians to Scotland as the price of peace. This decisive engagement led to the permanent loss of one of Bernicia's most prosperous provinces. The same battle signalled the end of even the pretence of independence for Strathclyde and Scottish kings were henceforth to be in direct control of territory only two days' ride from York itself.

After making pilgrimage to Rome, Cnut visited the north at some stage between 1027 and 1031. It was probably on this occassion that he came as a pilgrim to St Cuthbert's, ostentatiously approaching the shrine on foot from Garmundsway and bestowing on the church substantial estates in the vicinity. Having propitiated the principal religious establishment of the region, the king attempted to reconcile the leaders of Bernicia with Carl, *hold* of York, and Earl Ealdred of Bamburgh became Carl's sworn brother (either now or later). He then marched into Scotland and Malcolm recognized his superiority but the presence of neither the king nor his army could be permanent. Cnut did not control the resources necessary to sustain an army in the north and his war against Olaf of Norway required his attention on the other side of the North Sea.

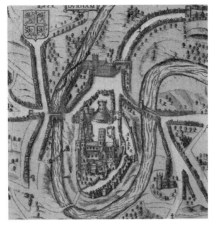

The unique defensive site finally chosen for the shrine of St Cuthbert is clearly shown in this inset map of Durham drawn by John Speed for his *Theatre of the Empire of Great Britain* (1611)

Earl Siward

The last, best-known and most successful of Cnut's earls was Siward, of *Macbeth* fame. Siward's origins are obscure. Like Godwin, Earl of Wessex, he was one of Cnut's new men and seems to have been appointed to the north in the 1030s, probably with a brief to bring to an end the feud which had broken out anew between Carl of York and the house of Bamburgh.

He was probably fortunate in the timing. Malcolm II died at last in 1034. He had attempted to alter the Scottish system of succession in favour of patrilinear descent and was succeeded by his grandson, Duncan. The young king sought to establish himself by attacking the territory of the Earls of Bamburgh and in turn besieged Durham at some date between 1035 and 1040. Once again this proved a disaster. Simeon was to recall in graphic detail the destruction of the Scottish army; Duncan escaped to Scotland with his reputation in tatters. It was probably this defeat which enabled Macbeth, the battle-hardened ruler of Moray, to rebel and kill Duncan at Pitgavery (near Elgin), probably in 1040. Macbeth moved south to Angus and Fife and made himself king. Duncan's brother and sons fled south, providing Siward with valuable claimants through whom he could destabilize the Scottish kingship.

Carl treacherously slew Earl Ealdred in 1038, causing the north to rebel once more. Indeed, it was probably at this stage that Duncan attacked Durham, seeking to repeat his forebears' success at Carham over a Bernicia isolated from the rest of England. The rising was extinguished by Siward. He was credited with killing Ealdred's brother and successor, Eadulf, in 1041, probably in battle. Within a year or two, Uhtred's last surviving son, Cospatric, was in exile with Macbeth in Scotland. When the death of Cnut's son, Harthacnut, brought Edward the Confessor to the throne in 1042, Siward was the ruler of all Northumbria from the Humber to the Tweed, bar the lands around the Solway Firth.

It is paradoxical that Uhtred's dynasty should have lost control of Bernicia in the very year in which Ethelred's son was raised to the throne. For Edward their collapse represented an opportunity lost and he found it necessary to acknowledge Siward's position in Northumbria. Over the next decade he even bolstered it with estates in the south and supplied ships and soldiers for his wars against Scotland. At some point Siward seized Cumberland. The evidence lies in a unique pre-Conquest grant pertaining to the Wigton area known as Cospatric's (or Gospatric's) Charter. He also invaded Scotland, placing Duncan's brother Maldred on the throne c. 1045–6.

His second and better-known invasion of Scotland was in 1054. Macbeth chose to fight, encouraged by his recruitment of Norman knights evicted from England in 1052, but Siward's forces were swollen by royal soldiers. On 27 July, in what was to be immortalized as the battle of Dunsinane, Siward defeated the Scots in a hard-fought battle, slaughtering the Normans. Although Macbeth escaped to Moray, his kingship was broken and he was killed in 1057 by Siward's nominee, Malcolm III. The old earl retired to York with his spoils.

Cospatric's Charter, a pre-Conquest grant of rights of lordship in the Wigton area of Cumberland

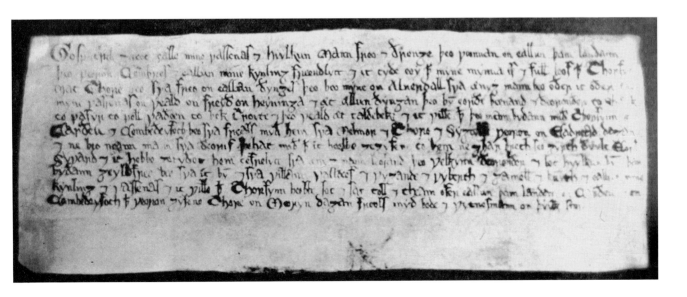

Alongside his military triumphs, Siward had made considerable efforts to achieve a political reconciliation with the Bernicians. There is some evidence that Cospatric was reconciled to him and his conquest of Cumbria and campaigns in Scotland must have relieved the northerners from Scottish and Cumbrian raids. Furthermore Siward took as his second wife Uhtred's daughter. Waltheof, his son by this marriage, certainly later identified with the house of Bamburgh, taking their feuds upon himself. Such marriages were a standard part of the peace process and had been used extensively in the past by Northumbrian kings. Siward may have intended that his elder son, Osbeorn, should succeed him at York and Waltheof in Northumberland.

Siward's relations with St Cuthbert's were rather less conciliatory. The canons selected one of their own number, Edmund, as bishop, c. 1020. Simeon noted that it was normal for the bishop to be a monk, so explaining Edmund's travelling south for instruction at Peterborough, his meeting with Cnut and his enthronement at Winchester. In practice, his recourse to royal patronage seems novel and proved the beginning of the end for the local right of election. Bishop Eadred was said to have bought the diocese from Harthacnut in 1042 and his sudden death thereafter at Durham may not have been entirely coincidental. Æthelric, a monk whom Edmund had brought back from Peterborough, was then selected but his 'foreign' ways led to his expulsion in 1044–5. He obtained the support of Earl Siward, who probably saw the controversy as an opportunity to assert his own authority over these independent-minded clerics. The restored bishop was later accused of behaving like an adventurer, patronizing his own brother, Æthelwine, and other fellow monks from the south and diverting to Peterborough a substantial cache of 'treasure' discovered at Chester-le-Street in the course of replacing the old wooden church with a stone one. When he eventually retired back to Peterborough, Æthelric engineered the succession of his brother with the support of Siward's successor, Tostig.

Siward's position was a curious mixture of royal appointee and client-ruler of a separate kingdom with its own very separate identity. His contemporaries, the Earls of Wessex and Mercia, were succeeded in their earldoms by their own sons and Siward probably anticipated a similar pattern in the north. However, his eldest son and his nephew were casualties of 'Dunsinane', although Shakespeare's reconstruction of Osbeorn's death at the hands of Macbeth owes more to his own sense of the theatrical than to history. With Waltheof too young to be granted the earldom, Edward's regime grasped the opportunity to propose its own solution to the problems of Northumbria's government. Siward died at York in 1055 and was buried in state in the minster which he had built at *Galmanho*, outside the north-west wall of the city, and dedicated to St Olaf. His choice of saint betrays the cultural outlook of an earl who had originally been an appointee of a Danish king and was, throughout, the ruler of the most 'Scandinavianized' province of England. With such men at the helm at this late date, it is hardly surprising that the Viking Age lived on at York through the reign of the Confessor.

This grave-cover at Auckland St Andrew dates from the mid-tenth to mid-eleventh century. It is decorated with plait-like strands

CHAPTER 8

The Destruction of Northumbria

At Siward's death, the bulk of the ancient kingdom of Northumbria was a single unit, subject to an earl at York and a king who normally resided below the Thames. By 1075, just two decades later, Northumbria had ceased to exist in any unitary sense, York was burnt and pauperized, its population decimated, and the members of Northumbria's several regional aristocracies were dead or had fled. Norman barons and their men-at-arms had barely begun the hard task of reconstruction following perhaps the most destructive single campaign in England's history – William's devastation of the north undertaken in the winter months of 1069–70.

As in so many respects, aspects of King William's relations with the north were presaged by those of King Edward. It was the decisions which were made by his *witan*, or council, in 1055 that began the sequence in which Northumbria was to perish.

Tostig

By 1055 Edward's councils were dominated by Harold of Wessex, the Confessor's eldest surviving brother-in-law. Although the promotion of Harold's brother, Tostig, to the vacant earldom of Northumbria has been interpreted as an attempt to tighten royal control of the north, it should be seen primarily as an element of the family's political and territorial aggrandizement, particularly given that it coincided with the outlawry of their principal rival, Ælfgar, son of Earl Leofric of Mercia. Relations between Harold and Tostig were mutually supportive. Tostig brought troops to support Harold in his war against Gruffydd in Wales in 1063 and it is important not to backdate to 1055 the hostility between these two brothers which was kindled in 1065–6. Tostig was probably ordered to reduce the southern subsidy to the government of the north; this was a means of selling his appointment to a king keen to

Harold at the court of Edward the Confessor, the opening scene from the eleventh-century Bayeux Tapestry

233

emulate the status of his forebears but trapped by the excessive power wielded by his principal lieutenants.

Despite his Danish mother, there can be little doubt that Tostig was viewed in the north as the first West Saxon to be appointed as earl. Siward's successes may have persuaded the *witan* that Northumbria was ripe for closer incorporation into England but Tostig's task was rendered far more difficult by his lack of local support, excepting that of Archbishop Cynesige (1051–60), who was probably a long-standing partisan of the Godwin family. Throughout, Tostig's power appears to have rested on his tenure of wide estates in Northamptonshire, Huntingdonshire and possibly Nottinghamshire which enabled him to fund a large contingent of 'housecarls' (soldiers) at York. It seems likely that these housecarls were drawn predominantly from his East Midlands interests. His overgrown establishment mirrored that of the Scandinavian kings of the later ninth and tenth centuries and was to be duplicated once more in 1068 when York's new castle was reputed to have been garrisoned by 500 men-at-arms.

Tostig appointed a lieutenant from the Anglo-Danish community as an intermediary between himself and the Northumbrians – one Copsig – and Simeon recorded the attempts of both to reconcile the community of St Cuthbert to their rule by gifts of land. However, the right of free election was a more critical issue for the canons. The much-resented Bishop Æthelric resigned only twelve months after the death of his protector, Earl Siward, but the succession of his brother Æthelwine – another monk from Peterborough of whom nothing good was reported at Durham – implies that Tostig's administration interfered decisively in the next election. Despite the warm tributes paid by Simeon to Tostig, Countess Judith and Copsig, there can be little doubt that their policies were much resented by the influential canons at Durham.

Had his frontiers held, then Tostig's private army, personal prestige and the political support of King Edward's court might have been enough to sustain his rule of the north. Unfortunately for him, Siward's settlement of the Scottish question proved transitory. In 1057–8, Malcolm III killed Macbeth and his successor, Lulach, and was free to turn south, where he had legitimate claims on English conquests in Cumbria. With Siward dead and his family without authority, there was no bond of gratitude to restrain him.

The first raid occurred in 1058. In 1059 the earl, Bishop of Durham and Archbishop of York, induced Malcolm to attend upon Edward the Confessor, who perhaps made a rare visit to York for the occasion. A general peace was concluded, the earl and king becoming sworn brothers – the normal expression in the north for an alliance. Yet Tostig's regime was about to suffer another savage blow. Archbishop Cynesige's death in 1060 deprived the earl of his most committed and experienced local supporter, whose ten years' residence in Yorkshire probably made him a valuable judge of northern politics. The Godwinsons engineered his replacement with another West Saxon, Ealdred, once a monk at Winchester and then Abbot of Tavistock. Ealdred had considerable experience of royal and ecclesiastical administration, particularly on England's other volatile border, with Wales, and had travelled extensively as an ambassador to Cologne (1054) and as a pilgrim to Jerusalem (1058). He was an obvious appointee to the vacant see and probably brought Tostig valuable political skills but he cannot have matched his predecessor's knowledge of the region.

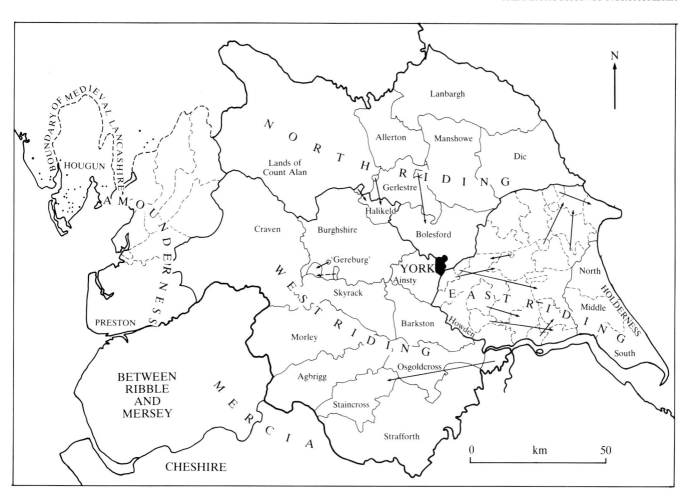

Northumbria in *Great Domesday Book* (based in part on Faull (ed.), 1986, vol. ii, map i)

In 1061 Tostig elected to follow in the footsteps of his deceased eldest brother, Swein, and himself accompanied Ealdred to Rome for the pallium, presumably relying on his treaty of the previous year to keep the north quiet. This proved a serious error. Malcolm wasted Northumberland, ravaging Lindisfarne and perhaps even County Durham and probably took this opportunity to re-secure his father's territory in Cumberland – a region certainly back in Scottish hands soon after the Conquest. The Domesday survey in northern Lancashire implies wasting and it is possible that this rather dubious evidence pertains to Malcolm's campaign.

On his return (1062), Tostig took no effective action against King Malcolm, yet he was not, on other occasions, slow to fight, as his participation in Harold's Welsh war of 1063–4 and in the 1066 campaigns clearly shows. His pacificatory policy in the north was presumably due to his growing political problems. As his credibility fell, so his rule came under increasing threat from the Bernician aristocracy, whose interests were jeopardized both by Tostig's Anglo-Danish administration and by Scottish control of the upper Tyne Valley. Tostig found his prestige caught in a downward spiral which was self-perpetuating and largely self-propelled.

He attempted to pre-empt opposition north of the Tees in time-honoured fashion, arranging through Queen Edith the murder of Cospatric (Uhtred's last surviving son) at King Edward's Christmas court in 1064 and himself murdering several of Cospatric's key supporters while under safe conduct at York. Thus had successive rulers of York attempted to retain control of the far north but Tostig had not even the committed support of the Yorkshire community to sustain his rule. Excluding only his own housecarls, the unpopular Bishop of Durham and Archbishop Ealdred, the earl was isolated. Indeed, his intelligence-gathering appears to have failed him. When, in the spring of 1065, the community of St Cuthbert chose to exhibit the relics of the murdered King Oswine of Deira, he should have anticipated that his enemies in the north had obtained the support of the Yorkshire community. Yet Tostig was absent from his earldom in the autumn, hunting with the king, when the rebellion occurred.

The revolt of the Northumbrians was the last great political event of King Edward's reign. It began in Bernicia but the rebels' unprecedented march south demonstrates that they were already assured of support there. At York they assembled, outlawed Tostig, killed his household retainers and seized his arsenal and treasury, before marching south to wreak vengeance on the east Mercian shires which had sustained his rule.

There are several extraordinary aspects of the revolt. One was the joint action of the aristocracy of Yorkshire and the far north which was made possible by the rule of an outsider, a West Saxon, unable to count on family and traditional ties of patronage in either community. That King Edward was asked to concede the law-code of Cnut to the rebels implies that Tostig had reneged on earlier undertakings to the Yorkshiremen concerning their use of Scandinavian law and legal procedures. The Confessor's first biographer confirms this charge, blaming the revolt on Tostig's law enforcement and his abuse of justice as a means of raising revenue. However necessary it was that Northumbria should pay for itself, Tostig's methods challenged northern privileges which probably dated back to the settlement of 954. Such disregard for local sensibilities may explain the willingness of the Anglo-Danish community to throw in their lot with their traditional enemies beyond the Tees.

Their march south was similarly unprecedented. Without an alternative claimant to the throne, the northerners were seeking the redress of northern issues in much the same way as northern rebels were to do in the sixteenth century. Their ability to cross the Humber and exert pressure on the government owed much to their alliance with the Mercian earl, Edwin. The willingness of the gentry of the north and the Midlands to march against royal authority under their own leaders implies a splintering of England into regions capable of action as independent of royal authority as Normandy or Anjou were of the French Crown. The initial meeting of the Northumbrian leadership at York behaved as if it were a royal council, implying that the Northumbrians believed themselves competent to act for Northumbria as Edward's *witan* did for the south, even in his absence.

Through their well-planned and forceful action, the Northumbrians discovered themselves to be a major force in English politics. They used this new-found power not to overthrow King Edward but to redefine the position of his lieutenant in the north and press home their demand for the earls of their own choice. They were thus demanding the same right of election in the appointment of a northern earl as was a customary element in the selection of an English king. The parallel is an

Edward the Confessor, from the Bayeux Tapestry

important one since it enshrines Northumbrian perspectives concerning the role of their province within England.

Their reasoning is undocumented but it may be reconstructed. To achieve an alliance of the house of Bamburgh with York, both had to abandon their claim to rule Northumbria. In the circumstances (Siward's youngest son, Waltheof, presumably being unacceptable at York), they had little choice but to demand another outsider as earl but from a family hostile to Tostig and his kin. The only family of sufficient status was the house of Leofric (Earl of Mercia, *d*. 1057), whose young grandson, Edwin, was Earl of Mercia. Edwin's younger brother, Morcar, was at this stage no more than a teenager but the Northumbrians secured his leadership while still at York, then followed him south. His participation assured them of the military support of Earl Edwin, whose west Mercian and Welsh forces joined the insurgents at Northampton.

The rebels therefore represented two of the three great earldoms and were too numerous to be outfaced by the king. In demanding Tostig's replacement by Morcar, the Northumbrians were effectively seeking self-government under the king. The antipathy between King Edward and Morcar's father, Ælfgar, is a matter of record and Morcar was extremely unlikely to be granted the southern estates which had enabled Tostig to maintain a small standing army. He would become a mere figurehead in Northumbria, with no option but to rule through consensus. It was a coup conceived and executed by the northerners with consummate skill, which reveals their full grasp of the intricacies of contemporary English politics.

To King Edward's chagrin, the demands of the rebels were conceded as Harold chose to abandon his brother rather than fight. With his eyes by this stage fixed on the succession, Harold presumably preferred to lose Northumbria to his family's rival rather than suffer the open wound and deep loss of fighting men which war would have entailed. He may in any case have decided by this stage that Northumbria was a poisoned chalice and virtually ungovernable by an outsider, and so unlikely to benefit its new earl in anything other than status. If so he was surely correct. Tostig, his wife and 'all those who were of one mind with him' went into exile among Countess Judith's kin in Flanders. Tostig's estates in and around Northamptonshire went to Waltheof, for whom an earldom was carved out as part of the peace plan, perhaps as a barrier between the Godwinsons of Wessex and East Anglia and Edwin in Mercia.

Whatever centralizing policies Tostig had espoused in the north were abandoned. For the remaining months of the Anglo-Saxon period, Northumbria would be a single earldom in little but name, with real power wielded in the far north by Osulf of Bamburgh and in Yorkshire by local leaders. By 1066 Morcar had not made good his title to the more distant estates of the earldom, in northern Lancashire and southern Cumbria, and his rule was sustained only by a group of estates in the vicinity of York and the Wolds and a handful of family holdings in western Mercia. His impoverished leadership may have suited the Northumbrians well but it could not provide effective military leadership or protection. The rebels had attained their aims but only time would tell if that would be to their own advantage.

1066

King Edward died on 5 January 1066 and was buried in his new West Minster in the morning of the following day. That afternoon Earl Harold was crowned in the same church, probably by Archbishop Ealdred of York. Harold's kingship met with little enthusiasm in the north, where many may have feared the return of Tostig, but Harold had visited York by Easter and been acknowledged there as king. His marriage to a kinswoman of Earls Edwin and Morcar clearly smoothed his path. His pact with them necessitated that his brother remain in exile.

This suited all parties, with the exception of Tostig, who attacked the Isle of Wight in April/May, then sailed into the Humber with a fleet reputedly of sixty ships. Tostig's enterprise was of the kind previously used to good effect both by the Godwinsons and Ælfgar, designed to be of sufficient nuisance value to obtain re-appointment to high office in England. In this instance, Earl Edwin, like King Harold in the south, was probably already mobilized to resist invasion, and he repulsed Tostig, probably in Lindsey. The latter's Flemish crews promptly returned home, leaving Tostig to make his way with a handful of small ships northwards, where he encountered both Copsig and Harald Hardrada, King of Norway, with the Norwegian fleet. With the arrival of one of the major foreign claimants to the English throne, Tostig's room for manoeuvre had evaporated. He is unlikely to have planned his meeting with King Harald but had little option but to join with him.

Hardrada was the greatest Viking leader of the day. Half-brother of St Olaf, he was a survivor of the battle of Stiklarstadir (July 1030), and had seen service in Sweden, Russia and Byzantium (as commander of the Varangian Guard) before returning to Norway to join his kinsman King Magnus in 1047. Succeeding to the throne, Harald fought a long and generally successful series of campaigns against Sweyn of Denmark until the two Viking kings agreed a peace formula in 1064 which freed

The death of Edward the Confessor is illustrated on the Bayeux Tapestry. Above, he utters his last requests, and, below, he is prepared for burial

The coronation of King Harold, as shown on the Bayeux Tapestry

Harald for the long delayed enterprise of England. Whatever modern opinion as to the legitimacy of his claim to the English throne might be, the Scandinavians had not forgotten the long reign of Cnut and a treaty between Cnut's son Harthacnut and King Magnus gave the Norwegians a claim of sorts to England. More important, Harald mobilized a credible force estimated at three hundred ships – perhaps upwards of nine thousand men – to whom others attached themselves *en route*. In the late summer Harald led his forces down the Bernician coast, which they ravaged, then entered the mouth of the Humber. Local English ships appear to have been stationed to guard the North Sea coast much as Harold Godwinson's fleet was marshalled in the Solent. They were heavily outnumbered, however, and retired upstream into the Wharfe to Tadcaster while the Norwegians disembarked on the Ouse at Riccall, only 10 miles (16 km) from York.

Earls Edwin and Morcar had had sufficient time to place themselves and their predominantly Mercian army between the Norwegians and York and it was at Gate Fulford, within sight of the city, that they stood at bay. The resolve shown by the two brothers at this critical moment is impressive. The king on whose behalf they fought had long been the enemy of their house and their opponent was a general without equal in northern Europe, heading the largest army of battle-hardened Vikings seen in Britain for half a century. Perhaps Edwin had calculated that a Norwegian succession would be as serious a disaster for his own interests as King Harold Godwinson's, but the inexperience of Edwin and his troops reinforces the impression of a desperate if heroic gamble taken in ignorance. That Edwin did not attempt to hold the walls of York itself implies either a lack of confidence in the defences there or in the men of York. The latter seems the more likely and was to be entirely justified. It was no coincidence that Hardrada had invaded via Yorkshire. He was probably anticipating considerable support for renewed Scandinavian kingship in that quarter.

The two armies fought a long and hard engagement at Gate Fulford on Wednesday 20 September 1066 and the Norwegians had the victory. Although Edwin extricated himself, his brother and the remnants of his army, he was in no condition to re-engage. The city of York joined Hardrada, promising to supply men who would march south with him to conquer England, and Hardrada withdrew to await the arrival of hostages at Stamford Bridge, apparently without doing any damage to the Yorkshiremen. The choice of this site implies that Harald was interested in communications in Yorkshire, establishing himself close to the Roman road network in the Derwent Valley – probably the ancient centre of Deira. He could expect no aid from the Bernicians.

Alerted to the unexpected arrival of the Norwegians, Harold Godwinson had already set off for the north before the battle of Fulford. He probably used the Great North Road, reaching Tadcaster on 24 September, where the presence of English ships implies that reinforcements awaited him and perhaps Earl Edwin himself. He then marched through York and on a further 17 miles (27 km) to deliver a surprise attack the following day on the Norwegians, whose leaders appear to have been entirely unaware of Godwinson's presence and had failed to adequately guard the bridge. The tactic was a complete success. The Norwegians were routed in one of the most convincing defeats ever inflicted on the Vikings by an English king. The remnants around Olaf, Hardrada's son, their bishop and the Earl of Orkney were harried as far as Riccall before being given quarter. The survivors departed on a mere twenty-four ships. Harald, supposedly shot through the throat, and Tostig were among the slain and the death of this most warlike Norwegian king is often held to symbolize the end of the Viking Age. A year after his death, his body was transported home for burial, in a church which he had himself founded.

Stamford Bridge: it was at a bridge at, or close by, this site that Harold Godwinson overwhelmed the Norwegians

Stamford Bridge was the last great victory of the Anglo-Saxon period and it is fitting that it was a great triumph over a Viking enemy. The campaign had, however, inflicted fatal damage on Harold's kingship. The destruction of the Mercian army, the proven unreliabilty of the Yorkshiremen, the absence of King Harold from the south and the losses and strain inflicted on his forces all contributed to the disaster to come. William the Bastard belatedly reached the Sussex coast while Harold was in the north. The latter's rapid march southwards and his attempt to repeat the surprise attack which had succeeded so brilliantly at Stamford Bridge utterly failed him. Harold, his brothers and the pick of their troops fell at Hastings on 14 October, just nineteen days after Stamford Bridge.

Sunset over the Mersey Valley

The leadership of England devolved upon the *witan* – primarily the bishops – who pledged their support to the young *ætheling*, Edgar, grandson of Edmund Ironside, but without competent military leadership his kingship could not be sustained against Duke William. Only Earl Edwin could have provided that leadership but his inactivity at London during the autumn suggests that his self-confidence had been another casualty of the battle of Gate Fulford. The Earls of Mercia and Northumbria were among those who abandoned Edgar and did homage to William at Berkhamsted, before attending his coronation on Christmas Day.

The Normans and the North

The Northumbrians took no part in the battle of Hastings. Although Earl Morcar was among those who recognized and crowned King William, it has been suggested that his connection with Northumbria was already at an end, having been replaced after Gate Fulford by Mærleswein, a nobleman from the Mercian Danelaw. The government of his furthest province is unlikely to have been high on William's long list of priorities in 1066–7 and the first Norman king initially attempted to govern the north through the local community. His pressing need was for taxes with which to satisfy the demands of his mercenary soldiers. He may have been led to believe that the adventurer Copsig, Tostig's erstwhile lieutenant, was a man capable of raising taxes from the north since he appointed him to the earldom of Northumbria beyond the Tyne in February 1067. However, Copsig's popularity in Bernicia had not been improved by his absence and, if known, his recent cooperation with Tostig and Hardrada would not have endeared him to the house of Bamburgh. After himself failing to capture Osulf of Bamburgh, he was taken by the Northumbrians and beheaded on 12 March 1067.

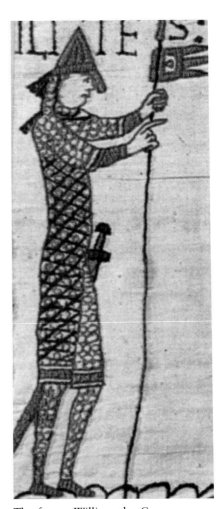

The future William the Conqueror, as shown on the Bayeux Tapestry preparing to meet Harold at the Battle of Hastings

Such a cavalier disregard of William's authority may have seemed justified. From what little direct experience they had had of the Normans, the Northumbrians had seen little to fear. Macbeth's Frenchmen had been cut to pieces by Siward's troops and Earl Ralph's had performed without distinction on the Welsh frontier. Fresh from a successful confrontation with Edward the Confessor, the northerners are unlikely to have considered his Norman successor a threat to themselves. They were to be proved fatally misled over the next few years.

William's authority was temporarily restored through an accident. Earl Osulf was killed by an outlaw late in 1067 and a northern nobleman related to his house in the female line, another Cospatric, bought the earldom from King William in December. However, Cospatric was no more able to deliver northern taxes to the king than had been Copsig. The levels of *geld* demanded by the Conqueror to pay off his mercenaries far outweighed those characteristic of the Confessor's reign. Edwin and Morcar headed a Mercian rebellion in the spring and, whether they formally recognized Morcar or not, the Northumbrians joined themselves to it, under Cospatric and the Yorkshire aristocracy. Precisely what they intended is unclear but the presence of Edgar the *ætheling* may imply a groundswell of opinion in favour of his kingship.

However, if the rebels expected to achieve their objectives as cheaply as they had in the autumn of 1065, they were to be rapidly disillusioned. William's construction of castles and stationing of garrisons at Warwick and Nottingham brought Mercia to heel and, rather than

York Castle: the medieval Clifford's Tower sits on top of an earthen motte

face him in battle, the leaders of the Northumbrians followed Edgar in flight to Scotland, where Malcolm gave them refuge in exchange for the hand in marriage of Edgar's sister, the Lady Margaret. William entered York, received the submission of the Yorkshiremen and constructed a castle there, in so doing flooding much of the Coppergate area with a defensive moat and pool created by damming the River Foss. He followed this up by negotiations with King Malcolm but, although Orderic Vitalis suggested that Malcolm did homage through his ambassadors, William failed to secure the northerners in exile. He built one further castle, at Lincoln, as he retired southwards.

At his departure, William left southern Northumbria in the hands of William Malet and Robert fitz Richard with troops enough to defend the castle – reputedly 500 in all. Domesday Book confirms William Malet's acquisition of substantial estates in Yorkshire and the *Anglo-Saxon Chronicle* alludes to a large treasure in York Castle by 1069. Both imply that the Norman occupation and governance of Yorkshire were rapacious. However, it was William's appointment of Robert de Commines as earl over the lands beyond the Tees which sparked off a new revolt. Robert treated his new command as a province in need of conquest, ravaging the winter countryside as he marched towards Durham in the bitter cold of January 1069. He entered Durham with

700 men, 'treating the men of the town as if they had been enemies' and looting their homes. They were taken entirely by surprise by a Northumbrian attack in the early hours of the following day (31 January) and, despite stiff resistance around the earl, they almost all perished by fire or the sword. Northumbria beyond the Tees was once more in open revolt against King William.

Simeon told at length, but in miraculous form, the story of the fate of the first punitive force despatched to avenge Earl Robert which, beset by mist in the Swale Valley, turned back at Northallerton, fearful that the fog was sent by St Cuthbert to confuse and destroy them. In Yorkshire Robert fitz Richard was caught outside the castle and killed, and a general rising ensued, aided and abetted by the return of the exiles from Scotland led by Edgar. William moved with his customary speed, confronted the rebels at York and defeated them. The city was treated as conquered territory – it was sacked and its churches robbed and outraged, including even the archdiocesan minster of St Peter.

William departed once more, this time leaving York with two castles and two garrisons, the larger under the leadership of his close friend and ally, William fitz Osbern. The latter had some success against the insurgents but new dangers were looming from the sea. The Northumbrians had long expected aid against the Normans from Denmark and King Sweyn's expedition, reportedly of 240 ships, duly arrived in the Humber on 8 September and combined there with Edgar, Earl Waltheof, Mærleswein and Cospatric. They were joined by the Northumbrians and the resulting army marched on York. It was at this critical

Baile Hill, the second Norman motte at York

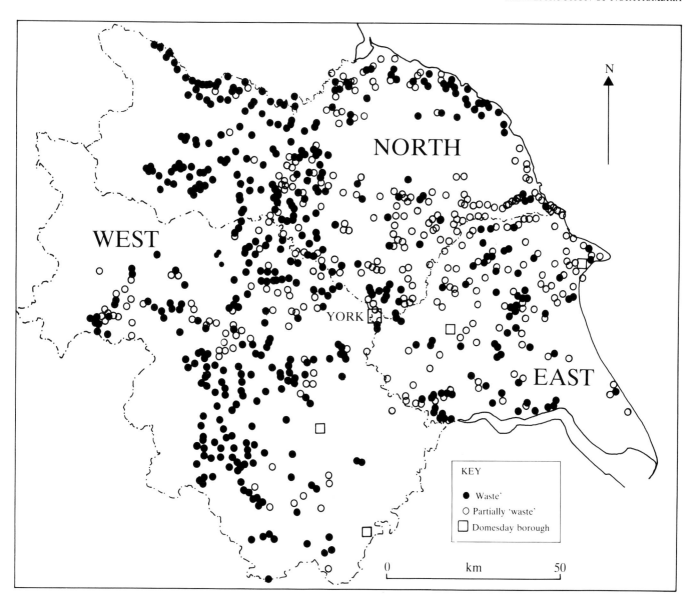

'Waste' manors in the Yorkshire Domesday

juncture that the widely respected Archbishop Ealdred died on 11 September, leaving the way open for a Norman appointee to this key episcopacy. Whether or not his death was precipitated by the ruin around him and his expectation of worse to come, his death removed the only man well acquainted with both King William and the Northumbrian leaders who might have worked to reconcile the two.

The Norman garrison fired the houses immediately around the castle within the city but lost control of the ensuing conflagration which engulfed the urban centre and finally destroyed St Peter's. Caught in the still burning streets, the Normans were killed or taken captive to the ships and the Danes were left in possession of the burned-out hulk of York. Its inadequacies as a base in which they could overwinter drove the Danes to attempt the fortification of Axholme in Lindsey but their efforts were frustrated by King William. They retreated to the ships in the Humber in considerable distress, finally agreeing to depart, without campaigning, in the spring in return for freedom from Norman attack and leave to gather provisions. The unwillingness of Sweyn's brother,

Earl Osbeorn, to fight King William left the north at his mercy and he 'ravaged and laid waste the whole shire and everything that was in it' (*Anglo-Saxon Chronicle*, 'C', 1069). Frustrated by the failure of his several attempts to both govern and exploit the north, and anxious to deny the Danish king the support and supplies of the Yorkshiremen on his expected springtime arrival, William seems to have broken up his army into small units and despatched them into the countryside to kill or drive out the peasantry, slaughter their plough animals and burn their ricks and cots. The widespread testimony of Domesday Book, assembled sixteen years later, is a grim witness to the thoroughness with which the Normans undertook the task, the record of waste spilling over widely from Yorkshire into the heartland of Mercian resistance in Cheshire, Shropshire and Staffordshire.

County Durham also felt the weight of William's savagery. Although the absence of the region from the folios of Domesday Book denies us a detailed inventory, Simeon recorded the flight of the community of St Cuthbert to distant Lindisfarne, bearing with them once more the relics of their patron saint. Their return to Durham on the kalends of April implies that Norman troops had by then departed but the precious ornaments which had been left within the church were gone, despoiled by William's men. Despite his promises, they had great difficulty in retrieving their possessions or obtaining justice against the perpetrators and William eventually recompensed them out of his own pocket.

The canons of Durham were among the lucky ones who had lived through the wasting and would have sufficient to eat for the following year, although the bishopric was to be impoverished for years to come. Most were less fortunate and the harrying of the north undermined the entire structure of the northern economy, creating famine. To escape it men and women sold themselves into slavery or fled south where their presence was noted as far away as Evesham. Others may have taken the unchronicled road into Scotland or Cumberland but for all, refugee, pauper or outlaw, the winter of 1069–70 was a major turning-point, beyond which Yorkshire at least was incapable of further resistance to the Normans.

The deaths of Ealdred and fitz Osbern and the flight of Bishop Æthelwine from Durham in 1069 enabled William to make new and crucial appointments in the north. He selected as archbishop a member of his half-brother's staff, Thomas of Bayeux, and followed Lanfranc's advice in requiring him to recognize the primacy of Canterbury, so denying the Danes of the opportunity to crown their own King of England at York, as Hugh the Chantor was to write over a generation later. William appointed a Lotharingian, Walcher, to Durham, a man who was a definite outsider and therefore perhaps rather more expendable than one of William's own clerks. He was also, unusually, a secular priest rather than a monk.

However, many of the leaders of the 1069 rising were still at large and active on the North Sea coasts, voyaging between their haven in Scotland and Hereward's rising in the Fens, and William had no immediate means of controlling Northumbria beyond the Tees. Perhaps for this reason he left it in Cospatric's hands between 1069–70 and 1072, but that summer the king undertook a major new initiative in the north, leading a combined army and fleet as far as Abernethy, where he received Malcolm's homage. The agreement apparently denied the English exiles a haven in Scotland, and henceforth they were forced to

A detail of the keep at Scarborough Castle. Constructed in the reign of Henry II, this fine window illustrates the interdependence of castle and church architecture in the Norman period

Richmond Castle is an early example of a stone-built courtyard castle in the north, to which a massive keep was added at the orders of Henry II in the later twelfth century

The stone keep at Newcastle, built in 1121 and refounded in 1164, as drawn by Francis Grose in 1768

turn to the far less convenient ports of Flanders. This done, William drove Cospatric into exile, installing Siward's son Waltheof in Northumberland. On his return south, William paused long enough at Durham to construct a castle for the bishop and, although Simeon recounted a curious tale of William's flight from St Cuthbert's city, the king's restoration of Billingham to Bishop Walcher demonstrates his attempts to protect the principal religious community of the region.

Yet even the roads between York and Durham were unsafe on account of robbers and wolves during the 1070s and settled life based on a sound agrarian economy returned only very slowly to Yorkshire, let alone to Northumbria beyond the Tees. Several more royal expeditions were launched into Northumberland before it was possible for Normans to establish a permanent garrison at the 'Newcastle' constructed by Robert, William's eldest son, in 1080 on the banks of the Tyne.

The new baronial geography which gradually emerged in the last two decades of the century differed markedly from Siward's earldom. Norman baronies were created by royal grants and castles constructed at their foci. York and Durham were initially isolated strongholds of royal authority but the habit of castle construction spread northwards to Tutbury, Tickhill and Peveril in the early 1070s and reached Pontefract and Richmond by 1080. Many of these honours were of vast size, even if the revenues from them were much reduced by the wasting. Count Alan's lordship of Richmond comprised a mass of 199 manors blocking the Stainmore crossing of the Pennines and it seems clear that this, like Skipton and Clitheroe, was an honour conceived in response

247

to widespread brigandage, itself the product of the political changes and the wasting of the north. Castles were eventually to be constructed at the centres of new honours even in Northumberland and would carry over during the following generation into southern Scotland. Within William's reign, that is, before 1087, the transfer of lands from Anglo-Saxon to Norman lordship was near completion in Yorkshire. When the Domesday surveyors examined Yorkshire in the spring of 1086, they encountered a landholding aristocracy dominated by men named Geoffrey, Hugh, Nigel, Ralph, Richard, Robert and William, all of whom had emigrated into the shire from the continent since 1070.

The revival of York was also underway. Its destruction was probably nearer total than that of any other city in Britain. Of the seven shires into which it was divided in King Edward's reign, one was lost through construction of the castles. In the remaining six there had been 1,607 inhabited houses. When King William took stock in 1086 his majority share of the town's dues came from only 391 inhabited properties, while 400 were not let as residences to burgesses and 540 were 'so empty that they render nothing'. The archbishop's shire amounted to only 100 (down from 189) and a further 145 residences were held by French immigrants – a proportion sufficient to change the entire complexion of the community. Numerous lodging-houses point to the continuing need of men to overnight in York on business. The pressure on space in the late Saxon town had been considerable – witness the several houses constructed in the city ditch and the rows of small hovels

Durham Cathedral and Castle overlooking the Wear

Earthworks of a motte and bailey castle at Tebay. This example was probably not constructed until the twelfth century but it exhibits the classic features of a high motte separated from the bailey by a ditch, with an entrance ramp and traces of internal buildings against the inside of the palisade around the bailey

Norman motte in southern Scotland, on the Irish Sea coast near Stranraer

One of the pillars of the early Norman minster at York

noted in Domesday Book. The houses inhabited in 1086 were easily fewer than half those in 1066, but the geography of the town and its tenements clearly survived largely intact. So too did royal dues, which, despite the crash in population and urban prosperity, William had seen fit to raise from £53 in 1066 to £100.

When Archbishop Thomas arrived in 1072, he was reported to have found everything deserted or wasted, the minster destroyed and few of its clergy remaining. It was he who first built on the site of the current minster, erecting a cruciform church apparently within the existing cemetery to the north-west of the burnt-out ruins of the Anglo-Saxon minster. It is elements of this building which are now visible in the crypt of York Minster. Thomas was also to divide the assets of the clerical community into prebends, ultimately thirty-two of them, in line with contemporary practice elsewhere. Thomas was by no means the only early Norman builder in the north. William St Calais, the second Norman Bishop of Durham and a man of independent means, set about the reconstruction of Durham Cathedral in 1093. The resulting building is today the finest example of Norman Romanesque in the region – some would say in Europe. Its boldly incised pillars supporting the nave and its early stone-rib vaulted ceiling remain, but its apse was later replaced by an eastwards extension of the church and the upper storeys of the towers are later additions. There were also to be numerous smaller churches built within the century or so over which the Norman style extended. Many of these were small, manorial churches, like Bossall in the Derwent Valley, but some were built on a comparatively grandiose scale. Mark, for example, the three arches and incised pillars on the north side of the nave of St Mary the Virgin, Kirkby Lonsdale, which were probably constructed by the same craftsmen responsible for the nave at Durham.

Kirkby Lonsdale, granted by Ivo de Taillebois, Baron of Kendal, to the Abbey of St Mary at York, was a product of monastic church-building which was to be typical of the period. The Conquest re-opened the floodgate of monastic patronage in the north, as new churchmen and magnates gathered its territorial resources and its churches into their own hands. In search of a better-educated clergy, some barons granted entire groups of churches to monasteries situated in the south or even in Normandy. Such occurred in northern Lancashire, where Roger of Poitou granted the rectories of nine churches and the tithes

The nave of the magnificent Norman cathedral at Durham

The remains of the monastery at Jarrow, viewed from the south-east by Francis Grose in 1773

from nineteen townships to the Abbey of Sées in Normandy as an inducement to found a priory beneath his castle walls at Lancaster.

However, much of the new monastic fervour came from the clerical establishment. In chapter fifty-six of his *History of the Church of Durham*, Simeon described the arrival in the north of the Mercian Aldwin, Prior of Winchcombe, with two English monks from Evesham, in search of the monastic sites of the early Northumbrian Church of which they knew only through Aldwin's reading (presumably of Bede). Under Bishop Walcher's patronage they re-occupied Jarrow,

> the roofless walls of which were all that remained, with little left of their ancient splendour. On those walls they constructed a roof of unsquared timbers, with thatch above, and began there to practise the offices of divine service. In the lee of the walls they erected a small shed in which to sleep and eat their food, and thus they kept up a life of poverty, supported by the alms of the pious. . . . many were persuaded by their example to give up the world and receive from them the cowl of a monk; and so experience taught them to be the soldiers of Christ under the discipline of monastic rule. A few of them were from Northumberland itself, but most were from the southern regions of England.

From there, Aldwin proceeded to refound Monkwearmouth and one of the two Evesham brethren, St Mary's at York. Whitby followed. That the primary movers in this process were southern Anglo-Saxons may reflect the Norman preferments to southern clerical positions during the 1070s, which were closing career paths to English clerics, however austere their habits and rigorous their asceticism. The new northern monasteries were as much a manifestation of southern dominance and intrusion as were the several castles of the Norman baronage.

CHAPTER 9

Settlement and Landscape: A Postcript

The northern landscape is today one of contrasts: there are few who do not admire the fells of the Lake District and Cheviots, or the Yorkshire Dales with their distinctive limestone scenery. These regions are slow-changing and provide considerable opportunity for scholars to research the complex processes of settlement history and landscape archaeology. Yet few areas are untouched by recent agriculture or building, and those which are are least likely to have been settled during the Anglian period. It was in the better-drained parts of the valleys and plains that early settlement was concentrated, however extensively farmers were grazing, felling or hunting over the uplands. It is the lowlands which have been most affected by modern activity. Large-scale industrial development, urbanization and dereliction, extractive industries and power generation, spoil tips, land-drainage, deep ploughing and much more have all rendered large expanses of the north inaccessible to the investigation of past human activities, the traces of which were never so deeply scored on the face of the earth as is the record of the last two centuries.

Less obvious but equally insidious was the impact of enclosure in the countryside which, between the fifteenth and nineteenth centuries, swept away unenclosed pastures on fell or moss and entire working landscapes of fields, villages and farms. As the new enclosures came into cultivation, so the surface imprint of older activity was gradually eroded. Unless deep cuts were made into the subsoil, such past activities are not now visible through aerial photography, and that technique of discovery is in any case effective only on land in current cultivation. Much of the northern plains and valleys are under pasture, yet have been ploughed sufficiently over the post-medieval period to have erased earlier features. The resultant grasslands pose an insuperable obstacle to those wishing to identify pre-Conquest activity in areas such as Lancashire and the West Riding. Even where agriculture is now present, the lack of diagnostic artefacts and pottery from the Anglo-Saxon

OPPOSITE: Hillfarming in Fuesdale, near Ullswater

The agricultural landscape of Upper Teesdale

OPPOSITE, ABOVE: Post-enclosure ridge and furrow at Barwick-in-Elmet, highlighted by a thin covering of snow; BELOW: Wigan Church preserves some later medieval fabric but this embanked thirteenth-century borough has been lost under the nineteenth-century townscape

period makes it impossible to identify farmsteads or landscapes of the early Middle Ages by techniques which have, in other regions, yielded useful results.

In some parts, enough of the open field and village landscape of the high Middle Ages remain in relic form – usually under permanent pasture – to obtain some idea of one chapter in the evolving medieval landscape. As a method of farming, open-field was popular across a wide front in temperate Europe between the ninth and fourteenth centuries and it seems probable that it would have reached the north even without the Normans. In Northumbria, its spread was always limited but 'Midland-type' open fields seem to have been associated with nucleated settlement. Both surviving and deserted villages are concentrated in the eastern lowlands, in an arc stretching from southern Yorkshire into Northumberland and spilling over the Pennines into Lonsdale and the Eden Valley.

Many examples display a highly regular form, with crofts all of one size sharing a common frontage to a roadway or green – a particularly prominent feature of villages in the north-east. They reveal a considerable degree of planning, the main lines of which are generally

255

still visible despite subsequent growth or settlement shifts. These villages were, therefore, generally founded with the full backing of manorial authority, coming into existence *in toto*, in conjunction with the laying out from scratch of one, two or occasionally three open fields.

When did this process begin? Although many archaeologists working in the region freely admit that the pottery evidence cannot be dated with any precision, most prefer to assign the onset of nucleation to the twelfth century. That is the period suggested for the organization of Wharram Percy into a regular, two-row village and seems to be the period when the only other extensively dug sites, West Whelpington, in Northumberland, and Thrislington in County Durham, were laid out. Such a date has yet to be contradicted by excavations on other village sites, as at West Hartburn, and Tollesby. In support, it was that century which was at the centre of the long period of warmer weather which was to characterize the central Middle Ages. This provided conditions conducive to investment in the countryside by landholders eager to increase output. The same period witnessed a rapid expansion of markets in the region, which spread during the twelfth and thirteenth centuries to provide a generally accessible network. The beginnings of commercial production of pottery coincides with the same period, and these factors appear to be interrelated.

The green at Piercebridge, across much of which the earthworks of the Roman town and fort are visible

The deserted medieval village of South Middleton, photographed under snow

The Norman castle and planned settlement at Church Brough. The earthworks of the Roman fort are clearly visible beneath the castle and the farms now occupying the planned settlement overlie the Roman civil settlement

The outline of a late medieval longhouse under pasture at Wharram Percy

Some of these new villages were on previously occupied sites, as at Wharram Percy, but, with many, previous occupation had ceased centuries before and direct links between Saxon settlement patterns and nucleated settlements so far remain sketchy. Iron Age or Roman sherds and ditches are commoner on village sites than evidence for Saxon settlement. Where nucleation occurred beside pre-Conquest churches, then we may be correct in assuming the presence of a late Saxon settlement, if only of the priest himself, and many churches were probably constructed close by the hall of their patrons. Elsewhere, as in the case of the small Norman planned town at Church Brough sited on the Roman *vicus* outside the Roman fort on which Brough Castle stood, there is every reason to believe the gap in occupation was a half-millennium or more. Many medieval villages were probably built on sites which had seen no previous occupation – this seems at present to be the case at West Whelpington, although further excavation may unearth fresh evidence.

The spread of nucleated settlement appears to have been associated with fundamental changes in the structure of territorial lordship and may have been facilitated by the rise of the single township manor. The Conquest provided an opportunity to rationalize seigneurial control of land without respect for existing patterns of tenure or the rights of local communities. So, for example, the regular open fields and nucleated

OPPOSITE: Greystoke village, with Lowther Castle and Park in the background. The modern enclosure walls respect much of the fabric of a planned medieval village, including back roads and open fields on either side

Broad ridges which have been lowered by modern ploughing, photographed in upper Weardale under light snow. Rapidly disappearing evidence of this kind is all that remains of what were once extensive field systems

settlements of the Eden Valley appear to have followed William Rufus's seizure of Cumberland from Scotland (in 1092), after which the author of the 'C' version of the *Anglo-Saxon Chronicle*, at Peterborough, recorded that he 'sent there many peasants with their wives and livestock to live there and cultivate the land'. Nucleated settlements of similar type are absent from other parts of north-western Northumbria, by then in southern Scotland.

That regular fields and nucleated communities of bondsmen appealed to Norman lords seems clear. The system offered them the opportunity to have demesne land cultivated by unpaid labour which would provide them with produce for their own households or for market. Open fields enabled peasant farmers to share plough teams and so reduced the number of ploughs and cattle to a minimum, and these efficiency savings enabled lords to exact higher rents. The need to keep livestock to a minimum may have been of little consequence in large parts of the north, where grazing was still comparatively plentiful in the twelfth century, but there were areas where the agricultural lands of the community stretched from one boundary of the estate to the other and here open fields and co-aration (ploughing with shared teams) made good economic sense. Open fields additionally reduced the labour expended on fencing and hedging and spread risks across the widest possible spectrum of soils. It was a system capable of supporting a large population and providing lords with high returns. Such returns, in cash, labour and kind, are best exemplified in the description of Boldon

in the Boldon Book, an inquest compiled in 1183 for the Bishop of Durham. On all counts, the arrival of this system in the north does look like an imposition from above, very largely by the first few generations of the new Norman aristocracy.

Significant changes in the structure of estates had, however, already occurred during the later Saxon period and particularly during the Viking Age. Domesday Book recorded some large estates in Yorkshire, perhaps worked as an integrated economic system, and the large numbers of manorial tenants, but small numbers of ploughs, on several of these implies that co-aration was taking place – a practice which was difficult to achieve without the farmers living in close proximity. Yet even if these farms were gathered into a village, they were no more than pools of nucleation within a dispersed landscape otherwise characterized by small hamlets or individual farms.

To take just one example, the archbishop's estate at Sherburn-in-Elmet owed *geld* assessed on ninety-six carucates and had arable enough to keep sixty ploughs busy, but it had attached to it an unspecified number of 'berewicks' (outlying parcels of demesne land). The breakdown of the estate into holdings in 1086 illustrates the general structure of the estate although the berewicks themselves were not named in the Domesday inquest: the archbishop had seven ploughs in demesne and thirty-eight assorted manorial tenants with ten-and-a-

Hay being dried in traditional fashion in Rossendale. Hay-making, like harvesting, was labour-intensive work for which boon-services were often demanded by the holders of estates from their tenants

half ploughs, whose farms may have lain cheek by jowl with open fields around them, but there were also free tenants and priests and fifty-two carucates held by the archbishop's soldiers (and one thegn), under whom there were 173 tenants of assorted status. On just ninety-three per cent of this estate (the Abbot of Selby had seven carucates), so on about fifty-six ploughlands, there were eighty-eight-and-a-half ploughs at work in 1086.

Sherburn was, therefore, a classic example of what has been described as an 'overstocked' manor, that is, one with more ploughs than ploughlands on which to work. This phenomenon was widespread in Domesday England, particularly in East Anglia, Danish Mercia and Yorkshire. Various attempts have been made to explain it, for example as the concentration of ploughs and teams with which it was intended to tackle the problems of under-cultivated manors in the near vicinity, and the disparity between ploughs and ploughlands has been a major plank in the proposal that ploughlands were not a unit of land. However, this pattern coincides closely with the distribution in England of small manorial holdings often comprising no more than a freeman's farm, and it probably represents the widespread under-utilization of ploughs which were capable of ploughing 100 to 120 acres per year, in a dispersed settlement pattern within which most farmers owned a plough but used it on land well short of a ploughland. Its significance in this instance would seem to be that nucleation of settlement and the rationalization of plough teams had made little progress on the archbishop's estate focused on Sherburn by 1086, much of the land being cultivated as individual scattered farms each smaller than a ploughland, with all the diseconomies which that entailed.

Most estates listed in Yorkshire were small, often comprising just a half or one ploughland and they seem to have been single farms. In numerous instances there are repeated references to manorial holdings in a single township, and in some several were amalgamated in the Domesday inquest into a larger unit – hence the six ploughlands liable for *geld* on twelve carucates at Great Ouseburn which, in 1066, had been held by five named late-Saxon tenants. Three carucates were in a separate lordship in 1086, implying a total of six separate estates in 1066 which are unlikely to have shared a settlement site or regular field system. The estate was the subject of one of Yorkshire's numerous disputes in Domesday Book, in this instance between Robert of Brus and the king, but this does not affect its structure.

Many of these small holdings were probably sub-tenancies, held within loose-knit estates from the greater aristocracy, but their separate listing in Domesday Book implies a contrast with the extensive holdings of the earl and a few great men in northern Lancashire, the royal hundred-wide manors of southern Lancashire and the vast estates of the Church in County Durham. It was these that seem to reflect older patterns of landholding, even though in each instance changes may have occurred in the actual estates and their boundaries since the ninth century. This earlier pattern was embodied in the shires of early Northumbria, some of which survived as wapentakes (equivalent to the English hundreds) of Domesday Book, so the *Borgescire Wapentake* – 'Burghshire' – in which lay Aldbrough.

The shire was in some ways comparable to the baronial honour of the post-Conquest period. It was a unit of tenure, of public jurisdiction and of social patronage. Shires arguably provided the geographical basis for the parish system in the centuries before that was subjected to massive sub-division into manor or township-parishes in the tenth, eleventh and twelfth centuries. Similarities between the Northumbrian shire and the medieval system of Welsh tenure have often been remarked upon and the parallels are unlikely to have been coincidental, the two descending from similar origins in the sixth and seventh centuries.

The eleventh-century shire was focused on a hall or court where members of the local community fulfilled their obligations by 'boon work' performed at seasons when farming was most labour-intensive, taking payments in cash and kind, the latter often being of a bewildering complexity. Something of its working can be seen in the Domesday description of King Edward's manor and hundred of West Derby (encompassing most of Merseyside), to which numerous local thegns paid rent and were responsible for boon works at harvest time and for the maintenance of the royal court and hunting apparatus. They were subject to courts for the shire and hundred by which they could be amerced for a variety of crimes. The Domesday commissioners were in some difficulty regarding how to denote such men, whose obligations included elements which they considered both free and bond, and other south Lancashire tenants were described variously as 'roadmen' (men who owed riding services) and 'drengs' – a term denoting something which, in Norman eyes, lay midway between free and unfree tenure and which was widespread in Northumbria.

The tumbled stone-walls of a medieval shieling on the lower slopes of Ingleborough Hill. Such sites were used as residences and bases by shepherds and herdsmen during the summer months

An express thunders by while a boy fishes in the River Idle. The river separates Bawtry from Scaftworth. It was the boundary between West Yorkshire and Nottinghamshire throughout the medieval period. Before the Conquest, it was probably the boundary between Hatfield (inside Northumbria) and Mercia

Shires were long-lived and self-contained economic systems within which a degree of specialization may have occurred, with one group of tenants responsible for renders of fish, another of honey, a third of barley, and so on. Given the variable quality of the environment confronting most northern communities, such specialization was probably a sound method of exploiting the natural resources of a territory and this element of specialization encouraged a degree of exchange within the several communities of the estate, without the need for an external system of markets. Additionally most shires probably practised common pasturage, using the extensive upland, woodland and moss-land grazings which were widely available. Seasonal use of upland pastures was to be a feature of the region throughout the Middle Ages, resulting in numerous shielings (summer pastures and graziers' huts), and the droveways used to move herds between upland and lowland are still recognizable in some areas, particularly along township boundaries. That these herd movements were practised in the seventh and eighth centuries is confirmed by the existence of 'the wood of Elmet' and 'of Deira', as well as incidental references in the earliest lives of the northern saints.

Many of these extensive estates were sufficiently long-lived to leave a permanent imprint on place-names. The agricultural core of most are characterized by place-names with settlement or topographical elements and ancient churches are concentrated there, generally at or close by the site of the court. Closer to the perimeter there is a tendency on the lowlands for woodland place-names – often with the element '-ley' – to predominate and these were probably associated with less open areas where pastoralism, forestry and food collecting predominated. Bands of woodland place-names are associated with long-standing boundaries, such as that running across southern Lancashire between the ancient hundreds or shires of Makerfield (split by the eleventh century into Newton and Warrington and perhaps West Derby hundreds) and Salford. Most boundaries followed watercourses where these were available, or cut across areas of land of little agricultural value, such as old mossland or fells.

Excepting the landholdings of the St Cuthbert community, such estates are poorly documented. Archaeology has so far been signally unsuccessful in researching any part of the mid- to late Saxon settlement hierarchy outside the monasteries and York itself – that is, those sites where settlement was unusually concentrated and which are well provided with identifiable artefacts. The richest parts of Northumbria's ploughlands are obscured by the very ridges and furrows and lynchets or plough-terraces which make later medieval farming accessible to the historian. Such massive earth movement necessarily obscures whatever preceded it, and the latter is not likely to be easily found when those ridges are ploughed away by modern farming.

Although there is a school of thought that would wish to push the heavy plough back to the Iron Age, there is a difference of scale between the ridges of the medieval open fields and those associated with late prehistoric or Roman fields. Medieval ridges are unlikely to predate the introduction of the eight-ox plough, which was clearly the standard in 1086 and on which Domesday ploughlands were based. It is unclear when this technology became available to the Northumbrians. The

Place-names in North Yorkshire derived from a mixture of settlement and woodland and grazing areas

Medieval plough-terraces or lynchets in Wharfedale, now preserved under permanent pasture

The foundations of a longhouse and auxiliary structure visible as earthworks on Orton Scar, Cumbria

language of the Danish unit of *geld* liability – the carucate – and its division into eight bovates clearly imply that the heavy plough and its large plough team was already commonplace when these terms came into use, so perhaps by the late ninth century.

Although it adopted a secondary meaning in the late Saxon period as a ploughland, there was no connection between the Old English hide and the heavy plough. The hide was the standard unit in which estates were valued during the seventh and eighth centuries, when the monastic landholdings were initially coming into existence. It was not a unit of area but one of value, measured in terms of the only thing of interest to its owners. One hide of land was an estate which could be expected to deliver annual renders sufficient to support a single household of free status – that of a *ceorl*. Some idea of what was entailed can be gleaned from Bishop Aidan's grant of just one hide to St Hilda (a lady of royal birth) and her companions for their maintenance. This was clearly far more than one peasant holding. An estate of forty hides was, therefore, an estate the renders of which could support forty households of *ceorl* status, not one on which there were forty households living. Clearly such an estate required a far larger peasant workforce than that, probably on a ratio approximating to ten peasant farms to the hide.

The settlements of the kings, thegns and *ceorls* of the early to mid-Saxon period are beginning to emerge through excavation. With the abandonment of furnished burials during the seventh century, the location of even high-status settlements becomes more difficult. Away from later cultivation, a handful of such sites have been identified on

the fells of the central Pennines and Lakeland. Examples at Ribblehead and Bryant's Gill (Kentmere) have been excavated but the quantity of finds is disappointing. Comparable examples known from aerial photography still await further research. These examples were all stone-founded and, without later ploughing, have survived as identifiable earthworks, comparable to those excavated at Braaid and Cronk ny Merriu on the Isle of Man but most Northumbrian residences, even of thegnly status, were probably devoid of building stone.

Peasant farms are the most elusive element in the Northumbrian settlement hierarchy. Despite claims that settlements such as that now under excavation at West Heslerton were villages inhabited by farmers, the storage facilities provided by sunken-featured buildings, the substantial post-built halls, the vast quantities of consumer goods and the close association with an Anglian-style cemetery all imply that such settlements were centres of consumption, not agricultural production. At such sites various crafts like weaving were practised but there is no evidence whatsoever that the inhabitants were farmers. The size of West Heslerton implies that it was the focus of a large territory, supplied from renders paid by a numerous producer class, the quantity of which enabled the establishment of increasing numbers of free households over several generations. Rapid growth is entirely understandable if it is remembered that the pagan Angles practised polygamy. As their sons came of age, sub-division of the renders from the family estates enabled them to establish separate households until those

One of a small group of buildings which comprise a Viking Age settlement at Braaid, Isle of Man. The prominence of some of the structural features today owes much to its presentation after excavation and should not be taken too literally

OPPOSITE: Late seventh-century ditches signal the end of the first phase of Anglian settlement at West Heslerton and the beginning of a more planned and controlled landscape

approximated to the number of hides available to them. Where this occurred on a single site, the type of settlement visible at West Heslerton was the likely result.

The implication must be that the peasantry do not emerge into archaeology until nucleation occurred in the central Middle Ages. Indeed, where nucleation failed to take hold – as across most of Lancashire and in parts of Yorkshire – the peasantry remain impervious to modern investigation for several more centuries. At least one entire layer of the settlement system remains to be identified, and this was necessarily the most numerous, but it is difficult to see how this is to be achieved. Without markets or direct contact with the tax-demanding kings, the northern peasantry had no access to the goods which were being fabricated at the behest of the élite and circulating only within their households before (in the pagan period) interment in their cemeteries. Like their Welsh, Pictish and Scottish contemporaries, they appear to have used no pottery or distinctive metalwork and their burial rites are obscure. Their settlements seem to have been constructed without deep foundations and they had no call to build sunken-featured buildings since their storage needs were few and the

Earth and turf bank on the Isle of Man. Such barriers are common of the island and were comparatively widespread in western Northumbria. Once removed they leave no trace and are, therefore, undetectable

Modern cultivation dominates large tracts of the eastern lowlands of Northumbria as far north as Fife (as shown here) and even Angus. The result is a loss of surface features and general smoothing of the ground surface

bulk of their surplus grain left the farm as render to the élite, filling the sunken-featured buildings which characterized their settlements.

The Dark Age farmer remains one of the greatest enigmas of British history and archaeology. His imprint on the landscape is not far short of invisible, yet the maintenance of clearance, of cultivation and of grazing, all of which are widely evidenced in the pollen record, make it certain that he was present in considerable numbers. How else were the warrior aristocracy and kings, monks and bishops of Northumbria provided with the renders that freed them from the necessity of themselves cultivating the soil? Their role within society is clear enough. It is their physical remains which are ethereal.

The clearest view of early farming comes not from archaeology but from the quills of early churchmen writing of the lives of their saintly forebears. Reference has been made already to the several lives of St Cuthbert, wherein there are fleeting sketches of timber houses and shielings. Perhaps the clearest witness was an Irishman, Adomnan, Abbot of Iona, who wrote a biography of St Columba at Iona,

Occupation and re-occupation: cropmarks of successive periods of settlement and enclosure at Ronaldsway, Isle of Man

c. 688–92. Whatever the historicity of the stories he recounted, the farming routine which provided their context was surely that of the Iona which he and his audience knew in the late seventh century. While this was always outside Northumbria, the influence of Iona in the Northumbrian Church, and particularly at Lindisfarne, makes it likely that the context of his descriptive passages would have been as applicable to the Northumbrian monasteries of the age of conversion as to the mother church itself. Adomnan wrote of a young man named Colman who chanced on the elderly St Columba while returning to the monastery from milking, a vessel of fresh milk on his shoulders:

> and he asked the saint to lay a blessing on his load, according to custom. Then the saint, being some way off, with hand upraised made the sign of the cross towards it in the air, and, in God's name, blessed the vessel, which was immediately shaken strongly. The fastening-peg of the lid was pushed out through the two holes and flung away; the lid fell to the ground; the bulk of the milk was spilt . . .
>
> (trs. A.O. and M.O. Anderson, 1961, II, 16)

This was, of course, the work of a demon, which was then successfully overcome by the saint, not the result of mere clumsiness on the part of a nervous youth.

Adomnan referred elsewhere to the practice of pasturing pigs in the autumn on the fruit of trees, acorns, beech mast and so on, but perhaps the most poignant material comes in his build-up to Columba's death (Ibid., III, 23):

the saint went out of the granary, and walking back towards the monastic buildings he sat down halfway. In that place a cross that was later set in a mill-stone is still today visible, upright by the roadside. And while the saint sat there, resting for a little while, being weary with age, lo, a white horse approached him, an obedient servant who normally carried the milk-vessels from the cow-pasture to the monastery . . .

Such mundane details were mere background in Adomnan's account but they offer us a vision of stored grain, of mills, of bacon from pigs fattened in the woods of autumn, of cows milked out in the pasture, the milk carried by man or horseback to the settlement. Of such elements in the farming cycle did the lives of most men consist, whatever the language they spoke and the names they gave their homes. Their deeds have left us little trace, crowded as they have been from the stage of history by the doings of their masters, monks or warriors, ship-borne raiders or kings.

Sunset from Hobthrush Island off Lindisfarne, the site of St Cuthbert's first hermitage

Further Reading

There follows a list of suggested further reading arranged chapter by chapter, with the exception that references appropriate to chapters seven and eight are listed together. These are amalgamated so as to avoid the undue repetition which would have resulted from the heavy concentration in these chapters on Viking Age York. An attempt has been made to avoid extensive repetition in these lists and the reader may find that it is necessary to refer to the lists appropriate to earlier chapters in pursuing any particular subject or title. For example, *The Northern Counties to AD 1000*, written by the author, is of relevance to every chapter but is listed only under chapter one.

The reader should be aware that these lists are very selective. For every item incorporated, many have been omitted. Those wishing to pursue more detailed study should use the bibliographies and lists of references attached to many of the works listed. There is a comparatively complete bibliography for England above the Tees up to 1984 in *The Northern Counties to AD 1000*.

CHAPTER 1

Place of publication given only if outside London.

Bidwell, P.T., (ed.), *The Roman Fort of Vindolanda*, HBMCE Archaeological Report 1, 1985.

Birley, A.R., 'Petillius Cerealis and the Conquest of Brigantia', *Britannia*, IV (1973), pp. 179–90.

Birley, E., *Roman Britain and the Roman Army*, Kendal, Titus Wilson, 1976.

Birley, R.E., *Vindolanda. A Roman Frontier Post on Hadrian's Wall*, Thames and Hudson, 1977.

Bishop, M.C. and Dore, J.N., *Corbridge: Excavations of the Roman Fort and Town, 1947–80*, HMSO, 1988.

Bowman, A.K. and Thomas, J.D., *The Roman Writing Tablets from Vindolanda*, Gloucester, Britannia Monograph series, IV, Alan Sutton, 1984.

Branigan, K., (ed.), *Rome and the Brigantes*, Sheffield, Deptartment of Prehistory and Archaeology, University of Sheffield, 1980.

Braund, D., 'Observations on Cartimandua', *Britannia*, XV (1984), pp. 1–6.

Breeze, D.J., *The Northern Frontiers of Roman Britain*, Batsford, 1982.

Breeze, D.J. and Dobson, B., *Hadrian's Wall*, Penguin, 1987.

Brewster, T.C.M., *The Excavation of Staple How*, Wintringham, East Riding Archaeological Research Committee, 1963.

Britton, D., 'The Heathery Burn Cave Revisited', in *Prehistoric and Roman Studies*, ed. G. de G. Sieveking, British Museum, 1971, pp. 20–38.

Burgess, C., *Bronze Age Metalwork in Northern England*, Newcastle, Oriel Press, 1968.

Burgess, C. and Schmidt, P.K., *The Axes of Scotland and Northern England*, Prähistorische Bronzefunde, 9/7, Munich, Beck, 1981.

Butler, R.M., (ed.), *Soldier and Civilian in Roman Yorkshire*, Leicester, Leicester University Press, 1971.

Carver, M., Donaghey, S. and Sumpter, A.B., *Riverside Structures and a Well in Skeldergate and a Building in Bishophill*, Council for British Archaeology, Archaeology of York, fasc. 4/1, 1978.

Challis, A.J. and Harding, D.W., *Later Prehistory from the Trent to the Tyne*, Oxford, British Archaeological Reports, 20, 1975.

Chapman, J.C. and Mytum, H.C., (eds), *Settlement in North Britain, 1000 BC–AD 1000*, Oxford, British Archaeological Reports, 118, 1983.

Clack, P. and Haselgrove, S., *Rural Settlement in the Roman North*, Durham, Council for British Archaeology, Group 3, 1981.

Collingwood, R.G. and Wright, R.P., *The Roman Inscriptions of Britain*, vol. 1, *Inscriptions on Stone*, Oxford, Clarendon Press, 1965.

Cunliffe, B., *Iron Age Communities in Britain*, Routledge and Kegan Paul, 2nd edn, 1978.

Curle, J., *A Roman Frontier Post and its People: the Fort of Newstead in the Parish of Melrose*, Glasgow, 1911.

Curwen, E, 'Ancient Cultivations at Grassington, Yorkshire', *Antiquity*, II (1928), pp. 168–72.

Daniels, C.M., *Handbook to the Roman Wall*, 13th edn, Newcastle, Hill, 1978.

Dent, J.S., 'Cemeteries and Settlement Patterns of the Iron Age on the Yorkshire Wolds', *Proceedings of the Prehistoric Society*, XLVIII (1982), pp. 437–57.

——, 'The Impact of Roman Rule on Native Society in the Territory of the Parisi', *Britannia*, XIV (1983), p. 35–44.

Dio, *Roman Histories*, 9 vols., trans. E. Cary, Loeb, 1914.

Dobson, B., 'The Function of Hadrian's Wall', *Archaeologia Aeliana*, 5th series, XIV (1986), pp. 1–30.

Dore, J.N. and Gillam, J.P., *The Roman Fort at South Shields*, Newcastle, Society of Antiquaries, Monograph series I, 1979.

Frere, S.S., *Britannia*, Routledge and Kegan Paul, 1978.

Gillam, J.P. and Daniels, C.M., 'The Roman Mausoleum at Shorden Brae, Beaufront, Corbridge, Northumberland', *Archaeologia Aeliana*, 4th series, XXXIX (1961), pp.37-61.

Gilyard Beer, R., *The Romano-British Baths at Wells*, Leeds, 1951.

Green, M.J., *A Corpus of Small Cult-objects from the Military Areas of Roman Britain*, Oxford, British Archaeological Reports, British series, 52, 1978.

——, *The Gods of the Celts*, Gloucester, Alan Sutton, 1986.

Hanson, W.S., *Agricola and the Conquest of the North*, Batsford, 1987.

Hanson, W.S. and Campbell, D.B., 'The Brigantes: from Clientage to Conquest', *Britannia*, XVII (1986), pp. 73–89.

Hanson, W.S., Daniels, C.M., Dore, J.N. and Gillam, J.P., 'The Agricolan Supply Base at Red House, Corbridge', *Archaeologia Aeliana*, 5th series, VII (1979), pp. 1–88.

Hanson, W.S. and Maxwell, G.S., *Rome's North-West Frontier: the Antonine Wall*, Edinburgh, Edinburgh University Press, 1983.

Harding, A.F., Excavations in the Prehistoric Ritual Complex near Milfield, Northumberland', *Proceedings of the Prehistoric Society*, XLVII (1981), pp. 87–135.

Harding, D.W., (ed.), *Later Prehistoric Settlement in South-East Scotland*, Edinburgh, University of Edinburgh, Occasional Paper 8, 1982.

Hartley, B. and Fitts, L., *The Brigantes*, Gloucester, Alan Sutton, 1988.

Haselgrove, C.C., 'The Later Pre-Roman Iron Age between the Humber and the Tyne', in *Settlement and Society in the Roman North*, eds. P.R. Wilson, R.F.J. Jones and D.M. Evans, Bradford, School of Archaeological Science, University of Bradford, and the Roman Antiquaries Section of the Yorkshire Archaeological Society, pp. 9–26.

Haselgrove, C.C. and Turnbull, P., *Stanwick: Excavation and Fieldwork. Second Interim Report*, Durham, University of Durham, Department of Archaeology, Occasional Paper 5, 1984.

Hayfield, C., *An Archaeological Survey of the Parish of Wharram Percy, East Yorkshire I. The Evolution of the Roman Landscape*, Oxford, British Archaeological Reports, British series, 172, 1987.

Heslop, D.H., *The Excavation of an Iron Age Settlement at Thorpe Thewles, Cleveland, 1980–82*, Council for British Archaeology, Research Report No. 65, 1987.

Higham, N.J., 'Dyke Sytems in North Cumbria', *Bulletin of the Board of Celtic Studies*, 28 (1978), pp. 142–55.

——, *The Northern Counties to AD 1000*, Harlow and New York, Longman, 1986.

——, 'Brigantia Revisited', *Northern History*, XXIII (1987), pp. 1–19.

——, 'Landscape and Land-Use in Northern England: a Survey of Agricultural Potential, *c.* 500 BC–AD 1000', *Landscape History*, IX (1987), pp. 35–44.

——, (ed.), *The Changing Past*, Manchester, Manchester University, Department of Extra-Mural Studies, 1979.

Higham, N.J. and Jones, G.D.B., 'Frontiers, Forts and Farmers, Cumbrian Aerial Survey, 1974–5', *Archaeological Journal*, CXXXII (1975), pp. 16–53.

——, 'The Excavation of Two Romano-British Farm Sites in North Cumbria', *Britannia*, XIV (1983), pp. 45–72.

——, *The Carvetii*, Gloucester, Alan Sutton, 1985.

Jobey, G., 'An Iron Age Homestead at West Brandon, Durham', *Archaeologia Aeliana*, 4th series, XL (1962), pp. 1–34.

——, 'Hill-forts and Settlements in Northumberland', *Archaeologia Aeliana*, 4th series, XLIII (1965), pp. 21–64.

——, 'Burnswark Hill'. *Dumfriesshire and Galloway Natural History and Archaeological Society Transactions*, LIII (1977–8), pp. 57–104.

——, 'Iron Age and Romano-British Settlements on Kennel Hall Knowe, North Tynedale, Northumberland', *Archaeologia Aeliana*, 5th series, VI (1978), pp. 1–28.

——, 'The settlement at Doubstead and Romano-British settlement on the coastal plain betweeen Tyne and Forth', *Archaeologia Aeliana*, 5th series, X (1982), pp. 1–23.

Jones, M., *England Before Domesday*, Batsford, 1986.

King, C.A.M., *Northern England*, Methuen, 1976.

MacGregor, M., 'The Early Iron Age Metalwork Hoard from Stanwick, North Riding, Yorkshire' *Proceedings of the Prehistoric Society*, XXVIII (1962), pp. 17–57.

Mann, J.C., 'The Function of Hadrian's Wall', *Archaeologia Aeliana*, 5th series, XVIII (1990), pp. 51–4.

Maxfield, V., 'Hadrian's Wall in its Imperial Setting', *Archaeologia Aeliana*, 5th series, XVIII (1990), pp. 1–28.

Miket, R. and Burgess, C., (eds.), *Between and Beyond the Walls: Essays on the Prehistory and History of North Britain in Honour of George Jobey*, Edinburgh, Donald, 1984.

Millett, M., *The Romanization of Britain: an Essay in Archaeological Interpretation*, Cambridge, Cambridge University Press, 1990.

Pausanias, *Description of Greece*, 6 vols., trans. W.H.S. Jones, Loeb, 1918.

Perrin, J.R., *Roman Pottery from the Colonia: Skeldergate and Bishophill*, The Archaeology of York, XVI, fasc. 2, 1981.

Piggott, C.M., 'The Excavations at Hownam Rings, Roxburghshire', *Proceedings of the Society of Antiquaries of Scotland*, LXXXII (1947–8), pp. 193–225.

Potter, T.W., *Romans in North-West England*, Kendal, Titus Wilson, 1979.

Ptolemy, *Geographia*, introduced by R.A. Skelton, Amsterdam, Theatrum Orbis Terrarum, 1969.

Raistrick, A., 'Prehistoric Cultivations at Grassington', *Yorkshire Archaeological Journal*, XXXIII (1937), pp. 116–74.

Raistrick, A. and Chapman, S.E., 'The Lynchet Groups of Upper Wharfedale', *Antiquity*, III (1929), pp. 165–81.

Ramm, H.G. *The Parisi*, Duckworth, 1978.

Richmond, Sir I.A., *Roman and Native in North Britain*, Edinburgh and Nelson, 1958.

Riley, D.N., *Early Landscape from the Air*, Sheffield, Department of Prehistory and Archaeology, University of Sheffield, 1980.

Ritchie, G. and Ritchie, A., *Scotland – Archaeology and Early History*, Thames and Hudson, 1981.

Rivet, A.L.F. and Smith, C., *The Place-Names of Roman Britain*, Batsford, 1979.

Royal Commission for Historic Monuments, *An Inventory of the Historic Monuments in the City of York I, Eburacum, Roman York*, HMSO, 1962.

Ross, A., 'The Horned God of the Brigantes', *Archaeologia Aeliana*, 4th series, XXXIX (1961), pp. 63–85.

Salway, P., *The Frontier People of Roman Britain*, Cambridge, Cambridge University Press, 1965.

——, *Roman Britain*, Oxford, Oxford University Press, 1981.

Simmons, I.G., 'Late Mesolithic Societies and the Environment of the Uplands of England and Wales', *Journal of Archaeological Science*, II (1975), pp. 1–15.

Simmons, I.G. and Tooley, M.J., (eds), *The Environment in British Prehistory*, Duckworth, 1981.

Spratt, D.A., (ed.), *Prehistoric and Roman Archaeology of North-East Yorkshire*, Oxford, British Archaeological Reports, 104, 1982.

Stead, I.M., *The La Téne Cultures of Eastern Yorkshire*, York, York Philosophical Society, 1965.

——, 'An Iron Age Hill-fort at Grimthorpe, Yorkshire', *Proceedings of the Prehistoric Society*, XXXIV (1968), pp. 148–90.

——, 'Beadlam Roman Villa: an Interim Report', *Yorkshire Archaeological Journal*, XLIII (1971), pp. 178–86.

——, *The Arras Culture*, York, York Philosophical Society, 1979.

Tacitus, C., *Historiae*, 2 vols, eds. E. Capps *et al.*, Loeb, 1925.

——, *De Vita Agricolae*, ed. R.M. Ogilvie and Sir I. Richmond, Oxford, Oxford University Press, 1967.

——, *Annales*, 5 vols, ed. J. Jackson, Loeb, 1970.

Turnbull, P., 'Stanwick in the Northern Iron Age', *Durham Archaeological Journal*, I (1984), pp. 41–9.

Turner, R., 'A Romano-British Cemetery at Lanchester, Durham', *Archaeologia Aeliana*, 5th series, XVIII (1990), pp. 63–77.

Varley, W.J., 'A Summary of the Excavations at Castle Hill, Almondbury 1939–72', in *Hill-forts: Later Prehistoric Earthworks of the British Isles*, ed. D.W. Harding, 1976, pp. 119–31.

Wacher, J.S., *Excavations at Brough-on-Humber, 1958–61*, Research Report of the Society of Antiquaries of No. 25, 1969.

Wenham, L.P., *The Romano-British Cemetery at Trentholme Drive, York*, Ministry of Public Buildings and Works, HMSO, 1968.

Wheeler, Sir R.E.M., *The Stanwick Fortifications*, Oxford, Oxford University Press, for the Society of Antiquaries, 1954.

CHAPTER 2

Alcock, L., 'Quantity or Quality: the Anglian Graves of Bernicia', in *Angles, Saxon and Jutes*, ed. V.I. Evison, Oxford, Clarendon Press, 1981, pp. 168–83.

Ammianus Marcellinus, *Historia*, ed. T.E. Page, Loeb, 1935.

Augustine, St, *Confessions*, trans. E.B. Pusey, ed. A.H. Armstrong, Dent, 1907.

Bede, *Historia Ecclesiastica Gentis Anglorum*, in *Baedae Opera Historica*, ed. C. Plummer, Oxford, 1896. Also available in various translations, such as: *Bede's Ecclesiastical History of the English People*, ed. and trans. B. Colgrave and R.A.B. Mynors, Oxford, Clarendon Press, 1969; *A History of the English Church and People*, trans. L. Sherley-Price, Penguin, 1955 and 1968.

Casey, P.J., (ed.), *The End of Roman Britain*, Oxford, British Archaeological Reports, 1979.

Chadwick, N.K., *Celtic Britain*, Thames and Hudson, 1964.

Daniels, C.M., 'Excavations at Wallsend and the 4th Century Barracks on Hadrian's Wall', in *Roman Frontier Studies XII*, eds. W.S. Hanson, and L.J.F. Keppie, Oxford, British Archaeological Reports, British series, 71 (1980), i, pp. 173–93.

Eagles, B.N., *The Anglo-Saxon Settlement of Humberside*, Oxford, British Archaeological Reports, British series, 68, i and ii, 1979.

Faull, M.L., 'British Survival in Anglo-Saxon Northumbria', in *Celtic Survival*, ed. L. Laing, Oxford, British Archaeological Reports, British series, 37 (1977), pp. 1–56.

Faull, M.L. and Moorhouse, S.A., eds., *West Yorkshire: An Archaeological Survey to AD 1500*, Wakefield, West Yorkshire County Council, 1981.

Gallagher, D.B., 'The Anglo-Saxon Cemetery of Hob Hill, Saltburn', *Yorkshire Archaeological Journal*, LIX (1987), pp. 9–28.

Gildas, *The Ruin of Britain*, ed. and trans. M. Winterbottom, Chichester, Phillimore, 1978.

Gillam, J.P., 'Romano-Saxon Pottery: an Alternative Explanation', in *The End of Roman Britain*, ed. P.J. Casey, Oxford, British Archaeological Reports, 1979, pp. 103–18.

Higham, N.J., 'The Origins of Inglewood', *Transactions of the Cumberland and Westmorland Antiquarian and Archaeological Society*, new series, LXXXVI (1986), pp. 85–100.

——, 'The Geographical Description of Britain', in the *De Excidio Britanniae* of Gildas: Old Light on the Dark Age Landscape', *Journal of Historical Geography*, 17 (1991), pp. 363–72.

——, 'Gildas, Roman Walls and British Dykes', *Cambridge Medieval Celtic Studies*, 22 (1991), pp. 1–14.

——, *Rome, Britain and the Anglo-Saxons*, Seaby, 1992.

Holder, P.A., *The Roman Army in Britain*, Batsford, 1982.

Hope-Taylor, B., *Yeavering: an Anglo-British Centre of Early Northumbria*, HMSO, 1977.

Hornsby, W. and Stanton, R., 'The Roman Fort at Huntcliff, near Saltburn', *Journal of Roman Studies*, II (1912), pp. 215–32.

Hornsby, W. and Laverick, J.D., 'The Roman Signal Station at Goldsborough, near Whitby', *Archaeological Journal*, LXXXIX (1932), pp. 203–19.

Jackson, K.H., *Language and History in Early Britain*, Edinburgh, Edinburgh University Press, 1956.

James, S., 'Britain and the Late Roman Army', Oxford, British Archaeological Reports, British series, 136 (1984), pp. 161–86.

James, S., Marshall, A. and Millett, M., 'An Early Medieval Building Tradition', *Archaeological Journal*, CXLI (1984), pp. 182–215.

Jones, G.D.B. and Shotter, D.C.A., *Roman Lancaster*, Manchester, Brigantia Monographs, 1988.

Laing, L. and Laing J., *Celtic Britain and Ireland 200–800: the myth of the Dark Ages*, Dublin, Irish Academic Press, 1990.

Lapidge, M. and Dumville, D.N., (eds), *Gildas: New Approaches*, Woodbridge, Boydell and Brewer, 1984.

Miket, R., 'A Restatement of Evidence for Bernician Anglo-Saxon Burials', in *Anglo-Saxon Cemeteries*, ed. P.A. Rahtz, T. Dickinson, and L. Watts, Oxford, British Archaeological Reports, British series, 82 (1980), pp. 289–306.

Miller, M., 'Stilicho's Pictish War', *Britannia*, VI (1975), pp. 141–50.

Myres, J.N.L., *Anglo-Saxon Pottery and the Settlement of England*, Oxford, Oxford University Press, 1969.

Myres, J.N.L. and Southern, W.H., *The Anglo-Saxon Cremation Cemetery at Sancton, East Yorkshire*, Hull, Hull Museum Publications, CCXVIII, 1973.

Orosius, Paulus, *Historiarum Adversum Paganos Libri VII*, trans. I.W. Raymond, New York, Columbia University Press, 1932.

Patrick, St, *Letter to Coroticus*, in *St. Patrick: His Writings and Muirchu's Life*, ed. and trans. A.B.E. Hood, Chichester, Phillimore, 1978.

Potter, T.W., *Romans in North-West England*, Kendal, Titus Wilson, 1979.

Powesland, D., 'West Heslerton, 1989: The Anglian Settlement. An Interim Report', unpublished interim report précised in *Medieval Settlement Research Group Annual Report*, IV (1990), p. 46.

——, 'Archaeological Excavations, 1987–90. An Interim Report on the Anglo-Saxon Village at West Heslerton, North Yorkshire', *Medieval Settlement Research Group, Annual Report*, V (1991), pp. 36–41.

Powesland, D., with Haughton, C. and Hanson, J., 'Excavations at Heslerton, North Yorkshire, 1978–82', *Archaeological Journal*, CXLIII (1986), pp. 53–173.

Rahtz, P., Hayfield, C. and Bateman, J., *Two Roman Villas at Wharram le Street*, York, York University Archaeological Publications, II, 1986.

Roberts, W.I., *Romano-Saxon Pottery*, Oxford, British Archaeological Reports, British series, 106, 1982.

Stead, I.M., *Rudston Roman Villa*, Leeds, Yorkshire Archaeological Society, 1980.

Thompson, E.A., 'Gildas and the History of Britain', *Britannia*, X (1979), pp. 203–26.

Watts, V.E., 'The Evidence of Place-Names, II', in *Medieval Settlement*, ed. P.H. Sawyer, Edward Arnold, 1976, pp. 212–22.

Williams, S., *Diocletian and the Roman Recovery*, Batsford, 1985.

CHAPTER 3

Ager, B. and Gilmour, B., 'A Pattern-welded Anglo-Saxon Sword from Acklam Wold', *Yorkshire Archaeological Journal*, LX (1988), pp. 13–24.

Alcock, L., 'Presidential Address: Gwyr y Gogledd: an Archaeological Appraisal', *Archaeologia Cambrensis*, CXXXII (1983), pp. 1–18.

Bartley, D.D., Chambers, C. and Hart-Jones, B., 'The Vegetational History of Parts of South and East Durham', *New Phytologist*, 77 (1976), pp. 437–68.

Blair, P.H., 'The origins of Northumbria', *Archaeologia Aeliana*, 4th series, XXV (1947), pp. 1–51.

Charles-Edwards, T.M., 'The Authenticity of the Gododdin: an Historian's View', in *Studies in Old Welsh Poetry*, ed. R. Bromwich and R.B. Jones, Cardiff, Cardiff University Press, 1978, pp. 44–71.

Colgrave, B., (ed.), *Two Lives of St. Cuthbert*, Cambridge, Cambridge University Press, 1940.

Colgrave, B., (ed.), *The Earliest Life of Gregory the Great by an anonymous Monk of Whitby*, Cambridge, Cambridge University Press, 1985 edn.

Donaldson, A. and Turner, J., 'A Pollen Diagram from Hallowell Moss, near Durham City', *Biogeography*, IV (1977), pp. 25–33.

Dumville, D.N., '"Nennius" and the *Historia Brittonum*', *Studia Celtica*, X–XI (1975–6), pp. 78–95.

——, 'On the North British Section of the *Historia Brittonum*', *Welsh Historical Review*, VIII (1976–7), pp. 345–54.

——, 'The Anglian Collection of Royal Genealogies and Regnal Lists', *Anglo-Saxon England*, V (1976), pp. 23–50.

——, 'The Historical Value of the *Historia Brittonum*', *Arthurian Literature*, VI (1986), pp. 1–26.

——, 'The Origins of Northumbria: Some Aspects of the British Background', in *The Origins of Anglo-Saxon Kingdoms*, ed. S. Bassett, Leicester, Leicester University Press, 1989, pp. 213–222.

——, 'The Tribal Hidage: an introduction to its texts and their history', in *The Origins of Anglo-Saxon Kingdoms*, ed. S. Bassett, Leicester, Leicester University Press, 1989, appendix 1.

Eddi[us Stephanus], *The Life of Bishop Wilfrid*, trans. and ed. B. Colgrave, Cambridge, Cambridge University Press, 1927.

Faull, M., 'The Semantic Development of Old Englsh *wealh*', *Leeds Studies in English*, VIII (1975), pp. 20–44.

——, 'Place-Names and the Kingdom of Elmet', *Nomina*, IV (1980), pp. 21–3.

Gates, T. and O'Brien, C., 'Cropmarks at Milfield and New Bewick and the Recognition of *Grubenhäuser* in Northumberland', *Archaeologia Aeliana*, 5th series, XVI (1988), pp. 1–9.

Higham, N.J., 'Cavalry in Bernicia?', *Northern History*, XXVII (1991), pp. 17–19.

——, 'Tacitus, the *Germania* and the Origins of 'Sunken-Featured Buildings', *Medieval Settlement Research Group, Annual Report*, V (1991), forthcoming.

Hogg, A.H.A., 'Llwyfenydd' *Antiquity*, XX (1946), pp. 210–11.

Jackson, K.H., 'The Britons in Southern Scotland', *Antiquity*, XXIX (1955), pp. 77–88.

——, 'Edinburgh and the Anglian Occupation of Lothian', in *The Anglo-Saxons*, ed. P. Clemoes, Cambridge, Cambridge University Press, 1959, pp. 35–42.

——, *The Gododdin: The Oldest Scottish Poem*, Edinburgh, Edinburgh University Press, 1969.

Miller, M., 'Historicity and the Pedigrees of the Northcountrymen', *Bulletin of the Board of Celtic Studies*, 3rd series, XXVI (1975), pp. 255–80.

——, 'The Commanders at Arthuret', *Transactions of the Cumberland and Westmor-*

land Antiquarian and Archaeological Society, new series, LXXV (1975), pp. 96–118.

——, 'Bede's Use of Gildas', *English Historical Review*, XC (1975), pp. 241–61.

——, 'The Dates of Deira', *Anglo-Saxon England*, 8 (1979), pp. 35–61.

Morris, J., ed., *Nennius: British History and the Welsh Annals*, Chichester, Phillimore, 1980.

Mortimer, J.R., *Forty Years Researches in British and Saxon Burial Mounds of East Yorkshire*, A. Brown and Sons, 1905.

Myres, J.N.L., 'The Teutonic Settlement of Northern England', *History*, new series, XX (1935–6), pp. 250–62.

Roberts, B.F., (ed.), *Early Welsh Poetry: Studies in the Book of Aneirin*, Aberystwyth, National Library of Wales, 1988.

Smith, A.H., *The Place-Names of the East Riding of Yorkshire*, Cambridge, Cambridge University Press for the Society for English Place-Name Studies, 1937.

St Joseph, J.K., 'Sprouston, Roxburghshire: an Anglo-Saxon Settlement Discovered by Air Reconnaissance', *Anglo-Saxon England*, X (1982), pp. 191–9.

Tacitus, C., *Germania*, T.E. Page and W.H.D. Rouse, Loeb, 1914.

West, S., *West Stow: The Anglo-Saxon Village*, East Anglian Archaeology, XXIV, 1985.

CHAPTER 4

Blair, P.H. and Lapidge, M., (eds), *Anglo-Saxon Northumbria*, London, Variorum Reprints, 1984.

Campbell, J., *Essays in Anglo-Saxon History*, Hambledon Press, 1986.

——, (ed.) *The Anglo-Saxons*, Phaidon Press, 1982.

Chadwick, N.K., (ed.), *Celt and Saxon: Studies in the Early British Border*, Cambridge, Cambridge University Press, 1963.

Colgrave, B. and Mynors, R.A.B., (eds), *Bede's Ecclesiastical History of the English People*, Oxford, Clarendon Press, 1969.

Cramp, R., 'Anglo-Saxon Settlement', in *Settlement in North Britain, 1000 BC–AD 1000*, eds. J.C. Chapman and H.C. Mytum, Oxford, British Archaeological Reports, British series, 118, 1983, pp. 263–97.

Craster, Sir E., 'The Patrimony of St. Cuthbert', *English Historical Review*, LXIX (1954), pp. 177–99.

Gelling, M., *Signposts to the Past*, Dent, 2nd edn, 1988.

——, 'The Early History of Western Mercia', in *The Origin of English Kingdoms*, (ed.) S. Bassett, Leicester, Leicester University Press, 1989, pp. 184–201.

Hart, C.R., *The Early Charters of Northern England and the north Midlands*, Leicester, Leicester University Press, 1975.

Higham, N.J., 'The Historical Context of the Tribal Hidage', in *The Burghal Hidage*, ed. D.H. Hill and A.R. Rumble, Manchester, Manchester University Press, forthcoming.

——, 'Medieval 'Overkingship' in Wales: The Earliest Evidence', *Welsh History Review*, forthcoming.

Kenyon, D., *The Origins of Lancashire*, Manchester, Manchester University Press, 1991.

Kirby, D.P., (ed.), *St. Wilfrid at Hexham*, Newcastle, Oriel Press, 1974.

——, *The Earliest English Kings*, Unwin Hyman, 1991.

Sawyer, P.H., *From Roman Britain to Norman England*, Methuen, 1978.

Wilson, D., 'A Note on Old English *hearg* and *weoh* as Place-Name Elements Representing Different Types of Pagan Saxon Worship Sites', in *Anglo-Saxon Studies in Archaeology and History*, ed. S.C. Hawkes, Oxford, Oxford University Committee for Archaeology, 1985, pp. 179–83.

Yorke, B., *Kings and Kingdoms of Early Anglo-Saxon England*, Seaby, 1990.

CHAPTER 5

Beresford, M. and Hurst, J., *Wharram Percy: Deserted Medieval Village*, Batsford, 1990.

Birch, W. de Gray, *Cartularium Saxonicum*, I, Whiting and Company, 1885.

Blair, P.H., 'The Northumbrians and their Southern Frontier', *Archaeologia Aeliana*, 4th series, XXVI (1948), pp. 98–126.

Bonner, G., Rollason, D. and Stancliffe, C., *St Cuthbert and his Cult and his Community*, Woodbridge, Boydell Press, 1989.

Clack, P.A.G. and Gill, B.H., 'The Land Divisions of County Durham in the Early Medieval Period (Fifth to Eleventh Centuries): the Uplands', *Medieval Village Research Group, Annual Report*, XXVIII (1980), 30–4.

Cramp, R., *Anglian and Viking York*, York, Borthwick Papers, XXXIII, 1967.

——, 'Excavations at the Saxon Monastic Sites of Monkwearmouth and Jarrow, Co. Durham: an Interim Report', *Medieval Archaeology*, XIII (1969), pp. 21–65.

——, 'Anglo-Saxon Monasteries of the North', *Scottish Archaeological Forum*, V (1973), pp. 104–24.

——, 'Monastic Sites', in *The Archaeology of Anglo-Saxon England*, ed. D.M. Wilson, Methuen, pp. 201–52.

——, 'The Window Glass from the Monastic Site of Jarrow', *Journal of Glass Studies*, XVII (1975), pp. 88–95.

Cramp, R. and Douglas-Home, C., 'New Discoveries at The Hirsel, Coldstream, Berwickshire', *Proceedings of the Society of Antiquaries, Scotland*, CIX (1977–8), pp. 223–32.

Cronyn, J.M. and Horie, C.V., *St. Cuthbert's Coffin*, Durham, Durham Cathedral, 1985.

Daniels, R., 'The Anglo-Saxon Monastery at Church Close, Hartlepool, Cleveland', *Archaeological Journal*, CXLV (1988), pp. 158–210.

Farrell, R.T., (ed.), *Bede and Anglo-Saxon England*, Oxford, British Archaeological Reports, British series, 46, 1978.

Fletcher, E., 'The influence of Merovingian Gaul on Northumbria in the Seventh Century', *Medieval Archaeology*, XXIV (1980), pp. 69–87.

Hamlin, A., 'Iona: A View from Ireland', *Proceedings of the Society of Antiquaries, Scotland*, CXVII (1987), pp. 17–22.

Hawkes, J. and Dixon, K.R., 'The Miracle-Scene on the Rothbury Cross-Shaft', *Archaeologia Aeliana*, 5th series, XVII (1989), pp. 207–11.

Hill, P., *Whithorn 2: Excavations 1984–1987: an Interim Report* Whithorn, Whithorn Trust, 1988.

Kirby, D.P., *The Earliest English Kings*, Unwin Hyman, 1991.

Kitzinger, E. and McIntyre, D., *The Coffin of St. Cuthbert*, Oxford, Oxford University Press for Durham Cathedral, 1950.

Lapidge, M., 'Byrhtferth of Ramsey and the Early Sections of the *Historia Regum* attributed to Symeon of Durham', *Anglo-Saxon England*, X (1982), pp. 97–122.

Mainman, A.J., *Anglo-Scandinavian Pottery from Coppergate*, London, Council for British Archaeology, Archaeology of York, fasc. 16/5, 1990.

Mc Gurk, P., *Latin Gospel Books, AD 400 to AD 800*, Paris, Brussells, Anvers Amsterdam, 1961.

Metcalf, D.M., 'Monetary Expansion and Recession: Interpreting Distribution Patterns of Seventh and Eighth-Century coins', in *Coins and the Archaeologist*, ed. J.Casey and R. Reece, Seaby, 1988, pp. 230–53.

——, (ed.), *Coinage in Ninth-Century Northumbria*, Oxford, British Archaeological Reports, British series, 180, 1987.

Morris, C.D., 'Pre-Conquest Sculpture of the Tees Valley', *Medieval Archaeology*, XX (1976), pp. 140–6.

Morris, R.K., 'Alcuin, York and the *alma sophia*', in *The Anglo-Saxon Church*, eds. L.A.S. Butler and R.K. Morris, Council for British Archaeology, 1986, pp. 80–9.

Parker, M.S., 'Some Notes on the Pre-Norman History of Doncaster', *Yorkshire Archaeological Journal*, LIX (1987), pp. 29–44.

Parkes, M., *The Scriptorium of Monkwearmouth–Jarrow*, Jarrow, the Rector, Jarrow Lectures, 1982.

Pirie, J.E., 'Finds of "sceattas" and "stycas" of Northumbria', in *Anglo-Saxon Monetary History: Essays in Memory of Michael Dolley*, ed. M.A.S. Blackburn, Leicester, Leicester University Press, 1986, pp. 67–90.

Plummer, C., (ed.), *Historia Abbatum Auctore Anonymo*, Oxford, Oxford University Press, 1896.

Royal Commission for the Ancient Monuments of Scotland, *Argyll*, IV (Iona), 1982.

Taylor, J. and Taylor, H., 'Pre-Norman Churches of the Border', in *Celt and Saxon: Studies in the Early British Border*, ed. N.K. Chadwick, Cambridge, Cambridge University Press, 1963, pp. 210–57.

White, A., 'Finds from the Anglian Monastery at Whitby', *Yorkshire Archaeological Journal*, LVI (1984), pp. 33–40.

Whitelock, D., (ed.), *English Historical Documents*, I, Eyre and Spottiswood, 1955.

CHAPTER 6

Archibald, M., 'The Dating of the Coins from the Cuerdale Hoard', in *Viking Treasure from the North-West: the Cuerdale Hoard in its Context*, ed. J. Graham-Campbell, Liverpool, National Museum and Galleries on Merseyside, Occassional Papers, forthcoming, pp. 15–20.

Arnold, T., (ed.), *Symeonis Monachi Opera Omnia*, Longmans, 1882–5.

Bailey, R.N., *Viking Age Sculpture*, Collins, 1980.

——, 'Aspects of Viking Age Sculpture in Cumbria', in *The Scandinavians in Cumbria*, eds. J.R. Baldwin and I.D. Whyte, Edinburgh, Scottish Society for Northern Studies, 1985, 53–64.

Bersu, G. and Wilson, D.M., *Three Viking Graves in the Isle of Man*, Society for Medieval Archaeology, Monograph series, I, 1966.

Blackburn, M.A.S., (ed.), *Anglo-Saxon Monetary History: Essays in Memory of Michael Dolley*, Leicester, Leicester University Press, 1986.

Cameron, K., 'Scandinavian Settlement in the Territory of the Five Boroughs', *Journal of the English Place-Name Society*, (1975) pp. 139–56.

Campbell, A., 'Two Notes on the Norse Kingdoms in Northumbria', *English Historical Review*, LVII (1942), pp. 85–97.

——, (ed.), *The Battle of Brunanburh*, Oxford, Oxford University Press, 1938.

——, (ed.), *The Chronicle of Æthelweard*, Nelson, 1962.

Collingwood, W.G., *Northumbrian Crosses of the Pre-Norman Age*, Faber and Gwyer, 1927.

Cramp, R.J., *The British Academy Corpus of Anglo-Saxon Stone Sculpture in England: I: County Durham and Northumberland*, Oxford, Oxford University Press for the British Academy, 1984.

Cramp, R.J. and Bailey, R.N., *The British Academy Corpus of Anglo-Saxon Stone Sculpture in England: II: Cumberland, Westmorland and Lancashire North of the Sands*, Oxford, Oxford University Press for the British Academy, 1988.

Cramp, R.J. and Lang, J.T., 'Northumbrian Sculpture', in *A Century of Anglo-Saxon Sculpture*, Newcastle upon Tyne, Frank Graham, 1977.

Craster, H.H.E., 'The Red Book of Durham', *English Historical Review*, XL (1925), pp. 504–32.

Dodgson, J. McN., 'The Background of Brunanburh', *Saga Book of the Viking Society*, XIV (1953–7), pp. 303–16.

Dolley, R.H.M., *The Hiberno-Norse Coins in the British Museum*, British Museum, 1966.

Fell, C., Foote, P., Graham-Campbell, J. and Thomson, R., *The Viking Age in the Isle of Man* Viking Society for Northern Research, 1983.

Fellows Jensen, G., 'Place-Name Research and Northern History: a Survey with a Bibliography', *Northern History*, VIII (1973), pp. 1–23.

——, 'Scandinavian Settlement in Cumbria and Dumfriesshire: the Place-Name Evidence', in *The Scandinavians in Cumbria*, eds. J.R. Baldwin and I.D. Whyte, Edinburgh, Scottish Society for Northern Studies, 1985, pp. 65–82.

——, *Scandinavian Settlement Names in the North-West*, Copenhagen, C.A. Reitzel, 1985.

Firby, M. and Lang, J., 'The Pre-Conquest Sculpture at Stonegreave', *Yorkshire Archaeological Journal*, LIII (1981), pp. 17–29.

Foote, P.G. and Wilson, D.M., *The Viking Achievement*, Sidgwick and Jackson, 1970.

Graham-Campbell, J., *The Viking World*, Frances Lincoln Publishers, 1980

——, 'Some Archaeological Reflections on the Cuerdale Hoard', in *Coinage in Ninth-Century Northumbria*, ed. D.M. Metcalf, Oxford, British Archaeological Reports, British series, 180, 1987, pp. 329–44.

——, (ed.), *Viking Treasure from the North-West: the Cuerdale Hoard in its Context*, Liverpool, National Museums and Galleries on Merseyside, 1992.

Hall, R. A. (ed.), *Viking Age York and the North*, Council for British Archaeology, 1978.

Hall, R., Daniels, M. and York, R., *1000 Years of York: The Archaeological Story*, York, York Archaeological Trust, 1978.

Hennessy, W.M., (ed.), *The Annals of Ulster*, vol. I, 1887.

Higham, N.J., 'The Scandinavians in North Cumbria: Raids and Settlement in the Later Ninth to Mid-Tenth Centuries', in *The Scandinavians in Cumbria*, eds. J.R. Baldwin and I.D. Whyte, Edinburgh, Scottish Society for Northern Studies, 1985, pp. 37–52.

——, 'The Cheshire *burhs* and the Mercian frontier to 924', *Transactions of the Lancashire and Cheshire Antiquarian Society*, LXXXV (1988), pp. 193–221.

——, 'Northumbria, Mercia and the Irish Sea Vikings AD 893–924', in *Viking Treasure from the North-West: the Cuerdale Hoard in its Context*, ed. J. Graham-Campbell, National Liverpool Museums and Gallerieson Merseyside, 1992, pp. 21–30.

Lang, J.T., 'Sigurd and Weland in Pre-Conquest Carving from Northern England', *Yorkshire Archaeological Journal*, XLVIII (1976), pp. 83–94

——, 'The Hogback: A Viking Colonial Monument', in *Anglo-Saxon Studies in Archaeology and History*, III, (ed.) D. Brown, Oxford, 1984.

——, (ed.), *Anglo-Saxon and Viking Age Sculpture and its Context*, Oxford, British Archaeological Reports, British series, 44, 1978.

Lyon, C.S.S. and Stewart, B.H.I.H., 'The Northumbrian Viking Coins in the Cuerdale Hoard', *Anglo-Saxon Coins*, ed. R.H.M. Dolley, 1961, pp. 96–121.

MacGregor, A., *Anglo-Scandinavian Finds from Lloyds Bank, Pavement and Other Sites*, Council for British Archaeology, Archaeology of York, 17/3, 1982.

Mainman, A.J., *Anglo-Scandinavian Pottery from Coppergate*, Council for British Archaeology, 1990.

Metcalf, M., (ed.), *Ninth-Century Coinage in Northumbria*, Oxford, British Archaeological Reports, British series, 180, 1987.

Morris, C.D., 'Northumbria and the Viking Settlement: the Evidence for Landholding', *Archaeologia Aeliana*, 5th series, V (1977), pp. 81–104.

Moulden, J. and Tweddle D., *Anglo-Scandinavian Settlement South West of the Ouse*, Council for British Archaeology, Archaeology of York, fasc. 8/1, 1986.

O'Connor, T.P., *Bones from Anglo-Saxon Levels at 16–22 Coppergate*, Council for British Archaeology, 1989.

Pirie, E.J.E., *Post-Roman Coins from York Excavations 1971–81*, Council for British Archaeology, Archaeology of York, fasc. 8/1, 1986.

Radner, J.N., (ed.), *Fragmentary Annals of Ireland*, Dublin, Dublin Institute for Advanced Studies, 1978.

Sawyer, P.H., *The Age of the Vikings*, Edward Arnold, 2nd edn, 1978.

——, 'The Causes of the Viking Expansion', in *Viking Civilization*, ed. R.T. Farrell, Phillimore, 1982.

Smyth, A.P., *Scandinavian York and Dublin*, 1975.

Wainwright, F.T., 'Ingimund's Invasion', *English Historical Review*, LXIII (1948), pp. 145–69.

——, *Scandinavian England*, Chichester, Phillimore, 1975.

Wilson, D.M., *The Vikings and their Origins*, Thames and Hudson, 1970, revised edn, 1989.

Wood, M., 'Brunanburh Revisited', *Saga Book of the Viking Society*, XX–XXIII (1980), pp. 200–17.

CHAPTERS 7 and 8

Because of the extensive overlap in subject matter in these two chapters a single list of subject literature is offered. For both, by far the most influential recent work of history is Kapelle's *The Norman Conquest of the North* (for full reference, see below).

Allsopp, B. and Clark, U., *Historic Architecture of Northumberland and Newcastle-upon-Tyne*, Stocksfield, Oriel Press, 1977.

Anderson, A.O., (ed.), *Early Sources of Scottish History, A.D. 500–1286*, 2 vols., Edinburgh, Edinburgh University Press, 1922.

Barrow, G.W.S., 'The Anglo-Scottish Border', *Northern History*, I (1966), pp. 21–42.

——, 'Northern English Society in the Early Middle Ages', *Northern History*, IV (1969), pp. 1–28.

——, *The Kingdom of the Scots: Government, Church and Society from the Eleventh to the Fourteenth Centuries*, Edward Arnold, 1973.

Bell, R.D. and Beresford, M.W., *Wharram Percy: The Church of St Martin*, vol. III of *Wharram: a Study of Settlement on the Yorkshire Wolds*, ed. J.G. Hurst, and P.A. Rahtz, Society for Medieval Archaeology, Monograph series, XI, 1987.

Butler, L.A.S. and Morris, R.K., *The Anglo-Saxon Church*, London, Council for British Archaeology, Research Report, LX, 1986.

Collingwood, W.G., 'Anglian and Anglo-Danish Sculpture at York', *Yorkshire Archaeological Journal*, XX (1908–9), pp. 149–213.

Cooper, J.M., *The Last Four Anglo-Saxon Bishops of York*, York, Borthwick Papers, 38, 1970.

Duncan, A.A.M., *Scotland: The Making of the Kingdom*, Edinburgh, Oliver and Boyd, 1975.
——, 'The Battle of Carham, 1018', *Scottish Historical Review*, 55 (1976), pp. 20–8.
Fernie, E., *The Architecture of the Anglo-Saxons*, Batsford, 1982.
Fisher, E.A., *Anglo-Saxon Towers: An Architectural and Historical Study*, Newton Abbot, David and Charles, 1969.
Hall, R., *The Excavations at York: The Viking Dig*, Bodley Head, 1984.
Harmer, F.E., *Anglo-Saxon Writs*, Manchester, Manchester University Press, 1952.
Holdsworth, J., *Selected Pottery Groups, AD 650–1780*, London, Council for British Archaeology, Archaeology of York, fasc. 16/1.
Jackson, K.H., 'Angles and Britons in Northumbria and Cumbria', in *Angles and Britons: O'Donnell Lectures*, ed. H. Lewis, Cardiff, University of Wales Press, 1963, pp. 60–85.
Jolliffe, E.A., 'Northumbrian Institutions', *English Historical Review*, 41 (1926), pp. 1–42.
Kapelle, W.E., *The Norman Conquest of the North*, North Carolina, University of North Carolina, and Croom Helm, 1979.
Kirby, D.P., 'Strathclyde and Cumbria: A Survey of Historical Development to 1092', *Transactions of the Cumberland and Westmorland Antiquarian and Archaeological Society*, new series, LXII (1962), pp. 77–94.
Magilton, J.R., *The Church of St Helens-on-the-Walls, Aldwark*, Council for British Archaeology, Archaeology of York, fasc. 10/1, 1980.
Robertson, A.J., (ed.), *The Laws of the Kings of England from Edmund to Henry I*, Cambridge, Cambridge University Press, 1925.
Rollason, D.W., 'Lists of Saints' Resting Places in Anglo-Saxon England', *Anglo-Saxon England*, VII (1978), pp. 61–94.
Royal Commission for Historic Monuments, *York: Historic Buildings in the Central Area*, HMSO, 1981.
Ryder, P.F., *Medieval Buildings of Yorkshire*, Ashbourne, Moorland, 1982.
Stenton, F.M., 'Pre-Conquest Westmorland', in *Preparatory to Anglo-Saxon England*, ed. D.M. Stenton, Oxford, Oxford University Press, 1970, pp. 214–23.
Stephenson, J., (trans.), *Simeon: a History of the Church of Durham*, Llanerch, Llanerch Enterprises, 1988.
Taylor, H.M. and Taylor, J., *Anglo-Saxon Architecture*, 3 vols., Cambridge, Cambridge University Press, 1965–78.
Walton, P., *Textiles, Cordage and Raw Fibre from 16–22 Coppergate*, Council for British Archaeology, Archaeology of York, fasc. 17/5, 1989.
Wenham, L.P., Hall, R.A., Briden, C.M. and Stocker, D.A., *St Mary Bishophill Junior and St Mary Castlegate*, Council for British Archaeology, Archaeology of York, fasc. 8/2.
Whitelock, D., 'The Dealings of the Kings of England with Northumbria in the Tenth and Eleventh Centuries', in *The Anglo-Saxons: Studies in Some Aspects of their History and Culture, Presented to Bruce Dickins*, ed. P. Clemoes, Bowes and Bowes, 1959, pp. 70–88.
Whittaker, N. and Clark, U., *Historic Architecture of Co. Durham*, Newcastle, Oriel Press, 1971.
Wilson, P.A., 'On the Use of the Terms "Strathclyde" and "Cumbria"', *Transactions of the Cumberland and Westmoralnd Antiquarian and Archaeological Society*, new series, LXVI (1966), pp. 57–99.

CHAPTER 9

Adomnan's Life of Columba, ed. A.O. and M.O. Anderson, Thomas Nelson, 1961.
Atkin, M.A., 'Some Settlement Patterns in Lancashire', in *Medieval Villages*, ed. D. Hooke, Oxford, Oxford University Committee for Archaeology, 1985, pp. 171–85.
Austin, D., *The Deserted Medieval Village of Thrislington, County Durham: Excavations 1973–1974*, Lincoln, Society for Medieval Archaeology, Monograph series, No. 12, 1989.
——, (ed.), *The Boldon Book*, Chichester, Phillimore, 1982.
Baker, A.R.H. and Butlin, R.A. (eds), *Studies in Field Systems in the British Isles*, Cambridge, Cambridge University Press, 1973.
Beresford, M. and St Joseph, J.K.S., *Medieval England: An Aerial Survey*, Cambridge, Cambridge University Press, 1958.
Bishop, T.A.M., 'Assarting and the Growth of the Open Field', *Economic History Review*, VI (1935–6), pp. 26–40.

Darby, H.C. and Maxwell, I.S., *The Domesday Geography of England*, IV, *Northern England*, Cambridge, Cambridge University Press, 1962.

Faull, M.L. and Stinson, M. (eds) *Domesday Book: a Survey of the Counties of England: 30, Yorkshire*, 2 vols., Chichester, Phillimore, 1986.

Harvey, M., 'Medieval Planned Fields in Eastern Yorkshire: Some Thoughts on their Origins', *Agricultural History Review*, XXXI (1983), pp. 91–103.

Harvey, S.P.J., 'Domesday Book and Anglo-Norman Government', *Transactions of the Royal Historical Society*, 5th series, XXV (1975), pp. 175–193.

Higham, N.J., 'Settlement, Land-use and Domesday Ploughlands', *Landscape History*, XII (1990), pp. 33–44.

Morgan, P. (ed.), *Domesday Book: a Survey of the Counties of England: 26, Cheshire*, Chichester, Phillimore, 1978.

Roberts, B.K., 'Village Plans in Co. Durham: a Preliminary Statement', *Medieval Archaeology*, XVI (1972), pp. 33–56.

——, *The Making of the English Village*, Harlow, Longman, 1987.

——, 'Norman Village Plantations and Long Strip Fields in Northern England', *Geografiska Annaler*, LXX (1988), pp.169–77.

Rowley, T., (ed.), *The Origins of Open Field Agriculture*, Croom Helm, 1981.

Taylor, C.C., *Village and Farmstead*, George Philip, 1983.

Vyner, B.E., (ed.), *Medieval Rural Settlement in North-East England*, Durham, Architectural and Archaeological Society of Durham and Northumberland, 1990.

Winchester, A.J.L., *Landscape and Society in Medieval Cumbria*, Edinburgh, Donald, 1987.

Picture Credits

The author and publishers wish to thank the following for permission to reproduce illustrations (numbers given refer to page numbers):

Peter Addyman of the Yorkshire Archaeological Trust, 209; Lindsay Allason-Jones, 47; Ashmolean Museum, 63, 166, 167, 200, 211; Bede Monastery Museum/St Paul's Church, Jarrow, 137; Biblioteca Medicea Laurenziana, Florence, 155, 156; the British Library, ii, 58, 127, 137, 146, 221; the Trustees of the British Museum, 12, 18, 51, 75, 116, 158, 185, 204; Cleveland County Council, 90, 91; the Master and Fellows of Corpus Christi College, Cambridge, 148, 191; the Department of Archaeology, University of Durham, 140, 150, 159, 162, 173, 176, 184, 189, 193, 195, 205, 212, 213, 218, 232; Durham Cathedral Library, 145, 153, 157, 159, 160, 175, 179, 182, 189, 190, 224; John Dore, 33; Dr Colin Haselgrove, 17; Historic Scotland, 227; David Hope, Dumfries, 164; Hull City Museums and Art Galleries, 40; John Hurst and the Wharram Research Project, 41, 170, 216; Professor G.D.B. Jones, 22, 35, 37, 46, 57, 62, 141, 229, 249, 270; Mick Jones and the Lincoln Archaeological Unit, 121; Bill Marsden, 13 (copyright of the Humberside Archaeology Unit); Gordon Maxwell, 93, 126 (copyright of the Royal Commission, Ancient and Historical Monuments, Scotland); National Museums of Scotland, 56; Museum of Antiquities, University of Newcastle-upon-Tyne, 128, 222, 256; Philip Nixon, 9, 81, 120, 128, 133, 152, 174, 217, 225, 255, 271; Colm O'Brien and the Archaeological Field Unit, University of Newcastle-upon-Tyne, 94; Dominic Powesland and the Heslerton Research Project, 102, 103, 104, 267; the Rector, St Paul's, Jarrow, 160; The Royal Commission on the Ancient and Historical Monuments of Scotland, 138; Somerset County Council, 180; Michael J. Stead, 136; the Syndics of Cambridge University Library, 155; Mrs M.J. Thorp, 248; Whitby Literary and Philosophical Society, Whitby Museum, 106, 135; Yorkshire Archaeological Trust Picture Library, 30, 92, 135, 167, 168, 207, 208, 214, 215; Yorkshire Museum, 66, 74, 130, 199.

Index

Page numbers in italic denote illustrations

Abercorn, 140, 150
Aberford, 87–8, *88*
Abernethy, *228*, 246
Acca, Bishop, 150, 165
Acca's Cross, 162, *162*
acculturation, *see* 'Anglicization', Romanization, Scandi-
    navianization
Acklam Wold, 90–1
Addingham, *197*
Adomnan, Abbot, 141, 269–71
Agmund, the *hold*, 186
Agricola, 18, 20
agriculture, 2, 5, 7, 8, 37–41, 74, 102, 106, 171, 252
agricultural climate, 6–7, *7*, 256
Aidan, Bishop, 99, 104, 111, 127, *128*, 133, 154, 222, 265
Alba, 228
Alcock, Professor Leslie, 71
Alcuin, 152, 154, 155, 159, 170, 173, 176
Aldborough, 13, *23*, 26, 27, 30, 41, 47
Aldfrith, 140–1, 154, 166
Aldwin, prior of Winchcombe, 251
Ælfflæd, Queen, 149
Ælfhelm, *ealdorman*, 211
Alfred, King, 184
Ælfwald I, 145, 149
Ælfwald II, 145, 149
Alhfrith, 134
Ælle, 79, 112
Ælle II, 145
Almondbury, 11–12, *13*, 14
amber, *208*, 209
Ammianus Marcellinus, 44, 45
Amounderness, 184, 192
Angeln, 69
Angles, 93
Anglesey, 116
Anglian,
    arrival, 60, 62–3, 65–7, 75
    cemeteries, 68–72
    culture, 75
    genealogies, *58*, 76, 78, *80*

geography, 79–90
paganism, 105–8
palaces, 94–6
raiders, 55
settlements, 94–6, 104
society, 68, 75, 91, 94, 96, 97, 123–4, 138–9, 147–9, 153,
    171
takeover, 76–82, 97–101
temples, 107
Anglian Tower, York, 174, *177*
'Anglicization', 70–1, 75, 99–101, 108, 111, 126
Anglo-Saxon Calendar, 106
Anglo-Saxon Chronicle, 95, 173, 174, 178, 179, 143, *172,
    173, 174, 178, 179*, 212, 259
Anglo-Saxons, in Northumbria, 60, 62–3, 65–7; *see also*
    Anglian
Anglo-Scandinavian art, 198
Annales Cambriae, 76, 82–5, 122
Antonine Wall, 21, 22, 23, 29, 62; *see also* Wall
Antonine Itinerary, 85
Antoninus Pius, 22
apostaty, 126
archbishops of York, 211, 212; *see also* York
Areani/Arcani, 49
Arfderydd, 82
army, late Roman, 43, 46–55
Arras culture, 12–13, 29, 70
Arthuret, 82
Æthelberht, of Kent, 112–3, 119
Æthelburh, Queen, 119
Æthelflæd, 'Lady', 184, 186
Æthelfrith, King, 1, 56, 76–9, 82, 85, 89, 99, *110*, 126–7, 129
Æthelric, King, 112
Æthelric, Bishop, 232, 234
Athelstan, King, 183, 188, 189, 219, 229
    coins of, 207
    rule of Northumbria under, 192
    usurpation of, 189
Æthelwald, King, 145
Æthelwulf, poet, 159
Æthilthryth, Queen, 136

Auckland St Andrew, *150*, 151, *232*
Aughertree Fell, *37*
Augustine, Archbishop, 119
Augustine's Oak, 120
Augustinian Monasticism, 150
Austerfield, 37

Balladoole, 199, *199*
Ballistae, 47
Bamburgh, 3, *60*, 79, 82, 97–8, 108, 133, 223, *225*, 229
  house of, 211, 212, 224, *226*, 227, 230, 231, 232, 234, 242
  kings of, 181, 188, 190, 204
barbarians, 43
Bardney, 128, 222
bargemen, Roman, 48
Barwick-in-Elmet, 11, *254*
baths, Roman, 28
Bayeux Tapestry, *233*, *236*, *238*, *239*, *242*
Bede, 1, 69, 71, 79, 85, 90, 103, 105–6, 108, 110, 112, 113, 115, 116, 119, 123, 125, 127, 130, 134, 135, 136, 138, 140, 151, 153, *221*, *222*
  reputed tomb of, *153*
Bede's letter to Ecgberht, 136, *146*
Belatucadrus, 31
Benedict Biscop, 137–8, 165, 222
Benedictine Monasticism, 151
Beowulf, 95, 110, 116, 154
Bernicia, 59, 71, 77–80, 82–3, 90, 92, 93, 98, 112–13, 118, 123, 127, 129, 186, 226, 230, 239, 240
Beverley, 169, 219
Bewcastle Cross, 32, 161, 162, *163*, 164, 165
Billingham, *219*, 247
Binchester, 48
Birdoswald, 55
Bishophill, St Mary, York, 25, 205, *205*, 214, 216
bishops, 2, 57, 154; *see also* Abercorn, Durham, Hexham, Lindisfarne, Whithorn
Blæcca, reeve, 122
Blackstone Edge, road, *23*
Bolanus, 18
Boldon Book, 259–60
bone, Anglian work in, *106*, *170*, 214
Boniface, Bishop, 157
Boniface, Pope, 106
boundary burial, 70
Bowness-on-Solway, 49
Braaid, 266, *266*
Brantingham, villa, 52–3
Brettas, 101
bridges, Roman, 20, 205
Bridlington, (?) Roman port, 24, 41
Brigantes, 15–18, *25*, 26, 40, 41, 47, 90
Brigantia/Bregans, 31
Brihtred (Berht), 141
Britannia Inferior, 24, 67
Britannia Secunda, 75
British,
  artefacts, 61
  burial practices, 59
  Church, 125
  clergy, 100
  courts, 60
  kingdoms, 61
  kings, 56, 59, 61
  place-names, *181*, 183, *264*
  taxation, 61

Brittany, 158
Brough-on-Humber, 24, 27, 29, 41, 49, 53, 62, 119
Bronze Age, 6
  metalwork, *12*
  settlement, 6
Bronze Age, late, 10
Burh, 142–3
burials,
  Anglian, 66, 68, *68*, 69, *69*, 70–1, *75*, 81, *90*, *91*
  British, 55, 59
  chariot/cart, 12, *13*
  Iron Age, 12
  Roman, 33
  sub-Roman, 55
Burnswark, 11
Burrow Walls, 48

Cædmon, 154, *155*
Cadwallon, 81, 92, 116, 124–6, 127, 129
Caledones, 44
Campodonum, 60, 85, 143
Candida Casa, 150
capital, Roman provincial, 24
Caracalla, 22
Caratacus, 16
Carham, battle of, 230, 231
Carl, *hold*, 225, 230, 231
Carlisle, 26, 29–30, 32, 52, 169, 183
Carl Wark, 86
Carolingians, 149
Carpow, 22
Carrock Fell, 11
cart burial, 12, *13*
Cartimandua, 16
Cartmel, 100
Carucates, 212, 214, 227, 265
Carvetii, 26, 31, 82
Carwinley, 82
Cassiodorus, *175*, 176
Castle Eden, *75*
Castleford, 70
castles, 234, 243–8
Catterick, 27–8, 48, 52, 60, 81, 83, 86, 90–1, 93, 97, 108, 130
cattle, 102–3, 210
Cearl, 112, 116
Cedd, 130, 135
Celtic culture, 57; *see also* British
Celtic kings, 61; *see also* British
cemeteries,
  Anglian, 66–69, *68*, *69*, *90*, *91*
  British, 59
  Roman, 33
  see also burials, inhumation
Ceolfrith, 141, 155, 170
Ceolwulf, 145, 149, 153
Ceorl, 104, 105, 133, 153, 265
Cerealis, Petillius, 18
Ceretic, 85–6
chariot burial, *see* cart burial
Charlemagne, 149
Chat Moss, 6
Chester, 18, 112, *112*, 119, 129, 154, 183, 184, 214
  submission of, 229
Chester-le-Street, 151, 183, *191*, 226, 232

Cheviot(s), 3, 9, 10
Christianity,
  Anglo-Saxon, 153; *see also* Church
  British, 58–9, 105, 108
  Viking Age, 196–7, 202–3, 215–22
Church,
  building, 215–19
  lands, 120–1, 132–3, 137, 219–22
  settlements, 257
Church Brough, 257, *257*
Civitates, 26, 36, 47
Civitas capital, 41
claw-beaker, *75*
clearance, woodland, 8, 37
Cleveland, 82
client rulers, 24
climate, 2, 6–7, 43, 256
Clitheroe, 248
Clodius Albinus, 22
Clovesho, 139, 150
Cnut, coinage, 183, 199, 203
Cnut, King, 199, 219, 225, 230, 236, 239
Coccium, 129; *see also Maserfelth*, Wigan
Cocidius, 32
Codex Amiatinus, 155–7, *155*, *156*
Coifi, 81, 106, 118
coinage,
  Anglian, 106, 118, 143, 166–71, *166*, *167*
  Viking Age, 192, 199–200, *200*, 203, 208, *211*, 214
  coiners, 206–7, 214
Colman, 135
Colonia, Roman York, 24, 25, 28, 34, 52, 205
Columba, St, 127, 269–71
combs, *106*, *170*, 214
Constantine I (the Great), 25, 47
Constantine III, 44, 54
Constantine, of Scots, 190, 192, 229
conversion, Northumbrian, 115, 119–24, *131*
Coppergate, York, 169, 205–7, *206*, *207*, 208–10, 214, 215, *215*, 243
Copsig, 234, 238, 242
Corbridge, 21, 22, 28, *45*, 52, 82, 151, 188
  Lanx, *51*
Corionototae, 82
corn dryers, 40
Coroticus, 59, 61
Cospatric I, 231–2, 235
Cospatric II, 242, 244, 246, 247
Cospatric's Charter, 231, *231*
councils, of Church, *see Clovesho*, Synod of Whitby
counties, 1
Coventina, 32
Craven, 111
Cronk ny Merriu, 266
Crosby Garrett, *36*, 69, 70
Crosby Ravensworth, 82
cross-carved slabs, 162
crosses, stone,
  Anglian, 161–4, *162*, *163*, *164*, *184*
  Viking Age, 192, 202, 203, 212, 213, 224
Cross Fell, 3
cross-slabs, *194*
Cuerdale Hoard, 185, *185*
Cuichelm, King of West Saxons, 150
Cumberland, 2, 181, *181*, 231
Cunedda, 76, 77

Cuthbert, St, 100, 102, 160, 173, 179, *191*, *221*, *230*, 244, 269, *271*
  altar of, *179*
  chapel of, *152*
  coffin of, *160*
  community of, 183, 186, *191*, 197, 218, 219, 224, 230, 232, 236, 246
  cross of, *159*
  stole of, *190*
  at Wells, 180
  see also Chester-le-Street, Durham, Lindisfarne
Cynesige, Archbishop, 234
Cynewulf, 148
Cynigils, King of West Saxons, 129

Dacre, 133, *159*, 190, *190*, 197, 229
Dal Riata, 57, 111, 140
Dalton Parlours, *39*, 41, 70
Danegeld, 223
Dane's Dyke, 87
Danes, 173, 178–84, 185, 222, 223, 245–6
Danish,
  client kings, 179
  immigration, 180
  kingdom of York, 180–3
  raids, 222, 223
  seizure of York, 178
  settlement, 179–80
Dark Ages, *see* Anglian, British, Celtic culture, Celtic kings, sub-Roman
Dearne, 142
defences, Roman York, 25
Degsastan, 99
Deira, 59, 67, 71, 78–81, 90, 98–9, 111, 112, 123, 129, 148, 183
Deirans, 127
Denisesburn, 127
Dere Street, 21, 127
Derwent Valley, 62, 67, 75, 81, *81*, 90, 98, 115, 116, 118, 240
Dicalydones, 44
Dio, 22
diocese, Roman, 54–5
Diocletian, 28
diplomacy, Roman, 44, 58
Don, 142–3
Doncaster, 60, 86, 143
Doon Hill, 60
Dore, 86, 143–4
Drax, *39*, 41
'Dream of the Rood', *164*
Dublin, 177, 178, 180, 184, 204
Dumbarton Rock, *57*, 60, 83, 126
Dumville, David, 76
Dunbar, 60, 142
Duncan, King of Scots, 230–1
Durham,
  bishops of, 2, 220, 232, 234, 260
  Castle, 247
  Cathedral, 153, 249, *250*
  City, 213, 222, 248
  County, 4, 49, 183, 186, 246
  foundation of, 222, 224, *230*
  crosses at, *213*, 224
  Gospels, *157*, *158*, *189*
  Norman seizure of, 243–4, 246

relics at, 222
  sieges of, 230
dykes, 36, 70, 87–8, 88, 142–3, 142, 143, 152

Eadred, Abbot, 183
Eadred, Bishop, 232
Eadred Cudel, earl, 230
Eadwig, King, 207, 214
Eadwulf, of Bamburgh, 181, 185
Ealdhun, Bishop, 224
ealdormen of Northumbria, 211–12
Ealdred, Archbishop, 234–5, 236, 238, 245
Ealdred, of Bamburgh, 188, 190
Ealdred, earl, 230, 231
Eamont, 183, 197
earls, 211–12, 224, 226; see also Morcar, Siward, Tostig
Eburacum, 71
Ecclesiastical History, 1; see also Bede
Ecgberht, King, 181, 183
Ecgfrith, 1, 78, 88–9
economy, Viking Age, 202–11
Edgar Ætheling, 242, 243, 244
Edgar, King, 81, 211, 213, 223, 229
  coins of, 211
Edinburgh, 60, 83, 91–2, 93, 228
Edmund, King, 193
Edward the Confessor, 231, 233, 233, 236, 238–9, 238
Edward the Elder, 186, 188, 228
Edward the Martyr, 223
Edwin, earl, 236, 237, 238, 239, 240, 242
Edwin, King, 78, 80–1, 89, 92
Eildon Hill, 10
Eliffer, sons of, 82
Elmet, 84–7, 84, 90
enclosure, Iron Age/Romano-British, 8, 38, 73–4; see also
  agriculture, farming, farmsteads, fields
Eoforwic, 71; see also York
Eric Bloodaxe, 193, 211
Eric of Hlathir, 225
erosion, 7
Escomb, 151, 161
estates, Viking Age, 195–7
Ethelred II ('the Unready'), 223, 224, 225, 230
Etton, 70

farming,
  Anglo-Saxon, 102–4, 266–70
  Medieval, 255
farmsteads,
  Iron Age/Romano-British, 8, 33–8, 34, 35, 36, 37, 42,
    53
Farne Islands, 3, 152
fields,
  Roman period, 33, 37–8, 37, 54
Fife, 20, 111, 140, 269
Filey, 49
Finan, 130, 134
Fingland Rigg, 36
Fishergate, York, 168, 168, 219
Flamborough Head, 87
Flavian occupation, 18–20, 19
Fleet,
  English, 239
  Roman, 49
'Florence of Worcester', 223, 229
fortlets, Roman, 21, 49–50

forts,
  British, 55, 94, 96–7
  prehistoric, see hill-forts
  Roman, 19–23, 29, 45, 46, 47, 48, 48
  sub-Roman, see British
fortress, legionary, 24, 45, 47
Frankia, 155, 157, 158
Frankish pottery, 170
Franks, 149
Franks Casket, 158, 158, 159, 160
Frenessici, 77
Frisians, 65, 77
  at York, 169, 170
'Frith Stool', 160–1, 161
frontier,
  Northumbrian, 142–4, 142, 143, 183, 197, 210
  Roman, 19–22, 21, 23
Fuesdale, 253
Fylde, 4

Gainford, 151, 212
Galloway, 59
Galmanho, 232
Gargrave, 39
Garrisons, Roman, 20–1, 25; see also army, forts, Roman
Garstang, 40, 52
Garton Slack, 68
Gask Ridge, 20
Gate Fulford, battle of, 239–40, 242
'gate' street-names, 212
Gaul, 13, 135, 151
geography,
  Norman, 247–8
  of Northumbria, 1–5
  sub-Roman, 79–89, 83
geology, of Northumbria, 2–4, 4
Germanic settlement, see Anglian, Anglo-Saxons
Germany, 155, 158
Gildas, 53, 59, 61–3, 67, 77, 94, 106
Gilling, 130
glaciation, 4
glass,
  Anglian, 66, 75, 137, 159, 174
  Viking Age, 206
Glen, baptism in, 119
Gododdin, 59, 83, 93, 96, 99, 111
Gododdin, 83, 91–3, 94, 105
Goldsborough, 55
Goodmanham, 67, 67, 81, 105, 106, 107, 108, 109, 118
Gosforth, 195, 198, 201, 201, 202, 203
government, Roman, 24
grain dryers, Roman, 41
Grassington, 38
graves, prehistoric, 13; see also burials
'Great Danish Army', 178, 186
Greatham, 161
Great Ouseburn, 261
Great Woolden Hall, Irlam, 35
Gregory, Pope, 106–7, 120
Greystoke, 258
'Grimston' hybrid, place-names, 196
gritstone, 3
Gunnar, earl, 81, 214
Guthfrith, King of York, 200
Gwenddolau, 82
Gwynedd, 59, 76, 93

hack-silver, *185*, 203
Hackthorpe, 149
Hadrian, Emperor, 21, 26
Hadrian's Wall, 2, *3, 20*, 21–4, *21, 23, 25*, 31, 44, 46, *52*, *65*, 77
hanging bowls, *74*
Harald Hardrada, King of Norway, 239–40
Harold Godwinson, 233, *233*, 238, 239, 240, 241
Harthacnut, King, 231, 239
Hartlepool, *166*
Hastings, battle of, 241
Hatfield, 1, 59, 80, 87–9, *138*
Healfdene, 181, 195
Heathery Burn, Bronze Age hoard, *12*
Heavenfield, *125*
hegemony, prehistoric, 13, 16
Helen's, St, on the Walls, York, *215*, 216
Hengest, 77
Herodian, 22
Heslerton, 68, 73, *102, 103, 104*, 266, *267*
Hexham, 82, 135–6, *136, 137*, 222
Heysham, *188, 192*
hides, 214, 227, 265
High Rochester, 47
Hilda, St, 265; *see also* Whitby
hill-forts, 10–13
History of the Britons, 76–9, 80, 82–4
Hobthrush Island, *271*
hogback tombstones, *192, 195, 198*, 200, *201, 203*
holds, 186, 202, 212, 225
Holme House, 40
Honorius, 43, *54, 55*
Housesteads, 46, 65
Humber, 2, 13, 67, 169
Humbrenses, 79, 80
Huntcliff, 49, *49*, 55
hunter gatherers, 5–6
Hurbuck, tools found, 203, *204*

Iceland, 178
Ida, King, 76–7, 79, 82, 98–9
Idle, River, battle by, 113, *263*
illuminated manuscripts, *ii, 148, 153, 159, 175, 182*
Inchtuthil, 20
Indigenes, Roman period, 23–8, 39, 42
Ingimund, 184
Ingleborough, *12*, 262
Inglewood Forest, *73*, 74
inhumation, 12, 33–4, 59, 68–71, 160, 161, 200–1
inscriptions,
    Anglian, 161
    Viking Age, *218*
Inter Ripam aet Mersham, 188, 214
Iona, 126–7, *126*, 133, 158, 177, 269–71
Ipswich ware, 169
Ireland, 56, 57, 59, 139, 184, 210
Irish Sea, Roman defences, 49
Iron Age,
    farming, 7–8, 35
    technology, 8
    tribes, 10–18
Ivar, Norse king, 178
'Iudeu', 97
Iurminburgh, Queen, 136

James the Deacon, 107–8, 122, 124, 134

Jarrow, 137, *137*, 155, 157, 161, *162*, 165, 222, 251, *251*
    dedication of church, 161, *162*
    sack of, 174
Jedburgh, *227*
Judith, Countess, 234, 238
Justinian, Emperor, 24

Kaims Castle, *22*
Keeills, 152
Kells, 177
    Book of, 158
Kenneth, King of Scots, 229
Kenneth MacAlpine, 228
Kent, 45
Kentigirn, St, *181*, 183
kingship,
    Northumbrian, 144–9, 171
    Viking, 208–10
Kirkby Lonsdale, 250
Kirkby Stephen, 36, 161, 198
Kirkdale, church dedication, 218, *218*
Kirk Hammerton, 218, *219*
Kirkmadrine, 58, *59*
Kirk Michael, Isle of Man, *177*
Kyle, Plain of, 141

Lady's Well, Holystone, *120*
Lake District, landscape, 3, 4, *5*, 252
Lancashire, 2, 118
Lancaster, 48
Lanchester, 47, 59, 151
landscape, evolution, 1–9
land-use, 252–6
    Anglian, 102–4, 170–1
    prehistoric, 5
    Roman, 36–42
Langdale, *5*
Langton, 40
Lastingham, 130, 132
late Bronze Age, *see* Bronze Age, late
Latenses, 86
Latin, 30
'Law of the Northumbrian Priests', 220
Leck Castle, *11*
Ledsham, 86, *216*
Ledston, 86
Leeds (*Loidis*), 84–6
legions, 24
Lérins, 155
Lichfield Gospels, 158
Limes, Roman, 20, 22; *see also* frontier
limestone, 3, *8*, 85
Limitatenses, 46
Lincoln, 97, 121, *121*, 210, 243
Lindisfarne, 99, *128*, 133, 134, 148–9, *150*, 173, 174, *174*, 246
    community in exile, 183; *see also* Chester-le-Street, Cuthbert, St, Durham
    Gospels, *ii, 158, 182*
    later priory at, *133, 176*
    sack of, 173, 177
    scriptorium, 148, 148, 153, 155
Lindsey, 1, 80, 88–9, 139
Liudger, St, 169, 170
Llwyfenydd, 82
London, 25, 90

Long Meg, *8*
Lonsdale, *or* Lune Valley, *50, 53, 255*
Lothians, 99, 228, 230
lots, in lawsuits, 154
Lowther, 162
Lul, Frankish bishop, 157
Lupicinus, 45
Lyme, 74
lynchets, 38, 264

Macbeth, 231–2, 234, 242
Maeatae, 21, 44
Maglocunus, 56, 63
Magnus Maximus, 45, 48
Makerfield, 84, 87, 101, 264
Malcolm I, of Scots, 193
Malcolm II, of Scots, 230, 234, 235, 243, 246
Malton, 18, 27, 29–31, 41, 49–50, 52, 65, 81
Man, Isle of, 116, *152,* 178, *194,* 199, *199,* 200, 230, 266, *268, 270*
Manaw Gododdin, 77
manors, 257
manuscript illumination, 148, 153, 158
Maponus, 32
Margaret, Queen, 243
markets, 210, 256, 263
Mærleswein, earl, 242, 244
Mars Riga, 31
Maryport, *46,* 47
Maserfelth, battle of, 129
masonry,
    Anglian, 160–1; *see also* stone-carving
    Roman, re-used, 151
Maughold, Isle of Man, *152, 194,* 198
Mellitus, 106–7
memorial stones, Christian, British, 58–9
Meols, 168, 210
merchants, 201, 207, 208–9, 210, 215
Mercia, 112–13, 116–17, 124
Mercians, 143–4
Mersey, 1, 2, 86, 143, 183, 186, *187, 241*
metalwork,
    Anglian, 159–60, *159*
    prehistoric, *12*
    Roman, 29
    sub-Roman, 55
    Viking Age, *185,* 203, *204,* 214, *219*
Micklegate, York, 25
Middleton Hall, 20, *53*
Milfield, 69–70, 94–5
Miller, Molly, 61
Minster clergy, 151
mints,
    Northumbrian, 167
    at York, 203–4, 211, 214
    see also, coinage
Mithraeum, 32–3, *32*
monasteries, Northumbrian, 133–7, 152–66
    architecture of, *151, 161, 166*
    decline of, 176
    libraries in, 159
    private, 153
    sack of, 171
    wealth of, 171
monasticism, 150–66
    'reform' of in tenth century, 213, 219, 220, 222

monks, pre-English, 53
Monkwearmouth, 137, 155, 157, 161, *165,* 251
    sack of, 174
Mons Graupius, 20
moorland, 5, 37
morality, 154
Morcar, earl, 237, 238, 239, 240, 242
Mortimer, John, 68–9
mosaics, 30, *30,* 39–40, *40,* 52
mosses, 264
Mote of Mark, 60, 96, *98*
Mount, The, York, 66
Mulling, Book of, 164
Mynyddog, 83, 91–2
Myres, John, 63

Neasham Fen, 74
Nechtanesmere, 88, 90, *138,* 139
Nennius, 76
Neolithic Revolution, 5–6
Newbald, 81, 214
New Bewick, *94, 95*
Newcastle, 247, *247*
Newton, hundred of, 101
Nico Ditch, 143, *143*
Ninian, St, 150
Norham, 174, 179
Norman churches, 249–51
Normans, 242–50
Norse, 173, 184–6, 228
Northern Army, 183, 185, 186, 203
North Ferriby, 13, 169
Northumbria,
    collapse of, 183
    in *Great Domesday Book,* 235
Northumbrian,
    Church, 130, 149–66
    manuscripts, 159
    military capability, 147, 153
    politics, 144–9
    privileges, 214, 236
    rebellion in 1065, 236–7
    rebellion in 1067, 242
    rebellion in 1069, 244–6
    resistance to Vikings, 177–9
'Northumbrians', the name, 1
North York Moors, 1, 3, 81
Norton, 68, 82, 90–1, *90, 91,* 216, *217*
Notitia Dignitatum, 46–8, *48*
Novantae, 82
nucleation of settlement, *see* villages
Nunburnholme, 184

Offa, son of King Aldfrith, 149
Offa, King of Mercians, 144, 149, 166–7, 173
Olaf Guthfrithson, 178, 193
Old Bylands, 161
open fields, 255, 257–61
oppida, 10, 16–17
Ordovices, 18
Orkneys, 77
Ormside bowl, *199*
Orton Scar, *8,* 265
Osbald, King, 145, 149, 153
Osbeorn, Danish earl, 246
Osbeorn, Siward's son, 232

Osberht, King, 145, 167
Oscytel, Archbishop, 220
Osfrith, son of Edwin, 124
Oslac, earl, 211, 212, 223
Osred I, 141, 144, 145, 149
Osred II, 145
Osric, King, 125–6, 145
Osthryth, Queen, 128
Ostia, bishop of, 154
Osulf, of Bernicia, 238, 242
Osulf, *ealdorman*, 211
Oswald, Archbishop and saint, 213, 220, 223
Oswald, King and saint, 77, 127–9, 134, 149, 222
Oswine, King and saint, 129–30, 154, 236
Oswiu, King, 77, 123, 129–32, 133, 135, 147
Oswulf, King, 145, 149
Œthelwald, 130
Outigern, 82
'Overkingship', 1, 77, 82, 98, 108, 111, 113, 116–18, 128, 129, 138–9, 140–1

Pabo, 84
paganism, 67, 105–8, *107*, 123, 130, 151, 153, 154, *177*
    Viking, 188–9, 198, 201, *212*
palace sites, 116, 118, 122, 142, 209–10, 212; *see also*
    Campodonum, Derwent Valley, Milfield, Yeavering,
    York
palisaded settlements, British, 60
papal visitation, 154
Parisi, 13, 18, 26, 29, 32, 41, 81
Patrick, St, 57, 59, 61, 127, 222
    chapel at Heysham, *188*, *220*
Paulinus, Bishop, 81, 100, 115, 119–20, 121, 122, 124, 135
Peak District, 3
peasantry, 266–9
Pecthelm, Bishop, 150
Penda, King of Mercians, 78, 97, 113, 124, 125, 129, 130,
    132, 133
Pennines, 3, 26, 41
Penrith, *140*
Penwortham, 188
Peter, St, coinage, 200, 204, 206–7
Peter, St, stone, Whithorn, *59*
Peter's, St, York, 245
Petillius Cerealis, *see* Cerealis
Pictish symbol stones, *228*
Pictland, 77
Picts, 44–5, 56, 93, 138, 140–1, 228
    (?) alliance with, 141–2
Piercebridge, 20, 27, 48, *256*
place-names, 71, 100, 107–8, *181*, *194*, 263–4, *264*
ploughlands, 261, 264–5
plough marks, prehistoric, 8
ploughs, Domesday, 261, 264–5
population, levels, 7–8, 12, 43
ports,
    Northumbrian, 169
    Roman, 24, 29
pottery,
    Medieval, 256
    Northumbrian, *63*, 169
    Roman, 29, 38, 52–3, 55
    Viking Age, 210, 214
Prata, military, at York, 26
prehistory, 5–15
prehistoric metalwork, 12, 18

Procopius of Caesarea, 106
provinces, Roman, 28, *50*, 56
Prosper Tiro, 45
Ptolemy, 13, 16, 29, 44

Rædwald, King of East Angles, 113–15, 124
Rædwulf, King, 145, 177
Ragnald, King of York, 186, 188, 197
Ragnarok, 198
raids, barbarian, 45, 48, 55–7, 75
Ravenglass, 48
regionalism, 7, 44, 168
regions, *2*
religion,
    Anglo-Saxon, 105; *see also* Christianity, paganism
    Celtic, 31
    Roman, 31–3, *31*, *32*
    sub-Roman, 58–9, 67
    Viking Age, 192, 197–201, 220
Rheged, 82, 90
Rhineland, 13, 65
Rhydderch Hen, 98
Ribblehead, 266
Riccall, 239
Richmond Castle, 247, *247*
ridge and furrow, 254, *254*, *259*, 264
Ripon, 99, 120–1, *135*, 153, 155, 160, 161, 174, 178, 222,
    224
roads, 20, 86, *122*, 240
Robert de Commines, 243
Robert fitz Richard, 243, 244
Roger of Poitou, 250–1
Roger of Wendover, 174
Roman,
    Britain, end of, 43, 54–5
    bureaucracy, 43
    church, 63
    civil settlements, 24, 29
    coinage, 51–5
    conquest, 15, *19*
    Empire, 41, 43–5
    farms/farming, 33–6, 42
    fleet, 49
    forts, 8, 20, 47, *47*, 48
    fortlets, 49–50
    frontier, or *limes*, 20, 22, 46–50
    garrisons, 20–1, 25, 42, 54–5
    government, 24, 27, 41–3
    inscriptions, 27
    markets, 51
    mosaics, 30, *30*, 39–40, *40*
    names, 58
    occupation, 22
    ports, 24, 29
    pottery, 29, 38–9, 52
    provinces, 62
    roads, 20, *23*, 86, 90
    signal stations, 20, *53*
    taxation, 42, 51, 60–1
    towns, 27–30, 41–2, 51
Romanization, 23–4, 27–8, 29–30, 36, 39–40, 42, 53, 62, 67
Romanized areas, 42, 44, 57, 62, 75
Romano-Saxon pottery, 65
Roman Ridge dykes, 142–4, *142*
Rome, 153
Ronaldsway, cropmarks, *270*

Rossendale, hay-making, *260*
Rough Castle, *62*
royal estates, 211
royal marriages, 149
Rudston, 40, *40*, 52, *52*
Ruin of Britain, by Gildas, 61; *see also* Gildas
runes, Anglo-Saxon, *106*, 161
Ruthwell Cross, 164–5, *164*

saga, 108, 154
St Andrew's, 228
St Ninian's Isle, treasure, 160
saints' cults, 222
saints' lives, 140
'Saint's tomb', Gosforth, 201, *201*
Salford hundred, 264
Saltburn, 70
Sancton, *63*, 66–7, *67*, 81, 118
Sawyer, Professor Peter, 176–7
Saxons, 62–3; *see also* Anglian, Anglo-Saxons
Saxon shore, 29, 49, 52
Scandinavianization, 70–1, 75, 99–101, 108
Scarborough Castle, *246*
sceattas, 166; *see also* coinage
Scone, 228
Scotch Corner, 17
Scotland, *228*, 231
    rise of, 228–30
Scots, 44–5, 140–1, 142, 183, 224
Scottish attacks on England, 228–30, 234, 235
Scottish Church, 127, 129, 130, *131*, 150, 153, 155
    bishops from, 132
    monks of, 134
Scriptoria, 148, 153, 155, 157–9; *see also* monasteries
sea travel, 170, 207
Selgovae, 10, 18, 82
settlement continuity, 72–5
settlement nucleation, 171
Severus, Septimius, 22, 26
Shap, 6
Sheaf, 86
Sherburn-in-Elmet, 86–7, *87*, 214, 260–1
shielings, 5, *262*, 263
shires, 101–4, 151
Shorden Brae, 33, *33*
signal stations, 20, 50, *53*
Sigurd, 198
Sihtric, King of York, 186, 188, 189
silver, 166, 203–4
Siward, earl, 225, 226, 230–2
Skipton Castle, *247*
slaves, 104, 177, 246
social hierarchies, prehistoric, 10
Sockburn, stonework at, *197*, *198*, 198, 202
Soemil, 79
soils, types and formation, 9, *9*
soldiers, 42, 46; *see also* Roman
Solway Plain, 4
Southern Uplands, 1, 3
South Middleton, *256*
South Shields, 22, 48
specialization, social and economic, 43
Sprouston, *95*
Staindrop, 151, 218
Stainmore, 20, 26, 193, 247
Stamford Bridge, 212, 240, *240*, 241

Stanegate, 20–1
Stanwick, 16–18, *16*, *17*, *18*, 90
Stilicho, 48
Stillingfleet, church, *219*
Stirling, *2*, 141–2, *141*
stone-carving,
    Anglian, *136*, *138*, *139*, *140*, 149, *150*, 159–61, *159*, *160*, *161*, *162*, *163*, *164*, *173*, *184*
    Viking Age, *190*, *192*, *194*, 195–9, *195*, *197*, *198*, *201*, *202*, *203*, *205*, *212*, *213*, *216*, *218*, *224*
Stranraer, 249
Strathclyde, 2, 83, 98–9, 141, 142, 181, *181*, 183, 229, 230
stycas, 167, *167*; *see also* coinage
sub-Roman,
    aristocracy, 67
    period, 55–62, 75, 94, 96; *see also* British
sundials, *218*
sunken-featured buildings, 72–3, 94, 95, *95*, 102, 266
Swale, baptism in, 119
Sweyn I, King of Danes, 224, 225
Sweyn II, King of Danes, 239, 244
Synod of Whitby, *see* Whitby

Tacitus, 18, 95, 105–6
Tadcaster, 27, 239, 240
Taliesin, 82
taxation, 171, 214, 242
Tay, River, 1
Tebay, castle, *248*
Teesdale, x, *255*
temples,
    Anglian, 107, *107*
    Roman, 27
Tettenhall, battle of, 186
Teviotdale, 10
textiles, 210, 214
Theodore, Archbishop, 88, 135, 139, 150
    penitentials of, 153
Theodoric, King, 98
Theodosian period, 47, 51
Thirlings, 95
thistle brooch, 204, *204*
Thomas of Bayeux, Archbishop, 246, 249
Thompson, Professor Edward, 61
Thored, earl, 223
Thorpe Thewles, 12
Thor's hammer, on coins, 200, *200*
Thrislington, 256
Tiddingford, Peace of, 184
Tollesby, 256
Tostig, earl, 232, 233–8, 239, 240
towers, of churches, 218
towns, of Viking Age, 210, 213
trade,
    Roman, 51–3
    Viking Age, 207–10, 214
transhumance, 5, 37, 102, 170, 263
Traprain Law, 10
    hoard found at, 56–7, *56*
Trent, battle of, 111, 139
Trentholm Drive, York, 33
tribal gatherings, South Scotland, 23, 58
Tribal Hidage, 111, *114*, 115–16, 124
tribes,
    prehistoric, 14, *14*
    Roman, 18, 25, 26

in Scotland, 44, *44*
   sub-Roman, 58, 59
Trumhere, Abbot and Bishop, 132
Tuda, St, 135, 222
Turgeis, 177
Tynemouth, 130, 133, 169, *180*, 222
   Danish occupation of, 179
   sack of, 174
Tynwald, *229*

Uhtred, earl, 211, 224, 225, 230, 231
urbanization, 27, 51, 207–10, 252
Urien, King, 56, 82–3, 98–9

Vale of York, *64*
vallum, 8, 21
Venutius, 16–18
Verturiones, 44
vici, 29–30, 39, 42, 50, 257
Viking Age,
   burials of, 199
   culture of, 194–202
   economy, 202–10
   second, 223–6, 232
   society, 202–10
   sculpture, 197–201, 205
Vikings, 57, 144, 154, 172–9; *see also* Danes, Norse
   attacks of, 167, 172, 173–4, 176–7, 222
   immigration of, 195
   interpretation of, 176–7
   in Irish Sea, 177
   on the Isle of Man, 178
Viking York, 204–10, *205*; *see also* York, Yorvik
villages, 171, 255, 257, 259, 260
villas, 39–42, *39*, 45, 52–3, 57
Vindolanda, 29, *29*, 42, 50
Vitris, 32
Vortigern, 67, 77
Votadini, 10, 18, 59, 83, 93

Walcher, Bishop, 246, 251
Wales, 116, 233
walh, place-name element, 101–2
Wall, Antonine, 21–2
Wall, Hadrian's, *see* Hadrian's Wall
Wall, Northumbrian church and palace, 130, 133, 151
Wallsend, 46
Waltheof, earl, 232, 237, 244, 247
wapentakes, 212, 227
Warden, cross at, *139*
warfare, 75, 77, 90–4, 97, 122, 132
warriors, 75
'Warrior tomb', Gosforth, *195*, 201, *201*
'Wasting of the north', 246
watch-towers, 49–50, *49*
weapons,
   Anglian, *92*, *116*, 130, 206
   Anglo-Viking, *130*
   prehistoric, 10
   sub-Roman, 59, 90–3
'week-work', 171
Well, Rudston, *52*
Wells, St Cuthbert's, *180*
Welsh Annals, The, see Annales Cambriae
Welton, 40, 52
wergild, 201–2

Wery Wall, 48
Wessex, 116, 129
West Derby, 101, 262
West Heslerton, *see* Heslerton
West Saxons, 234
West Stow, 95–6, *95*, *96*
West Whelpington, 256, 257
Whalley, 222, *222*, 223
Wharfedale, *15*, *85*, *264*
Wharram (Percy), 35–6, 38, *41*, 72–3, *72*, 169, *170*, *216*, *257*
Wheeler, Sir Mortimer, 16–17
Whin Sill, 3, *3*
Whitby, *106*, 133, 135, *135*, *136*, 168–70, *169*, 251
   Synod of, 135, 149, 153, 154–5
Whitham, 1
Whithorn, 59, *59*, 150–1, *151*, 165, 168
wic sites, 168, 171
Wigan, 129, 254; *see also Coccium*
Wigtown, 2
Wilfrid, St, 99, 120, 123, 134, 135, 136, 137, *137*, 138, 140, 147, 150, 153, 155, 222
William, I, 233, 241
William fitz Osbern, 244
William Malet, 243
William Rufus, 259
William St Calais, 249
Winwaed, battle of, 130
Wirral, 184
Woden, 78–9, 105, 123, 127
Woden Law, 10, *10*
wolds, 3, 11, 12, 29, 35–8, 66, 81
woodland, 5, 37, 74–5
   clearance, 7, 37
wool, 210
Wreay Hall, 50

Yanwath, *34*, *54*
Yeavering, 60, 70, 94–5, *94*, 126
   auditorium at, 111, 118–19, *118*
   church at, 133–4, *134*
   pagan temple at, 107–8, *107*
   palace site, 111
York, *193*, *209*
   accommodation with England, 211, 212
   Anglian, 65, 66, *66*, 68, 81, 90, 92, 125, 135, 153, 161, 174
   archbishops of, 150, 192, 213
   battle of, 145, 178–9
   castles at, 234, 243, *243*, 244, *244*
   churches at, 216, 244, 245
   coins from, *167*
   defences of, 174, *174*
   destruction of, 233
   in *Domesday Book*, 248–9
   early Christian site, 119, 124
   helmet from, 92, 206
   imports to, 207–10
   library at, 159
   mint at, 183, 192, 211, 214
   name, 71
   palace at, 209–10
   Roman, 18, 24–8, *24*, *25*, 30, *30*, 32, *41*, 45–7, *45*, 52, 57
   St Peter's (York Minster), 155, 249, *249*
   sea routes to, 170, 178
   trade at, *168*, *169*, 207–10
   Viking kingdom of, 180–6, 193–210
   Viking seizure of, 178–9

Yorkshire, 1, 49, *64*, 93, 180, 183, 214, 223–4, 227
   attitude towards Danes in, 210, 224, 225
   attitude towards Harald Hardrada, 239–40
   attitude towards Tostig, 236–8
Yorvik, 204, *205*
   excavations in, 205, 215
   wealth of, 207–10, 215